W0112725

FILM SCRIPTS FOUR

FILM SCRIPTS FOUR

Edited by
George P. Garrett
O. B. Hardison, Jr.
Jane R. Gelfman

Applause Theatre & Cinema Books
An Imprint of Hal Leonard Corporation

First Applause printing 2013 by arrangement with Ardent Media Inc.
Copyright © 1971 by Meredith Corporation

All rights reserved. No part of this book may be reproduced in any manner whatsoever, including information storage, or retrieval, in whole or in part (except for brief quotations in critical articles or reviews), without written permission from Ardent Media Inc. For information, contact info@ardentmediainc.com or fax 1-212-861-0998.

Distributed by Applause Theatre & Cinema Books
An Imprint of Hal Leonard Corporation
7777 West Bluemound Road
Milwaukee, WI 53213

Trade Book Division Editorial Offices
33 Plymouth St., Montclair, NJ 07042

Acknowledgments:
A Hard Days Night   Published by permission of Felix de Wolfe.
The Best Man   Copyright © 1960 by Gore Vidal. Reprinted by permission of Gore Vidal.
Darling   Published by permission of Bernard Sheridan & Co. (London).

These film scripts in their present form are designed for the reading public only. All dramatic rights are fully protected by copyrights and no public or private performance—professional or amateur—may be given.

Originally published by Appleton-Century-Crofts/Meredith Corporation in 1972
Reprinted by Irvington Publishers Inc. in 1989

Front cover design by Mark Lerner

Printed in the United States of America

The Library of Congress has cataloged the Irvington Publishers Inc. printing as follows:

Film scripts / edited by George P. Garrett, O.B. Hardison, Jr.,
    Jane R. Gelfman
            p.   cm.
    Reprint. Originally published: New York: Appleton-Century-Crofts, 1971-
        1. Motion picture plays.   I. Garrett, George P., 1929-
II. Hardison, O.B. III. Gelfman, Jane R.
PN1997.AIG25 1989
791.43'75—dc19
                                        89-2004
                                        CIP

ISBN 978-1-4803-4206-4

www.applausebooks.com

CONTENTS

FILM SCRIPTS FOUR

INTRODUCTION

The first movie in the modern sense of the word was made by the Thomas A. Edison laboratories and shown in the unlikely location of West Orange, New Jersey, on October 6, 1889. It was produced by the marriage of Edison's sprocket-controlled motion picture camera with the new nitrocellulose film developed by George Eastman of Rochester, New York. Because the early Edison movies had to be viewed individually, through a peephole exhibiting device, they remained curiosities. During the early 1890s attempts were made by Major Woodville Latham, Louis and Auguste Lumière, Thomas Armat, and others to wed Edison's films to the magic lantern to permit film showings for large audiences. Armat's projector was put in regular use at Koster and Bial's music hall in New York City on April 23, 1896. In spite of a series of ills, including a disastrous fire in a Paris theater that killed some 180 spectators, legal battles by Edison over foreign patent rights, and various attempts to regulate the new industry by monopoly control, motion pictures flourished. The final step in the emergence of the modern film industry was taken by Edwin S. Porter, an Edison cameraman, in 1903. Dissatisfied with the vaudeville acts and sporting events that were the staple of early film, Porter made a narrative film crowding as many thrills as possible onto a standard thousand-foot reel. *The Life of an American Fireman* was sufficiently successful to justify a second effort, which emerged as *The Great Train Robbery* (1903). This film was the first commercially important narrative movie. When it opened in 1905 in a theater specifically designed for film showing and dubbed the *nickelodeon* on the basis of the five-cent admission price, the film industry was fairly launched on its amazing twentieth-century career.

For the first decade of the new century the movie industry was dominated by eastern producers (the Motion Picture Patents Company licensed by Edison). A group of independents using French equipment soon arose to challenge the monopoly of Edison's "movie trust." Partly as a result of competition, the independents moved to Southern California, where labor was cheap, the terrain varied, and the climate mild, an important consideration at a time when almost all movies were made outdoors. In 1911 the Nestor film company, under David Horsley, leased a studio site on Sunset Boulevard in Hollywood, and by the end of the year some fifteen companies had followed suit.

During the decade from 1910 to 1920, Hollywood became the film capital of the world. Cecil B. De Mille, Jesse Lasky, Samuel Goldwin, D. W. Griffith, Charlie Chaplin, Douglas Fairbanks, Sr., and a host of others came to Hollywood during this period and were to remain dominant for years to come, some, like De Mille and Goldwin, until after World War II. It was during this decade that movies found their audience. Regarded by intellectuals as crude popular entertainment, they quickly became the cultural staple for the unwashed millions. As success strengthened the financial position of the theater owners and Hollywood studios, movies challenged the supremacy of almost every form of popular entertainment—fiction, Victorian stage melodrama, and vaudeville—except sports. An awkward symbiosis, in some ways closer to an armed truce than peaceful coexistence, eventually developed between Hollywood and the legitimate theater, but movies badly upset the economy of stage drama. Touring companies were broken up. Smalltown theaters were everywhere converted into moving picture houses. Only the large cities—eventually, only New York—continued to support a vital stage drama. Many of the refugees from legitimate drama, of course, later found their way to Hollywood.

During the twenties and thirties movies reigned supreme in the mass entertainment field, and Hollywood was the undisputed center of world cinema. After World War I, while Europe's picture-making capacity was disrupted, the American industry quickly, and with little additional cost, peddled prints of its films abroad. By 1925, American films had captured 95 percent of the British market, 70 percent of the French, and 68 percent of the Italian; elsewhere the situation was much the same.[1]

The "Hollywood approach" was the hard sell. Hollywood producers based their work on what paid off at the box office, not on what film directors or critics claimed would make great art. They gave the public what the public wanted—slick photography, fast-paced plots, action for the men, and tear-soaked sentiment for the ladies. "Eventually two kinds of film

[1] Thomas H. Guback, *The International Film Industry: Western Europe and America Since 1945* (Bloomington: Indiana University Press, 1969), pp. 8–9; supporting references here omitted.

would dominate the screen: the peep show and the chase. As primitive tribes described them to Hortense Powdermaker, 'kiss-kiss' and 'bang-bang' stories are right for the screen." [2]

So successful was Hollywood that after 1915, the date of D. W. Griffith's *Birth of a Nation*, the film industry in England, France, Germany, and Italy never offered serious competition. But, in spite of Hollywood's unchallenged position in America as well as Europe through the twenties and thirties, the market at home still accounted for most of its income.[3] As the world's screen capital, it could afford to be as provincial and inward-looking as the country itself. To accommodate ever-larger audiences, enormous cathedrals or palaces of film were built in the major cities. The forerunner of these citadels was Mitchell Mark's Strand, opened in New York in 1914, with a seating capacity of 3,000. In the twenties the cathedral/palaces rivalled in glitter and luxury the fabled opera houses of Paris, Vienna, and Milan. The Roxy Theater in New York, for example, cost some $8,000,000 and had a seating capacity of over 6,000. But every small town had its moviehouse of some sort, and throughout America, Saturday night became almost synonymous with "going to the movies." Meanwhile, in addition to satisfying the popular craving for entertainment, movies created something like an American equivalent of European royalty. The star system fed the public on dreams of glamour, embodied in such popular idols as Theda Bara, Lillian Gish, Rudolph Valentino, Greta Garbo, William S. Hart, and others, whose exploits were followed obsessively not only on the screen but also in the gossip columns of newspapers and in the screen magazines that were by-products of the star system.

The introduction of sound in 1928 greatly increased the range of artistic effects possible in movies. At the same time it created a group of artistic problems that are still unresolved in the 1970s. Sound tended to nationalize movies. The silents spoke the universal language of visual imagery. Their few subtitles could easily be translated into French, Thai, Hindustani, or what have you, with no leakage of meaning. Talkies, however, relied heavily on rapidly spoken dialogue and often on fairly subtle vocal nuances. This was particularly true in their early years when directors tended to stress sound at the expense of image simply because sound was new, and when many Broadway plays—together with many actors— were translated bodily from the legitimate stage to film. To sell such films abroad it was necessary either to add subtitles or to dub in native-language dialogue. Neither expedient was satisfactory. Subtitles are a poor substitute for the spoken word. They can never translate more than a fraction of what is spoken in fast dialogue. And, of course, they make the unwarranted as-

[2] Roy Huss and Norman Silverstein, *The Film Experience: Elements of Motion Picture Art* (New York: Dell, 1969), p. 15; citing Hortense Powdermaker, *Hollywood: The Dream Factory* (Boston: Little, Brown, 1950), p. 14.
[3] Guback, p. 9.

sumption that the audience is literate! Dubbed dialogue, while better than subtitles, is also awkward. The actors who do the dubbing are usually poorly paid hacks. The dialogue itself is often crudely translated. Perhaps most distressing, the words on the sound track seldom correspond to the lip movements of the actors on the screen, a situation that undercuts, if it does not destroy, the dramatic illusion. Thus, in spite of the growing international character of the film industry, the serious viewer still suffers an annoying distortion and dislocation if he must experience, say, Michelangelo Antonioni's *L'Eclisse* (1961), which is set in contemporary Rome, under the amplification of an English-language sound track. Equally disturbing, on the other hand, is an encounter with the same director's *Blow-up* (1967), which is set in London of today, in any tones other than those of British English.

More fundamental, sound brought with it the unanswerable question of whether movies are a visual or a verbal art. The accident of limited technology forced the directors of the silent era to concentrate on the visual aspect of film. They explored a remarkable range of techniques for telling stories visually. In the opinion of many students of film, sound caused a regression in film technique that lasted until after World War II. Sound made it too easy to tell a story. Cinematic techniques that were commonplace to producers like Griffith and actors like Chaplin were replaced by stale devices imported from Broadway along with playscripts and actors. Not until after World War II, when a new breed of filmmakers formed by the realities of invasion, military defeat, and economic collapse made its vision felt, was Hollywood shaken out of its complacency.

While Hollywood continued to dominate world cinema between the two world wars, Europeans did produce many films that gained international attention either for their intrinsic qualities or innovative techniques. Sergei Eisenstein, the great Russian director, is a towering figure both in the art of making films and of analyzing principles of cinematography. Several of his films, notably *Potemkin* (1925), *Alexander Nevsky* (1938), and *Ivan the Terrible* (1944–46), have had worldwide influence. The silent, *The Cabinet of Dr. Caligari* (1919), by the Austrian director Robert Wiene, remains a classic of expressionism in the theater adapted to film while *The Blue Angel* (1930), a talking picture directed by Josef von Sternberg and starring Marlene Dietrich and Emil Jannings, remains a classic of harsh realism, social and psychological, which was inspired by the disillusionment that pervaded Germany in the last years of the Weimar Republic. Among the French, René Clair produced charming, socially cutting, film fantasies like *À nous la liberté* (1932) and *The Ghost Goes West* (1938); and Marcel Pagnol revealed with tender luminosity in *La Femme de boulanger* (1938) and a trilogy—*Marius* (1929), *Fanny* (1931), and *César* (1936)—complexities of feeling among the petty bourgeoisie of provincial France.

But it was not until 1945, following World War II, that European cinema began to challenge Hollywood and the economic situation for American producers began to change completely. In such films as Rossellini's *Open City* (1945), De Sica's *Shoe Shine* (1946), and his *Bicycle Thief* (1948), Italian filmmakers achieved sensitive but unsentimental renderings of the physical and emotional realities of German occupation, American liberation, and the struggle to rebuild a peacetime society with habits and outlooks conditioned by years of learning how to survive only from moment to moment. This new spirit of filmmaking, *cinéma vérité* (or direct cinema), came as a refreshing new perspective for American audiences when experienced against their own long exposure to Hollywood's vision, subsidized by our government, of a world at war. The newsreel-like verisimilitude of scenes shot on location where local inhabitants played the lesser roles was a radical break with the controlled and insulated environment of the sound studio and its professional actors.

This new and less-expensive procedure opened the door for shooting other films—from British comedies to Scandinavian psychocinedramas—out-of-doors. As the impressionists liberated painting during the last quarter of the nineteenth century by taking their canvases out of the studio and into the fields and streets, European directors led a similar revolution in filmmaking out of necessity after World War II. *Cinéma vérité* also restored to the directors some of the preeminence they had enjoyed during the silent era. They thus opened the way for such meditative, director-dominated films as *8½*, *Last Year at Marienbad* (1962), *Juliet of the Spirits* (1964), and *Blow-up*. French cinema has also been influential, though perhaps experimental, beginning with the postwar classic *Les enfants du Paradis* and extending through the *nouvelle vague* movement of the 1960s. Many isolated but major contributions have also come from Japanese and Scandinavian filmmakers, most notably Akira Kurosawa and Ingmar Bergman.

During the sixties British and American filmmakers began to draw on continental techniques. *A Hard Day's Night* (1964) is a brilliant English contribution which manages the difficult task of carrying its unorthodox techniques so lightly that they seem entirely natural expressions of the dominant tone of exuberant, uninhibited play. In the United States, as the photographic industry produced less cumbersome and expensive cameras and more light-sensitive film, a new kind of movie, one of *personal statement,* emerged. "Underground"—or "independent" as most of them preferred to be called—filmmakers could dissent "radically in form, or in technique, or in content, or perhaps in all three" from the offerings of commercial cinema, and all for an outlay of about a thousand dollars.[4] In the fifties

---

[4] Sheldon Renan, *An Introduction to the American Underground Film* (New York: Dutton, 1967), p. 17.

and sixties a subculture whose important personages included Stan Brakhage, Kenneth Anger, Stan VanDerBeek, and Andy Warhol established themselves as the heirs of an earlier generation of avant-gardists and experimentalists such as Jean Cocteau (*Le sang d'un poète,* 1930) and Luis Buñuel (*Un chien andalou,* 1928).

The response of the major American studios to the new freedom has been slow, but there are signs of change, principally in the form of more flexible use of visual strategies—jump-cuts, flash cuts (forward or backward), slow and accelerated motion, form cuts, zoom-freezes, and the like. *Petulia* (1968), *The Graduate* (1967), *The Wild Bunch* (1969), and *The Landlord* (1970) are excellent films which illustrate this tendency, and they doubtless indicate the direction of much future development. Whatever the case, the pressure on Hollywood to experiment is constant, especially (and ironically) from the screen of commercial television, which feeds heavily on Hollywood's past to keep its viewers awake and watching between plugs for automobiles, beer, and carpets. To compete, the motion picture industry, which is increasingly worldwide in every respect, must either seek a different audience from television or offer the average addict of the tube a positive inducement to leave his living room with its easy chair, ash tray, and nearby supply of cold beer for the privilege of spending from two to five dollars for a *new* movie.

The future of commercial filmmaking is now being shaped by pressures from several, and often conflicting, directions. In terms of revenues for a new feature film "just four countries in Western Europe—the United Kingdom, Italy, France, and West Germany—can yield almost half of the domestic [i.e., United States] gross for a film." [5] Indeed, as early in the postwar years as 1953, Hollywood producers conceded, through Eric Johnston, their industry spokesman, that "9 out of 10 United States films cannot pay their way on the domestic market alone." Simultaneously with greater dependence on foreign markets, other important economic shifts have occurred at home and abroad. Moviegoing in the United States, as reflected in average weekly attendance at theaters, is "but slightly more than half the 1941 figure, while population growth in the intervening years has stretched the imbalance." [6] Even though admission prices have risen steeply, they do not offset the loss of volume. In addition, the suppression of the "block-booking" system by forced separation of Hollywood's production facilities from its distribution outlets through action of the federal government (1948) early deprived major Hollywood studios of assured domestic showcases for each of their products, whatever their individual cinematic or other merits.

Since then, a number of forces are at work to push and shove the world's film capital into its future. Increasingly, "one centrally located, fully equipped permanent facility" makes little economic sense because

[5] Guback, p. 4.
[6] Guback, p. 3.

of high labor costs in the United States when compared with the rest of the world; access to remote corners of the world for airborne men and equipment becomes ever easier; an improved technology offers better and more portable cameras and more sophisticated editing equipment as well as film stock that is both more sensitive to light and less sensitive to extremes in climate; a new generation of filmmakers are as concerned about experimenting with the technical and psychological aspects of the medium as they are in exploring a variety of social themes; major studios are steadily absorbed by vast financial conglomerates which, though sensitive to costs and attentive to balance sheets, are insensitive to Hollywood's traditions and indifferent to established patterns of production.[7]

In addition to all of these pressures, American capital investment, starting in the early 1950s, has gone abroad and offered to national film industries, which welcomed aid from the United States, financial backing of production costs and the guarantees of an international distribution system for completed films. In two decades the rest of the world has, for better or worse, increasingly lost its independence. In other words, the internationalization of the film industry under American auspices has inevitably meant the diminishing of "chances for diversity and different points of view." Film, however, which is "not only a business commodity but a vehicle of communication . . . , is important not only for what it says but for what it does not say. The boundaries of human experience . . . expand or contract on the basis of what people have presented to them." [8]

The purpose of this thumbnail sketch of the history of film is not to outline or even block out a subject whose dimensions are so large that they are still partly unexplored. Rather, it is to document the basic contention of the present anthology: that film is not *an* art form of the twentieth century, it is *the* art form of the twentieth century. If sculpture was the glory of Periclean Greece, architecture of Augustan Rome, painting of Renaissance Italy, and drama of Elizabethan England, cinema has been both the major contribution of America to world culture and the dominant mode of world culture itself for the last fifty years.

In its brief history, the film has assimilated the photograph variously filtered and focused, motion near and far, sound from one or several directions, color in all of its subtle gradations, screens of great breadth both indoors and out, and lenses that give a visceral feeling of depth and movement. Within these expanding dimensions, filmmakers have elaborated techniques of transition and dislocation from frame to frame which dissolve rigidities of time and space as its audiences know them in everyday life. As a result, the tension achievable in film between order and chaos, between control and chance—which lies at the heart of every art regardless

[7] "Movies Leaving 'Hollywood' Behind," *The New York Times* (May 27, 1970), p. 36.
[8] Guback, pp. 203, 4; see also pp. 94–95.

of its media—is more dynamic and capable of greater complexity than in any other art. Film is far from exhausting its possibilities for artistic triumphs.

In the years since World War II a new medium and industry, television, has emerged not only to challenge established patterns of filmmaking and moviegoing but also to create intricate and reciprocal relations with cinema. Even a partial profile of the mutual impact of film and television on each other would take us too far afield from our primary concern, feature films and their scripts. But certain aspects, some of which we have already discussed, should be noted in passing. The advent of television in the United States has coincided with a reduction in selected subjects, especially newsreels and weekly serials, at moviehouses and their reintroduction in contemporary forms on home screens. Television has also relied heavily on films of the thirties through the sixties from its sister industry in order to sustain the commercial messages of its own advertisers. And, in the postwar years, while the large Hollywood production companies have redefined themselves—lost their chains of tied moviehouses, dismantled their sound stages, and dissolved the star system—commercial television has formed three major networks with affiliated stations across the country, fostered its own production facilities, and created its own stellar personalities—the hosts of its talk, news, and variety shows. At the present time, the internationalism that the film industry has gradually achieved since 1945 is only just becoming possible for television, thanks in part to the broadcast potential of transmission satellites.

The place of film in twentieth-century culture can be demonstrated in another, equally dramatic way. The average nineteenth-century child was illiterate. He was effectively isolated from the culture of the dominant class. As he matured, his entertainment, when he could afford it, consisted of dance-hall reviews, vaudeville, and, occasionally, a melodrama by Dion Boucicault or one of his imitators. Conversely, middle- and upper-class children were brought up on books. They were introduced to the world of art through the printed page. As adults they consumed a constant fare of novels, some good, most bad or indifferent. Theater and opera were significant, but the novel formed the core of the cultural life of the literate population. The modern child, by contrast, is exposed to the visual world of movies and television long before he can read. There is no class distinction in this exposure. It is experienced equally by rich and poor, and it becomes more rather than less intense as the typical modern child matures. College students read more than the general public, but it has been estimated that in the United States a typical freshman has seen twenty movies for every book he has read—and this does not include an average of some 15,000 hours of exposure to television by age 18![9] After college, the student tends

[9] *Man and the Movies*, ed. W. R. Robinson (Baton Rouge: Louisiana State University, 1967), pp. 3–4.

to fall back into habits like those of the population in general, which means that he reads less, while his consumption of movies and television remains constant or increases. Clearly, film and television now form the cultural medium in which twentieth-century men—from the illiterate to the affluent —are immersed.

The consequences of the dominance of film and television as twentieth-century culture media have often been discussed. Marshall McLuhan feels we are being (or have been) pushed abruptly into a new phase of world culture, the post-Gutenberg era. Sounds and images, rather than printed words, shape our imaginative apprehension of the surrounding world. Sounds and images are not only far richer than printed words, they are also less "linear"—less dominated by the sequential logic of the sentence or paragraph or chapter—less constrained by the need to avoid redundancy or contradiction, and far more accessible since they do not assume literacy. McLuhan's theories imply that the printed word may be growing archaic: that some day the reading of printed books may be an antiquarian pursuit, a little like reading books written in Greek and Latin.

Whatever the future of the printed word, today's educational curricula are shaped around it to a degree that seems exaggerated on the secondary level and nearly obsessive on the college and university level. The higher-education establishment does obeisance to the printed word as devoutly as primitive tribes worship the idols of gods. While harmless in the area of the physical sciences, this behavior is questionable in the area of the humanities. Our literature departments boast of their concern for relevance—for significant examination of every aspect of modern culture. They actively encourage the study of modern fiction, modern poetry, modern drama, and modern criticism. Yet a Martian, after taking the "modern lit." curriculum at a typical American college, might emerge with no other knowledge of cinema than the vague realization that from time to time earthlings of the twentieth century went (probably furtively) to certain entertainments called movies. He might realize that plays and novels were occasionally made into movies, but he would have no inkling of the influence that movies have had on twentieth-century drama and fiction. At best, he would conclude that movies were a minor diversion appealing chiefly to the lower classes, the illiterate, the vulgar, the naive, the deviant.

Granted that film is the cultural medium characteristic of our age, that its neglect has been unfortunate, and that a proper understanding of its values and achievements would enrich studies of twentieth-century fiction, drama, and poetry, not to mention studies of modern psychology and sociology—the question remains: how does one study film?

In general, three approaches to film are possible: the technical, the historical, and the aesthetic. The technical is perhaps the most common one. Presently, some 850 courses on film are being taught at American colleges. The majority are technical in orientation. They are usually taught in departments of radio-television-film, of drama, and of speech, by individuals who are interested in how films are made.[10] Their common feature is their stress on making films—on script writing, photography, film acting, and film direction and editing. They are valuable, but they tend to be professionally oriented. In other words, they are primarily for those who hope to find a career (or, at least, an avocation) in film. They bear the same relation to the study of film that courses in creative writing bear to courses in literature and literary criticism, with the difference that, being much more technical, they are more numerous and less standardized in content.

No one who is interested in film can afford to be ignorant of the technical side of filmmaking, but the limitations of the technical approach should be recognized. One does not need to know how to write a novel in order to appreciate a good one once it is written: to respond to it, to observe its artistry, its literary relations, its form, and its thematic and historical significance. The same holds true for the study of film. Most films are made to be appreciated by audiences who could not care less about how they are made. Occasionally we have a technical *tour de force* like *The Cabinet of Doctor Caligari*, Cocteau's *Orpheus* (1949), or *Blow-up;* but the sheer cost of making a major film means that all but a few experimental directors use technique functionally—a point equally illustrated by Alfred Hitchcock's thrillers and Ingmar Bergman's meditative studies of the human psyche. Hitchcock and Bergman are both masters of film technique, and their technique is always part of their expression. Never present for its own sake, it serves as the medium of our vision, and, while we are members of an audience, we need be no more conscious of it *as technique* than the botanist examining plant cells is conscious of the complex arrangement of lenses that makes his observations possible.

The historical approach to film is also well-defined. Like the technical approach, it offers a valuable, even essential, body of information to the student. Although less common than the technical approach, it appears widely in the curriculum in the form of courses on "The History of Film," "The Silent Film Era," and the like. Historical courses are organized on analogy to the standard courses in the history of literature. Like the "surveys of English lit.," they tend to emphasize chronology, biography, and historical context, and to concentrate on early landmarks—the silent era— rather than later achievements. Their limitation is intrinsic to their approach. They are necessarily oriented toward history rather than toward the achievement of individual films.

The battle begun in the 1930s between historical scholars and the new critics of literature has given way to a generally peaceful coexistence. We recognize that there were (and are) important verities on both sides. In general, however, the basic contentions of the new critics have been established. We accept the idea that the study of literature is primarily a study

[10] *Film Study in Higher Education*, ed. D. C. Stewart (Washington, D.C.: American Council on Education, 1966), pp. 164–67.

of works of literature, not of dates, genres, influences, or biographies. This is why the old-fashioned sophomore literature survey has been replaced at most schools by courses in literary appreciation or literary masterpieces.

Surely, the same principles should apply to the study of film. It should be oriented toward our interest in ourselves and the culture within which the self is defined. The emphasis should be on individual films. Their artistic and cultural significance, rather than their technique or relation to the history of film, should receive first priority. Beyond that, if the films are considered in chronological order, the approach will take on an historical coloring; if they are considered by genres like the Western, the thriller, or the social documentary, the coloring will be formalist; if they are approached in terms of theme, the coloring will be sociological, philosophical, or theological. Some such coloration is inevitable and proper. It supplements the aesthetic approach, as long as it does not threaten to compromise examination of individual films.

To examine a film with the same care and thoroughness as a novel or a poem is difficult. The authoritative text of a film is the master print on which all prints made for commercial distribution are based. In the first place, the master print is never available. All films that are shown commercially and for educational purposes are later prints, and these are often edited silently to conform to local censorship laws, time requirements, and the like. Since many master prints have been lost, the later prints now available may or may not be edited versions, and for many early films, there is no way of knowing what the original really was.

Such bibliographical problems need not concern the average viewer. He can assume that the print of the film which he sees is reasonably close to the master print unless warned otherwise. His problem is of a different order. It stems from the fact that films are dynamic. They move. And as they move they convey more information than the human mind can retain. An experienced critic can pick up an impressive amount of detail from a single viewing of a film, but even the best observer has his limits and they are soon reached. The viewer of a film is the witness of a complex but significant series of events. We know how fallible even the most intelligent witnesses can be from the conflicting testimony that is always generated by a sensational public event. A vivid case in point is provided by the assassination of President Kennedy. We have to recognize the same propensity to error in ourselves. Yet the study of film demands accurate recall not only of what happened but what was said, how it was said, and—film being visual as well as verbal—how it was conveyed in images. That is, we certainly need to know that the hero married the heroine in the last reel. Depending on the aspect of the film that catches our interest, we may also need to know whether or not the butler was wearing gloves, whether the father drove a Ford or a Chevrolet, whether the heroine's costume in the first reel was red to foreshadow the sunset in the last, or whether there was a cut, a fade, or a dissolve from the chapel to the mountains. Moreover, if we wish to discuss our observations, we need some means of verifying them. If we disagree on the color of the heroine's costume, for example, the only way to decide who is right is to go to the film or an authoritative substitute.

Apparently, the ideal way of solving this problem is through movie archives and a viewing machine like the movieola, which permits the observer not only to see the film but to stop the action on a given frame, reverse it, and begin again. Comprehensive film archives would make it possible to document discussions of film in the same way that discussions of poems and novels are documented. An archive would have the further advantage of allowing interested critics to view films as often as necessary to refine and extend their observations.

But this solution, though ideal, is at present impracticable. No archive can accommodate the large numbers of individuals interested in film, and even if it could, the constant use of films quickly destroys them. A much more practical solution is to coordinate viewing of films with reading of scripts. Unlike reels of film, a script is easily portable; it can be read anywhere; it resists wear; notes can be written in its margins; and it is not "time bound," that is, it does not move continuously forward. If the critic comes to the last scene and wants to compare it to the first, he can simply turn back. Although a film can be reversed, the process is time-consuming, particularly if it has to be repeated several times.

Evidently, if film is to be studied as a cultural form in something of the same way that we study poetry, fiction, and drama, the script is a necessary adjunct to viewing the film. Note that it is an adjunct, not a replacement. A faithful copy of the master print must remain the final, authoritative text for the public at large. Normally, however, it is seen only once. At best it can be seen two or three times since rental schedules are fixed and viewing facilities (not to mention the time of the viewer) are limited. The script, which can be read as preparation for viewing the film, can also be annotated while the memory of the film is still fresh, reviewed easily and conveniently as often as needed, and can serve as documentation in resolving doubts about the filmmaker's intentions.

Note, too, that the importance here assigned the script does not imply that film is primarily verbal. The relative importance of image and word is a question in film aesthetics that will probably be debated as long as the question of what Aristotle meant by catharsis. The only assertion being made here is that if film is to be given its proper place in the study of modern culture, then viewing must be supplemented by use of scripts. In fact, a shooting script of the sort included in the present anthology often contains comments and revisions that call attention to effects that might otherwise be missed.

A final word may be useful concerning the scripts selected for the present volume. Silent films are not represented because they had no scripts in the modern sense of the term. Foreign films are excluded because they necessarily lead to awkward—usually misleading—compromises. Any-one who has read a translated script will be aware that its dialogue usually bears little relation to the dialogue in the film. The translator who provides subtitles works directly from the original shooting script, but within the economies of space and time in the footage. Many foreign films today are shown with dubbed-in dialogue. The alternative to a translation is thus a script transcribed from the English dialogue of a dubbed-in sound track. Such a script is next to worthless since the quality of the acting—the tonality, expression, gestures, and the like—was dictated by the nature of the *original* dialogue as well as the linguistic and cultural inheritance of the director and actor, not the words chosen by the English-language editor because they happen to fit the lip movements on the screen.

The scripts selected are entirely from the period between 1945 and 1970. The complicated legal status of prewar scripts makes permission to print difficult to obtain, and, evidently, many shooting scripts have been lost because they were not thought to have any intrinsic value. This limita-tion is not, however, without advantages. Hollywood's most vital periods were the silent era and the period following World War II. Postwar films are generally more serious in theme, more flexible in technique, and, of course, more directly relevant to contemporary life than their prewar fore-runners. Since this anthology is intended for the study of film as an art form rather than the history or technique of film, the basis of the selection has been the quality and intrinsic interest of the film itself. Each selection at-tracted the serious attention of reviewers and critics when it originally ap-peared; and each still repays thoughtful critical analysis. Given the abun-dance and excellence of English and American films during the period covered, no more than a sampling of them can be offered. But an effort has been made to represent the more important types—comedy, satire, costume-movie, social criticism, psychological study, thriller, and fantasy— as well as the more important ways in which a story comes to the screen— from a novel or short story, from a drama, from television, and from an original screen play. Although every reader will inevitably miss several of his favorites, the editors believe that each film selected has a legitimate claim for inclusion.

Most of the scripts are shooting scripts; that is, they represent the written version of a story as it was available to director, actors, and camera-man before and during the making of the film itself. Because shooting scripts differ from dramatic scripts, a brief discussion of their characteris-tics will be helpful.

Place and Use of the Script

The true text of any film is the film itself, or, more strictly speaking it is the final negative, called the *master film*, from which all prints are made.

The relationship between a shooting script and a finished film is complex and depends upon a large number of variables, mostly upon the intentions and practices of the director. Some of the most outstanding directors, Alfred Hitchcock, for example, work with most explicit and detailed scripts and follow the script with much the same precision as a builder does the blueprints of an architect. (Hitchcock, of course, always works very closely with his writer at every step of the way in preparing his own kind of script.) Other directors prefer a loosely defined scenario so that they have a maximum amount of margin for revision and improvisation during the shooting stage. Some cineasts believe, quite wrongly, that many contemporary pictures are made without scripts. In general, this is simply not true, although the form of the script may vary widely from neatly bound scripts to pencilled scribblings done moments before shooting or even during the shooting of a scene. Granted the powerful aesthetic influence of *cinéma vérité* in our time, which some critics see as a new development in the medium and others as a return to the classical purity of improvisation that characterized the making of many of the greatest silent films, the fully developed script remains a key step in the creation of most films.

To be sure, a certain kind of film, increasingly popular and becoming well-known, dispenses with the rigidities of conventional plot and conventional story line, in favor of working out, directly before the camera, improvisations, ad lib dialogue, and even events or happenings. A conventional script obviously serves little or no purpose in such a scheme. In addition, as the old, arbitrary lines of distinction between fiction and nonfiction, fable and fact, continue to break down, even the feature-length documentary film will be affected by this new creative energy. The work of the American filmmaker Fred Wiseman is an excellent example. Using his team of cameramen to record actual people engaged in actual events, he might once have been called a documentary filmmaker, and judged by old-fashioned standards and classifications. Today he is regarded simply as a filmmaker. His *Titicut Follies* (1967), *High School* (1968), *Law and Order* (1969), and *Hospital* (1970) are, indeed, documentaries taken on the scene at particular times and places and using real people, not actors. Yet these films are also examples of advocacy reporting, designed to make strongly felt social and political points. He exercises the filmmaker's art in choosing to film the events that support his views and feelings and also in the most careful editing of the film to make "reality" coincide with his personal vision. He is thus as much a deliberate fabulator as any other filmmaker, an honest and engaged artist for whose work the old distinctions between "fiction" and "nonfiction" are largely irrelevant. But his method, at least in these films, precludes the use of any ordinary script.

Allowing for notable exceptions, however, it is still generally true that all feature films intended to be shown to audiences in theaters have a script. They may differ in form and format. The script may exist in many copies, available and known to all concerned, or it may be the private property of only a few key figures in the production process. But there is almost always a script, and that script precedes the making of the film.

The process of filmmaking and the unique nature of the medium are such that a script may be considered as raw material for the finished product. It helps to initiate the process of making, serves as a guide to director, actors, and technicians, and is then finally, to a greater or lesser degree, expendable. To the student of cinema, however, a script can be of real value. Close reading of it, in conjunction with an attentive viewing of the film, will demonstrate a great deal, which otherwise might be difficult to learn, about the nature of this twentieth-century art form. And such a procedure can offer substance for the purposes of query, discussion, and debate, the give-and-take and discovery that is learning.

The primary value of using shooting scripts in the study of films is that this method reflects honestly the first critical phase in the process of filmmaking. Although the outlines have been publicly available for a full half-century and have changed only slightly and very gradually during all that time, the process of making pictures is surprisingly little known. Or, when known, it is all too often ignored. Critics and reviewers are, for their own reasons, frequently indifferent to the process of making; or, what is perhaps less defensible, sometimes imply a very different sort of process than the one actually followed by the makers of films. Audiences, even some of the most appreciative and sophisticated, are frequently unfamiliar with the basics of the craft. This ignorance may be partially advantageous; for films, perhaps more than any other art form, depend almost as much upon sleight-of-hand, upon the magicians's art, for their effect upon the viewer as they do upon what is literally shown and seen. Often what is not shown, but is instead evoked in and imagined by the audience, is as viable as what is really shown. Good film shows us a great deal, but we perceive more than what is shown. From Eisenstein to Hitchcock to McLuhan and including the young filmmakers and cinema buffs around the world, directors and producers of films as well as critics and scholars of the art have sought to define theoretically and to name and classify the elements that combine to create the aesthetic effects of film. Their explorations, especially those of the makers of films, are a fascinating subject for research and study and are extremely important in the cultivation of a finer cinematic sensibility. The views of these men, although not to be ignored or slighted, in theory and practice, are far from definitive, whether they be interpreted singly or in any combination. The rules of the game, as even a slight reading of items listed in the bibliography will show, keep changing. One of the surest signs of vitality is the resistance of film art to every attempt at definitive classification, even the most subtle and persuasive. A rudimentary knowledge and general familiarity with the basic steps in the process of making a film should, however, at least serve to increase one's sense of appreciation, to refine one's taste and judgment rather than strip the cinematic experience of its human magic.

And that is the aim of this collection of scripts: to give the reader a means of seeing how films evolve from words to something else and, ideally, something much more than a script, namely, a complex of images, arranged in careful sequence, supported by sound and by music, dramatized by actors, and controlled by the intelligence and sensibility of a director.

Although most scripts are much transformed in the sequential processes of shooting and editing, the ideal of filmmakers, from producer to prop man, is to translate the script into the language and idiom of cinematography and to realize in doing so the script's full potential. This goal is an elusive one at best because of the nature of the process of making films and the many variables involved. All of the artists, craftsmen, and technicians who work at the making of a picture bring to it both skill and creativity. Each is a maker who seeks by his own skills to create something new and good. But even the best results have never given us "perfect" films, only truly fine films whose magic succeeds in spite of their imperfections.

A film script, even when published with care to reflect in detail the copy provided by the film's proprietors, is at best a verbal outline, a blueprint of what one sees and experiences in viewing a film. It is in no way a substitute for the actual experience of seeing a clear, unbutchered print of the film. But as an aid to memory, it helps us recall what we have already experienced as an ordering of meaningful sights and sounds.

Although the script writer is a valuable contributor to the total experience of a film, he is only one of many. Insofar as a single controlling sensibility unifies the entire process and experience, it is always that of the director. The director, of course, cannot possibly do everything himself or know in detail everything necessary to make a moving picture. But he, in the last analysis, is held responsible for all that happens or fails to happen. In recent years, especially with the decline of the large corporate producers in Hollywood, we have come to perceive this fact more clearly. The director's name rather than that of the producer or his imprint is the one we associate with a film in allotting praise or blame. In a very real sense the French critics of our time have been more accurate than innovative in naming the director of a picture its *auteur*. No full and easy analogy, however, quite explains the role of the director. His function is at once that of quarterback, orchestra conductor, building contractor, trail boss, company commander, and, sometimes, lion tamer—the latter image amusingly exploited by Fellini in 8½. The director rules, benevolently or despotically, over a little kingdom. The writer, though absolutely essential to the process and especially to the beginning of it, remains his majesty's loyal servant.

This book contains several sorts of film scripts in a variety of formats. Most are final shooting scripts, that is, examples of the very form which director, cast, and crew worked with when a film first went into production. In many cases additions and deletions and rearrangements and revisions of material take place during the period of shooting the film and, again, during the period of editing the film. Freedom and flexibility are basic characteristics of the creative process of filmmaking. The possibilities for revision are always present when a scene is being filmed, and equally so in the cutting room and laboratory as the film is being edited and polished into its finished form. The final shooting script is the first part of the production process, but it should be remembered that even in this form a script has usually been through many stages already and has been much revised.

Two scripts in this entire collection are not precisely final shooting scripts: those of *Henry V* (1944) and *The Pumpkin Eater* (1964). Each of these British scripts is designated, in British film terminology, as a *release screenplay*. That is to say, each has been more or less adjusted to conform as closely as possible to the edited film, its basic camera angles and shots, its frames and footage. These screenplays, in comparison with final shooting scripts, offer a fuller description of sound and music devices, present many more separate camera shots, and include such elements of the finished and released film as the full title and credits. Necessity requires the inclusion of these release screenplays; for, unlike their American counterparts, it is not the custom of British production companies to preserve copies of the earlier versions of scripts on file. We are most fortunate, however, thanks to the writers themselves, to have obtained rare versions of the shooting scripts of *A Hard Day's Night* (1964) and *Darling* (1965) for this collection. Yet even these release screenplays are somewhat different from and fall short of what is generally known as the *final* official form of a film script—the *combined continuity*. Created by a specialist (usually designated as *script girl*) who follows the shooting and editing of a film from beginning to end, based entirely upon the completed and commercially released form of the film, with all of the separate camera shots listed and all details of footage and running time of individual shots and scenes, etc., carefully recorded, a combined continuity is at once a sort of chart or graph of a finished film and the very last *word* of the film. Close as these two British release screenplays are to what is seen in the films, they are not combined continuities; and differences exist between them and the films. The alert student will note slight changes in each of them.

All of the other scripts in this collection are final shooting scripts. If the release screenplay comes near the end of the process of filmmaking, a final shooting script represents a true beginning. It is the demarcation point—many filmmakers would call it "the point of no return," the place where the production of the film really begins. From there on it goes first before the cameras, then, perhaps most crucially of all, into the movieola of the film editor to be cut and arranged before the finished film is to be projected upon a screen. Next to the director the film editor has, in a literal and physical sense, more control over what will be seen by an audience than anyone engaged in the making of a picture. The director remains responsible for the results and thus supervises the editing process closely. Some directors are engaged in the cutting and editing of a film in all details. Others prefer to give their film editor considerable freedom and to act in a critical capacity, viewing sections of the film in the projection room and offering general advice, suggestions, and criticism as, bit by bit, the whole film is put together. (Sometimes the screenwriter is called upon to participate at this stage as well.) The film editor, of course, is a highly professional craftsman, often an experienced artist in his own right. How he works with the director and others, and how much the actual labor is overseen and divided is a subtle matter involving diplomacy, tact, and personal relationships. Theoretically, in any event, the director has the last word in this area and is held responsible for the quality of the editing.

The Process of Filmmaking

In the beginning someone has an idea for making a picture. Once this "someone" was almost always a producer. Now, increasingly, it is a director, a writer, or occasionally a star who initiates the process. As witnessed by the scripts in this collection, the idea, the source of original inspiration for a movie, may come from almost anywhere—a novel or short story, a play for stage or television, another film old or new, something from the newspapers or magazines, or something that has captured an artist's attention and can lead to an original screenplay. However the idea may begin, it soon becomes a *property*. This term, though unfortunate in its connotations, is almost universally used by filmmakers and is used in a neutral rather than a pejorative sense. In any case, the original desire and intention to create a film becomes a matter of real property when a producer involves himself by means of an option or outright purchase of film rights.

Enter the writer (if he has not arrived already) to set about building a story and writing a script. Whether the picture is an adaptation or an original screenplay, as soon as a producer is involved, commerce begins to make its claims. The making of all pictures to be shown in theaters, where audiences buy tickets of admission, is an elaborate (and sometimes lucrative) business as well as an art. Each year the cost of making films increases. The producer must be able to raise the capital necessary to make the film from one or more sources. Perhaps, under ideal circumstances and blessed with a reputation for success, he can tentatively arrange the financing, sign options with leading actors and the right director, and gather the essential elements of the crew on the strength of the property alone. But sooner or later, and usually sooner, he will need a script to present to both potential backers and key coworkers before any firm commitments can be made, contracts signed, and a budget and production schedules devised. The writer thus comes in early. If he is lucky he stays late and sees the picture through production.

A very large number of projects, begun with high hopes and much enthusiasm, never reach the point of a workable script, one that is satisfactory to everyone who must be satisfied. A large percentage of properties never become films. And a very large number of the films we see have had more than one screenwriter and many preliminary versions and drafts of the script. Only writers whose material is actually used in the film receive *film credit,* even though a number of writers may have worked on the property earlier.

For simplicity and assuming ideal circumstances, let us imagine one writer working on a script. It should also be understood that though the stages described here are customary and conventional, they vary considerably according to the experience and reputation of the writer and his personal relationship with the producer and the director. Usually the writer will first produce a brief *synopsis* that is basically a literary outline of how he proposes to deal with the story in cinematic terms. If this proves satisfactory, he then writes a *treatment,* a much longer and detailed development of the synopsis, an extended outline of the potential script. The treatment is still more or less literary in form, descriptive rather than dramatic, though it may very well include some individual scenes done in dramatic form and with some dialogue.

Many filmmakers find the treatment a vital stage in the development of script into film. A commonplace among filmmakers says, "If it isn't in the script, it won't be in the picture." What is not meant, of course, by this aphorism is the picture's style, direction, cinematography, cutting, or any matter of filmmaking technique. What is meant is what has always concerned writers as storytellers—structure, character, motivation, tone, etc. Some filmmakers themselves apply this rule of thumb to the treatment and swear that if a script—and hence the film—takes a wrong turn, the flaw can be found in the treatment.

Following the treatment comes the *first draft screenplay,* now employing one of the conventional formats used for film scripts. These forms, as you will see, have slight differences, but there are some general things that apply to all the shooting scripts in this collection. A script is broken down into separate units. Usually, though not always, these are numbered sequentially, and are called *master scenes.* These units may be many or relatively few in number, depending on the detail called for in order to help the translation of dialogue and action as written into camera frames, angles, depth-of-field, transitions, sound, etc. Compared to continuities all scripts are sparse in this kind of explicit direction. A master scene is, then, simply a single dramatic unit at a single location or setting. Within this unit any number of shots and camera angles may be used to shoot many feet of film—versions of the same scene from a variety of angles and points of view. Though the method is changing, the traditional one still employed by most directors requires that all actions in a given master scene be shot at least five times (sometimes the number can be as high as twelve) in order to insure proper *coverage* of the scene. The purpose here is not only to allow for different readings on the part of actors or, say, different lighting conditions, but to provide the director and the film editor with enough footage of the same basic dramatic unit so that they may cut and splice with a maximum of freedom and choice. In the cutting, which comes later, they may well use and juxtapose frames and pieces from all the separate versions of a photographed master scene. This rule does not apply easily, of course, to scenes (or entire films) based upon spontaneity and improvisation.

In addition to specifying a sequence of master scenes and calling for certain specific camera angles in the cinematography of a film, the writer may or may not specify the use of certain kinds of transitions from one unit to the next. Transitions from one scene to the next, from one piece of film to the next, are the concern of the editor. It is not properly a part of the writer's job to tell director, cameraman, or editor how to do theirs; nor will they heed his suggestions to the disadvantage of the film or the inhibition of their own talents. There are a number of reasons, however, why a writer will offer some directions, camera angles, and transitions in his script. First, he will do so in order to make clear a point within his proper area of concern—a story or plot point, a bit of characterization, a structural device, or, perhaps, an occasional suggestion as to the rhythm of a scene or sequence of shots. For the rhythm of a film is intricately wedded to its dramatic structure. Unless elapsed time, for example, is being used functionally for suspense, as in *High Noon* (1952), film is not concerned with what we call "real" time. Instead one has a sense of continual present, a sense that is created by the rhythm of the film. Context may make two scenes of approximately the same footage seem radically different. One may appear slow and lyrical whereas the other may seem jagged, jazzy, and quick. With a full awareness that his views are largely speculative suggestions and may frequently be ignored, the writer is within his rights in dealing with these elements. His views may give director, cameraman, or editor a clearer idea of the intent and inner quality of the script. He will be at fault only in persuading himself that his own visualization of the finished film ought to be binding on the director, actors, and technicians.

There is also another value in the writer's use of at least a few technical devices in his script. Although the script is mainly intended to lead towards the creation of the film, it must be read by a great many people, some very knowledgeable in cinematic technique, others less so. In addition to being examined by the cast and crew, the script is read by bankers and financial backers, by lawyers and talent agents and casting agents, by potential distributors, sometimes even by the owners of theaters, and by publishers and journalists, etc. And each of these readers must be given a sense of the finished film, enough detail to imagine, however, vaguely, the style, form, and content of the film itself. Whether or not the details are ever used as they are indicated in a shooting script depends upon many things, but clearly one function of the script writer, though it is secondary, is to produce a readable film script.

The writer writes his first draft screenplay and the drafts and versions that follow with the criticism, encouragement, and, to an increasing degree as he comes closer to the final shooting script, the collaboration of others who will be making the picture.

The *production manager* worries about the budget, tries to eliminate what seem to him unnecessary scenes and characters wherever possible. And he arranges his own *sequence* for the shooting of the picture, a sequence designed to use talent, sets, material, etc., as efficiently as possible. Almost all pictures made these days, anywhere is the world, are shot *out of sequence* because of the enormous expense of making films. The actual sequence of production and shooting thus hardly ever parallels the sequential structure of the script. Major parts, the leads, have the whole script to study and, with the help of the director, can, even out of proper order, build a character. The minor actors with bit parts are frequently given only *sides*, that is, those specific pages of the script which involve them. They are thus much more dependent on the director. Producer, director, actors, production manager, cameraman, editor, art director, set dresser, and even the prop man, these and many more all have legitimate interests and concerns, and they may exert a considerable influence before the final shooting script is ready.

Once the picture goes into production, collaboration is increased both because more people are involved at that stage and because of the necessity of meeting a fairly strict schedule, within the terms of a fixed budget. If the writer continues on the job, working through the period of production, he will make many changes on the spot to fit unforeseen circumstances. If he does not, there will be changes anyway. Like the diagram of a football play, the script, though well-conceived and planned, does not always work out on the ground exactly as anticipated.

Revision and repeated possibilities for revising, changing, and rearranging occur in every stage of the filmmaking process. Everyone involved has to make constant choices. With liberty to choose and change comes an increased responsibility. For often the choices that must be made are not clear-cut, not between good and bad, but, like many political choices, are decisions between imperfect options for the sake of expediency and in hope and faith that results may serve to justify what is finally decided.

Hence, everyone involved in the making of a film, and not least of these the writer, must always allow for the unexpected and for the possibility of change throughout the entire production. Even then, with the production finished and "in the can," the possibilities of change and (sometimes) improvement remain. Many films are slightly revised following their first previews. Some are revised even later, after their initial premiere openings and in response to reviews. One of the most famous of American filmmakers, the late Irving Thalberg (who served as the model for the producer in F. Scott Fitzgerald's last and unfinished novel, *The Last Tycoon*) is frequently quoted as describing the filmmaking process: "Pictures are not made, they are remade."

Sometime after the final shooting script is finished, the picture goes into actual production, following the shooting schedule. There are rehearsal periods (and, usually, subsequent changes) sometimes before the shooting begins, and always on the set during daily shooting. Scene by scene, the material to be shot is rehearsed until the director is ready to photograph the scene. Then, with everything in place, lighting arranged, camera and sound equipment ready to record, there is the *take*. There may be many takes before the director is satisfied and signifies that a particular take is a *print*. As the shooting schedule progresses the director and editor are regularly viewing the prints called *rushes* or *dailies* as they are delivered from the photographic laboratory. Always bearing in mind their aim of assembling the best possible scenes, they study the prints to decide if it is necessary (and possible) to reshoot sequences that seem to have failed.

When the shooting schedule has been completed and most of the cast and crew are gone, then the stage of full-scale editing commences. It is an intense time which, by traditional rule of thumb, is at least equal to the time spent shooting. All the prints must now be assembled into a single form, a sort of rough draft of the film called the *work print* or *rough cut*. Some figures will give an indication of the magnitude of the task facing the editor and the director. The average feature film runs approximately ninety minutes or, in footage, 8,100 feet of film. It is not unusual for the director and editor to have at least 200,000 feet of prints to work with, from which the film must be composed. And it is also common to have on hand another 100,000 feet of film which represent prints put aside in reserve but not yet discarded during the daily viewing of the rushes. These reserve prints are called *bolds*.

Now the director and editor begin the task of composing and arranging all of this material, through constant revision, into the order and form of the rough cut. When the rough cut is ready, the director can for the first time know with some degree of accuracy how long his film, in its present stage, runs. It is not uncommon for a rough cut to be very long indeed, sometimes an hour or even several hours too long for a feature film. When this is the case, a process of cutting back and simplifying begins. In editing, whole scenes from the script can be shortened or, in some cases, ruthlessly eliminated as being, in terms of the context of the entire picture, no longer necessary. Whole scenes and even larger blocks of script material can be easily rearranged. Both sequence and structure are relatively flexible again.

When the director and the producer are satisfied with the work print, more work still remains to be done. Although this custom is changing, the services of the *composer* are called upon at this late stage. He views the work print, studies the script, then writes music for the picture, which is arranged, performed, and recorded. The contribution of music to the total experience of the film can be enormous. From the beginning, even before the advent of sound, when pianos accompanied the silent pictures in theaters, music has been an integral part of the aesthetic experience of movies. The full implications and possibilities of the use of music in support of and conjunction with all the elements of the film are only now being systematically explored and understood. At least it is clear to all that composer and musicians make a really major contribution to the totality of a film.

With the music ready and recorded and all the various sound effects (for example, the ringing of a doorbell, traffic noise, a jet passing overhead, train and boat whistles, etc.) on hand, then, music, dialogue and sound effects are *mixed* by a careful and complicated electronic process to become the *sound track*, a permanent part of the *negative* and, thus, of the *composite print* made from it. At that point the film is done, the picture is finished and ready to be previewed and put into release.

From this oversimplified account of the making of a film several basic generalizations can be drawn:

(a) Filmmaking is complex and collaborative to an extent beyond any of our other media or art forms.

(b) The writer has a critical part to play in the collaboration, for he makes what is at once a blueprint for and the raw material of the finished film. But nonetheless his part is only one among many.

(c) The script is only the first tentative draft text of the film. The extent to which it is followed, closely or freely, literally or with much embellishment, depends on many variable factors.

(d) The effect of the finished film as experienced by an audience is simultaneous, a happening in which all the individual parts, done separately and in bits and pieces, come together at once. Only in the film, and to a lesser extent in the shooting script from which it evolved, is this unity possible.

(e) The making of pictures is a process allowing for many stages of revision, for an extraordinary number of choices to be made. Choices, even bad choices, are exercises of reason. Filmmaking becomes, by definition, one of the most rational art forms man has known. The writer shares in this process, and there is a reason for everything in his script. But in the end, since a film must evoke emotional and imaginative responses from the audience, all the reasons of the makers of the film become means to an end, tools to accomplish a task.

Perhaps the finest picture concerned with the process of filmmaking is Fellini's 8½, in which the protagonist is a gifted director trying to make a picture. Although he fails in his intention, he does succeed in creating the picture we have seen. At the end, the next-to-last scene of the film, the director and his writer sit in a lonely car and the writer, most reasonably, tells him all of the reasons why he has failed. The writer's arguments are irrefutable. Except . . . except precisely at that point a mind reader, a kind of magician who had appeared much earlier in the film, reappears and summons the director to come and do his proper job. The characters from all of the story's episodes reappear at once and, following the instructions of the director, come together hand in hand in a beautiful dance. As they fade out and we are left to confront a dark screen, the truth brightens at the last: out of all the confusion and chaos of this collaborative enterprise, out of all the choices and reasons, good and bad, comes something marvelous, a kind of magic. All the craft of filmmaking conspires to strive towards what Alexander Pope called "a grace beyond the reach of art."

Films are the art form of our tribe, our modern cave paintings. To study the script and to see the film is only the beginning, a preliminary stage in acquiring a finer appreciation of the medium and a greater refinement of taste and judgment. It is fitting and proper to begin where the filmmakers begin, with the script, and to retrace, partly by the evidence and partly by educated surmises, their journey to the final destination of the finished film.

Film Terms in Context

The grammar and syntax of film are not verbal. In the complete cinematic experience words play a part, a very small part, in the form of dialogue. And words are important in the creation of film, beginning with the written script. But when creators, critics, and scholars speak of the *language* of film they are very seldom referring to words. Rather they are speaking of all aspects of cinematic technique as they apply to the making of films and as they are part of the aesthetic experience of the finished film. Though the language of film is essentially nonverbal, a *vocabulary* for film exists to describe the steps taken in the making of films and the effects of films upon appreciative viewers.

The terminology associated with film is complex at its best and esoteric at its worst. It is often confusing to the uninitiated when it is not apparently contradictory. A classic example is the word *montage*. Originally it was the French filmmaker's technical term for the entire process of editing. Great Russian theorists and filmmakers, notably Lev Kuleshov, Vsevolod Pudovkin, and Eisenstein, pioneers of film art, took over the term and changed its meaning. It replaced for them what they had earlier called *the American cut* and was used more strictly to describe both their theory and practice of the art of rapid cutting. (See below for definition of a *cut*.) Because the art and critical theory of these men, and others who followed, have been extremely influential and remain so today, their definitions and classifications of montage are widely used. At the same time, however, American filmmakers incorporated the term montage to describe a very different thing, and their definition is also current and is sometimes called for in scripts. They used the word to describe a series of shots rapidly *dissolving* (see below) over each other. Today the word is used in either sense. Its meaning depends upon context.

The shifting values of montage, both denotative and connotative, are typical of many words in the glossary of film. Context tends to make meaning clear even when there is disagreement about the precise definition. Critics and reviewers, looking at films from the point of view of the effect of the experience of viewing, use their own words and definitions, some of these used exclusively in this critical language. Scholars and specialists in the history of film art are often inclined to use other words, or to use more common words within the limits of special connotation. Makers of films, usually quite aware of both these "dialects," have another vocabulary to describe the technical details of making. They can communicate to each other easily enough, even across the barriers of national language, as witnessed by the fact that in our time international pictures made by multilingual casts and crews are not a novelty. A great many terms in the filmmaker's lexicon are thus more or less meaningless to all those outside of the craft. Fortunately, an appreciative student of film art need not master a very large vocabulary of technical terms at the outset to speak to the basic aspects of scripts or finished films. From an understanding of some of the elementary terms and experience with the things they signify, the student of film can go on to increase his knowledge and refine his understanding through reading the work of outstanding historians, critics, and filmmakers.

In recent years, precisely the years covered by the volumes of *Film Scripts*, it has been the custom of filmmakers to hire writers of all kinds—dramatists, novelists, poets, journalists—to write screenplays. Most of these writers at least begin their association with filmmaking without any previous experience, except for the great, common, shared experience of moviegoing. The days of great production studios, each with its building where a corps of full-time script writers was kept busy, are gone for good. A writer is generally hired to work on one particular project. The common experience of the beginner, frequently described by these writers in interviews and written accounts of their experience, has been doubt at the ability to master the form of the medium, a doubt followed by a sense of surprise and relief that the fundamentals of the vocabulary of filmmaking are not so complex as to demand years of expert experience.

The purpose here is to offer a limited glossary needed for the reading of these scripts and the viewing of the films which came from them. (A full glossary will be found in the back of the book.) Some terms have already been isolated and defined in the preceding section. Others are briefly defined and discussed below.

Those readers who wish to seek out deeper and more inclusive working definitions and examples, will find them in a number of readily accessible books.

(a) *The Filmviewer's Handbook* by Emile G. McAnany, S.J., and Robert Williams, S.J. (Glen Rock, N.J.: Paulist Press, 1965). The chapter entitled "The Language of Film" (pp. 42–69) offers excellent and precise definitions of many terms in a general introduction to the subject.

(b) *A Grammar of the Film* by Raymond Spottiswoode (Berkeley, Calif.: University of California Press, 1965). The chapter "Definitions" (pp. 42–53) offers some useful definitions, though some of his terminology is eccentric when seen beyond the context of this volume.

(c) *A Dictionary of the Cinema* by Peter Graham (New York: A. S. Barnes, 1964). Essentially a brief listing of people in films, this book does offer some definitions of film terms and, notably, some of the special terms used by British and European filmmakers.

(d) *People Who Make Movies* by Theodore Taylor (New York: Doubleday, 1967). Though intended for younger readers, this introduction is exceptionally clear and fine in its coverage of many parts of the filmmaking process. Basic terms, together with examples, are used throughout the text. A brief but accurate glossary is appended.

(e) *Behind the Screen: The History and Techniques of the Motion Picture* by Kenneth MacGowan (New York: Delacorte Press, 1965). This massive compendium of information gives examples and illustrations by a distinguished producer and deals with all aspects of picture-making. Pages 333–501, concerned in depth with technical aspects of filmmaking, present a great many useful terms with full, accurate definitions.

The scene as unit

The opening unit of the script *High Noon*, the first capitalized section, incorporating scenes 1–8 in a descriptive passage, is a useful example. Its format is conventional enough to be called standard.

1–8 EXT. OUTSKIRTS OF HADLEYVILLE—DAY

First, the numbering indicates that eight separate shorter "scenes" are here incorporated into one unit. This device, which is somewhat literary, is designed to make the script more readable at the outset, to set the tone and style before any reader contends with the difficulty of trying to visualize and imagine a large number of separate scenes, 426 in all, many of which are to be very short, individual shots. In the capitalized identification the abbreviation "EXT." establishes that the shooting of the scene is *exterior,* outdoors. The abbreviation "INT." would have established an *interior* location, a setting within some structure. Though this identification may seem so obvious as to be silly to the reader, it serves both a narrative purpose in the script and a technical purpose in making the film. A number of important members of the crew, for example the production manager and the cameraman, not to mention a host of minor functionaries, use this information at a quick glance in their preparation for a scene. Since a film can seldom be shot in the order and sequence of scenes found in the script, the production manager must devise a schedule in which exterior scenes, or nearby parts of them, can be used in a single shooting sequence. At the same time he must be ready not to lose a full day's shooting on account of weather. In the event of rain, for example, he has ready a *backup schedule,* or alternate shooting plan that uses interior sets. These sets must be in order and ready, lighting and sound facilities available, and other members of the cast alert to be called. The script and the schedule also give the cameraman and his crew or *unit* some of the basic information they need to work efficiently. Their equipment for outdoor shooting, the size and composition of the crew, will be different than for interior work.

Because the action of *High Noon* takes place within a small span of time and entirely by daylight, the convention "DAY" is not repeated after the initial heading. In other scripts, however, this traditional direction is frequently used, either regularly with each separate scene, wherever context requires it, or the information is necessary for the crew. Very often scenes supposedly set at night are photographed during the day since the illusion of darkness can be created by the use of appropriate lens and filters as well as by the type and the quality of the film. If the scene must in fact be shot at night, then the proper artificial illumination must be on hand.

Occasionally a more specific direction will be found, such as "DAWN," "TWILIGHT," or "DAY FOR NIGHT," the latter calling explicitly for the daylight shooting of a night scene. These notations tell the cameraman and his unit the kind of light qualities they must capture on film.

The scene

Generally, the breakdown of scenes, headed by the capitalized line and separated by space from other scenes, is determined not only by place, but also by the primary *setup* of the camera and other equipment necessary for shooting. Although all of this equipment cannot easily be displaced in most instances from one setting to another, within a single setting the camera is readily movable. A scene combines, therefore, the physical setting and the primary placement of camera and equipment. In all of the scripts different "scenes" occur from time to time within the larger scene. These separate units, which are part of the same setting and sequence of action, can be used to identify a new and specific setup or to isolate a particular kind of shot.

The filmmaking technique of Alfred Hitchcock is an exception to the rule. Hitchcock prepares, simultaneously with the preparation of the final shooting script, an elaborate and detailed series of sketches (rather like an oversize comic strip) visualizing the film-to-be scene by scene. These sketches are called *continuity sketches*. Script and continuity sketches together, and coordinated as to camera angles and shots, are the material upon which the production of the film is based. Many other directors use continuity sketches as a part of their working strategy, for at least parts of a film, as a guide to the shooting and editing of difficult scenes and transitions. (See "Editorial Terms" below.)

Camera shots

Many kinds of shots are possible, but basically all of them are variations upon a few standards.

Three are defined by proximity of the camera to the subject, whether literally by distance or by use of special lenses. These shots—*long, medium,* and *close*—are only relative and not specific measures. The long shot includes details of an entire setting. Its subject may be on the horizon, for example, a distant ship, the buildings of a city, an expanse of open country, or it may be as close as, say, fifty yards. In order to emphasize great distance, an *extreme long shot* is sometimes called for. A medium shot is of a distance to include, if necessary, a group of two or more people and at least part of the surroundings. A close shot, also called *closeup,* focuses closely on its subject in isolation. It may be of the face or hands of a character or of some single object. Close shots, of course, can be photographed quite separately, even at another time and place, and inserted later in the action of a sequence. For further definition close shots may be *extreme* or *tight* on the one hand or a *medium close shot,* which is indefinite in scope, but nearer at hand than a standard medium shot and at the same time not so tight as the standard closeup.

Two other shots, in which the proximity may vary, are usually included in the five basic shots. They are the *two-shot,* or *group shot* if more than two characters are involved, and the *over-shoulder* shot. The first, at whatever distance, focuses attention on two characters or the group. Sometimes the cameraman is asked in this context to center attention on one of the characters by *featuring* or *favoring*. The over-shoulder shot is, in fact, a variation of the two-shot or group shot; for, in the foreground is the back of the head of one character and in the background we see what the character sees.

Occasionally other kinds of shots are called for, which the context makes clear. For example, a *full shot* does not specify distance, merely that the shot should be fully inclusive of the subject.

In scripts the term *montage* is sometimes used to describe a shot. It then signifies a "series of rapid dissolves," which was mentioned earlier, and involves both cameraman and editor in its creation.

A *stock shot* is a shot or sequence not filmed specifically for the picture but taken from the stock of available footage of any given subject or event. A frequently used stock shot is that of a commercial jet taking off or landing.

A *process shot* is a shot in which actors in the foreground play out a scene in front of a screen that is itself filled with a photograph or movie. The most familiar conventional example occurs in traffic scenes. The characters are photographed in the shell of a stationary automobile while a film of traffic, visible through the rear window, gives the impression of movement and traffic. Process shots may also be used to give the impression of some background or setting far from the studio and set where the actors are being photographed.

Camera angles

In addition to the specific kind of shot sometimes explicitly called for in a script, camera angles may be stated. Just as in the case of shots, these suggestions by the writer will be actually followed by the director and cameraman only insofar as they are deemed valid and functional.

The camera may photograph from certain basic *angles* and, as well, it may shoot from a particular *point of view* (usually abbreviated POV). Point of view need not include the observing character, whose presence on the screen would constitute an over-shoulder shot. A character, for example, looks up; the next shot, made as if to represent what he sees, is of a buzzard in the sky.

Camera angles can be reduced to three principal types: a *regular* or standard angle, unnamed and unspecified since it is assumed to be taken from the camera as set up, straight up and down; a *high angle* (looking from above); and a *low angle* (looking up).

Occasionally the angle is assumed and the direction *shooting up* or *shooting down* is given. The high angle is sometimes simply described as a *high shot*.

Camera and movement

In shooting a camera may be either *fixed* or *moving*.

A fixed camera is set up at one spot. But a fixed camera can nevertheless be used to create a sense of movement or action.

The fixed camera can *tilt*, be moved upward or downward on its single axis while shooting.

And the fixed camera can *pan*. The word is a contraction of the original term used—*panoramic shot*. It is a pivotal movement, usually lateral, made by turning the camera on its axis from one side or part of a scene or setting to another.

Two other customary movements of a fixed camera are the *zoom* and the *whip*.

The zoom is achieved by lens adjustment during photographing so that, without any break, the camera may move (*zoom in*) to a quick closeup of a particular subject.

The whip is a variation on the pan. The camera, focused on one object in a scene, is suddenly and swiftly moved (whipped) to focus upon another subject.

But, since the earliest days, it has not been necessary to depend exclusively upon a fixed camera. The camera may be moved while shooting in what are called *moving* or *running* shots.

One method of moving the camera is by means of a *dolly*. Mounted upon a short set of tracks or a level platform with wheels, the camera can be moved along to follow action, and it can *pull back* from or *come in* on the action. A *crab dolly* is a small platform on wheels designed to move in any direction.

More extensive movement over a larger area than can be accomplished by dollying is achieved by mounting the camera on a platform on a car or truck or other moving vehicle for what are called *trucking* or *tracking* shots. A well-known example of extensive tracking, praised by some critics and censured by others, is to be seen in Olivier's direction of the Battle of Agincourt in *Henry V.*

Still another form of using a mobile camera is by means of the *crane* or *boom*. A small camera platform is set at the end of a long crane, and the crane may be moved up and down or laterally across a set.

Another basic photographic effect, increasingly popular in recent times, is most often described as the use of a *hand-held* camera. The term is most accurately used to differentiate the filmic qualities obtained by a small camera held in the hands while shooting from those created by a standard studio camera which is balanced, level, and set on its tripod, a dolly, or platform. Ironically, the results of the hand-held camera, rather like that of home movies, can be duplicated by more conventional (and more expensive) camera setups. Combined by laboratory work with grainy prints of high or low key, the camera work appears to be less smooth and even in the recording of subjects and action. What is deliberately achieved is a certain urgent and amateurish quality, associated in the minds of the contemporary audience with the verisimilitude of newsreels and documentaries and, as well, with the art films of certain prominent European directors in the immediate postwar years, the *réalismo* of Roberto Rossellini and Vittorio De Sica, for example. The effects of the hand-held camera seem more "realistic" however they are manufactured, and call attention to the cameraman's struggle and the immediacy of his work. Because of the artifice of film techniques, however, these effects may in fact be as "artificial" as those usually associated with only the highest standards of cinematography.

Editorial terms

The process of editing, which has already been mentioned, is highly technical and requires specialized study and experience. Some basic editorial techniques should, however, be understood by any student of film. One of these is the method of *transition* from one unit of film or larger sequence to another. Although the screenwriter must concern himself to some extent with the transitions, his part is marginal and limited to suggestions. For the editing of a film is exclusively the director's concern and that of his editor, or *cutter* as he is usually called by filmmakers.

There are essentially three kinds of transitions, with variations and, in some cases, different ways of accomplishing the same effect. The three forms of transition are the *cut*, the *dissolve*, and the *fade*.

The cut is, quite simply, a break or cut in the film. A sequence of images photographed from the same setup and angle is literally cut off, then spliced to another sequence. Cutting is, inevitably, continuous in a film, so frequent a pattern that we seldom notice it—unless it is the intention of the editor and the director that we should. The use of the word cut is somewhat confused by a number of other definitions of the term. For example, a cut may be used to describe a single strip of film. Many filmmakers call shots cuts, as in "Let's have a cut of the charging Indians here." And cut may mean *take out* or *add to*.

Professionals have no difficulty with this burden of possible meaning because context makes the particular case clear. But in terms of transitions, some examples may be in order. One of the most frequent cuts occurs when a character in an exterior setting starts to open a door to go into an unseen interior. We see him turn the handle of the door and start inside. The next shot will likely be a *reverse*, taken from within the interior set. The door is opening and he is coming in. Another common example of the conventional direct cut is frequently found when two characters are in conversation. At the outset we may see them both together in a two-shot. Then we cut back and forth from their separate faces as they speak to each other and react.

For the most part we do not consciously notice simple cuts. We imaginatively supply the missing connections and, so long as we are engaged in the viewing of the film, the action may seem smooth and continuous. Part of our reaction comes from experience and the habit of response; for the fundamentals of cutting have remained much the same since the days of D. W. Griffith. In *Birth of a Nation* he effectively used five-second shots, cut and joined together, in many places to establish a pattern for future editing.

Equally conventional is the use of the cut for a special effect in unexpected circumstances. An excellent example of the cut, used for humor, occurs in the fine Italian comedy *Big Deal on Madonna Street* (1959). Vittorio Gassman, arrested and awaiting trial, confidently reassures his weeping girl friend that he has an excellent lawyer and that the prosecution has no case against him. Nothing to worry about. From his smiling self-assurance there is a *direct cut* to a line of convicts, Gassman among them, marching doubletime around the yard of a penitentiary.

A *dissolve* or *lap dissolve* is a different sort of transition, sometimes called a *special effect* because it involves laboratory work. It is a process of superimposition by which one image gradually vanishes to be simultaneously replaced by another image without any perceptible fading of the light. The result is often a graceful sort of transition, traditionally used to indicate shifts of time and place without appearing to break the continuity of the film.

A variation on the dissolve is the *swish-pan,* a very swift dissolve which seems to be the result of camera movement, but is in fact a laboratory process.

A fade, used within the film as a transition, begins as a *fade out.* Both light and images fade into darkness and the screen goes (briefly) black. Following that a new image slowly *fades in.* Traditionally a fade acts as a definite break in the action of a film, somewhat analogous to the use of the curtain in the proscenium theater. It is also traditional to begin a script with the direction "Fade In" and to end it with "Fade Out."

There are a number of variations which can be used in lieu of a dissolve or fade. One is the *wipe,* in which the scene we are watching appears literally to be wiped away or erased from the screen, horizontally, vertically, or diagonally.

The *flip* is an effect in which a frame of film and its images appear to be flipped over like a card, either horizontally or vertically, to be replaced by another frame of images.

One of the oldest means of transition in the history of filmmaking, once widely used before the fade was possible, but still in use today, is the *iris.* As in fades, we *iris out* or *iris in.* The effect of irising out may occur in one of two ways. Either, within the frame, black seems to come from all sides diminishing the area of the image seen so that the image itself appears to recede or dwindle until it vanishes; or a single spot of black in the frame may appear to grow larger, going outward in all directions until the entire frame is dark. To iris in is to reverse the process.

The extent to which any of these editorial devices of transition—or, for that matter, the full variety of camera shots and angles—is employed depends, of course, on such things as current cinematic fashion and the nature and treatment of the subject of a script and a film. It also depends in large part upon the taste and aesthetic predilections of the director. On the one hand is Richard Lester, who opened up a full, rich bag of tricks, and most appropriately, to enliven *A Hard Day's Night,* whose shooting script gives very little indication of the style of the finished film. On the other hand is Billy Wilder; his scripts for *Some Like It Hot* (1959) and *The Apartment* (1960) are almost equally bare of explicit or suggested directions to cameraman or editor. Although Wilder is no stranger to the use of tricks, witness his *Sunset Boulevard* (1950), he has long been outspoken against depending too much on techniques to do the work of actors and directors. Kenneth MacGowan quotes him as saying: "If the scene is well directed from the point of view of its feelings, the camera can be set down, forgotten, and allowed to record." Wilder is, as ever, more careful than he seems at first glance. While he proposes limitations on the camera as writer-director, Wilder does not place limits upon the techniques of the editor.

Sound

Though sound as a part of motion pictures was technically possible much earlier, it did not become commercially feasible until the mid-1920s, and silent films continued to thrive until 1930. With the advent of sound as an integral part of the film art, this element became a part of the editor's general responsibility. In preparing the sound track, he has a number of technicians to help him. A *sound crew,* which works during the shooting of the picture, usually consists of a *mixer,* a *recordist,* and a *sound boom man.* Once the editing process begins a *sound effects editor* and a *music editor* are usually on hand in addition to a number of mixers who work on the final synchronization of all sounds and images in creating the composite print.

For a beginning, the editor has at his disposal the sound crew's original recordings taken during shooting. When synchronized with the rough cuts these recordings comprise the *wild track.* Where dialogue needs correction and better quality, which is often the case, the actors redo their lines in a controlled sound studio where *off-screen* or *voice over* dialogue is also added. This process of recording in synchronization with the film is called *dubbing* or *looping.* The opposite procedure, the deletion of sound effects or unwanted noises, is called *dialing out.*

The technical resources and possibilities of filmmaking, as even this brief glossary makes clear, are enormous. The greatest problem facing all of a film's creators is to choose among all of the possibilities the most efficient and most suitable means. The director, aided and advised by other artists, bears final responsibility for the choices made.

The writer's special responsibility is to create a script which, whatever its format, speaks to the needs of all the cast and crew, points directions by suggestion, and yet leaves each artist and technician free to create within the framework of his own competence. Within this context the technical terms of filmmaking should be understood. The value in application can be measured only by close viewing of films.

A Note on the Text of These Scripts

In preparing *Film Scripts* for publication, the editors have tried to present, as closely as is reasonable and possible, the version of each script acquired in the form in which it originally came to them. Because no two are precisely the same in all details, the special characteristics of each are mentioned in the appropriate headnote.

All of the American scripts included here are final shooting scripts. Some were more "finished" and "clean" than others; some contained pencilled revisions, made on the spot during the process of making.

In order to facilitate comparative study of word and image, the following conventions have been observed in reproducing facsimile versions of the scripts:

Deletions (of a passage, line, speech, direction, etc.) are indicated by asterisks plus any end punctuation.

New passages are underlined with dashes. Where there was a deletion involved this is likewise indicated by asterisks.

Deleted material is given in the form of annotation at the foot of the page. Large brackets have been placed around each continuous deletion. Small brackets are used to indicate changes in material that was later discarded.

The purpose here is not to provide a description or analysis of bibliographical changes; for the true bibliography of a film would chiefly be concerned with the text of the film—the master film and the prints made from it. But since revisions, even of the final shooting script, are parts of the process of making a film, these changes are indicated where evidence of them in the script was decipherable.

The most important revisions and changes, however, are manifest in the difference between the script and the finished film. The reader, who should also be a viewer, may wish to keep his own notes, perhaps in the margin of the text, on the basis of his own seeing of the film. This anthology can thus lead the reader/viewer to a better and more detailed understanding of the process of filmmaking. For, by having the script in handy and readable form, he not only has points of reference for testing his own memory of a screening but also, at least in a number of cases, a base line for questioning the possible function and purpose of some of the filmmaker's visions and revisions.

A HARD DAY'S NIGHT

1964—A Proscenium Films Production;
released in the United States by United Artists
Director Richard Lester
Script Alun Owen
Source Original screenplay
Stars John Lennon, Paul McCartney, George Harrison,
Ringo Starr

A Hard Day's Night sneaked up on the critics. It was to be what is known as an "exploitation picture," that is, a film designed to exploit other things —in this case the Beatles and their records. Therefore the critics, in general, approached it warily. (Audiences did not. It was a smash hit wherever it played.) What could be expected? A fairly "thin" script, an occasion, a vehicle for the musical numbers. And whatever clever tricks the young American Richard Lester had learned from making TV commercials. What the film critics did not realize was how sophisticated the audience, after some years of bombardment, had become in viewing TV commercials where, with almost unlimited budget, the makers were forced to experiment, and could afford to, in order to keep up with the competition. Nor, until this picture, did the intellectual establishment know a great deal about the Beatles, one way or the other.

The critics were surprised and pleased. Bosley Crowther recognized it as "a wonderfully lively and altogether good-natured spoof of the juvenile madness called 'Beatlemania'." He praised it as "a fine conglomeration of madcap clowning in the old Marx Brothers' style." This was a notion he repeated four days later (August 16). "It is a joyous reminder of the sort of fun the Marx Brothers used to spread, done up in the cluttered climate of the television age." *Time* called it "one of the smoothest, freshest, funniest films ever made solely for the purposes of exploitation." Philip Hartung of *Commonweal* called it "delightful" and praised its zany surrealistic poetic quality. *Newsweek* emphasized the modernity and eclecticism of its style—"Sight gags and documentary realism, semi-abstract, Antonioni-ish chases, a Fellini helicopter at the end, the meagerest possible plot line—all contribute to making *A Hard Day's Night* a truly fresh, lively length of film."

The most serious appraisal of the film, a bit later (October 10) than the other reviewers, was by Elizabeth Sutherland for *The New Republic*. While acknowledging that both Richard Lester and Alun Owen had done the best they could do with this assignment, she was not so much impressed by the quality of the direction or the character of the humor (which she called "rather sophomoric") as by the characters of the Beatles themselves. In effect she praised the moviemakers for letting the Beatles *be*. "The beauty of the film lies in its integrity, an integrity based upon the Beatles as individuals and as a collective," she wrote, "and it is no insult to the director, Richard Lester, or to the writer, Alun Owen, to say that in a sense *A Hard Day's Night* isn't really a movie."

No one could have guessed the enormousness of the film's success. And, not able to guess that, they could hardly have foreseen the extent of its almost-instant influence, not only on the making of feature films all over the world, but also upon television, and, as if in final irony, upon the making of television *commercials*. For better or worse, nothing would ever be the same after *A Hard Day's Night*. At worst, the result has been poor imitation and a whole new set of conventions and mannerisms. At best, the odd example and great success of *A Hard Day's Night* has been a genuine breakthrough, liberating audiences and moviemakers alike from the constraints of many clichés and conventions.

For Richard Lester, though he has been roundly chastised by the critics for repeating his successful mannerisms, it has meant the successful films *Help!* (1965) and *The Knack* (1965), and the opportunity to direct major feature films in his own country, beginning with *Petulia* (1968).

And as for the Beatles, they couldn't lose for winning.

The Script   Note that the script was originally titled simply *The Beatles*. This is a clean, crisp, conventionally organized script, relatively short, having only 41 master scenes. There is a good deal of description of action within these master scenes, and there are minimal camera directions. There is a good deal of dialogue also, but a large part of this is not so much deleted as lost in the rush and style of the film. This script is a superb example of the place and use of a shooting script in filmmaking; for there is no explicit indication of the style of the film itself, nor is there any sense of the music which, throughout, was at once the key to and the occasion of the film. What we have is a clean sketch which was designed to challenge and inspire the director and to give the Beatles a chance to perform their music.

Credits   Producer, Walter Shenson; Director, Richard Lester; Art Direction, Ray Simm; Music (Director), George Martin; Photography, Gilbert Taylor; Editor, John Jympson.

Cast   John: John Lennon
         Paul: Paul McCartney
         George: George Harrison
         Ringo: Ringo Starr
         Grandfather: Wilfrid Brambell
         Norm: Norman Rossington
         Shake: John Junkin
         Television Director: Victor Spinetti
         Shirt Advertising Man: Kenneth Haigh
         Millie: Anna Quayle
         Police Sergeant: Deryck Guyler
         Pompous Traveler: Richard Vernon
         Club Manager: Michael Trubshawe
         Waiter: Eddie Malin

1. EXTERIOR STREETS OUTSIDE RAILWAY TERMINAL DAY

   The film opens with crowds of girls, shot in a sequence of
   CLOSE-UPS, chasing after GEORGE, JOHN and RINGO. The boys
   hare off just ahead of them. They take a turn down a back
   alley way and the crowd of screaming girls are after them.

2. EXT. TERMINAL

   They rush on through the narrow cobbled passageway and into the
   main station, quickly show their tickets at the barrier for
   the London train and get onto the platform as hordes of yelling
   and screaming girls reach the closed gates.

3. EXT. TERMINAL PLATFORM

   We see the fans rushing to the few platform ticket machines and
   endless pennies being dropped and tickets torn out in their
   haste to get on to the platform to see the boys.

   NORM has been waiting for the boys and he hurries them to
   where all their baggage, instruments and the drums are waiting,
   piled up to be put into the guards' van. The boys turn and
   see the oncoming stream of girls pushing through the barriers
   and descending on them with yells and shouts. They grab their
   instruments, RINGO makes for the drums. NORM plugs into a
   handy transformer and using their instruments like a gun volley
   to stop the onrush of females, the boys blast fire into a
   number and start to sing. This stops the girls in their tracks
   and they settle down on whatever they can to listen to them
   playing.

   As the boys are playing we CUT BACK into the crowds. In the
   centre we see PAUL struggling and pulling to fight his way
   through the girls to join the other boys. He is dragging a
   very reluctant old man behind him. The old man seems most
   disgruntled and we can see by his gestures how unwilling he is
   to be pulled and pushed forward through all the girls.

   At last PAUL reaches the other boys. He sits the old man down
   on a pile of cases and joins in the number to the squeals of
   delight from the fans. The old man sits aloof and proud,
   ignoring the whole proceedings. JOHN, GEORGE and RINGO look
   enquiringly at PAUL, who gives a noncommittal shrug of the
   shoulders as if to say, "It's not my fault," and the number
   proceeds.

   SHOT of sudden horror on JOHN's face, PAUL follows his eyeline
   only to see the old man has doffed his cap and is busily collecting

money from a disconcerted crowd. PAUL dives hastily into the
crowd, and with suitable apologies extracts the old man, and
with a long suffering sigh drags him back to the group. GEORGE
and PAUL hold him firmly as they finish the number, the old man
standing there between them.

As the number finishes and the girls scream and shout with
delight, the guard blows his whistle. NORM and SHAKE grab the
instruments and the drums, and with the rest pile the lot into
the guards' van. The boys head into their reserved compartment
pursued by the fans, but the train moves off. They have
successfully repelled all extra boarders.

The boys stand and wave to the fans until out of sight line . . .
the girls running along to the end of the platform waving and
calling out.

4. <u>INTERIOR   RESERVED COMPARTMENT IN THE TRAIN</u>

The boys relax, sitting down on one side of the compartment.
They are about to settle down and make themselves at home when
first RINGO nudges GEORGE who in turn nudges JOHN. Opposite
them is sitting the LITTLE OLD MAN. He is holding himself stiff,
erect and very aloof.

The three boys look at him enquiringly, but with an elaborate
sniff he looks away from them and out of the window.

PAUL catches his eye and winks at the LITTLE OLD MAN. He winks
back at PAUL, scowls at the other three, then looks firmly out
of the window again.

The boys turn on PAUL, crowding around him.

                         JOHN
          Eh . . . pardon me for asking but who's that
          little old man?

                         PAUL
          What little old man?

                         JOHN
                    (pointing)
          That little old man.

                         PAUL
          Oh, that one. That's me Grandfather.

> GEORGE
> That's not your Grandfather.

> PAUL
> It is, y'know.

> GEORGE
> But your Grandfather lives in your house.
> I've seen him.

> PAUL
> Oh, that's me other Grandfather, but this
> one's me Grandfather and all.

> JOHN
> How d'you reckon that one out?

> PAUL
> Well . . . everyone's entitled to two, aren't
> they, and this one's me other one.

> JOHN
> (long-suffering)
> Well, we know that but what's he doing
> here?

> PAUL
> Well, me Mother said the trip 'ud do him
> good.

> RINGO
> How's that?

> PAUL
> Oh . . . he's nursing a broken heart.

The lads all look intently at the GRANDFATHER.

> JOHN
> Aah . . . the poor old thing.

He leans across to GRANDFATHER.

> JOHN
> Eh, Mister . . . are you nursing a broken
> heart then?

The GRANDFATHER glares at him, in a way that indicates yes.

                    PAUL
                (whispering)
You see, he was going to get married
but she threw him over for a butcher.

                    GEORGE
A butcher?

                    PAUL
Yeah, she was fickle.

                    JOHN
Aye, and fond of fresh meat and all.

                    PAUL
                (seriously)
No . . . it was his sweetbreads. She
was dead kinky for sweetbreads. Anyroad,
me Mother thought it'ud give him a change
of scenery, like.

                    JOHN
Oh, I see.

He inspects GRANDFATHER carefully.

                    JOHN
                (to Paul)
Eh, he's a nice old man, isn't he?

                    PAUL
Oh yeah, he's very clean, y'know.

They all agree with PAUL.

JOHN has been examining GRANDFATHER. He now leans forward
to him.

                    JOHN
                (in an over-
                friendly voice)
Hello, Grandfather!

                    GRANDFATHER
Hello.

                    JOHN
                (delightedly)
He can talk then?

                          PAUL
                    (indignantly)
            Course he can talk. He's a human being,
            like. Isn't he?

                          RINGO
                     (grinning)
            Well . . . if he's your Grandfather, who
            knows?

The lads all laugh.

                          JOHN
            And we're looking after him, are we?

                          GRANDFATHER
            I'll look after meself.

                          PAUL
            Aye, that's what I'm afraid of!

                          JOHN
            Has he got you worried?

                          PAUL
            Him, he costs you a fortune in breach
            of promise cases. He's a villain, and a
            right mixer as well.

                          GEORGE
                    (disbelieving)
            Gerron.

                          PAUL
            No, straight up.

                          GRANDFATHER
            The lad's given you the simple truth. I'm
            cursed wid irresistible charm, I'm too
            attractive to be let loose.

At this moment, SHAKE, a tall man who works with the boys,
pulls open the door of the compartment.

                          SHAKE
            You got on all right then?

                          BOYS
            Hi, Shake.

                    SHAKE
We're here. Norm'll be along in a mo'
with the tickets.

He sees GRANDFATHER.

                    SHAKE
    Morning!
              (whispers)
    Who's that little old man?

                    GEORGE
    Paul's Grandfather.

                    SHAKE
    Oh aye, but I thought . . .

                    JOHN
              (cutting in)
    No, that's his other one.

                    SHAKE
    That's all right then.

                    JOHN
              (displaying Grandfather)
    Clean though, isn't he?

                    SHAKE
    Oh yes, he's clean all right.

NORM the road manager appears behind SHAKE.

                    NORM
    Morning, lads.

                    BOYS
    Morning . . . Hi, Norm.

                    NORM
              (checking them quickly)
    Well, thank God you're all here. Now,
    listen, I've had this marvellous idea . . .
    now just for a change, let's all behave like
    ordinary responsible citizens. Let's not
    cause any trouble, pull any strokes or do
    anything I'm going to be sorry for, especially
    tomorrow at the TV Theatre, because . . .

He looks sharply at JOHN who is polishing his nails.

Are you listening to me, Lennon?

                    JOHN
               (off-hand)
You're a swine, isn't he George?

                    GEORGE
               (disinterested)
Yeah . . . a swine.

                    NORM
               (just as indifferent)
Thanks.

He sees the GRANDFATHER.

                    NORM

Eh . . .

                    BOYS IN CHORUS
. . . Who's that little old man?

                    NORM
Well, who is he?

                    RINGO
He belongs to Paul.

                    NORM
               (accepting the
                situation)
Ah well, there you go. Look, I'm going
down the diner for a cup of coffee, are
you coming?

                    PAUL
We'll follow you down.

GRANDFATHER rises.

                    GRANDFATHER
I want me coffee.

                    NORM
He can come with Shake and me if you
like.

                    PAUL
Well, look after him. I don't want to find
you've lost him.

                    NORM
Don't be cheeky, I'll bind him to me with
promises. Come on, Grandad.

GRANDFATHER joins SHAKE and NORM.

                    NORM
              (over Grandfather's
              head)
He's very clean, isn't he?

SHAKE and NORM collect GRANDFATHER and are in the process of
leaving the compartment when an upper-class city Englishman,
JOHNSON, attempts to enter. There is a bit of confusion and
they get tangled up with each other.

                    JOHNSON
Make up your minds, will you!

At last SHAKE, NORM and GRANDFATHER sort themselves out and
JOHNSON enters with his case. The other three go to coffee.

JOHNSON puts his case up on the luggage rack, then sits down.
All his movements are disgruntled . . . he finally picks up his
copy of the <u>Financial Times</u> and, burying himself behind it,
starts to read. After a moment he looks up, notices the
compartment window is open. He gets up and without so much as
a "by your leave" he closes it, glares at the boys and sits down
again.

The boys exchange looks as if to say . . . "Hello, Saucy!!"

                    PAUL
              (politely)
Do you mind if we have it opened?

                    JOHNSON
              (briefly)
Yes, I do.

                    JOHN
Yeah, but there are four of us, like,
and we like it open, if it's all the same
to you, that is.

> JOHNSON
> (rudely)
> Well, it isn't. I travel on this train
> regularly twice a week, so I suppose
> I've some rights.

> RINGO
> Aye, well, so have we.

He disappears behind his paper before the boys can say another
word.

RINGO pulls a face at the raised paper and switches on his
portable radio. A pop number is playing.

JOHNSON puts down his paper firmly.

> JOHNSON
> And we'll have that thing off as well, thank
> you.

> RINGO
> But I . . .

JOHNSON leans over and switches it off.

> JOHNSON
> An elementary knowledge of the Railway
> Acts would tell you I'm perfectly within
> my rights.

He smiles frostily.

> PAUL
> Yeah, but we want to hear it and there's
> more of us than you. We're a community,
> like, a majority vote. Up the workers
> and all that stuff!

> JOHNSON
> Then I suggest you take that damned thing
> into the corridor or some other part of
> the train where you obviously belong.

> JOHN
> (leaning forward
> to him)
> Gie's a kiss!

                              PAUL
              Shurrp! Look, Mister, we've paid for
              our seats too, you know.

                              JOHNSON
              I travel on this train regularly, twice
              a week.

                              JOHN
              Knock it off, Paul, y' can't win with his
              sort. After all, it's his train, isn't it,
              Mister?

                              JOHNSON
              And don't you take that tone with me, young
              man!

                              GEORGE
              But . . .

                              JOHNSON
                          (accusingly)
              I fought the war for your sort.

                              RINGO
              Bet you're sorry you won!

                              JOHNSON
              I'll call the guard!

                              PAUL
              Aye . . . but what? They don't take kindly to
              insults. Ah, come on, you lot. Let's get a
              cup of coffee and leave Toby the manager.

The boys troop out of the door into the corridor. JOHNSON
smiles triumphantly. He is about to settle down to his paper
when there is a tap on the corridor window. He looks up and
we see pressed against the window a collection of hideous
Beatle faces.

                              PAUL
              Eh, Mister . . . can we have our ball back!

The man jumps to his feet.

5. <u>INTERIOR   OF THE CORRIDOR</u>

The boys run away like a pack of school boys and disappear round
the corner.

6. INTERIOR OF THE TRAIN CORRIDOR

From the P.O.V. of the door leading to the restaurant car.

The boys come down the corridor in full flight, laughing away
like happy idiots. GEORGE and PAUL pull open the sliding doors.
The boys look inside.

7. INTERIOR RESTAURANT CAR

From their P.O.V. we see the car is half empty and at a table
in the centre SHAKE and NORM and GRANDFATHER are sitting. On
the table is a pile of photos of the boys. NORM and SHAKE are
arguing. NORM is being very agressive, much to SHAKE's discomfort.

                    NORM
Yeah, you want to watch it.

                    SHAKE
                (unhappily)
It's not my fault.

                    NORM
Well, you stick to that story, son.

                    SHAKE
I can't help it, I'm just taller than you.

                GRANDFATHER
             (to NORM slyly)
They always say that.

                    NORM
Yeah, well I got me eye on you.

                    SHAKE
I'm sorry Norm, but I can't help being taller
than you.

                    NORM
Well, you don't have to rub me nose in it.
I've a good mind to . . .
             (he is about to thump SHAKE)

                    JOHN
               (enjoying himself)
If you're going to have a barney I'll hold
your coats.

                    NORM

He started it.

                    SHAKE

No, I didn't, you did . . .

                    GEORGE

Well, what happened?

                    SHAKE

The old fella wanted these pictures and
Norm said he couldn't have 'em, all I
said was 'aw go on, be big about it.'

                    PAUL

And?

                    NORM

Your Grandfather pointed out Shake was
always being taller than me to spite me.

                    PAUL

I knew it, <u>he</u> started it, I should have known.

                    NORM

Y'what?

                    PAUL

You two have never had a quarrel in your life
and in two minutes flat he's got you at it.
He's a king mixer. Adam and Eve, meet the
serpent. Anthony and Cleopatra, there's
your asp. Divide and Conquer, that's this
one's motto. He hates group unity so gets
everyone at it.

The boys, i.e. JOHN, GEORGE and RINGO, look at each other, then
at PAUL.

                    PAUL

Aye and we'll have to watch it and all.

                        GEORGE
          I suggest you give him the photos and have
          done with it.

                        NORM
          You're right. Here you are, old devil.

SHAKE and NORM leave. GRANDFATHER grins triumphantly
and collects them, then with a sweet smile he turns to PAUL.

                        GRANDFATHER
          Would you ever sign this one for us, Pauly?

PAUL does so automatically, but in the middle of signing he gets
suspicious. GRANDFATHER smiles at him charmingly so PAUL
finishes signing.

                        JOHN
          Come on, let's get this coffee.

                        GRANDFATHER
          Before you go, I think it's only fair to warn
          you about me Grandson . . . don't let our Paul
          have his own way all the time, 'cos if you do
          he won't respect you!

JOHN, RINGO and GEORGE take this up straight away. They all
pretend to be girls, RINGO jumps into PAUL's arms.

                        GEORGE
                   (coyly)
          Oh, Paul, you can't have your own way!!!

                        JOHN
                   (invitingly, in a Marlene Dietrich
                   voice)
          If I let you have your own way, you little
          rascal, will you respect me?

                        PAUL
                   (choked)
          I'll murder you, Grandfather!

JOHN waltzes PAUL down to an empty table and the lads sit down.

                        GEORGE
          Eh, look at that talent.

They all gaze across the aisle. From their P.O.V. we see two
very attractive young girls, RITA and JEAN, having coffee.

> JOHN
>
> Give 'em a pull.

> PAUL
>
> Shall I?

> GEORGE
>
> Aye, but don't rush. None of your five bar
> gate jumps and over sort of stuff.

> PAUL
>
> Now what's that mean?

> GEORGE
> (grinning)
> I don't really know, but it sounded
> distinguished, like, didn't it?

> JOHN
>
> George Harrison, The Scouse of Distinction.

We follow PAUL as he crosses over to the two girls. He places
a bowler on head.

> PAUL
> (in posh accent)
> Excuse me, but these young men I'm sitting
> with wondered if two of us could join you,
> I'd ask you meself only I'm shy.

The two girls giggle together.

JOHN and GEORGE are about to move over when GRANDFATHER suddenly
appears by their sides.

> GRANDFATHER
> (sternly)
> I'm sorry, miss, but you mustn't fraternise
> with my prisoners.

> JEAN
>
> Prisoners!!

> GRANDFATHER
>
> Convicts in transit to Wormwood Scrubs.
> Typical old lags, the lot of 'em.

                              THE BOYS
             Y'what!!!

                              GRANDFATHER
             Quiet, you lot, or I'll give you a touch of
             me truncheon.
                         (He points at Ringo)
             That little one's the worst. If we don't
             keep him on tablets he has fits.

                              RINGO
                         (protesting)
             Now look here!!

GRANDFATHER grabs two lumps of sugar from the table and forces
them into RINGO's mouth.

                              GRANDFATHER
             Get out while you can, ladies, his time's
             coming round for one of his turns.

The girls scurry out of the restaurant car. We are not sure if
they recognised the boys who look in amazement and horror at
GRANDFATHER. They are completely flabbergasted. GRANDFATHER
smiles at them benignly.

8. <u>INTERIOR OF RAILWAY COMPARTMENT</u>

SHAKE and NORM are seated. SHAKE is buried in a science fiction
book.

NORM looks at his watch, slightly worried.

                              NORM
             He's been gone a long time.

                              SHAKE
                         (without looking up)
             Who?

                              NORM
             Paul's Grandfather.

                              SHAKE
             Oh, I didn't notice, where'd he go?

                              NORM
             Down the . . . er . . .

SHAKE

Oh, down the . . . er . . . ?

NORM

Yeah, down the . . . er . . .

SHAKE

Well, give a couple of minutes . . .

He resumes reading.

But NORM goes on worrying.

9. <u>INTERIOR OF ANOTHER COMPARTMENT ON THE TRAIN</u>

GRANDFATHER is in full flight of conversation with a charming elderly lady, AUDREY, who is listening intently.

GRANDFATHER
(proudly)

Yes, I'm their manager, I discovered them.

AUDREY

Did you indeed, Mr. McCartney?

GRANDFATHER

Now, Audrey, I told you, the name's John.
We Show Biz people are a friendly lot.

AUDREY

Of course.

GRANDFATHER

Yes, they were playing the queues outside
the picture palaces of Liverpool. Scruffy
young lads, lacking even the price of a jam
roll. Orphans, every Paddy's son of 'em,
I saw their potential at once although I had
me doubts about the little fella, a savage
primitive, that Ringo, but it was him what
gave in first. He picked up a brick and heaved
it at me and I quelled him wid one fierce flash
of me eyes. 'Mister, can you spare us a
copper?' he said. I was disarmed by the grubby
little outstretched mauler . . . So, I took them
under me managerial banner.

AUDREY

The usual ten per cent?

                    GRANDFATHER
        Oh, not at all, I let them have twenty-five;
        sure aren't there four of them?

                      AUDREY
                (her eyes lighting up)
        How fascinating. Do go on . . .
                    (pause)
        . . . John.

                    GRANDFATHER
        . . . Oh, I'm all heart, Ma'am, all heart . . .
        Well, I let . . .

10. <u>INTERIOR   CORRIDOR OF TRAIN</u>

    NORM and SHAKE meet with the boys as they are returning from
    coffee.

                      NORM
        Eh, have you got Paul's Grandfather?

                      JOHN
        Of course, he's concealed about me person.

                      NORM
        No . . . he's slipped off somewhere.

                      PAUL
                  (accusingly)
        Have <u>you</u> lost him?

                      NORM
        Don't exaggerate.

                      PAUL
        You've lost him.

                      SHAKE
        Put it this way, he's mislaid him.

                      PAUL
        You can't trust you with anything, Norm,
        if you've lost him, I'll cripple you.

                      SHAKE
        He can't be far.

                    JOHN
I hope he fell off.

                    PAUL
                 (mildly)
Don't be callous.

                    RINGO
He doesn't like me, honest, I can tell . . .
it's 'cos I'm little.

                    GEORGE
You've got an inferiority complex, you
have.

                    RINGO
Yeah, I know, that's why I took up the drums.
It's me active compensatory factor.

JOHN and PAUL run down the corridor. SHAKE and NORM turn from
the door and go in the opposite direction, GEORGE and RINGO
follow after the other two boys.

11. INTERIOR CORRIDOR OF THE TRAIN

PAUL and JOHN look into various compartments. CLOSE SHOT of
RINGO looking into compartments in the manner of Groucho Marx.
In one of the compartments we see from RINGO'S P.O.V. the
occupant, a glamorous woman, TANIA, with a small lap dog.

She is beautifully and most expensively dressed. She looks up
and sees RINGO.

RINGO smiles at her and she smiles back. She then beckons him
to join her.

He looks around to see if she means someone else. She nods a
negative. RINGO looks back enquiringly then points at himself
as if to say: "Who, me?"

TANIA smiles enthusiastically.

GEORGE has been watching all this.

                    GEORGE
Are you going in?

>   RINGO
>   No, she'll only reject me in the end and
>   I'll be frustrated.
>
>
>   GEORGE
>   You never know, you might be lucky this
>   time.
>
>
>   RINGO
>   No, I know the psychological pattern and it
>   plays hell with me drum skins.

He blows the glamorous lady a kiss, then moves sadly on.

12.   <u>INTERIOR   FARTHER DOWN THE CORRIDOR</u>

PAUL enters a compartment followed by JOHN.

The two girls, RITA and JEAN, from the restaurant car are sitting there.

>   PAUL
>   Excuse me, but have you seen that little
>   old man we were with?

The girls jump up, surprised.

>   JOHN
>   We've broken out, oh, the blessed freedom
>   of it all!
>   (he extends his hands
>   as if handcuffed)
>   Eh, have you got a nail file, these handcuffs
>   are killing me.
>
>
>   PAUL
>   Will you stop it! Sorry to disturb you,
>   miss . . .

He starts to drag JOHN after him.

>   JOHN
>   I was innocent, I was framed, I won't go
>   back.

JOHN is now by the door; he leers at the girls horribly.

>   I bet you can guess what I was in for.

He cackles like a maniac before disappearing, the door closing after him.

A waiter carrying a tray with champagne and glasses on it passes into one of the compartments with the blinds down.

> PAUL
> How about that one?

He moves towards the compartment.

> PAUL
> (to Ringo and George)
> Did you look in there?

> GEORGE
> No. I mean, it's probably a honeymoon couple or a company director or something.

> PAUL
> Well, let's broaden our outlook.

PAUL opens the door of the compartment.

13. <u>INTERIOR OF COMPARTMENT</u>

From the BOY'S P.O.V. we see GRANDFATHER and the elderly lady, AUDREY, sipping champagne and nibbling caviar on toast.

> GRANDFATHER
> (looking up)
> Congratulate me, boys, I'm engaged.

PAUL enters and crosses over to him.

> PAUL
> Oh no, you're not. You've gone too far this time . . . and who's paying for all this?

> GRANDFATHER
> It's all taken care of. It's down on our bill.

> PAUL
> Oh, well that's all right.
> (Realising)
> What?

                              AUDREY
              Young man, kindly moderate your tone when
              you address my fiancé.

                              PAUL
              I'm sorry, Missus., but the betrothal's off.
                         (He grabs GRANDFATHER
                          by the arm)
              I'll refuse me consent, he's over-age!

AUDREY grabs GRANDFATHER's other arm and pulls back.

                              AUDREY
              Leave him alone. After all he's done for you
              is this the way you repay him?

A tug of war now starts between PAUL and AUDREY.

                              PAUL
                         (pulling)
              Him? He's never done anything for anybody
              in his life.

                              AUDREY
                         (pulling)
              You dare to say that when even those
              ridiculous clothes you are wearing were
              bought when you forced him to sell out his
              gilt-edged Indomitables!!

JOHN and GEORGE jump on the seat egging PAUL and AUDREY on.

                              JOHN
              Come on, Auntie, you're winning.

                              GEORGE
              Get in there, Paul, she's weakening.

RINGO attempts to interfere.

                              RINGO
              Look, Missus, this is all a misunderstanding,
              you see, he's . . .

                              AUDREY
              Keep away from me, you depraved lout, I
              know all about your terrible past.

RINGO

Y'what?

She hits RINGO with her handbag and continues struggling with
PAUL for GRANDFATHER. RINGO grabs her handbag to stop her
hitting him.

RINGO

> He's given me a bad character, blackguarding
> me name to all and sundry. He's got to be
> stopped. It's not fair.

RINGO pushes out into the corridor, forgetting that he is
holding the woman's handbag.

A voice shouts off from outside.

VOICE OFF

> That's one of them . . . stop thief!

14. <u>INTERIOR   CORRIDOR</u>

From RINGO'S P.O.V. we see down to the right the city man,
JOHNSON, approaching with a GUARD. RINGO turns the other way
to the left when he is joined by three other boys. From their
P.O.V. down the corridor we see the two girls, autograph books
in hand, followed by ten girls from the same school.

Both groups are closing in on the boys. There is no escape.

RINGO
(looking down at the
handbag in his hand)

Oh Mother!!

15. <u>INTERIOR   LUGGAGE VAN</u>

Very dark, and behind bars we see GRANDFATHER. He is sitting
crouched up on a wooden box tea chest and looks pretty miserable.
He turns towards the CAMERA; in the foreground of the SHOT we
see PAUL standing. In the background an impassive GUARD is
reading a paper which he does throughout the scene.

GRANDFATHER
(bitterly)

> And to think me own grandson would
> have let them put me behind bars!

                              PAUL
        Don't dramatise.

The CAMERA PULLS BACK and we see GRANDFATHER in the luggage
compartment of the guards' van. In with him are a crate of
chickens and a dog. The chickens peck at him; GRANDFATHER
moves listlessly away.

                              PAUL
        Let's face it, you're lucky to be here. If
        they'd have had their way you'd have been
        dropped off at Stafford.

GRANDFATHER proudly turns away from PAUL, who dodges round so
he can still see his face.

                              PAUL
        Well, you've got to admit you've upset a
        lot of people.

GRANDFATHER turns away again.

                              PAUL
        All right, how about Ringo? I mean . . . he's
        very upset, you know . . . and as far as your
        girl friend, little Audrey's concerned, she's
        finished with men for the rest of her natural,
        and another thing . . .

                           GRANDFATHER
                          (cutting in)
        You're left-handed, aren't you, Paul?

                              PAUL
        Yeah . . . so what?

                           GRANDFATHER
        Why do you always use your left hand?

                              PAUL
        Well, don't be daft, I've got to.

                           GRANDFATHER
        And I take a left-handed view of life, I've
        got to.

PAUL grins. After a moment of looking at him, PAUL opens the
door of the luggage compartment and joins GRANDFATHER on a box.

                        PAUL
        Shove up!

GRANDFATHER produces a penny.

                        GRANDFATHER
        Odds or evens?

PAUL sighs.

                        PAUL
        Odds.

GRANDFATHER flips the coin.

The guards' van door opens and JOHN, GEORGE and RINGO come in.
With them are the two girls, RITA and JEAN.

                        JOHN
                (as he sees PAUL behind the bars)
        Don't worry, son, we'll get you the best lawyer
        trading stamps can buy.

                        PAUL
        Oh, it's a laugh a line with Lennon.
                (to Ringo)
        Anyroad up . . . It's all your fault.

                        RINGO
        Me? Why?

                        GEORGE
        Bag-snatcher.

                        GRANDFATHER
        That's right; convict without trial . . .
        Habeas corpus.

                        JOHN
                (casually)
        Every morning.

JOHN has been looking around the guards' van.

                        JOHN
        Gaw, it's depressing in here, isn't it? Funny . . .
                (he pats the dog)
        'cos they usually reckon dogs more than

                              JOHN (Cont.)
                people in England, don't they? You'd
                expect it to be palatial.
                              (he shudders)
                Come on, let's have a little action.

                              PAUL
                Like what?

                              JOHN
                Well, I've got me gob stopper.
                              (he produces his mouth
                              organ)
                Look, a genuine Stradivarius, hand tooled
                at Dagenham.

And to RINGO's beat on a tea chest they are off, PAUL and GEORGE
improvising other sounds, much to the girls' delight. During
the number, GRANDFATHER quietly lets the latch off the chicken
crate and chickens begin to wander through the scene.

16. EXTERIOR TRAIN IN MOTION FROM ABOVE (NIGHT)

While the number is progressing the train is getting nearer and
nearer to London.

17. EXTERIOR PLATFORM TERMINUS (NIGHT)

SHOTS of the station full of GIRLS waiting for the BOYS.

18. INTERIOR GUARDS' VAN

By the time the number finishes the train pulls up with a sharp
halt that sends all the passengers sprawling, boys and girls.

NORM enters the guards' van.

                              NORM
                Don't move, any of you. They've gone
                potty out there. The whole place is surging
                with girls.

                              JOHN
                Please, can I have one to surge with?

                              NORM
                No.

> JOHN
> Ah, go on, you swine.

> NORM
> No, you can't. Look, as soon as I tell you,
> run through this door and into the big car
> that's waiting.

He points and we see a big car parked across the road.

The boys prepare to depart, lining up with GRANDFATHER at the
door.

19. <u>EXTERIOR PLATFORM TERMINUS</u> (NIGHT)

Just as they are ready to go a line of taxis draws up parallel
to the train and now separates them from the big car waiting
for them.

> NORM
> Oh no!

GRANDFATHER pushes past the boys, holding his coat closed.

> GRANDFATHER
> All right, lads, follow me.

And before NORM can stop him, he darts out of the door, PAUL
after him. The fans farther down the platform see PAUL and
charge forward . . . in a panic NORM and the others follow,
JOHN just having time to kiss both the girls.

> JOHN
> Vive l'amour!

NORM drags him away.

20. <u>EXTERIOR RAILWAY STATION</u>

The BOYS manage to follow GRANDFATHER by leaping onto a motorized
luggage carrier, GEORGE driving and the other three posing as
a frozen tableau on the back. GRANDFATHER has arrived at a taxi
door. He flings it open and runs through, opening the other
door, thus making a safe bridge to the car.

The BOYS follow. They run towards GRANDFATHER's taxi. The
FANS have followed the BOYS and we see streams of GIRLS piling

through all the taxis, one of which contains JOHNSON the city
man, opening and shutting the doors to get through, much to the
indignation of the TAXI DRIVERS.

21. INTERIOR BIG CAR

NORM is sitting in front with the DRIVER, FRANK. The four BOYS
and GRANDFATHER are squashed together in the back.

NORM
(to the driver)
Go like the clappers, son!!

FRANK
(smoothly)
That was my entire intention, sir.

22. EXTERIOR STATION

The car moves off surrounded by the FANS; from a height we see
them converge on the car but it moves forcefully out of the
station and off.

It moves into the traffic in the main road and the journey to
the hotel begins.

23. INTERIOR HOTEL SUITE NIGHT

There is a reception room and off it lead rooms that are
presumably bedrooms, bathroom, etc. JOHN is lying sprawled
out on a settee listening to a transistor radio, demolishing
a basket of fruit. PAUL is sitting at an upright piano and
GRANDFATHER is mooching about the room. One of the doors
opens and GEORGE enters followed by RINGO. None of the boys
are wearing coats.

RINGO
I don't snore.

GEORGE
You do -- repeatedly.

RINGO
(to John)
Do I snore?

JOHN
(eating a banana)
You're a window rattler, son.

                    RINGO
Well that's just your opinion. Do I snore,
Paul?

                    PAUL
              (stopping playing)
With a trombone hooter like yours it'ud be
un-natural if you didn't.

                    GRANDFATHER
Don't mock the afflicted, Pauly.

                    PAUL
Oh for Pete's sake, it's only a joke.

                    GRANDFATHER
Well, it may be a joke, but it's his nose. He
can't help having a horrible great nose, it's
the only one he's got. And his little head's
trembling under the weight of it.

NORM enters with three piles of fan mail and places them in
front of JOHN on a table. RINGO is almost in tears, examining
his nose in a mirror.

                    NORM
Paul, John, George, get at it.

                    JOHN
Hello, the income tax have caught up with
us at last.

PAUL and GEORGE gather round the low table. RINGO is left out
of it.

                    RINGO
None for me, then?

                    NORM
Sorry.

He hands RINGO a single envelope.

                    JOHN
That'll keep you busy.

                    GRANDFATHER
It's your nose, y'see. Fans are funny that
way. Take a dislike to things. They'll

                        GRANDFATHER (Cont.)
        pick on a nose . . .

                        RINGO
        You go and pick on your own.

SHAKE enters with a stack of mail about three times larger than
all the others put together.

                        JOHN
        Is that yours?

                        SHAKE
        For Ringo.

He dumps it in RINGO's arms who staggers into an armchair. The
boys send him up.

                        JOHN
        That must have cost you a fortune in
        stamps, Ring.

                        GEORGE
        He comes from a large family.

                        RINGO
                (dumping the letters)
        Well.

RINGO opens his letter and reads it. It contains a large embossed
card.

                        RINGO
        Eh, what's Boyd's Club?

The lads gather round him and PAUL takes the card from him and
reads.

                        PAUL
        "The Management of Boyd's Club takes
        pleasure in requesting the company of
        Mr. Richard Starkey in their recently
        refinished gaming rooms. Chemin de Fer.
        Baccarat, Roulette, and Champagne Buffet."
        Blimey!

                        RINGO
                (surprised)
        And they want me?

                          JOHN
          Oh it's got round that you're a heavy punter.

                          NORM
                    (snatching the card)
          Well, you're not going.

                          RINGO
          Ah.

                          GRANDFATHER
                    (taking card from
                    Norm)
          Quite right, invites to gambling dens full
          of easy money and fast women, chicken
          sandwiches and cornets of caviar, disgusting!

He pockets the card himself.

                          RINGO
          That's mine.

                          NORM
          Have done, and you lot get your pens out.

                          BOYS
          Why?

                          NORM
          It's homework time for all you college puddings.
          I want this lot
                    (he indicates the
                    fan letters)
          all answered tonight!

The boys all protest.

                          NORM
          I'll brook no denial!

                          JOHN
          It's all right for you, you couldn't get
          a pen in your trotter, you swine.

                          NORM
          Come on, Shake, we'll leave 'em to their
          penmanship.

He goes followed by SHAKE.

There is a pause, and JOHN deliberately rises slowly and crosses to
his coat. He puts it on and walks to the door.

                    JOHN
          While the swine's away the piglets can
          play. Well come on, what are we waiting
          for?

With a whoop PAUL, GEORGE and RINGO collect their coats and head
for the door.

                    GRANDFATHER
          What about all these letters?

                    BOYS
          Read em!

They disappear. After a moment GRANDFATHER takes out RINGO's
card.

C.U. GRANDFATHER

And a free champagne buffet.

He grins to himself.

At this moment a waiter enters with a tray. He is clad in tails
and GRANDFATHER eyes them longingly, measuring himself the while
alongside the startled waiter. He leaves us with no doubt in
our minds what he wants, i.e., the waiter's suit.

24. INTERIOR DANCING CLUB NIGHT

    The club is the latest in modern decor and full of teenagers
    all enjoying themselves. The CAMERA wanders around the club
    till it finally picks out JOHN, PAUL, GEORGE and RINGO all
    crowded around one small table. The music is blaring away from
    a juke box and the boys join the dancers. They are recognised
    and given smiles and nods of encouragement by all the other
    customers. During this scene we

                                        CUT AWAY

25. INTERIOR BOYD'S CLUB NIGHT

    The whole atmosphere is of quiet elegance and loud wealth.
    Around the baccarat table the rich, bored customers sit barely
    moving a face muscle as they languidly murmur "Suivez" and

"banco" to the dealer as he operates the shoe. The manager of
the club is beaming with satisfaction as he surveys his customers.
One of these customers is clad in evening dress and he has his
back to us. The rest of the players (male) are in suits. By
each of them is standing a lush lady with a bored sophisticated
face that looks as if it has been painted on. From the REVERSE
of the LAST SHOT we now see the solitary evening dress player is
GRANDFATHER. He looks around him and wipes off his look of
enjoyment and elaborately out-bores everyone in the room.

                    DEALER
          Alors, M'sieur?

                    GRANDFATHER
                  (nonchalant)
          Souflée.

He turns to the buxom BLONDE, who is dripping over him.

                    GRANDFATHER
          I bet you're a great swimmer. My turn?
          Bingo!

                    CROUPIER
          Pas "Bingo", M'sieur . . . Banco.

                    GRANDFATHER
                  (taking cards)
          I'll take the little darlings anyway.

He takes up the cards and can't understand that they are
unnumbered.

                    GRANDFATHER
          Two and one is three, carry one is four.

The buxom BLONDE leans over him.

                    BLONDE
          Lay them down.

                    GRANDFATHER
                  (disturbed by his eyeline)
          Eh?

                    BLONDE
          Lay them down.

                        GRANDFATHER
          We'd be thrown out.

                        BLONDE
          Your cards . . . lay them down . . . face up.

He does so.

                        CROUPIER
          Huit à la pointe . . . et sept.
                    (he pushes chips and
                    box to Grandfather)

                        BLONDE
          You had a lovely little pair, y'see.

                        GRANDFATHER
          I did?

CROUPIER taps impatiently on box (shoe).

                        BLONDE
          They're yours.

                        GRANDFATHER
          They are?

                        BLONDE
          The cards . . . you're bank.

26. INTERIOR DANCING CLUB

    The BOYS are having a rare old time and the place is really moving.

27. INTERIOR BOYD'S CLUB

    GRANDFATHER is playing and a waiter is checking the requirements
    of the players.

                        GRANDFATHER
          Bingo!

                        CROUPIER
                    (wearily)
          M'lord dit "Bingo".

                        WAITER
                    (to Grandfather)
          A little light refreshment.

> GRANDFATHER
> (lordly)
> A glass of the old chablis to wash down a
> gesture of giblets wouldn't go amiss.
> (he resumes his game)
> Souflée, chop chop.

The CROUPIER uses the spatula to pick up a card. GRANDFATHER
grabs it and scoops some sandwiches off a passing tray.

28. <u>INTERIOR DANCING CLUB</u>

The boys are at their table again laughing and enjoying themselves
when suddenly their faces freeze.

From their P.O.V. we see NORM standing glowering down at them;
with him is SHAKE. Reluctantly the boys rise and follow NORM out.

29. <u>INTERIOR BOYD'S</u>

GRANDFATHER is looking worried, and at the call of the card he
loses and we see that all his chips have gone. He notices the
waiter delivering snacks and champagne to a couple, so quick as
a flash he places a handkerchief over his arm and, writing a bill
out on a piece of paper, presents it to the couple and collects
payment in chips. He then resumes playing.

30. <u>INTERIOR HOTEL ROOM</u>

Waiter is sitting on chair in underclothes, reading. He hears a
noise, says "The Manager!" and hides in outer clothes closet.
NORM and the boys enter saying

> NORM
> Now get on with it.

> JOHN
> We were going to do it.

> NORM
> Aye, well now!
> (he goes through bedroom)

RINGO goes to hang up coat in closet. He does so, then crosses
to rest.

> RINGO
> Any of you lot put a man in that cupboard?

                              ALL
          A man?   No.

                              RINGO
          Well somebody did.

GEORGE goes to cupboard. We see the waiter from his P.O.V. He
closes door, returns to group.

                              GEORGE
          He's right, y'know.

                              BOYS
                         (disinterested)
          Ah well, there you go.

SHAKE enters front door, goes to hang up coat and drags waiter
out.

                              SHAKE
          Eh, what's all this?

                              PAUL
          Oh, him . . . He's been lurking.

                              JOHN
          Aye, he looks a right lurker.

                              SHAKE
                         (to waiter)
          You're undressed. Where are your clothes?

                              WAITER
          The old gentleman borrowed them to go
          gambling at Boyd's.

                              PAUL
          No!

                              RINGO
          Oh, he's gone to my club, has he?

                              PAUL
                         (turning on Ringo)
          Yeah, it's all your fault, getting invites
          to gambling clubs. He's probably in the
          middle of an orgy by now.

                              JOHN
              Well, what are we waiting for?

                              SHAKE
              Aye, come on, honest, that Grandfather
              of yours is worse than any of you lot.

31. <u>INTERIOR BOYD'S CLUB</u>

    GRANDFATHER is drinking champagne in locked arms with BLONDE.

                              MANAGER
              Encore de champagne, Monsieur?

                              GRANDFATHER
              Yes, and I'll have some more champagne
              as well.

    He takes another swig of his glass.

                              MANAGER
                           (beaming)
              Lord John McCartney, he's the millionaire
              Irish peer, filthy rich of course.

                              CUSTOMER
              Oh I don't know, looks rather clean to me.

    The MANAGER comes to GRANDFATHER's side.

                              MANAGER
              Play is about to resume, m'lord.

                              GRANDFATHER
                        (handing him a chip)
              Lead me to it, I've a winning itch that only
              success can pacify.

    He takes his place at the table. The MANAGER watches for a moment,
    then moves away from the table towards the club reception desk.

32. <u>INTERIOR RECEPTION DESK BOYD'S CLUB</u>

    JOHN, PAUL, GEORGE, RINGO, NORM and SHAKE are trying to gain
    entrance.

                              ATTENDANT
              I'm sorry sir, members and invited guests
              only.

                              PAUL, GEORGE, RINGO, JOHN
          I've got to get in.
          It's urgent and important.
          I've had an invite.
          Take me to your leader.

                    NORM

          Shurrup.

The BOYS do and meanwhile the MANAGER has walked into SHOT. He
recognises the BOYS and welcomes them with false enthusiasm.
They all start to enter the main room.

                    NORM
          All we want to know is have you got a
          little old man in there?

                    MANAGER
                 (pleasantly)
          Do you mean Lord McCartney?

CLOSE UP   PAUL

                    PAUL
          He's at it again. Look, I'm his grandfather
          . . . I mean . . .

                    BLONDE
                 (standing next to
                 Grandfather)
          Oh, it must be the dolly floor show.

                    JOHN
          Stay where you are everybody, this is
          a raid and we want him.

                    GRANDFATHER
          Who are these ruffians? . . . I've never seen
          them before in my life! . . . (etc.)

They grab the protesting GRANDFATHER and drag him into the
reception area. He keeps trying to return to BLONDE and table.
GEORGE and RINGO take an end each of the velvet cord hanging
between the two stanchions. They exchange ends and re-hook it,
thus encircling GRANDFATHER by the entrance desk. They then go
to settle up.

                    MANAGER
               (with false charm)
     Before you go, gentlemen, there's the
     small matter of the bill.

He snaps his fingers and a waiter hands him the bill.

                    NORM
                 (taking it)
          I'll settle that.

He glances at it.

                    NORM
          A hundred and eighty quid!

                    MANAGER
                  (icily)
     I beg your pardon, guineas.

At that moment a WAITER appears with a tray full of pound notes.

                    WAITER
     Your winnings, my Lord, one hundred
     and ninety pounds.

The MANAGER tears up the bill and takes the money.

                    GRANDFATHER
     How about me change?

                    MANAGER
     Cloak room charge.

He hands GRANDFATHER his old mackintosh.

                    RINGO
                 (brightly)
     Ah well, easy come, easy go.

The others glower at him.

     Well.

33. <u>INTERIOR BIG CAR (MOVING ON WAY TO STUDIOS)</u>

The BOYS have settled down.

                    JOHN
        Should I say it?

                    GEORGE
        Follow your impulse.

                    RINGO
        It'll only get you into trouble.

                    JOHN
                 (to RINGO)
        Aah, shurrup, misery!

JOHN slouches forward.

                    JOHN
                 (urgently)
        O.K. Driver, follow that car!!

The driver is an urbane man in a handsome grey uniform.

                    FRANK
              (indicating the traffic)
        Would you like to be a little more precise, sir?

                    JOHN
        Well, that's the wrong line for a start.

                    FRANK
        Sorry?
                 (meaning: "I beg your pardon")

                    GEORGE
        Oh, don't pay any attention to him, he was
        just fulfilling a lifelong ambition.

                    FRANK
        I see.

                    JOHN
        Yeah, you know, "O.K. Buster, follow that
        car, there's a sawbuck in it for you if you
        get real close!"

                    FRANK
        Oh, yes, now I'm with you.
        But, gee, Mister, I've got my licence
        to think of . . . we're doing a hundred now . . .

The car is stopped in traffic behind a bus. JOHN gets out of
car and walks to the front. JOHN leans in window delightedly,
he flashes his wallet. The car starts again.

> JOHN
> (walking alongside)
> Ever seen one of these before?

> FRANK
> Ah . . . a shamus, eh?

> JOHN
> I see you go to the night court.

> FRANK
> I've made the scene.

> JOHN
> (jumping into car)
> Well, remember, it's Leathery Magee
> up ahead in that convertible, so cover
> me in the stake-out.

> GEORGE
> I don't think that bit's right.

> JOHN
> What do you expect from an ad lib . . .
> Raymond Chandler?

34. EXTERIOR STREET

As the big car overtakes a Company Director's Rolls. JOHN
lowers his window and the boys let out an imaginary hail of
bullets at the Executive in the back. He reacts violently and
starts to shout at them. As he does so, he presses the button
of his window, so that we hear only part of it. But what we
do is unpleasant. He immediately presses the button and the
window rises.

RINGO and PAUL jump out of the car. RINGO takes two drumsticks
from his coat pocket and, using them as banderillas, inserts
them with style into the radiator grill (V.O. "Ole" from the
BOYS). PAUL then, using his coat as a matador's cloak, does a
butterfly pass at the car which has just started up, narrowly
missing him, but he keeps in the matador position.

35. INTERIOR CAR

                         NORM
            Will you all stop it, you're like a gang
            of school kids, I knew this was going to
            happen one day.

                         JOHN
                    (as Ringo and Paul
                     climb in)
            Well, you shouldn't have had bacon for
            your breakfast, you cannibal.

                         FRANK
                    (to Norm)
            We're nearly there, sir.

                         JOHN
            Eh . . . don't call him sir, he's got enough
            delusions of power as it is.

CLOSE SHOT of a long-suffering NORM.

                         NORM
            And I was happy in the bakery. I'll never
            know why I left.

36. <u>EXTERIOR OF AN OLD VICTORIAN MUSIC HALL THEATRE</u>

    <u>which has been converted to the T.V. Studios.</u>

    There are a few groups of GIRL FANS standing outside the front
    of the theatre, but against the curb of the pavement is a
    night-watchman's canvas hut and brazier.

    The car approaches.

37. <u>INTERIOR OF THE CAR</u>

                         NORM
            Get ready John, open the door and as it
            draws up, out you go and straight in.

    JOHN nods and opens the door. The FANS start to swarm round
    them. To escape, the BOYS dash into the night-watchman's canvas
    hut, pick it up and run with it to the stage door, revealing the
    night-watchman, staring in astonishment.

    At the door the BOYS put the hut down and enter the theatre.

38. <u>INTERIOR STAGE DOOR ENTRANCE</u>

As the BOYS enter, two P.R.O. men in dark suits, stiff white
collars and old school ties step forward and smile menacingly.

                    FIRST P.R.O. MAN
                  (menacingly)
          Press conference, they're waiting for you.

                         NORM
                  (jovially)
          Give us a couple of shakes to get our breath.

                    FIRST P.R.O. MAN
                  (more menacingly)
          They're waiting now!

And without more ado they grab an arm each and march the
protesting NORM towards the stairs that lead to the dress
circle.

                         PAUL
          Eh, this lot means it. They're even taking
          hostages.

The BOYS, SHAKE and GRANDFATHER rush after the rapidly disappearing
NORM, who by now is half way up the stairs.

39. <u>INTERIOR OF DRESS CIRCLE LOUNGE</u>

It is empty except for two BARMAIDS poised ready to serve,
standing behind trestle tables full of drinks and sandwiches.
The dark-suited MEN enter with NORM and close behind them follow
GRANDFATHER, SHAKE and the BOYS. The group arrives at the centre
of the lounge and have time to look about and see the food but
before they can get to it, from all directions NEWSPAPERMEN
and PHOTOGRAPHERS converge upon them.

Now begins an elaborate tug-of-war between various PHOTOGRAPHERS
using their flash attachments and REPORTERS to capture a
Beatle, and in the midst of this running battle a man with a
portable recorder is trying to interview them. Together and
singly the BOYS are pushed about the room and while this goes
on a hard core of NEWSPAPERMEN are busily devouring sandwiches
and pouring themselves drinks, to the annoyance of the BARMAIDS.

Every time one of the BOYS attempts to get a sandwich or a drink,
it is either too late, the plate is empty, or they are intercepted.
The single and constant thing we see in the scene is the pushing
and pulling, heavy impersonal handling, the BOYS are just things

to be placed like still life in one advantageous position after
another. During the scene these individual exchanges take
place:

> SOUND REPORTER
> What's your philosophy of life?

> JOHN
> I'm torn between Zen and I'm all right Jack.

> REPORTER
> Has success changed your life?

> RINGO
> Yes.

> REPORTER
> Do you like playing the guitar?

> GEORGE
> Next to kissing girls it's favourites.

PAUL surrounded by NEWSPAPERMEN:

> PAUL
> No, actually, we're just good friends.

HIGH SHOT of the Press Reception, and we see the BOYS ease their
way out until they get to the curtained entrance to the Dress
Circle; completely unnoticed, they slip through.

40. <u>INTERIOR THEATRE DRESS CIRCLE</u>

The BOYS come up the stairs into the Dress Circle proper.
GRANDFATHER and SHAKE are sitting there having a picnic of beer
and sandwiches.

> PAUL
> (ironically)
> Anything to spare?

> GRANDFATHER
> We've just finished, Pauly. George, write
> us your John Henry on this picture.

> GEORGE
> Sure.
> (He does so)

                          PAUL
              Ah well. Eh, look!

He points, and from PAUL's P.O.V. we see, on stage, the setting
up of the show. Scenery and lights, cameras and sound equipment
are being put into position by a small army of studio staff.
DANCERS and SINGERS are milling about as well.

                          PAUL
              Let's go and muck in.

                          JOHN
              Aye, before anyone stops us.

They exit to rows of the Dress Circle and go through the entrance
down the narrow stairs to the stalls and onto the stage that is
built and extended right into the stalls, which are partly covered
up.

41. INTERIOR STAGE

Everyone is so busy that they hardly notice the BOYS, who wander
about examining the studio equipment. A load of three drum sets
are being brought on stage and a voice shouts out:

                          VOICE
              Here, what about these electric guitars?

                          SHAKE
              Where are they?

                          VOICE
              Back here, mate.

                          SHAKE
                    (going towards the voice)
              I'm coming.

RINGO is busy setting up his drums, and MEN are setting up the
other sets. He drops a stick and the FLOOR MANAGER retrieves it
and is about to tap the drum. The FLOOR MANAGER is a languid
young man.

                          RINGO
              Leave them drums alone.

                          FLOOR MANAGER
              Oh, surely one can have a tiny touch.

                              RINGO
          If you so much as breathe heavy on them, I'm
          out on strike.

                         FLOOR MANAGER
          Aren't you being rather arbitrary?

                              RINGO
          That's right, retreat behind a smoke screen of
          bourgeois clichés. I don't go round messing
          about with your ear-phones, do I?

                         FLOOR MANAGER

          Spoil sport!

                              RINGO

          Well!

RINGO fusses like a mother hen clucking over his drums. The
FLOOR MANAGER is furious.

                             GEORGE
          He's very touchy about those drums, they loom
          large in his legend.

RINGO gives his drums a defiant crash, and JOHN and PAUL stop
whatever they are up to and hurry over.

                              PAUL
          What's up?

                             GEORGE
                         (pointing)
          He's sulking again.

                              JOHN
          I'll show him.

He picks up a set of drum sticks and bashes back at RINGO, who
does a more complicated drum roll. GEORGE now joins in and to
PAUL's encouragement a drum duel starts completely naturally
and improvised. During this encounter the work proceeds around
them and the guitars are brought on and SHAKE sets them to
working order. PAUL first, then JOHN and GEORGE take up their
own instruments and out of the drum duel emerges one of their
numbers.

42. INTERIOR RAMP

As the number finishes, a baldheaded man (he is the T.V. DIRECTOR) storms down the ramp that leads from the control box under the Dress Circle.

>   DIRECTOR
>   (with over-exaggerated calm)
>   All right, I'm sorry and let's hear no more
>   about it. If that's your opinion you're probably
>   right. Look, if you think I'm unsuitable let's
>   have it out in the open, I can't stand these
>   back-stage politics.

By the end of this speech he is standing in front of JOHN who takes the scene in his stride.

>   JOHN
>   Aren't you tending to black and white this
>   whole situation?

>   DIRECTOR
>   Well, quite honestly I wasn't expecting 'a
>   musical arranger' who would question my
>   ability . . . picture-wise.

>   JOHN
>   (to the others)
>   I could listen to him for hours.

>   PAUL
>   Heave to, what's all this about a musical
>   arranger?

>   DIRECTOR
>   Mr. McCartney Senior!

The BOYS have a giggle at the very idea and at this moment GRANDFATHER appears from behind the DIRECTOR.

>   GRANDFATHER
>   Pauly, they're trying to fob you off wid
>   this musical charlatan but I've given him
>   the test.

>   DIRECTOR
>   (bravely)
>   I'm quite happy to be replaced.

                         GRANDFATHER
                    (indicating the Director)
          He's a typical buck-passer.

                         DIRECTOR
          I won an award.

                         JOHN
          A likely story.

                         DIRECTOR
          It's on the wall in my office.

At this moment NORM comes on the stage, confident, cigar in
mouth and serene.

                         NORM
          Hello our lot, everyone happy?

The BOYS, the DIRECTOR, FLOOR MANAGER and GRANDFATHER turn on
him and stare silently.

                         NORM
              All right, all right. If you don't need
              this lot, I'll lock 'em up in the dressing
              room till you do.

                         DIRECTOR
              Please do, I'll not need them for fifteen
              minutes. Thank you.

He glares at GRANDFATHER who glares right back. The DIRECTOR
walks away with the FLOOR MANAGER pacifying him.

                         DIRECTOR
              Give me a bottle of milk and a packet of
              Oblivion. Oh, it's a plot, I see it now, it's
              all a plot.

They go left towards the back-stage.

                         NORM
                    (producing key)
          Now, come on, I've got the key.

He leads the lads off right. RINGO is last as he is putting his
drum sticks down safely.

NORM and the BOYS turn on him.

                              NORM
          Let's have you?

                              JOHN
          Come on speedy!

                              PAUL
          Ringo!

                              GEORGE
          Wake up!

RINGO glares at them and follows quickly. As the BOYS move off
after NORM, they pass the next act waiting for rehearsal. It is
an elegant man in full-tail suit meticulously adjusting his
cuff-links. Beside him is a free-standing sign reading "Leslie
Jackson and his ten disappearing doves." The BOYS pass him and
go through the door. GRANDFATHER stops and looks at the performer
with respect.

                         GRANDFATHER
               I can't tell you how much I've enjoyed
               your act.

He slaps the man on the back with happy camaraderie. There is
the sound of a dove, a few feathers fall out of the sleeve of the
man's coat and he and GRANDFATHER look down at the floor. The
man glares at GRANDFATHER, takes out a pen from his pocket,
crosses out "10" on his sign, and writes "9" in its place, puts
the pen back in his pocket and starts towards the centre stage
putting on a false performer's smile as he does.

43. <u>INTERIOR THEATRE BACK-STAGE CORRIDOR</u>

The BOYS move down the narrow stairs, and out of the ground floor
dressing rooms stream steady flow of costumed actors and
actresses. They engulf the lads and force them against the
wall -- the actors are all making for the stage door. As the
actors push past the BOYS we see the BOYS' excited faces, their
mouths watering for the costumes. JOHN touches the costume on
one actor.

                              JOHN
                         (to Actor)
               Gear costume!

                              ACTOR
                         (eyeing him)
               Swap?

                              NORM
              Right, first floor and no messing about.

NORM, leading the way, goes up the stairs, but as they turn the
first corner they are confronted by a group of GIRLS; a game of
manners starts: "After you," "No, after you." NORM, who is ahead
of the group, looks down on them in disgust.

                              NORM
              Lennon, leave them girls alone or I'll
              report you.

The BOYS let the GIRLS pass and resume the journey, always
surrounded by people.

44. INTERIOR   DRESSING ROOM AND CORRIDOR

     RINGO's attention is caught by a door. He crosses and opens it,
     looking out onto a fire escape. The others join him and the four
     BOYS step through the door and onto the fire escape.

45. EXTERIOR   TOP OF THE FIRE ESCAPE

     From the BOYS' P.O.V. we see down below into the property yard
     behind the theatre. It is a long narrow yard full of old coaches,
     motor cars and all the general debris of hundreds of sets from
     past theatre shows. Through the piles of heaped high junk there
     are a couple of narrow alleyways.

     The BOYS scamper down the fire escape.

     When they reach the bottom there is a large door. They open it
     and look through.

     From their P.O.V. we see a large green field quite empty.

     The BOYS step through the doorway into the field. We now see
     from a HELICOPTER SHOT the four BOYS standing together surrounded
     by space.

     It is the first time they have been alone and unconfined all day.

     They look at each other and grin . . . then first GEORGE and
     PAUL let out a whoop and run towards the centre of the field;
     after a moment JOHN and RINGO follow them. The BOYS pick up some
     loose straw and insert it under JOHN's cap and sleeves, turning
     him into a scarecrow.

The four BOYS dash about madly calling to one another and generally
horsing around. Out of this emerges an imaginary game of soccer
and although there is no ball the game is fast and furious.
RINGO is goalkeeper. GEORGE is the referee. JOHN has his name
taken by the referee. PAUL takes the penalty kick. RINGO dives
the wrong way and disgustedly kicks the imaginary ball into the
back of the net. After a few moments the long shadow of a man
falls across the grass.

                         MAN'S VOICE (off)
           I suppose you know this is private property.

The BOYS freeze.

From their P.O.V. we see a big burly middle-aged man glowering
at them. The BOYS exchange rueful glances and, under the big
man's eye, mooch back towards the gateway they came in by. JOHN
is the last to go through. He turns to the man.

                         JOHN
           Sorry if we hurt your field.

46. INTERIOR CORRIDOR BACK-STAGE

    GRANDFATHER is sneaking down the corridor, a pile of photos under
    his arm.

47. INTERIOR T.V. THEATRE UNDERNEATH THE STAGE

    Under the stage the usual set of wooden columns that support the
    stage with lots of furniture and a single light is on; it is
    placed by the orchestra's entrance to the orchestra pit.
    GRANDFATHER comes down the stairs and winds his way through the
    columns until he finds himself a safe little cubby hole and
    settles himself under the light. He spreads the signed photos
    of the boys in front of him and, adjusting an old-fashioned pair
    of glasses, ball-point pen in hand, begins to copy the boys'
    signatures onto the fresh photos, tutting at his failures and
    chuckling at his successes. After a moment, there is a sound of
    someone coming down the stairs. GRANDFATHER darts into a dark
    patch out of sight.

    The menacing shadows appear on the stairway.

                         NORM (voice off)
           There's no one here.

                         SHAKE (voice off)
           This is the only way they could have gone.

We now see GRANDFATHER holding himself stiffly in; he is on some
sort of raised platform and he fidgets and in doing so he knocks
a lever of some sort. Slowly GRANDFATHER ascends OUT OF SHOT
with a light that grows bigger above him.

48. INTERIOR T.V. THEATRE STAGE

A rehearsal of the toast scene from a Strauss operetta. The
entire stage is full of SINGERS. Glasses in hand they are singing
away at each other but in true opera tradition they are addressing
out to the audience. Slowly in between the leading man and leading
woman, who are about to embrace, a stage trap opens and a blinking,
surprised GRANDFATHER appears. Here we INTERCUT to the T.V.
control room for amazed REACTION SHOTS of the DIRECTOR and control
room CREW.

Back now on the stage the toast song reaches its climax and the
LEADING MAN and WOMAN rush into each other's arms. GRANDFATHER
sandwiched between them.

48A. INT. CORRIDOR AS BOYS PASS THRU ON WAY TO DRESSING ROOM

JOHN is behind them.

JOHN, BOYS and MILLIE are walking towards each other.

> MILLIE
> (as all pass)
> Hello.

> JOHN
> (stopping . . . The boys
> carry on past, not noticing
> her)
> Hello.

> MILLIE
> Oh, wait a minute, don't tell me you're . . .

> JOHN
> No, not me.

> MILLIE
> (insistently)
> Oh you are, I know you are.

> JOHN
> No, I'm not.

                    MILLIE
You are.

                    JOHN
I'm not. no.

                    MAGGIE
Well, you look like him.

                    JOHN
Oh do I? You're the first one who ever
said that.

                    MILLIE
Oh you do, look.

JOHN looks at himself in the mirror.

JOHN examines himself in the mirror carefully.

                    JOHN
My eyes are lighter.

                    MILLIE
                 (agreeing)
Oh yes.

                    JOHN
And my nose . . .

                    MILLIE
Well, yes your nose is. Very.

                    JOHN
Is it?

                    MILLIE
I would have said so.

                    JOHN
Aye, but you know him well.

                    MILLIE
                 (indignantly)
No I don't, he's only a casual acquaintance.

                    JOHN
                 (knowingly)
That's what you tell me.

                              MILLIE
                          (suspiciously)
                    What have you heard.

                              JOHN
                          (blandly)
                    It's all over the place, everyone knows.

                              MILLIE
                    Is it? Is it really?

                              JOHN
                    Mind you, I stood up for you, I mean I
                    wouldn't have it.

                              MILLIE
                    I knew I could rely on you.

                              JOHN
                          (modestly)
                    Thanks.

          MILLIE touches his arm, then walks away. After a moment she turns.

                              MILLIE
                    You don't look like him at all.

          JOHN winks at her and she winks back.

49. INTERIOR   DRESSING ROOM

          NORM and SHAKE enter the room. The BOYS' TAILOR is there waiting
          for the BOYS.

                              SHAKE
                    Oh they've probably gone to the canteen, cup
                    of tea, like.

                              NORM
                    That's too easy for Lennon.

          He crosses to door leading to the fire escape.

                              NORM
                          (dramatically)
                    He's out there somewhere, causing trouble just
                    to upset me.

                    SHAKE
You're imagining it. You're letting things
prey on your mind.

                    NORM
Oh no . . . this is a battle of nerves between
John and me.

                    SHAKE
But John hasn't got any.

                    NORM
What?

                    SHAKE
Nerves.

                    NORM
I know, that's the trouble.

He puffs nervously at his cigarette.

Oh, I've toyed with the idea of a ball and
chain but he'd only rattle them at me . . . and
in public and all. Sometimes I think he enjoys
seeing me suffer.

He hears something.

Get behind that door, they're coming.

The two men hide behind the door. The BOYS enter the room.
As JOHN is last he shuts the door and faces SHAKE and NORM.

                    JOHN
What are you doing there?

                    SHAKE
Hiding.

                    JOHN
I think you're soft or something.

                    NORM
We weren't hiding.

                    TAILOR
Now?

                              NORM
             Now. We were trying to catch you red-
             handed. I thought I told you to stay here?

                              RINGO
             Well . . .

                              NORM
             When I tell you to stay put, stay put.

                              JOHN
                       (down on his knees)
             Don't cane me, sir, I was led astray.

                              NORM
             Oh shurrup and come on. They're waiting
             for you in the studio.

                              RINGO
             Oh dear, I feel like doing a bit of work.

                              NORM
             Good lad, Ringo.

                              PAUL
             Oh, listen to teacher's pet.

                              GEORGE
             You crawler.

                              JOHN
             He's betrayed the class.

                              RINGO
             Oh, leave off!!!

                              JOHN
             Temper! Temper!

                              RINGO
             Well . . .

     CLOSE UP on NORM's long-suffering face.

                              NORM
             Will you all get a move on! They're waiting
             for you!

By this time the TAILOR has his tape stretched between his hands
to measure GEORGE's shoulders. But since GEORGE has moved away,
he is measuring space. JOHN takes up his scissors and cuts the
tape.

                         JOHN
           I now declare this bridge open.

The BOYS run out the door.

50. <u>INTERIOR BACK-STAGE AREA</u>

Five beautiful MODELS are standing about in costume. One is
knitting a loose wool sweater which is almost completed. There
is the sound of a juggling act's music off and a few of the girls
are looking off towards the centre stage. At the edge of frame is
a collapsible table covered with green baize. On it are three
spaced white plates.

From the door off stage above which is a sign "To Canteen and
Production Offices", GRANDFATHER enters eating a plate of
spaghetti on toast. The knitting GIRL sees him and, in mime,
asks him to stand still so that she can measure the sweater
against him. GRANDFATHER, eager to help, puts his plate of food
on the green table between plates two and three. He goes to
be measured with the sweater.

From the onstage area, a juggler's assistant (pretty girl) in
costume backs up and with the usual theatrical flourishes picks
up, without looking, plate number ONE and throws it off screen
towards centre stage. There is a drum roll from orchestra. She
then throws plate number TWO. We CUT on stage to the JUGGLER
now balancing the two spinning plates on two poles, one in each
hand. He has another pole in his mouth and nods to his assistant,
asking for the THIRD plate.

We CUT BACK to the assistant who, still not looking, throws plate
THREE which is GRANDFATHER's. There is the sound of an orchestra
raggedly stopping and all the hangers-on in the scene look off
interestedly.

We hear the DIRECTOR's voice.

                         DIRECTOR (V.O.)
           All right, hold it, hold it . . . O.K.
           John, wipe him down and we'll carry on
           with the next act.

We

                                                            CUT TO

Centre stage. The JUGGLER is as before but the spaghetti is
covering his head, having slipped off the third plate.

The FLOOR MANAGER is bustling around, trying to help.

We CUT BACK to back-stage. GRANDFATHER has finished being
measured and goes to the green table where he put his plate
down. He picks up the only remaining plate, looks at it,
wondering where his food has gone, shrugs and heads back
towards the exit door as we hear the DIRECTOR'S VOICE.

51. INTERIOR T.V. STUDIO FLOOR

CLOSE UP on the distraught DIRECTOR.

                         DIRECTOR
             Where are they? I said, where are
             they?

                         FLOOR MANAGER
                      (placating)
             They're coming, I promise you.

                         DIRECTOR
                      (fiercely)
             Now look, if they're not here on this
             floor in thirty seconds there's going to
             be trouble . . . understand me . . . trouble!!!

Two STAGE HANDS are walking disinterestedly past, they look at
the DIRECTOR.

                         1st STAGE HAND
             What's he on about, Taff?

                         WELSH STAGE HAND
             Well . . . he's being the director. Of course,
             he lives in a world of his own, mind.

At this moment the BOYS, NORM, SHAKE and GRANDFATHER appear.
The BOYS grab their instruments and prepare to play.

                         JOHN
                      (to the Director)
             Standing about, eh? Some people have it dead
             easy, don't they?

The DIRECTOR is about to blow his top but manages to hold on and mutter to the heavens.

> DIRECTOR
> (to himself)
> Of course, once you're over thirty, you're finished. It's a young man's medium and I just can't take the pace.

> RINGO
> Are you as young as that, then?

> BOYS
> Shurrup!

> GRANDFATHER
> Isn't it always the way? Picking on us little fellas.

> PAUL
> (to Shake)
> Shove the gentleman jockey in the make-up room and keep your eye on him, will you?

> SHAKE
> I'm an electrician, not a wet nurse, y'know.

> PAUL
> (threateningly)
> I'll set John on you!

> SHAKE
> (hastily)
> Oh, anything you say, Paul.

He leads GRANDFATHER away.

The BOYS are placed in position, instruments ready. The boom moves in near them. There is a mike hovering just over JOHN's head. JOHN starts attacking it.

> DIRECTOR'S VOICE (over Tannoy)
> Run through the number and try not to jiggle out of your positions.

The BOYS start the number, as the stage hands adjust their settings, and when they've finished they stand about spare.

52. INTERIOR T.V. CONTROL ROOM

The room is crowded with the usual personnel, P.A., elecs, racks, etc. . . . make-up supervisor and wardrobe mistress.

> DIRECTOR
> That was more or less all right for me. I'll give them one more run-through then leave them alone until the dress . . .
> > (to make-up woman)
> Oh, how about make-up?

> MAKE-UP WOMAN
> Not really, they don't need it. We'll just powder them off for shine.

> DIRECTOR
> Good. Norm, get them along to make-up will you?

> NORM
> > (rising)
> Sure.

> DIRECTOR
> > (looking into the monitor)
> And hurry, they're not looking too happy.

From the DIRECTOR'S P.O.V. we see into the monitor. The BOYS crowding around RINGO.

[Scene 53 deleted in revision.]

54. INTERIOR MAKE-UP ROOM

A smallish room with a line of chairs facing a wall mirror and a long table. Each place is clearly marked and above each mirror a girl's name: Betty, Angela, Deirdre, Jenny.

SHAKE and GRANDFATHER are sitting in splendid isolation. They are staring each other out.

> SHAKE
> You blinked!

> GRANDFATHER
> I never did, you did.

The BOYS enter.

>   SHAKE
> Hello, he's not talking to me. He's having
> a sulk.

>   GEORGE
> Well, it must be catching. He's given it to
> the champ here.

He indicates RINGO, he ignores him.

>   NORM
> Stop picking on him.

>   RINGO
> I don't need you to defend me, y'know, Norm.

>   JOHN
> Leave him alone, he's got swine fever.

>   NORM
> Sit down, the lot of you.

At this moment several ACTORS come into the room. They are all
dressed in the uniform of officers in Wellington's army. Together
with the BOYS they sit down, Beatles and soldiers all mixed up.

Now a group of several pretty make-up girls make an entrance and
the BOYS herald their arrival with a chorus of "aye aye's" and
wolf whistles. JOHN meanwhile has helped himself to a big beard
and the other lads are generally messing about with assorted
make-up things.

>   HEAD MAKE-UP GIRL
> Oh, this is impossible! We'll never get you all
> done in time.

>   ACTOR
> Well, you'll just have to do us first . . . it
> makes no difference to them whether they're
> made up or not . . .
>   (sees John with beard)
> And who's me, then?

>   JOHN
>   (charmingly)
> My name's Betty . . .
>   (pointing to the name
>   on the mirror)
> Do you want a punch up your frogged tunic?

NORM fights his way to JOHN.

> NORM
> Now listen, John, behave yourself or I'll
> murder you and, Shake, take that wig off,
> it suits you.

SHAKE has a long blonde girl's wig on. With the assistance of the
girls, NORM gets the BOYS seated into the chairs nearest the
door. For some reason RINGO now has a Guardsman's busby wedged
down almost over his eyes and is sitting with it on under a hair
drier, reading a copy of "Queen" magazine.

> NORM
> (to Ringo)
> What do you think you're up to?

> RINGO
> Someone put it on me.

> JOHN
> Excuses, that's all we get and you know
> you fancy yourself in the Coldstreams.

The girls now move in and put make-up bibs on the BOYS and start
to powder them off.

> JOHN
> You won't interfere with the basic rugged
> concept of my personality, will you, girl?

> PAUL
> Eh, don't take out me lines.

> GEORGE
> Yeah, they give him that "Je ne sais quoi"
> rakish air.

The lads laugh with pleasure.

RINGO decides to try a little joke.

> RINGO
> (indicating the busby he is still
> wearing)
> Short back and sides, please.

The others look at him with mock disgust.

                    PAUL
Behave . . .

                    JOHN
Foreign devil . . .

                    GEORGE
Control yourself . . .

GRANDFATHER has been watching the powdering process.

                    GRANDFATHER
In my considered opinion you're a bunch
of sissies.

JOHN grabs a powder puff from his girl.

                    JOHN
You know you're only jealous!

And dabs the old man liberally with the powder much to GRANDFATHER's
annoyance.

                    NORM
Leave him alone, Lennon, or I'll tell
them all the truth about you.

                    JOHN
You wouldn't!

                    NORM
I would though.

NORM goes out.

                    PAUL
What's he know?

                    JOHN
Nothing, he's trying to brainwash me and
give me personality doubts . . . oh, he's a
swine but a clever swine, mind.

                    GRANDFATHER
                    (impatiently)
Lookit, I thought I was supposed to be getting
a change of scenery and so far I've seen a
train and a room, a car and a room and a

                    GRANDFATHER (Cont.)
room and a room. Well, that's maybe all right
for a bunch of powdered gee-gaws like you lot
but I'm feeling decidedly strait-jacketed.
This is no life for a free-booting agent of my
stamp, I'm a frustrated man and that class of
McCartney is a dangerous McCartney.

                    GIRL
                (admiringly)
What a clean old man.

                    GRANDFATHER
                (touchily)
You're too young for a fella of my cosmopolitan
tastes, so don't press your luck.

                    JOHN
He's sex-obsessed, the older generation are
leading this country to galloping ruin.

NORM returns leaving the door open; the BOYS hear the sound of
music coming from the studio.

                    NORM
They're nearly ready for you. They're just
finishing the band call.

                    JOHN
                (jumping up from his seat)
Gear! Come on, girls, let's have a bit of a
dance.

                    JOHN'S GIRL
I don't think it's allowed.

                    JOHN
Well . . . it wouldn't be any fun if it was!

The BOYS drag the make-up girls out of the room and into the
studio.

The GIRLS are still trying to finish making the BOYS up.

As the BOYS and MAKE-UP GIRLS dance past, we see one of the
"Strauss" singers combing his long hair straight back. Two
STAGE HANDS swing a windmachine past him and his hair is blown
straight forward into a Beatle cut.

> JOHN
> (passing him)

Never.

During dance, GEORGE takes off wig and places it on dummy, revealing identical hair underneath.

55. INTERIOR T.V. STUDIO FLOOR

The work is still going on and the music is up full blast, the BOYS enter and with the girls they start a wild dance, hippy, shake, zulu, blue beat, the lot. LIONEL and DANCERS are doing their routine on one side of stage . . . it becomes a challenge dance between both groups. JOHN swings his GIRL onto the motorised CAMERA, Western style, and starts to track through the GROUP. GEORGE is on another CAMERA.

56. INTERIOR CONTROL ROOM

The whole control room crew are watching the dance on all the monitors. The DIRECTOR is about to stop the BOYS but his GIRL P.A. glares at him. With a shrug he lets the dance go on.

We now CUT between the dancers on the monitors and the BOYS' actual dancing down on the studio floor. When the recorded music stops, they grab their instruments and go into a number.

So we can watch every aspect of their work and with so many monitors it gives the impression that there are many more boys than just four.

When the number finally ends we are back in the studio on the floor.

57. INTERIOR T.V. STUDIO FLOOR

> DIRECTOR'S VOICE OVER TANNOY
> Thank you, gentlemen, you can break now
> while we push on with the show.

The BOYS acknowledge this with a quaver of guitar chords and a drum roll.

NORM is on them at once.

> NORM
> That was great, you've got about an hour
> but don't leave the theatre.

JOHN grabs the arm of a sexy girl dancer.

                    JOHN
          She's going to show me her stamp collection.

                         PAUL
                    (grabs a showgirl)
          So's mine.

NORM grabs JOHN's arm.

                         NORM
          John, I was talking to you. The final
          run-through is <u>important</u>. Understand,
          important!

                         JOHN
                    (like a pig)
          Oink! Oink!

They dash off with the two beauties.

GRANDFATHER is hovering in the background with SHAKE.

                              GRANDFATHER
          I want me a cup of tea.

                         NORM
          Shake.

                         SHAKE
          I'm adjusting the decibels on the inbalance.

                         NORM
          Clever.
                    (he turns)
          George!

But GEORGE is disappearing out of the door.

NORM turns to RINGO.

                         NORM
          Look after him.

                         RINGO
          But . . .

                    NORM
Do I have to raise me voice?

                    RINGO
                 (choked)
Oh, all right. Come here, Grandad.

And the two of them walk off, RINGO leading.

57A. <u>INTERIOR BACK-STAGE</u>

A man, whose act is playing tunes by hitting himself on the head,
is swallowing a handful of aspirin tablets. He starts rehearsing
his act, which consists of throwing his head back and slapping his
cheeks. Next to him, a JUGGLER is practising with four table
tennis balls.

GRANDFATHER passes him and bumps his arm slightly. Only 3 balls
come down. There is the sound of coughing off.

We

                                                        CUT TO
THE HEAD-PLAYER being patted on the back. The ball drops out
of his mouth and bounces slowly on the studio floor.

58. <u>INTERIOR T.V. STUDIO CANTEEN</u>

The canteen is about half full of actors, many of whom are dressed
as Nazi Soldiers, with mock blood bandages and arm bands. Also
there are a sprinkling of T.V. people. At a table sit GRANDFATHER
and RINGO. RINGO is deeply engrossed in a book and GRANDFATHER
has a near-empty cup of tea in front of him. The old man is
bored and looks about him slyly. He then looks at RINGO, who is
innocently occupied. A malicious gleam comes in to GRANDFATHER's
eye. He decides to have a go at RINGO and sits staring at him.
RINGO gradually becomes aware of the stare and shifts uncomfortably,
then tries to continue reading his book.

                    GRANDFATHER
               (disgustedly to no one
                in particular)
Will you ever look at him, sitting there
wid his hooter scraping away at that book!

                    RINGO
Well . . . what's the matter with that?

                    GRANDFATHER
              (taking the book from
              him)
Have you no natural resources of your own?
Have they even robbed you of that?

                    RINGO
              (snatching back his
              book)
You can learn from books.

                    GRANDFATHER
Can you now? Aah . . . sheeps heads!
You learn more be getting out there and
living.

                    RINGO

Out where?

                    GRANDFATHER
Any old where . . . but not our little Richard
. . . oh no! When you're not thumping them
pagan skins, you're tormenting your eyes wid
that rubbish!

                    RINGO
              (defiantly)
Books are good!

                    GRANDFATHER
              (countering)
Parading's better!

                    RINGO

Parading?

                    GRANDFATHER
              (marching up and down
              the canteen)
That's it, parading the streets
trailing your coat . . . bowling along
living!

                    RINGO
Well, I _am_ living, aren't I?

                    GRANDFATHER
You're living, are you? When was the
last time you gave a girl a pink-edged

                         GRANDFATHER (Cont.)
daisy? When did you last embarrass
a sheila wid your cool appraising stare?

                         RINGO
Eh . . . you're a bit old for that sort of
chat, aren't you?

                         GRANDFATHER
At least I've a back-log of memories, but
all you've got is that book!

                         RINGO
Aaah . . . stop picking on me . . . you're
as bad as the rest of them.

                         GRANDFATHER
So you are a man after all.

                         RINGO
What's that mean?

                         GRANDFATHER
Do you think I haven't noticed . . . do you
think I wasn't aware of the drift? Oh . . .
you poor unfortunate scuff, they've driven
you into books by their cruel unnatural
treatment, exploiting your good nature.

                         RINGO
                  (not too sure)
Oh . . . I dunno.

                         GRANDFATHER
                  (confidingly)
And that lot's never happier than when
they're jeering at you . . . and where would
they be without the steady support of your
drum beat I'd like to know.

                         RINGO
Yeah . . . that's right.

                         GRANDFATHER
And what's it all come to in the end?

                         RINGO
                  (defensively)
Yeah . . . what's in it for me?

                    GRANDFATHER
        A book!

                    RINGO
        Yeah . . . a bloomin' book!

He throws the book down.

                    GRANDFATHER
        When you could be out there betraying a rich
        American widow or sipping palm wine in
        Tahiti before you're too old like me.
        A fine neat and trim lad the class of you
        should be helping himself to life's goodies
        before the sands run out. Being an old age
        pensioner's a terrible drag on a man and
        every second you waste is bringing you nearer
        the Friday queue at the Post Office.

                    RINGO
        Yeah . . . funny really, 'cos I'd never thought
        of it, but being middle-aged and old takes up
        most of your time, doesn't it?

                    GRANDFATHER
                    (nodding)
        You're only right.

                    RINGO
                    (nodding back)
        I'm not wrong.

There is a pause, then RINGO rises and croses to the door.

                    GRANDFATHER
        Where are you off to?

                    RINGO
        I'm going parading before it's too late!

RINGO leaves and GRANDFATHER laughs at what he has done, then
realizes its full meaning and looks worried.

59. <u>INTERIOR   CORRIDOR AND STAIRWAY</u>

RINGO comes along the corridor then down the narrow stairs.
Half-way down he comes face to face with GEORGE who is coming
up the stairs.

> GEORGE
> Eh, Ringo, do you know what happened to me?

> RINGO
> (passing him)
> No. I don't.

As he goes round the corner RINGO turns on the surprised GEORGE.

> RINGO
> You want to stop being so scornful, it's
> twisting your face.

60. <u>INTERIOR T.V. THEATRE NEAR STAGE DOORMAN'S OFFICE</u>

JOHN and PAUL are chatting up a couple of GIRLS. When they see
RINGO approaching they break off the conversation.

> JOHN
> Here he is, the middle-aged boy wonder.

RINGO looks at JOHN hard.

> PAUL
> Eh. I thought you were looking after the
> old man.

> RINGO
> (with simple dignity)
> Get knotted!

PAUL and JOHN gape at him. For good measure RINGO takes a quick
photograph of them before he leaves them flabbergasted and walks
off into the street.

> PAUL
> We've got only half an hour till the
> final run-through. He can't walk out on
> us.

> JOHN
> Can't he? He's done it, son!

GEORGE runs towards them.

> GEORGE
> Eh, I don't know if you realise it but . . .

PAUL

We do.

GEORGE

Yes. Your Grandfather's stirred him up.

PAUL

He hasn't.

GEORGE

Yes, he's filled his head with notions
seemingly.

PAUL

The old mixer, come on, we'll have to put
him right.

The three of them go into the street.

61. EXTERIOR T.V. THEATRE STAGE DOOR ENTRANCE

The boys look up and down but RINGO has completely disappeared.

PAUL

We'll split up and search for him, he
can't be far.

They now all start to go off in the same direction, they pause,
there are three roads they can take but each time they begin to
move they all go the same way.

JOHN

It's happened at last, we've become a
limited company.

PAUL gives him a push to the left and GEORGE to the right, and
going straight ahead himself, they part and go their separate
ways.

62. EXTERIOR STREET

RINGO is walking along taking photographs with his camera when
some girls recognise him and start to follow him. They quicken
their pace and RINGO runs ahead of them. In the background a
policeman watches him. He turns and comes into another street.
He sees a second-hand clothes shop with a sign saying "We buy
Anything" and enters the shop just before the pursuing girls
come round the corner. The girls stand about looking in all
directions. After a moment RINGO comes out of the shop. He is

wearing a long mackintosh and a natty cap pulled well down. He is ignored by the girls who don't recognise him -- Realising this he goes back and ogles one of them. She glares at him.

> GIRL
> Get out of it, short house!

CLOSE-UP on RINGO's secret but happy smile as he walks briskly down the road.

63. <u>EXTERIOR   TOW PATH   CANAL</u>

RINGO kicks at a brick. He kicks stylishly but misses, so tries again, misses again, but finally kicks the stone, which doesn't budge, so he bends down and pulls it out of the ground. It is quite big, three quarters of it being below surface. Having got it he now decides to throw it away. As he does so the same POLICEMAN rides past on a bicycle.

> POLICEMAN
> Ain't you got no more bleeding sense than
> to go round chucking bricks about?

Before RINGO has time to answer the man has disappeared.

> RINGO
> (shouting after him)
> Southerner!

He looks at the canal water moodily; at this moment a large lorry tyre rolls down the incline and bashes him slap in the back, sprawling him on the path, the tyre on top of him. A small boy appears after the tyre and stands over the prostrate RINGO.

> BOY
> Here, mate, that's my hoop, stop playing
> with it.

> RINGO
> Hoop, this isn't a hoop, it's a lethal weapon.
> Have you got a licence for it?

> BOY
> Oh don't be so stroppy!

> RINGO
> (getting up)
> Well! A boy of your age bowling <u>"hoop"</u>
> at people. How old are you anyway?

                    BOY
               (aggressively)
Nine.

                  RINGO
Bet you're only eight and a half.

                    BOY
               (countering swiftly)
Eight and two thirds.

                  RINGO
Well, there you are and watch it with
that hoop.

                    BOY
Gerron out of it, you're only jealous 'cause
you're old.

                  RINGO
Shurrup!

                    BOY
I bet you're
               (searching for an age)
-- sixteen!

                  RINGO
Fifteen and two thirds, actually.

                    BOY
Well --

                  RINGO
All right, take your hoop and bowl.

He moves off and the BOY follows.

                    BOY
Oh you can have it, I'm packing it in --
it depresses me.

                  RINGO
Y'what?

                    BOY
You heard, it gets on my wick.

                    RINGO
Well that's lovely talk, that is. And another
thing, why aren't you at school?

                    BOY
I'm a deserter.

                    RINGO
          (smiling in spite of himself)
Are you now?

                    BOY
Yeah, I've blown school out.

                    RINGO
Just you?

                    BOY
No, Ginger, Eddy Fallon and Ding Dong.

                    RINGO
Ding Dong? Oh Ding Dong Bell, eh?

                    BOY
Yeah, that's right, they was supposed to
come with us but they chickened.

                    RINGO
And they're your mates?

                    BOY
          (sighing)
Yeah.

                    RINGO
Not much cop without 'em, is it?

                    BOY
          (defensively)
Oh, it's all right.

                    RINGO
          (disbelievingly)
Yeah?

                    BOY
Yeah.

                              RINGO
          What they like?

BOY is glad to have something to talk about.

                               BOY
                         (enthusiastically)
          Ginger's mad, he says things all the time and
          Eddy's good at punching and spitting.

                              RINGO
          How about Ding Dong?

                               BOY
          He's a big head and he fancies himself
          with it but it's all right 'cos he's one of
          the gang.

RINGO nods his head understandingly and they mooch on together.

                               BOY
          Why aren't you at work?

                              RINGO
          I'm a deserter, too.

                               BOY
          Oh.

At this moment a child's voice shouts out "Charley" and from
RINGO'S P.O.V. we see three kids. RINGO turns to the BOY and
looks at them enquiringly.

                               BOY
                           (to RINGO)
          See you.

The BOY runs off to join his mates. As he joins them they punch
and scuffle together. They are obviously a gang. RINGO is left
alone.

64. INTERIOR   CORRIDOR   T.V. THEATRE

GEORGE comes round the corner, looking for RINGO, then grins and
walks past a sign saying "Canteen and Executive Office opposite".
He comes to the exit door, crosses to a modern building across
from the theatre. He enters building.

65. INTERIOR   OFFICE

It is a reception room that leads to an inner office. Behind a
desk sits a smart young woman typing busily as GEORGE enters. He
is surprised when he sees the girl, she looks up and speaks to
him at once.

                    SECRETARY
          Oh, there you are!

                    GEORGE
          Oh, I'm sorry, I must have made a
          mistake.

                    SECRETARY
                    (tartly)
          You haven't, you're just late.
                    (she rises and crossing
                    over to him examines
                    him critically)
          Oh, yes, he's going to be very pleased
          with you.

                    GEORGE
          Is he?

                    SECRETARY
          Yes, you're quite a feather in the cap.
                    (she crosses to the
                    desk and picks up the
                    inter-office phone)
          I've got one . . . oh, I think so . . .
          yes, he can talk . . . Well . . . I think you
          ought to see him.
                    (she smiles)
          Of course, right away.

She crosses to the inter-office door. On the door is written
SIMON MARSHALL . . . she opens it.

                    SECRETARY
          Well . . . come on.

                    GEORGE
          Sorry.

He follows her quickly in.

66. <u>INTERIOR THE INNER OFFICE</u>

A large room, part production office with models and sets, drawing board with ground plans, the other part of the room a mixture of Pop and Queen's magazine decor.

Behind a large desk sits SIMON MARSHALL, a bland but slightly irritable young man of about thirty-five. He is wearing the ultimate in the current smart-set fashion. He is attended by a couple of underlings (ADRIAN and TONY) and behind him on the wall is a poster of a girl. Across the poster is printed, "Way Out, your own T.V. Special with Susan Campey. Director, Simon Marshall."

> SECRETARY
> (proudly)
> Will this do, Simon?

> SIMON
> (looking at George)
> Not bad, dolly, not really bad.
> (he motions to
> George)
> Turn around, chicky baby.

GEORGE does so.

> SIMON
> Oh yes, a definite poss. He'll look good
> alongside Susan.
> (he indicates the girl
> on the poster)
> All right, Sonny Jim, this is all going to
> be quite painless. Don't breathe on me,
> Adrian.

ADRIAN has recognised GEORGE and is trying to stop SIMON.

> GEORGE
> Look, I'm terribly sorry but I'm afraid
> there's been some sort of a misunderstanding.

> SIMON
> (sharply)
> Oh, you can come off it with us. You don't
> have to do the old adenoidal glottal stop and
> carry on for our benefit.

> GEORGE
> I'm afraid I don't understand.

                    SIMON
Oh, my God, he's a natural.

                    SECRETARY
                 (anxiously)
Well, I did tell them not to send us any
more real ones.

                    SIMON
They ought to know by now the phonies are
much easier to handle. Still he's a good type.

He now speaks to GEORGE in the loud voice that the English reserve
for foreigners and village idiots.

                    SIMON
We want you to give us your opinion on some
clothes for teenagers.

                    GEORGE
Oh, by all means, I'd be quite prepared for
that eventuality.

                    SIMON
Well, not your real opinion, naturally.
It'll be written out and you'll learn it.
                 (to Secretary)
Can he read?

                    GEORGE
Of course I can.

                    SIMON
I mean lines, ducky, can you handle lines?

                    GEORGE
I'll have a bash.

                    SIMON
Good. Hart, get him whatever it is they
drink, a cokearama?

                    GEORGE
Ta.

                    SIMON
Well at least he's polite. Tony, show
him the shirts.

A collection of shirts is produced and GEORGE looks at them.
While he is doing this SIMON briefs him.

> SIMON
> You'll like these. You really "dig" them.
> They're "fab" and all the other pimply
> hyperboles.

> GEORGE
> I wouldn't be seen dead in them. They're
> dead grotty.

> SIMON
> Grotty?

> GEORGE
> Yeah, grotesque.

> SIMON
> (to Secretary)
> Make a note of that word and give it to
> Susan. I think it's rather touching really.
> Here's this kid trying to give me his utterly
> valueless opinion when I know for a fact
> within four weeks he'll be suffering from a
> violent inferiority complex and loss of status
> if he isn't wearing one of these nasty things.
> Of course they're grotty, you wretched nit,
> that's why they were designed, but that's
> what you'll want.

> GEORGE
> But I won't.

> SIMON
> You can be replaced you know, chicky baby.

> GEORGE
> I don't care.

> SIMON
> And that pose is out too, Sunny Jim. The new
> thing is to care passionately, and be right wing.
> Anyway, you won't meet Susan if you don't
> cooperate.

> GEORGE
> And who's this Susan when she's at home?

                    SIMON
              (playing his ace)
Only Susan Campey, our resident teenager.
You'll have to love her. She's your symbol.

                    GEORGE
Oh, you mean that posh bird who gets
everything wrong?

                    SIMON
I beg your pardon?

                    GEORGE
Oh, yes, the lads frequently gather round
the T.V. set to watch her for a giggle. Once
we even all sat down and wrote these letters
saying how gear she was and all that rubbish.

                    SIMON
She's a trend setter. It's her profession!

                    GEORGE
She's a drag. A well-known drag.
We turn the sound down on her and say
rude things.

                    SIMON
Get him out of here!!

                    GEORGE
              (genuinely surprised)
Have I said something amiss?

                    SIMON
Get him out of here. He's knocking the
programme's image!!

The underlings hustle GEORGE to the door.

                    GEORGE
              (smiling)
Sorry about the shirts.

He is ejected through the door.

                    SIMON
     Get him out.
              (he stops in mid-
              shout)

> SIMON (Cont.)
> You don't think he's a new phenomenon
> do you?

> SECRETARY
> You mean an early clue to the new
> direction?

> SIMON
>   (rummaging in his
>   desk)
> Where's the calendar?
>   (he finds it)
> No, he's just a trouble maker. The
> change isn't due for three weeks. All
> the same, make a note not to extend
> Susan's contract. Let's not take any
> unnecessary chances!

67. <u>EXTERIOR   STREET   PUB ON THE CORNER</u>

The sign on the pub is Liverpool Arms. RINGO is standing looking
up at it. He decides to go in and does so.

68. <u>INTERIOR   T.V. CONTROL ROOM</u>

The atmosphere is tense. GRANDFATHER is standing miserable
in front of the director, the criminal confronted by the judge.
SHAKE and NORM are flanking him grimly.

> GRANDFATHER
> I'm sorry lads, I didn't mean it,
> honest.

> DIRECTOR
> If he says that again, I'll strike him.

> SHAKE
>   (unconvincingly)
> They'll be back, they're good lads, they'll
> be back.

> DIRECTOR
> Yes? Well, they've got only 10 minutes to the
> final run-through.

> GRANDFATHER
> I meant no harm. I was only trying to
> encourage little Ringo to enjoy himself.

NORM
(grimly, C.U.)
God knows what you've unleashed on the
unsuspecting South. It'll be wine, women
and song all the way with Ringo once he's
got the taste for it.

69. INT. PUB PUBLIC BAR

CLOSE-UP on RINGO. He is eating a bone dry sandwich that curls
up at the end. He puts it down with disgust. He has a lager
glass in his hand.

BARMAID
(accusingly)
That was fresh this morning.

We now see the pub is full of enormous cockney workmen downing
pints. RINGO is very much alone. He moves away from the bar
towards a group that is standing together, they've an average
height of over six foot. There is a group at a dart board.
Another group are playing bar skittles and a third group are
around a pin-ball table.

Near the bar is a shove-halfpenny board with two players. There
is a caged parrot nearby.

BARMAID
(to Ringo)
That'll be two and nine . . .

RINGO fumbles some change out of his pocket. A few coppers fall
from his hand onto the shove-halfpenny board just as the crucial
point has been made. The men glare at him. Embarrassed, he
moves away and without looking, places his glass on the skittles
table just as a player swings the string, which hits RINGO's
glass. More embarrassed, RINGO backs away, unfortunately into
the pin-table, just as a winning score is about to be reached.
He bumps it very slightly, but enough to cause it to TILT. He
then moves to the dart board. By this time, most of the pub is
staring at him. With great style, he takes the darts. The first
throw goes into a cheese sandwich which a man is pointing in
demonstration. The second we see arrive into a pint of bitter
and when we see RINGO shoot the third dart and hear the sound
of the parrot shout angrily off, the BARMAID has had enough.

BARMAID
Right . . . On your way!

                              RINGO
            Y'what?

                              BARMAID
            You heard, on your way, trouble maker!

Now the centre of attention, RINGO backs out of the pub,
followed by every eye in the place, the BARMAID and a few
players following him to the door . . .

70. <u>EXTERIOR   STREET OUTSIDE PUB</u>

    RINGO comes out and crosses road, watched by the POLICEMAN
    who is now quite suspicious.

71. <u>EXTERIOR   STREET</u>

    PAUL comes down the street looking about him for RINGO. In the
    street is an old building, the sort of place that is highly
    favoured for TV rehearsals. There is a sign on door saying "TV
    Rehearsal Room". As PAUL draws near, a load of actors and extras,
    etc., are leaving, they are in costume, they are the ones who
    earlier had been going to a word rehearsal. When PAUL gets
    near the entrance he decides to go inside.

72. <u>INTERIOR   HALL</u>

    PAUL enters and wanders about. He reaches a door, pushes it
    open and looks in. He sees a girl clad in period costume. She
    is moving around the room and obviously acting. PAUL watches
    her for a moment and then decides to go in.

73. <u>INTERIOR   REHEARSAL ROOM</u>

    PAUL goes into the room. The girl is in mid-flight. She is
    very young and lovely and completely engrossed in what she is
    doing. The room is absolutely empty except for PAUL and herself.
    She is acting in the manner of an eighteenth-century coquette,
    or, to be precise, the voice English actresses use when they
    think they are being true to the costume period . . . her youth,
    however, makes it all very charming.

                              GIRL
            If I believed you, sir, I might do these
            things and walk those ways only to find
            myself on Problem's Path. But I cannot
            believe you, and all those urgings serve only
            as a proof that you will lie and lie again to
            gain your purpose with me.

She dances lightly away from an imaginary lover and as she turns she sees PAUL, who is as engrossed in the scene as she was.

> GIRL
> (surprised)
>
> Oh!

> PAUL
> (enthusiastically)
>
> Well . . . go 'head, do the next bit.

> GIRL
>
> Go away! You've spoilt it.

> PAUL
>
> Oh, sorry I spoke.

He makes no attempt to go. He simply continues to look steadily at the girl, then he smiles at her. She is undecided what to do next.

> GIRL
>
> Are you supposed to be here?

> PAUL
>
> I've got you worried, haven't I?

> GIRL
>
> I'm warning you, they'll be back in a
> minute.

> PAUL
>
> D'you know something, "they" don't worry
> me at all. Any road, I only fancy listening
> to you . . . that's all but if it worries you . . .
> well . . .

> GIRL
>
> You're from Liverpool, aren't you?

> PAUL
> (ironically)
>
> How'd you guess?

> GIRL
> (seriously)
>
> Oh, it's the way you talk.

                        PAUL
                    (innocently)
        Is it . . . is it, really?

                        GIRL
                    (suspiciously)
        Are you pulling my leg?

                        PAUL
                    (looking her straight in
                    the eye)
        Something like that.

                        GIRL
                    (unsure)
        I see.
                    (airily)
        Do you like the play?

                        PAUL
        Yeah . . . I mean, sure, well, I took it at
        school but I only ever heard boys and masters
        saying those lines, like, sounds different on a
        girl.
                    (smiles to himself)
        Yeah, it's gear on a girl.

                        GIRL
        Gear?

                        PAUL
        Aye, the big hammer, smashing!

                        GIRL
        Thank you.

                        PAUL
        Don't mench . . . well, why don't you give us a
        few more lines, like?

GIRL pouts.

                        PAUL
        You don't half slam the door in people's
        faces, do you? I mean, what about when
        you're playing the part, like, hundreds
        of people'll see you and . . .

                    GIRL
               (cutting in)
I'm not . . .

                    PAUL
Oh, you're the understudy, sort of thing?

                    GIRL
No.
               (aggressively)
I'm a walk-on in a fancy dress scene.
I just felt like doing those lines.

                    PAUL
Oh, I see. You are an actress though,
aren't you?

                    GIRL
Yes.

                    PAUL
Aye, I knew you were.

                    GIRL
What's that mean?

                    PAUL
Well, the way you were spouting, like . . .
               (he imitates her)
"I don't believe you, sir . . ." and all that.
Yeah, it was gear.

                    GIRL
               (dryly)
The big hammer?

                    PAUL
               (smiling)
Oh aye, a sledge.

                    GIRL
But the way you did it then sounded so
phony . . .

                    PAUL
No . . . I wouldn't say that . . . just like an
actress . . . you know.
               (He moves and stands about
               like an actress)

                         GIRL
          But that's not like a real person at all.

                         PAUL
          Aye well, actresses aren't like real people,
          are they?

                         GIRL
          They ought to be.

                         PAUL
          Oh, I don't know, anyroad up, they never
          are, are they?

                         GIRL
                    (teasingly)
          What are you?

                         PAUL
          I'm a group; I mean . . . I'm in a group . . .
          well . . . there are four of us, we play and sing.

                         GIRL
          I bet you don't sound like real people.

                         PAUL
          We do, you know. We sound like us having
          a ball. It's fab.

                         GIRL
          Is it really fab or are you just saying that
          to convince yourself?

                         PAUL
          What of? Look, I wouldn't do it unless I was.
          I'm dead lucky 'cos I get paid for doing
          something I love doing.

He laughs and with a gesture takes in the whole studio.

          . . . all this and a jam butty too!!

                         GIRL
          I only enjoy acting for myself. I hate
          it when other people are let in.

                         PAUL
          Why? I mean, which are you, scared or
          selfish?

                          GIRL
Why selfish?

                          PAUL
Well, you've got to have people to taste your
treacle toffee.

She looks at him in surprise.

                          PAUL
No, hang on, I've not gone daft. You see
when I was little me mother let me make some
treacle toffee one time in our back scullery.
When I'd done she said to me, "Go and give some
to the other kids." So I said I would but I
thought to meself, "She must think I'm soft."
Anyroad, I was eating away there but I wanted
somebody else to know how good it was, so in the
end I wound up giving it all away . . . but I
didn't mind, cos <u>I'd</u> made the stuff in the
first place. Well . . . that's why you need other
people . . . an audience . . . to taste your treacle
toffee, like. Eh . . . does that sound as thick-
headed to you as it does to me?

                          GIRL
Not really but I'm probably not a toffee maker.
How would you do those lines of mine?

                          PAUL
Well, look at it this way, I mean, when
you come right down to it, that girl, she's
a bit of a scrubber, isn't she?

                          GIRL
Is she?

                          PAUL
Of course . . . Look, if she was a Liverpool
scrubber . . .
                    (Paul starts acting a Liverpool girl,
                    he minces about then turns, extending
                    his leg)
Eh, fella, you want to try pulling the other
one, it's got a full set of bells hanging off it
. . . Y'what? . . . I know your sort, two cokes and
a packet of cheese and onion crisps and suddenly
it's love and we're stopping in an empty shop doorway.

                         PAUL (Cont.)
You're just after me body and y'can't have it . . .
so there!!

                         GIRL
                    (shattered)
And you honestly think that's what she meant?

                         PAUL
Oh, definitely, it sticks out a mile, she's
trying to get him to marry her but he doesn't
want . . . well . . . I don't reckon any fella's
ever wanted to get married. But girls are
like that, clever and cunning. You've got
to laugh.
                    (he laughs)

                         GIRL
Well, it's nice to know you think we're clever.

                         PAUL
                    (grinning)
And cunning.

                         GIRL
And what do you do about it?

                         PAUL
Me? Oh, I don't have the time, I'm
always running about with the lads . . . no
we don't have the time.

                         GIRL
Pity.

                         PAUL
                    (not noticing the invitation)
Aye, it is but as long as you get by, it's
all right, you know . . . bash on, happy valley's
when they let you stop. Anyroad, I'd better
get back.

                         GIRL
Yes.

                         PAUL
                    (going)
See you.

GIRL

Of course.

PAUL stands at the doorway, shurgs then goes out.

74. EXT.   STREET

In the street, workmen are collecting shovels, drinking tea and doing all the things people do around building sites. RINGO mooches around. In the road is a hole with a diameter of about 3 feet, and at least 6 feet deep. RINGO looks down and a man is busily working at the bottom of the hole. He glares at RINGO. After a moment RINGO turns away. We now see a very elegant young lady coming towards RINGO. She is daintily avoiding a series of puddles. RINGO has an idea and does a Sir Walter Raleigh with his large Mac, spreading it over one of the puddles. The girl walks across it smiling graciously. RINGO proceeds with the coat to the next puddle and to the next backing gradually towards the hole. At last he spreads the coat, without noticing what he is doing, over the hole. The girl steps onto the coat and disappears sharply. RINGO looks down the hole where the girl is held in the workman's arms. The WORKMAN rises out of the manhole until he is waist height. At this point an elegantly dressed gentleman appears (the girl's husband) he looks at his wife in the WORKMAN's arms and hits the WORKMAN. RINGO backs away through the puddles, and is nicked by the POLICEMAN.

[Scenes 75 and 76 deleted in revision.]

77. INTERIOR   T.V. THEATRE   NEAR STAGE DOOR

The DIRECTOR is pacing up and down the corridor. NORM is also walking up and down, SHAKE is leaning against the wall quite unconcerned. NORM gives SHAKE a push.

NORM

Worry, will you!

SHAKE adjusts his features to a worrying expression.

DIRECTOR
(bitterly)
Well, that's it, two minutes to the final
run-through . . . They're bound to miss it . . .

NORM
I'll murder that Lennon.

                         DIRECTOR
          But I suppose we can survive a missed run-
          through as long . . .

                         SHAKE
          . . . as they head up for the show. Oh yes,
          well I mean it'ud be a pity to miss the show,
          wouldn't it like.

                         NORM
          Shurrup, cheerful.

The horrible prospect hits the DIRECTOR.

                         DIRECTOR
          You don't think . . .

                         NORM
                    (reassuring him)
          They'll be here.

                         DIRECTOR
          Oh now, they can't do that to me.
                    (turning on Norm)
          It's all your fault.
                    (overriding Norm)
          Oh yes it is and if they don't turn up I
          wouldn't be in your shoes for all the . . .

                         SHAKE
                    (helping out)
          . . . tea in China. Oh you're right, neither
          would I.

He steps away from NORM and stands near the DIRECTOR.

                         NORM
          Traitor!

SHAKE nods his agreement to this assessment of his character.

                         SHAKE
          Of course.

At this moment JOHN, GEORGE and PAUL enter from the stage door.
They are completely unconcerned and walk past the DIRECTOR,
SHAKE and NORM.

                    JOHN
               (as he passes by)
          Hi Norm!

                    NORM
               (preoccupied)
          Hi, our lot!

The BOYS walk on when after a moment NORM snaps to.

                    NORM
          Our lot!

                    GEORGE
               (mildly)
          Did you want something?

                    NORM
               (beaming with delight)
          I could eat the lot of you.

                    JOHN
          You'd look gear with an apple in your gob.

                    DIRECTOR
               (accusingly)
          You could have missed the final run-through.

                    GEORGE
          Sorry.

                    SHAKE
          Eh, there's only three of them.

                    PAUL
          Aye, we were looking for Ringo. But we
          realised he must have come back.

                    DIRECTOR
          Do you realise we are on the air, live,
          in front of an audience in forty-five minutes and
          you're one short.

                    JOHN
          Control yourself or you'll spurt. He's
          bound to be somewhere.

                    NORM
          Aye, let's try the dressing room.

Everyone starts along the passage. NORM and PAUL last.

> PAUL
> Eh, where's my Grandfather?

> NORM
> Don't worry about him. He can look after himself.

> PAUL
> Aye, I suppose so.

They run after the others.

78. EXTERIOR T.V. THEATRE

C.U.

> GRANDFATHER
> Here they are, personally signed and hand written by your own sweet boys. The chance of a lifetime. Be the envy of your less fortunate sisters!

The CAMERA PULLS back and we see GRANDFATHER is surrounded by girls who have broken from the queue and are doing a brisk trade with the old man. He has a large sign on which is written: "Get your genuine autographed Beatles photographs." On the edge of the crowd two POLICEMEN are trying to force the girls back into the queue. Finally they wade through the girls and confront GRANDFATHER. They look at the old man quizzically, he stares back coldly. They indicate he should hop it and quick, but GRANDFATHER defiantly glares back at them, so with a sigh they grab an arm each and escort the old man off.

79. INTERIOR POLICE STATION

It is the reception desk and behind it is the Desk Sergeant. After a moment RINGO is dragged in by the POLICEMAN we saw him with before.

> RINGO
> Look, I'm Ringo Starr . . . I've got a show to do in a few minutes . . . you've got to let me go . . . I'm Ringo . . .

> POLICEMAN
> Sure, they all say that these days . . . Anyway . . . I don't care who you are . . . you can

                    POLICEMAN (Cont.)
save that for the stipendary. Here you
are, Sarge.

                    SERGEANT
What is he?

                    POLICEMAN
              (reeling off the list)
Wandering abroad. Malicious intent.
Acting in a suspicious manner. Conduct
liable to cause a breach of the peace. You
name it, he's done it.

                    SERGEANT
Oh, a savage, is he?

                    POLICEMAN
A proper aborigine.

                    RINGO
              (on his dignity)
I demand to see me solicitor.

                    SERGEANT
What's his name?

                    RINGO
Oh, well if you're going to get technical --

At that moment there is a loud series of noises off camera,
furious shouting and dull crashes of wood.

                    SERGEANT
Hello, it's going to be one of those nights,
is it.
              (to Policeman)
Sit Charley Peace down over there.

The Policeman takes RINGO to a bench and sits him down as
GRANDFATHER and the two policemen who were with him enter.
The sign is tattered and is being lugged after them.

                    GRANDFATHER
Well, you got me here so do your worst,
but I'll take one of you with me.
              (kicks the nearest
              policeman)

                              GRANDFATHER (Cont.)
              Oh, I know your game, get me in the tiled
              room and out come the rubber hoses but I'll
              defy you still.

                              SERGEANT
              Is there a fire, then?

GRANDFATHER leans across the desk and hisses at the SERGEANT.

                              GRANDFATHER
              You evil brute you, you have sadism
              stamped on your bloated British kisser.

                              SERGEANT
              Eh?

                              GRANDFATHER
              I'll hunger strike. I know your caper. The
              kidney punch and the rabbit clout. The third
              degree and the size-twelve boot ankle-tap.

                              SERGEANT
              What's he on about?

                              GRANDFATHER
                         (squaring up)
              I'm soldier of the republic. You'll need the
              mahogany truncheon for this boyo. A
              nation once again.

                              SERGEANT
                         (to Policemen)
              Get Lloyd George over there with that
              mechanic in the cloth cap while I sort
              this lot out.

The policemen hurl GRANDFATHER firmly but gently over to the
bench on which RINGO is sitting and then return to the desk
for a whispered conference with the Sergeant. Meanwhile in
full conspiratorial fashion GRANDFATHER talks to RINGO out of
the side of his mouth.

                              GRANDFATHER
              Ringo, me old scout, they grabbed yer leg
              for the iron too, did they?

                              RINGO
              Well I'm not exactly a voluntary patient.

                    GRANDFATHER
Shush! Have they roughed you up yet?

                    RINGO
What?

                    GRANDFATHER
                (whispering)
Keep your voice down, this lot'll paste you,
just for the exercise. Oh, they're a desperate
crew of drippings and they've fists like
matured hams for pounding defenceless lads
like you.

                    RINGO
                (disturbed)
Have they?

                    GRANDFATHER
That Sergeant's a body-blow veteran if
ever I measured one. One of us has got
to escape, hold on son. I'll be back for
you.

                    RINGO
                (horrified)
Me!

                    GRANDFATHER
And if they get you on the floor watch out
for your brisket.

                    RINGO
                (hopefully)
Oh, they seem all right to me.

                    GRANDFATHER
That's what they want you to think. All
coppers are villains.

                    SERGEANT
                (calling)
Would you two like a cup of tea?

                    GRANDFATHER
You see, sly villains.

                    RINGO
                (miserable)
No thanks, Mr. Sergeant, sir.

We now have a CLOSE SHOT of Policemen round the Sergeant's desk.

                    SERGEANT
          So you just brought the old chap out of the crowd
          for his own good.

                    POLICEMAN
          Yeah, but he insisted on us bringing him
          to the station.

                    SERGEANT
          Well, he can't stop here.

Shot of GRANDFATHER watching POLICEMEN intently and muttering
words as he does.

                    RINGO
          What you doing?

                    GRANDFATHER
          Lip reading.

                    RINGO
          What are they saying?

                    GRANDFATHER
          Nothing good.

The Policemen make a move towards GRANDFATHER and RINGO.

                    GRANDFATHER
          Well son, it's now or never.

He jumps to his feet and scurries towards the door.

                    GRANDFATHER
          All right, you paid assassins, John McCartney'll
          give you a run for your threepence ha'penny.

He dashes out of the door followed by the Policeman who has his
pile of photos.

                    SERGEANT
          Now, what's he up to?

                    RINGO
          He's allergic to Bobbies, especially English
          Bobbies.

The Policeman with the photos returns.

> POLICEMAN
> (Irish accent)
> Your man disappeared like a leveret over
> a hill.

> RINGO
> Turncoat!

The Policemen turn on RINGO and walk towards him.

C.U. RINGO

> RINGO
> Mother!

80. <u>EXTERIOR STREET</u>

GRANDFATHER is running at top speed down the street, he is
breathing heavily and runs as if pursued by the hounds of
hell. The street however is entirely empty and no one is even
in sight. As he reaches the top of the street he pauses and
turning, looks around him. From his P.O.V. we see just how
empty the street is and heaving a sigh of relief GRANDFATHER
cackles to himself. His triumph is short-lived. At this
precise moment down the street comes a parade of police
vehicles, a Black Maria, an escorting police motor bike patrol
and an ordinary squad car. The procession draws up and the
street is full of policemen getting out of the Black Maria and
squad car and off motor bikes.

C.U. GRANDFATHER's horrified face.

> GRANDFATHER
> Be God, they've called up reinforcements,
> the dragnet's out!

He dashes off wildly in the general direction of the theatre.
He has been completely unnoticed by the Policemen who are lining
up for a last-minute inspection by the Inspector in charge. The
Inspector is like a commander-in-chief of a spear-head attack
force.

They smartly march off in the direction taken by GRANDFATHER.

81. <u>INTERIOR T.V. THEATRE   CONTROL ROOM</u>

                         DIRECTOR
                    (watching the clock)
          Only half an hour and you're on!

                          GEORGE
          Can I say something?

The Director clutches at any straw.

                         DIRECTOR
                      (hopefully)
          Yes, anything.

                          GEORGE
                      (earnestly)
          It's highly unlikely we'll be on . . . I mean
          the law of averages are against you and it
          seems that, etc., etc. . . .

But his speech is drowned by the pitiful moans of the Director.

82. EXTERIOR   STAGE DOOR   T.V. THEATRE

The four little boys from the canal are being driven away by
the security guard.

                          GUARD
                 (going back into theatre)
          I'll have the hides off of you lot.

The kids retreat as GRANDFATHER pants into shot. Ignoring the
kids he enters the stage door but in a second he is out again,
grasped firmly round the collar by the security guard.

                          GUARD
          You ought to be ashamed of yourself.
          Go home!

                       GRANDFATHER
          I must see Pauly.

                          GUARD
          Go home then, and watch him on the telly.

The Guard re-enters the stage door.

GRANDFATHER looks about him and sees the four kids. He hustles
over and after a whispered conference we hear his offer.

                              GRANDFATHER
          Sixpence.

                                   BOY
          Each?

GRANDFATHER is about to argue.

                              GRANDFATHER
          Oh, all right.

                                   BOY
          And in advance.

                              GRANDFATHER
                               (disgusted)
          Mercenary!

But hands over the money. The kids rush in the stage door and
after a moment the furious security Guard chases them out and
down the alley. GRANDFATHER, chuckling, nips in the door.

83. INTERIOR T.V. THEATRE ON STAGE

GRANDFATHER is being chased by several studio attendants; he is
dodging behind equipment. He finally gets on a sound boom
trolley and uses it as a weapon to keep his pursuers at bay.

84. INTERIOR T.V. CONTROL ROOM

The Director, the BOYS and NORM and SHAKE see GRANDFATHER on
the monitors. They dash out of the room and onto the stage.

                              DIRECTOR
                               (shouting)
          It's all right, leave him alone.

                                   PAUL
          Grandad, where's Ringo?

                              GRANDFATHER
          The police have the poor unfortunate lad
          in the Bridewell.

                                   BOYS
          The police station.

                              GRANDFATHER
          He'll be pulp be now.

                         JOHN
           Well, what are we waiting for?

                         GEORGE
           Come here.

PAUL, JOHN and GEORGE dash off.

C.U. DIRECTOR

                         DIRECTOR
           We've only got twenty minutes.

85. <u>EXTERIOR   STREET OUTSIDE POLICE STATION</u>

PAUL, JOHN and GEORGE come running down the street in single
file, their knees high in the air; they skid to a halt at the
police station and without pausing they dash inside. After a
moment they reappear -- only this time RINGO is behind them.
They dash off down the street. They are followed at once by
ten Policemen also in single file. They are also pounding along
knees high in the air. The BOYS and the coppers disappear round
the corner. At once they re-appear from the other direction,
they run down the street still followed by the policemen. When
they reach the police station another group of police bars their
way so they are forced to run up the stairs and inside.

86. <u>INTERIOR   POLICE STATION</u>

The desk Sergeant is standing behind his desk looking very
surprised. At this moment the boys run in and stand panting in
front of the desk. Before the Desk Sergeant can speak the pursuing
Policemen arrive. They, too, are out of breath.

                         SERGEANT
           What is all this?

                         JOHN
                    (heaving and panting)
           Hold on till we get our breath.

The BOYS and the Policemen pant on until finally JOHN seems to
have recovered.

                         SERGEANT
           All right now?

                         JOHN
     Sure.
                    (to the boys)
     Ready?

The BOYS nod and without more ado they turn and run through the
surprised rank of Policemen and out into the street.

87. <u>EXTERIOR STREET</u>
    THE CHASE CARRIES ON.
    Shots of Boys being pursued (still in single file) by the police,
    including the Sergeant, with one shot which is where the Boys are
    chasing the Policemen. Finally, as they approach the theatre,
    they are seen by the girl fans who swarm around the police, over
    running them. The boys grin to each other and are about to make
    off when from their P.O.V. we see the Inspector and Policemen
    blocking it.

                          JOHN
          Ah well, it was worth a try.

                        INSPECTOR
                   (calling to Sergeant)
          What do you think you're up to?

                        SERGEANT
                   (struggling in crowd)
          Arrest those boys, sir.

                        INSPECTOR
          That's all we need to start a real riot!
                        (to Boys)
          Come on lads, they're waiting for you.

<u>INT. THEATRE BACK STAGE</u>
The Inspector now hustles the BOYS through the crowds and in
through the main entrance of the theatre where SHAKE and NORM
are waiting. NORM looks suspiciously at RINGO who is still
wearing his cap. RINGO whips it off and NORM delightedly hugs
him. The BOYS dash through the stalls entrance and on stage.
The Director sees them and bursts into tears with relief.
NORM hustles the lads into the wings to be changed into their
show costumes. All around them last-minute preparations are
going on.

                        DIRECTOR
          Boys, you don't know what this means to
          me. If you hadn't come back it would
          have been the epilogue or the news in Welsh
          for life.

                    NORM
          Aren't you supposed to be in that box?

The Director gives NORM a final glare and dashes off.

                    PAUL
          And another thing, where's that old
          mixer?

                    GRANDFATHER
          Here, Pauly.

And sitting on a box sadly chastened sits GRANDFATHER.

                    PAUL
          Well, I got a few things to say to you,
          two-faced John McCartney.

                    JOHN
          Aw, leave him alone Paul, he's back,
          isn't he? And it's not his fault he's
          old.

                    PAUL
                 (hotly)
          What's old got to do with it?

                    JOHN
          You needn't bother.

                    PAUL
          Y'what?

                    JOHN
          Practising to be thick-headed, you're
          there already.

                    PAUL
          Look, he's a mixer and a trouble maker!

                    JOHN
          That's right, but he's only asking us
          to pay attention to him, aren't you?

From JOHN'S P.O.V. we see GRANDFATHER. He looks what he is,
a tired old man.

                    JOHN
          You see.

                    JOHN (Cont.)
                   (to Grandad)
You know your trouble -- you should have
gone West to America. You'd have wound
up a Senior Citizen of Boston. As it is
you took the wrong turning and what happened,
you're a lonely old man from Liverpool.

                  GRANDFATHER
                 (fighting back)
        But I'm clean.

The BOYS giggle and slap him on the back.

88. <u>INTERIOR T.V. THEATRE AUDITORIUM</u>

We see the audience of girls streaming in and settling down in
their places for the show. There is the usual business of getting
the show ready and we see SHOTS of the girls' faces, then JOHN,
PAUL, RINGO and GEORGE looking at them. At last on cue from
the floor manager the BOYS start their act to the audience's
screams. During the number we constantly CUT away to the
audience with various SHOTS of the ecstatic girls. In the
middle of these shots we see NORM standing at the side of the
audience, his face glowing with satisfaction. We follow his
gaze and from NORM'S P.O.V. we see GRANDFATHER handcuffed to
SHAKE, but in spite of this the old man is enjoying himself.
The BOYS now perform a medley of numbers, i.e., a little of all
the songs we have heard during the story. While they are doing
so they look again in the general direction of SHAKE and
GRANDFATHER and from their P.O.V. we see SHAKE is beating time
to the music, but from his wrist dangles an empty set of
handcuffs. GRANDFATHER has gone again. As the BOYS are reacting
to GRANDFATHER's disappearance once again, the trap door on the
stage opens and GRANDFATHER appears in the centre of the group
as they finish their act and take their final bows.

89. <u>INTERIOR STUDIO CORRIDOR</u>

NORM is waiting for the boys. With him are two studio attendants
carrying the boys' luggage. As the BOYS excitedly appear he
speaks to them.

                    NORM
        I've got the stuff. Come here.

                    PAUL
        Aren't we . . .

                              NORM
              No, we're not!

He hurries them along.

                              NORM
              The office was on the phone, they
              think it'd be better if we pushed straight
              to Wolverhampton.

                              JOHN
              Tonight? We can't make it . . .

                              NORM
              You've got a midnight matinee.

                              JOHN
              Now look here, Norm.

                              NORM
              No, you look here John. I've only
              one thing to say to you.

                              JOHN
              What?

                              NORM
              You're a swine. So hurry up . . . we're
              travelling!!

NORM turns down a side exit where the door is open to the field.
In it is an eight-passenger helicopter.

90. <u>EXT. STAGE DOOR T.V. THEATRE</u>

The boys and NORM come out of the building and start to run towards
the helicopter.

                              PAUL
                       (looking behind him)
              Where's my Grandfather?

                              NORM
                       (arriving at helicopter door)
              Don't start. Look.

The boys look in the passenger bay and there is GRANDFATHER.
He is still handcuffed to SHAKE but clutching his pile of
photos.

                    GRANDFATHER
              (beckoning them in with his
              free hand which holds the photos)
         Come on, you're hanging up the parade.

The boys shout "Get rid of those things" etc.

91. <u>EXT. FIELD</u>

The final shot is of the helicopter rising up (SHOT FROM BELOW).
As it disappears, a shower of photos comes from its window.

We cut to a CLOSE-UP of one signed photo as it hits the ground
and super the closing credits over it.

THE BEST MAN

1964—A Millar-Turman Production;
released by United Artists
Director Franklin Schaffner
Script Gore Vidal
Source Play, *The Best Man*, by Gore Vidal
Stars Henry Fonda, Lee Tracy, Cliff Robertson,
Edie Adams, Shelley Berman

The Best Man had been a successful Broadway play, but the adaptation of a proscenium drama to the screen is perhaps the most difficult translation from one literary medium to another. All success is *tour de force*, requiring extraordinary virtuosity of both the writer and the director. Gore Vidal, ever a virtuoso performer, was equal to the task of adapting his own play, with the happy result that Roger Manvell declares in *New Cinema in the USA* that Vidal's script is "one of the most intelligent scripts the American cinema has had in recent years." Schaffner, quite new to pictures following an apprenticeship as a television director, and Vidal both received praise from most of the reviewers. Philip Hartung gave the film a good notice in *Commonweal*, praising it for its satire and humor. Bosley Crowther, in two reviews (April 7 and April 12) in the *New York Times* praised the film as an "excitingly ruthless melodrama about the nature of American politics, particularly as played in the national conventions where there's a Presidential nomination up for grabs." He especially praised the choice of Schaffner to direct "the film to emphasize the rasp of a convention as well as individuals," adding, "Against this background or feeling the contours of a sensitive, scrupulous man appear that much more incongruous—and that much more gratifying too." Brendan Gill of *The New Yorker* applauded the work of Gore Vidal and "particularly admired Mr. Robertson and Mr. Berman, whose acting career is, oddly, in jeopardy because of his too great fame as a nightclub comedian."

On the same day that Brendan Gill's review appeared, Stanley Kauffmann published a long review which disagreed with Gill's on both script and acting. He rapidly disposed of Berman: "Shelley Berman plays an informer with his eye on the audience as vulgarly as the worst vaudevillian." While allowing that some of the satire was successful and that some fair targets and abuses were "nicely stung," Kauffmann quibbled with Vidal's script on two counts. He was critical of the blackmail plots, taken directly from the stage play to the screen: "Some plot devices that are credible onstage do not convince when magnified on screen." His second objection was moral, posed in the question "Why is it a more fitting discharge of moral obligation to help elect an unknown as President, after fighting to protect the office from inadequacy?" And he concludes, "This comedy about the need for intelligent idealism in politics ends up by calling down a plague on all the houses."

Both questions raise important points in any consideration of this script.

Meanwhile Gore Vidal has enjoyed more dramatic success, most recently in the extraordinary novel *Myra Breckenridge*. And *The Best Man*, with a four-star rating, has enjoyed considerable popularity on television.

The Script The "Final Revised Shooting Script" is dated August 28, 1963. Individual sections and pages, dated, indicate six further stages of revision, from September 3, 1963, to October 28, 1963; and, as the printed text of the script shows, there were further minor revisions after that date. The opening section, scenes X1–X10, was added on September 11, 1963. The reader will note occasional camera directions, specifying the angle or distance of a particular shot, and there are a few editorial directions in the script. But essentially the script consists of rather large master scenes only. There are fewer than 100 master scenes, a small number for a feature film, and all involve a considerable dependence, in the script, upon dialogue rather than action or cinematic effects. The result is a fairly long script built around a limited number of settings. For the most part, then, author Vidal leaves the handling of the master scenes in cinematic terms to the director and the crew.

Credits   Producers, Stuart Millar and Lawrence Turman; Director, Franklin Schaffner; Author, Gore Vidal; Screenplay, Gore Vidal; Art Direction, Lyle R. Wheeler; Music, Mort Lindsey; Photography, Haskell Wexler; Editor, Robert E. Swink.

Cast

William Russell:	Henry Fonda
Joe Cantwell:	Cliff Robertson
Mabel Cantwell:	Edie Adams
Alice Russell:	Margaret Leighton
Sheldon Bascomb:	Shelley Berman
Art Hockstader:	Lee Tracy
Mrs. Gamadge:	Ann Sothern
Don Cantwell:	Gene Raymond
Dick Jensen:	Kevin McCarthy
Herself:	Mahalia Jackson
Himself:	Howard K. Smith

Awards   *The Best Man* received the Special Jury Prize awarded at Karlovy Vary, the biennial Czech film festival.

"THE BEST MAN"

BEFORE TITLES

X1. EXT. -- LONG SHOT -- DAY

Los Angeles Sports Arena. Pickets are marching up and down.
People are milling about the doors; cars approach; State
Troopers troop. HOWARD K. SMITH, with a neck mike, faces
a TV camera, arena behind him.

> HOWARD K. SMITH
> This is Howard K. Smith. I'm standing
> in front of the Sports Arena in Los
> Angeles, California. Inside that big
> building a thousand delegates from all
> over the United States are about to
> select a man who will be their party's
> candidate for President of the United
> States. Every four years the two major
> political parties have one of these
> conventions. There is nothing quite
> like one of our conventions. Part
> circus . . .

CUT TO:

X2. CIRCUSY SHOTS OF PAST CONVENTIONS

> HOWARD K. SMITH'S VOICE
> Part secular rite . . .

CUT TO:

X3. FULL SHOT

Solemn convention moments: anthem singing, rapt attention.

> HOWARD K. SMITH'S VOICE
> And all politics.

CUT TO:

X4. SHOTS OF MEN

Knots of politicking men at various conventions.

X5. <u>EXT. SPORTS PALACE</u>

> HOWARD K. SMITH
> The political party that is meeting
> today is pretty sure to win the
> election which will be held six
> months from now, on the second
> Tuesday in November, according to
> our Constitution. Confident of
> winning, the delegates realize
> that it is particularly important
> that this time the man they choose
> is The Best Man.

On this phrase, THE BEST MAN title comes onto the screen;
credits begin.

> HOWARD K. SMITH'S VOICE
> The first convention of modern sort
> was held in 1860 at Chicago, when a
> brand new party called the Republicans
> nominated Abraham Lincoln.

SHOTS of Lincoln's convention from drawings, early photos.

> HOWARD K. SMITH'S VOICE
> In the century since, all of our
> Presidents have gone through the
> same process. It is a cruel, hard
> business, but those who survive it
> tend to be remarkable men.

From this point on, we show shots of the presidents from
Lincoln to Kennedy. Some should be stills; some old films.
There is no narration during the first melange of 19th-
century presidents. But in the 20th century, Smith will
identify, with voice over, each president as he appears on
the screen, starting with Teddy Roosevelt. After Kennedy:

> CUT TO:

X6. <u>EXT. SPORTS ARENA</u>

> HOWARD K. SMITH
> Today, the convention will nominate
> five men. Tomorrow they will begin
> to vote. Or to ballot, as they call
> it. Occasionally, nominees are chosen
> on the first ballot. But usually it

HOWARD K. SMITH (Cont.)
takes several ballots. One convention,
in 1924, took 103 ballots before they
could agree on a candidate.

This particular convention could
become a deadlock. On the first
ballot we have a good idea who will
have what votes, because the two
principal candidates, William Russell . . .

CUT TO:

X7. STILL SHOT OF RUSSELL

HOWARD K. SMITH'S VOICE
He was Secretary of State under
former President Hockstader . . .

X8. BACK TO HOWARD K. SMITH

HOWARD K. SMITH
And Joseph Cantwell . . .

CUT TO:

X9. STILL SHOT OF CANTWELL

HOWARD K. SMITH'S VOICE
The brilliant young United States
Senator . . .

X10. EXT. SPORTS ARENA

HOWARD K. SMITH
. . . have both been campaigning through
the fifty states, getting delegates
to support them. To win tomorrow,
the candidate will need 761 votes.
At the moment, Russell probably has
hit the 600 mark. Cantwell is somewhere
between 500 and 550 . . . There are
also three favorite sons in the race,
local politicians who will be nominated
even though they have no hope of
winning. They will hold onto their
votes for at least one ballot, then,
for one reason or another, they will
decide which man to support.

                              HOWARD K. SMITH (Cont.)
                         (smiles)
              It is what we call a horse race.

                                               CUT TO:

A. INT. ARENA

Senator Lazarus is on the podium. He roars into the microphone.

A. CLOSE SHOT: CHAIRMAN LAZARUS, STATE DELEGATION

                              SENATOR LAZARUS
                This great honor which has fallen to
improve/   me, to put in nomination for President
                of the United States that great   * * * 2 extra
                American and Secretary of the State, the   lines of
                next President of the United States: peroration
                The Honorable William Russell!

As pandemonium breaks loose, bands start to play; the
pageant of a planned demonstration begins, Confederate lad
& N.Y. Negro -- Cantwell girls --

                                               CUT TO:

1. INT. PALM COURT -- CLOSE SHOT -- WILLIAM RUSSELL

He watches the television set with an odd mixture of intense
excitement and amusement.

2. MED. SHOT

But this silent communion with his noisy destiny does not last
more than an instant. He is in the press room of the Ambassador
Hotel, surrounded by journalists who are also watching a
series of television sets as well as milling about, filing
stories, etc. This set could be along the lines of the press
room at the Biltmore (1960) when each paper and wire service
had its own cubicle, with an open area at one end containing
TV sets, chairs, telephones, etc. Russell is surrounded now by
newsmen. DICK JENSEN is close beside him.

                              JENSEN
                Now for the demonstration . . .

                              REPORTER #1
              How long will it last?

                         RUSSELL
                    (smiles)
     This is a spontaneous demonstration . . .

                         JENSEN
          Carefully planned . . .

                         RUSSELL
          We expect about twenty-two minutes of
          spontaneity. Now, gentlemen, I am
          officially a nominee and I must be on
          my way . . .

Jensen and Russell start to door; while they maneuver to
door through hordes of reporters, the following dialogue
takes place.

                         REPORTER #1
          What about ex-President Hockstader?

                         REPORTER #2
          Yes, he's here in the hotel?

                         RUSSELL
          What about him?

                         REPORTER #3
          Do you have his support?

                         REPORTER #4
          He's going to speak tonight at the
          banquet . . .

                         REPORTER #1
          It's between you and Cantwell, which
          one he's for.

                         RUSSELL
          We'll just have to wait 'till tonight.
          Now I'm afraid . . .

Someone thrusts Russell's book, "The American Vision," at
him to autograph.

                         FAN
          Could you write "to Bruce and Farina . . .
          F-a-r-i-n-a . . . "

Russell pluckily scribbles something.

                        RUSSELL
The nice thing about running for
President, you sell so many books . . .

                   * * *

          (hands book back)
My best to Farina.

                    REPORTER #1
About the platform yesterday . . .

                        RUSSELL
I'm very pleased with our party's
platform . . .

                    REPORTER #5
Senator Cantwell isn't.

                        RUSSELL
I'm <u>not</u> very pleased with Senator
Cantwell . . .

                    REPORTER #1
On integration you felt . . .

                        RUSSELL
          (serious)
That it is the federal responsibility
to guarantee the rights of all our
citizens. If our party had not
endorsed that point of view, I would
not be a candidate.

---

2.   [REPORTER #5
Did you write your book all by
yourself, Mr. Secretary?

                    JENSEN
That is a vicious question . . .]

                    [RUSSELL
Anyway, I read it all by myself.
Every candidate should read his
own book . . . most instructive.]

* * *

REPORTER #5
        (triumphantly)
But * * * the property rights on which this
country was based . . .

RUSSELL
The country was based, I always thought,
on life, liberty and the pursuit of
happiness, even for Negroes.

REPORTER #3
Would you consider Senator Cantwell
as a possible running mate? If you
are nominated, that is?

RUSSELL
No, but I might consider his brother.
        (laughter)
No, seriously, I like his big brother.
After all, politics is a family
affair nowadays. I'm handicapped of
course. I am the only only child in
Presidential politics today.

* * *

JENSEN
Look, we've got a full schedule and
I'm happy to announce that we are
only an hour late for everything today.

2.

[REPORTER #5
Senator Cantwell feels that the states
should look after this. Now are you in
favor of states' rights or not? I mean
the right of people who own property
to decide who uses that property?

RUSSELL
If the property is used commercially,
then everyone can use it . . .]

[that is an invasion of]

[REPORTER #4
Would you consider Governor John
Merwin as a running mate?

RUSSELL
He's one of a number of competent men.]

                    REPORTER #3
          Mr. Secretary, how did you interpret
          the Gallup poll this morning?

                    RUSSELL
          I don't believe in polls, accurate or
          not.

                         * * *

                    REPORTER #3
          Do you think the people mistrust
          intellectuals, like you, in politics?

                    RUSSELL
          Intellectual? You mean I . . . <u>we</u> wrote
          a book?
                    (laughter)
          Well, Bertrand Russell once said that
          the people in a democracy tend to
          think they have less to fear from a
          stupid man than from an intelligent
          one. Yet it's usually the other way
          round, the stupid . . .

                    REPORTER #1
          Bertrand . . . ?

                    RUSSELL
          Bertrand Russell.

                    REPORTER #1
                    (slow, false dawning)
          Oh, the same name . . .

---

2.   [JENSEN
          That's because we're nine per cent
          ahead of Cantwell . . .

                    REPORTER #5
          But you just lost two per cent . . .

                    JENSEN
          With only eight per cent "Don't know."

                    RUSSELL
          Some day the people are going to
          elect *Don't Know* for President.]

                        RUSSELL
                (amused)
Yes. But no relative. Unfortunately.

                        REPORTER #5
                (the taste of blood)
Wasn't Bertrand Russell <u>fired</u> from
City College of New York?

                        RUSSELL
                (sadly)
Yes, he was fired. But only for
teaching free love . . . <u>not</u> for
incompetence as a philosopher.

                        REPORTER #1
How do you feel -- personally -- about
Senator Cantwell?

                        RUSSELL
I told you, I like his brother.

Reporters laugh.

                        REPORTER
What image do you feel * * * he's
projecting at the moment?

                        RUSSELL
I'm afraid I don't know much about
images. That's a word from advertising
where you don't sell the product, you
sell the image of the product. And
sometimes the image is a fake.

                        REPORTER #5
                (slyly)
But after all, your own image . . .

                        RUSSELL
Is a poor thing but mine own. Paint
me as I am, warts and all.

                        REPORTER #1
What?

_____

2.   [Senator Cantwell is]

                         JENSEN
          Oliver Cromwell.

                         REPORTER #4
          Mr. Secretary . . .

They are now at the door.

                         RUSSELL
                    (through attempted
                    questions)
          Now I should like to leave you with
          but one thought. As Senator Cantwell
          has already put it so well . . . and so
          often: "May the best man win."

Reporters laugh. Russell and Jensen go.

3. <u>EXT. PALM COURT -- DAY</u>

People wearing badges -- CLAYPOOLE, MERWIN, ANDERSON,
CANTWELL, RUSSELL banners.

                         JENSEN
          Bertrand Russell at a press conference.

                         RUSSELL
                    (grins)
          I couldn't resist it.

Russell goes to a telephone.

                         RUSSELL
          Operator -- this is William Russell.
          Yes. Would you try that long-distance
          call again?
                    (exchanges worried look
                    with Jensen)
          What? Yes, it's to my wife. To
          Mrs. Russell in New York . . . The number
          doesn't answer? Yes, keep on trying.

He hangs up.

                         JENSEN
          Will Alice show?

Russell gives him a long, grim look: Your guess is as good
as mine.

>   JENSEN
>   If she isn't at that banquet tonight,
>   you'd better become a Mormon and get
>   yourself another wife. Quick.

>   RUSSELL
>   Or a Moslem. A white Moslem. What a
>   mess!

Russell and Jensen go to door and start back to the hotel through
the pool area.

4. EXT. POOL -- DAY -- LONG SHOT

Russell and Jensen have been stopped by the pool. The bathers
who have recognized Russell force him to shake wet hands,
autograph bar checks, etc. He complies good-humoredly while
Jensen tries to get him free of them. Suddenly Jensen looks
past the crowd to the hotel. Out of the great glass door
comes a resolute figure of a WOMAN. She carries a parasol.
She heads purposefully for them.

5. TWO SHOT -- JENSEN AND RUSSELL

As Russell beams and shakes hands and autographs, murmuring
politely, Jensen speaks into his ear.

>   JENSEN
>   Here she comes!

>   RUSSELL
>   Who?
>   (to bather)
>   Thank you very much. I hope so.

>   JENSEN
>   Our national committee-woman.

>   RUSSELL
>   Mrs. Gamadge!

He looks up.

6. LONG SHOT -- RUSSELL'S POV

Mrs. Gamadge draws closer. She waves gaily.

7. CLOSE SHOT -- RUSSELL

He looks slightly pained.

>   RUSSELL
>   The only link between the N.A.A.C.P.
>   and the Klu Klux Klan. Well, we're
>   in for it.

A sex symbol BATHER wriggles up to him.

>   GIRL
>   I'd vote for you if I was old enough . . .

>   RUSSELL
>   (overwhelmed)
>   Well . . . so would I . . . I mean --
>   (stammers with charm)
>   -- that's very nice of you . . .

Jensen draws him away from the group.

>   RUSSELL
>   Unusual idea; a convention with a
>   swimming pool . . . stimulating . . . triumph
>   of the American way . . .
>   (grimly)

MAN with Cantwell button holds out paper to be autographed;
Russell does so squarely.

>   JENSEN
>   Okay. Brace yourself.

>   RUSSELL
>   Keep walking.

Mrs. Gamadge arrives.

>   MRS. GAMADGE
>   Bill Russell! My favorite candidate,
>   how are you!

Hearty handshakes all around.

>   RUSSELL
>   Wonderful to see you again, Mrs.
>   Gamadge! You know my campaign
>   manager, don't you? Dick Jensen.

>   JENSEN
>   Nice to meet you . . .

              MRS. GAMADGE
I'm glad to meet you, Mr. Jensen. I
love eggheads in politics.

              JENSEN
    (taken aback)
Oh, well . . .

              MRS. GAMADGE
Professors like you give such a tone
to these conventions. No, I really
mean it. Of course, a lot of
women don't like them, but I do. You
don't mind my speaking like this?

              JENSEN
Certainly not, Mrs. Gamadge. After
all, talking to you is like . . . well,
like talking to the average American
housewife.

Jensen is aware that Mrs. Gamadge has frozen on "average."
He stammers.

              JENSEN
I mean you're not average but you
speak for them . . .

              MRS. GAMADGE
Very nicely put, Mr. Jensen.
      (to Russell)
You don't mind if I talk turkey?

              RUSSELL
No. By all means . . . turkey.

              MRS. GAMADGE
You are not the ideal candidate for
the women.

              RUSSELL
<u>Which</u> women do you have in mind?

              MRS. GAMADGE
    (coldly)
The women don't like your trying to
be funny all the time.

              RUSSELL
No, no. It is a flaw, I agree.

                    MRS. GAMADGE
They like a <u>regular</u> kind of man, like
General Eisenhower, that nice smile.
And he's not pushy or aggressive.
Why, you could imagine him washing up
after dinner or listening to * * *
Mamie's views on important matters.
- - - -

                    RUSSELL
Yes. Indeed you can.

                    MRS. GAMADGE
So just don't try to be smart-aleck
and talk over our poor heads. Now
we want to see more of your wife. A
lot more.

                    JENSEN
Mrs. Russell was sick during the
primaries . . .

                    MRS. GAMADGE
She must be at your side at all times.
She must seem to be advising you. It
did Adlai Stevenson great harm, not
having a wife, and trying to be funny
all the time, too. Great harm. Now
I want to ask you a blunt question:
What truth is there in the rumor that
there has been . . . marital discord
between you and Mrs. Russell?

                    RUSSELL
                 (evenly)
My wife will definitely campaign with
me, if I'm nominated, of course.

                    MRS. GAMADGE
She <u>is</u> here, isn't she?

                    JENSEN
Of course she's here.

                    MRS. GAMADGE
Could I see her?

_____

7.   [his wife's]

                    RUSSELL
              (smoothly)
     Why, yes. Come on up to the suite.
     Unless . . .

Russell looks at Jensen: Your cue.

                    JENSEN
     I'm afraid we have a meeting with
     Governor Merwin right now.

                    RUSSELL
     Maybe later this afternoon.

                    MRS. GAMADGE
     Good! Now Mabel Cantwell is such a
     nice woman. Really one of the girls.

The television unit at the pool briefly stops them for a
picture. Mrs. Gamadge holds up Russell's arm like a
prize-fighter.

                    FEMALE TV INTERVIEWER
     Mrs. Gamadge, do you . . .

                    MRS. GAMADGE
     Us girls are going to hustle with
     Russell! He's our candidate.

In his agony, Russell continues to beam.

                    TV INTERVIEWER
              (to Russell)
     Has Mrs. Russell arrived yet?

Mrs. Gamadge answers for him.

                    MRS. GAMADGE
              (brightly)
     Of course she's here! And they'll
     make a fighting team. A pair of
     winners. Bill and Alice Russell!

Jensen and Russell move on.

                    JENSEN
              (aside)
     George and Martha Washington.

                         RUSSELL
                     (delicately)
          Shut up.

They enter lobby.

                         MRS. GAMADGE
                     (in background)
          More women in government. That's my
          motto!

Mrs. Gamadge hurries after Russell and Jensen.

8. <u>INT. LOBBY</u>

                         MRS. GAMADGE
          Oh, by the way, a little bird tells
          me that Joe Cantwell's getting ready
          to smear you with something . . .

                         RUSSELL
                     (startled)
          Smear . . . <u>me</u>? With what?

                         MRS. GAMADGE
          Something pretty bad, so they say. But
          here I am telling you something you already
          know . . . I'm sure you can handle it. Anyway,
          <u>go</u> <u>to</u> <u>it</u>, <u>Bill</u>! . . . I'm in your corner.

                         RUSSELL
          You don't know how much that means, Sue-Ellen.

Mrs. Gamadge plunges into the hotel. Russell and Jensen
exchange anxious looks.

                         RUSSELL
                     (frowns)
          What do you think it is? Alice and
          me?

                         JENSEN
          Who knows? But if Joe tries anything . . .
                     (a throat-cutting gesture)
          People in glass houses . . .

                         RUSSELL
          Or White Houses . . .

JENSEN
(nods)

Shouldn't throw mud.

They move on, past lipstick sign.

9.   <u>INT. HOTEL CORRIDOR</u>

Russell and Jensen are seen fighting their way through a mob
of reporters, TV men, tourists, to a door marked "WILLIAM
RUSSELL -- PRIVATE."

10.   <u>INT. NERVE CENTER</u>

Here three television sets are placed against one wall,
many telephones, etc. This is one of several connected rooms.
Through a doorway we can see additional staff working in the
next room. Both rooms are filled with campaign literature,
posters of Russell. On the walls are layouts of magazine
pieces on the Russell family in LIFE, TIME, LOOK, NEWSWEEK.
Prominent in many of them are Alice Russell and two young
sons. Also, charts, graphs, etc.

While one AIDE engages Russell in the background (as he
simultaneously picks up the telephone), another button-holes
Jensen.

AIDE

We're going to pick up three more from
Texas on the second ballot.

Jensen and Aide cross to men on walkie-talkie. In front of
man is TV set of the convention. The Russell demonstration
continues.

MAN
(into walkie-talkie)

Where's that snowball? Well, I can't
see it on the set. Yeah. The snowball.

AIDE
(to Jensen)

The demonstration's going very well . . .

JENSEN

Where is the snowball?

                         AIDE
                      (proudly)
          It's the largest snowball since Adlai
          Stevenson's . . .

                        JENSEN
          But where is it?

                         MAN
                      (to Jensen)
          They're having trouble . . .
                      (looks at set, now
                      filled with snowball)
          There she comes.

                        JENSEN
          Very satisfying.

                         MAN
          More music.

                         AIDE
          We're hooked up by walkie-talkie with
          every delgation in the arena.

                         MAN
          Cue the girls with the hats.

                        JENSEN
          When is Joe Cantwell being nominated?

                         AIDE
          As soon as we're finished, then
          Governor Claypoole.

          Jensen crosses to Russell, who is on the telephone, with two
          key AIDES. Both are talking simultaneously.

                        AIDE A
          Texas says if you hold the line on
          depletion of resources . . .

                        AIDE B
          The ADA says you've got to nail those
          oilmen . . .

                        RUSSELL
                      (into phone)
          Tell President Hockstader I was trying

                        RUSSELL (Cont.)
        to get him.
                (hangs up)

                        JENSEN
        We're so close! We can almost make
        it on the first ballot.

                        RUSSELL
        If I can swing Art Hockstader.

                        AIDE
        Where do we stand on tideland oil?

                        RUSSELL
        Drink more oil. No, that's milk.
        Jensen, a position paper on oil.

Beautiful GIRL AIDE approaches.

                        WORKER
        Sorry to interrupt you, Mr. Secretary.

                        RUSSELL
        That's all right.

                        MAN
        Where are the girls?

A swift look between the two. Jensen is also aware:
One of Russell's girls.

                        WORKER
        Mrs. Russell wants to see you right
        away.

                        MAN
        Okay. I see them.

                        RUSSELL
                (taken aback)
        What? Where?

                        WORKER
        Why, right here. In your suite. She
        just telephoned.

Russell and Jensen: Saved-by-the-bell response.

                           RUSSELL
          Thank you, Janet.

He starts to the door. Over shoulder to Jensen:

                           RUSSELL
          I've got a call in to Hockstader . . .

                           JENSEN
          Okay.
                    (to aide)
          Here's the speech for tonight.
          Alert mimeo.

Russell is gone. Jensen crosses to board of convention
votes; over shoulder to turn-on-walkie-talkie:

                           JENSEN
          Too much snowball.

                           JANET
          Funny, Mr. Russell acted like he was
          surprised his wife was here.

                           JENSEN
          When this is all over, Janet, I plan
          to divorce my wife, put my children
          out to adoption and make an honest
          woman of you in Phoenix, Arizona.

                           JANET
          I've heard that before.

                           JENSEN
          I hope not. Get me Senator Lazarus,
          Pennsylvania delegation. And remember,
          our lips are sealed.

11. INT. RUSSELL SUITE

Russell enters the living room of the suite, which is located
across the hall from the Nerve Center. It is large; the
inevitable bar, mountain of fruit; telegrams and newspapers
are piled on chairs. He crosses tentatively to the bedroom
door which is open.

                           RUSSELL
          Alice?

12. <u>INT. BEDROOM</u>

ALICE RUSSELL, a handsome woman, is hanging up clothes in the closet. She is very businesslike. She ignores him as she concentrates on what she is doing. Russell enters the bedroom; twin beds.

> RUSSELL
> (expectantly)
> Well . . .

She continues her work.

> RUSSELL
> (brightly)
> Hello there. Did you have a nice flight?

She gives him a look; that line was unworthy of him.

> RUSSELL
> (slightly rattled)
> Everyone's been asking . . . where you were and . . . so on. I'm certainly glad you got here.

Another pause.

* * *

> ALICE
> I am here because I read the Gallup Poll and apparently you are going to be the next President.

> RUSSELL
> (lightly)
> Join the bandwagon! I like that. No sentimentality. No nonsense. No . . .

12.

> [ALICE
> Well, as someone is bound to say: politics make strange bedfellows.

> RUSSELL
> I'd hoped it wouldn't be *you* who said it.]

                    ALICE
"No nonsense." That's it. I mean
it, Bill. I've had twenty years
of nonsense, of being a good sport.
A good front. While all the time
my husband was devoting himself
to his favorite hobby --

                    RUSSELL
I've never embarrassed you . . .

                    ALICE
          (drily)
And what would you like for that?
Some sort of gold star? Now, Mr.
President-To-Be, you are going
to make your first treaty.
          (looks at key)
The treaty of Suite 674. I'll
stay with you through the convention,
through the election, in the White
House, but on one condition -- that
you give up your hobby.

                    RUSSELL
It was never as much a hobby as
you . . .

                    ALICE
Yes, yes, * * * you need love . . . As your
psychiatrist said, you want everyone to
love you. Bill, we love you!

                    RUSSELL
For someone who wants to be loved,
I do a lot of unpopular things,
politically.

                    ALICE
Because you want history to love
you, too.

---

12.   [we've had that out before.
       When your psychiatrist discovered
       what everyone else knew: that you
       need love. But not just from me.
       . . . Including a majority of the
       voters all shouting: . . . All thirty
       million fans!]

                    RUSSELL
              (ruefully)
You've been working on the case,
haven't you?

                    ALICE
For the first time since we were
married, you need me. Because if
I were to ask for a divorce now
you couldn't be President, could
you?

                    RUSSELL
I wouldn't <u>count</u> on that, but . . .

                    ALICE
But it would make it awfully rough.
It's considered bad form to get
rid of * * * the old wife.
             — —

                    RUSSELL
Especially when I don't want to
get rid of her.

                    ALICE
You mean you <u>can't</u> get rid of her.
              (sighs)
You know, I find I'm unexpectedly
ambitious. I'd <u>like</u> to be First
Lady. I really would. I'd like
to re-redecorate the White House.
And I wouldn't mind seeing you
every now and then. Just occasionally,
an ambiguous encounter in the Lincoln
Bedroom.

                    RUSSELL
I didn't know you cared.

                    ALICE
              (a real question)
Do I?
              (pause)
Anyway, I insist on my one condition:
there is to be no house on K Street
or wherever it was President Harding

                              ALICE (Cont.)
          used to go. And no girls in the
          White House or ever on tour. That
          is the Treaty of Suite 674, agreed
          this fourteenth day of May, in
          Los Angeles County.

                              RUSSELL
          Agreed . . .
                    (softly)
          Thank you.

They look at one another, close to affection, old antagonists
quite used to this familiar warfare.

                              ALICE
                    (suddenly)
          How does it look?

                              RUSSELL
          Close.

                              ALICE
          I hope you make it.

                              RUSSELL
          I think we will.
                    (takes paper from
                    pocket)
          Here's your schedule for the day.

                              ALICE
          You knew I'd come?

Russell smiles.

                              ALICE
                    (laughs)
          I really think you will be a good
          President.

                              RUSSELL
          But what happens to the treaty
          if I lose?

                              ALICE
                    (suddenly bleak)
          We go our separate ways. Which
          is what you want.

Jensen enters with papers.

Alice continues unpacking.

>   JENSEN
> Glad you dropped in, Alice . . .

>   ALICE
> Hello, Dick . . .

>   JENSEN
>   (to Russell)
> Hockstader's disappeared. Nobody
> can find him. Stop looking in the
> mirror.

>   RUSSELL
> I never pass a mirror I don't look
> in it. I wonder why.

>   * * * JENSEN
> Vanity, Narcissus, vanity.

Jensen is correcting two documents.

>   RUSSELL
> I look to remind myself I really
> exist. One needs constant proof.

>   ALICE
> Do your shy smile, the one the
> housewives adore.

Russell does a shy smile.

>   JENSEN
> Here's your speech for tonight.
> I think you'll enjoy it. It's
> one of your best. Read it.

Jensen starts to go.

>   RUSSELL
> I'll wait till I speak it. I like
> to surprise myself.

Jensen goes. Alice crosses to bathroom door. She opens it
and there, smiling, is the former President Art Hockstader.

> ALICE
> (gasps)
> Mr. President! What . . . are you doing
> there . . . ?

> HOCKSTADER
> Hi, Miss Alice, you going to give
> me a big hug?

Hockstader embraces her. Russell comes forward, beaming.

> RUSSELL
> Mr. President, I'm really glad . . .

> HOCKSTADER
> Plain old Art to you.
> (indicates bathroom)
> I didn't want anybody to see me
> just yet. So I got into the next
> suite and snuck in through the
> privy.

Both Russell and Alice are looking somewhat nervous.
Hockstader grins.

> ALICE
> Mr. President . . .

> HOCKSTADER
> No. I didn't hear any marital
> secrets, if there are any. I'm
> deaf.

13. INT. LIVING ROOM

During this, they have gone into living room. Russell crosses
to bar.

> ALICE
> (to Hockstader)
> You look wonderful after your
> operation!

> RUSSELL
> What can I get you to drink? No,
> no, don't tell me . . . bourbon and
> branch water.

Russell goes to the living-room bar.

>   HOCKSTADER
> With which I shall strike a blow
> for liberty.
>   (to Alice)
> Don't let anyone know I'm here.

Alice nods and goes into bedroom.

>   HOCKSTADER
> Well, son, how do you like politics?

>   RUSSELL
> I like it so much I'm beginning
> to worry.

>   HOCKSTADER
> Awful, ain't it? Worse than gamblin'.
> I was hooked when I was no more
> than this high . . .
>   (indicates a child)
> . . . and a certain fourflusher named
> William Jennings Bryan came to town.

>   RUSSELL
>   (orates)
> "You shall not press down upon the
> brow of labor this crown of thorns."

>   HOCKSTADER
>   (nods)
> "You shall not crucify mankind
> upon a cross of gold!" Oh, that
> was a speech!

Russell gives Hockstader his drink.

>   RUSSELL
> But then Bryan lost the election.

>   HOCKSTADER
> So he did. So he did.

>   RUSSELL
>   (carefully)
> Art, your endorsement is a very
> important thing for anybody who
> wants to be nominated.

                    HOCKSTADER
        I know it is.
                (smiles)
        So, indulge an old duffer! After
        all, gettin' you fellows to listen
        to my stories and squirm a bit,
        waitin' to see who I'm goin' to
        put my money on, why I tell you
        it's about the only pleasure I
        got left.

                    RUSSELL
        I'm squirming.

                    HOCKSTADER
        Politics has changed a lot since
        my day. The Age of the Great Hicks
        to which I belong is over. You
        rich boys have it all sewed up.
        Hell, you got to be a millionaire
        to run for President nowadays,
        and it's usually your Daddy's
        million . . .

                    RUSSELL
        I didn't know you were a Marxist.

                    HOCKSTADER
                (serenely)
        Marxist? Never heard the word.
        No, time was you rich boys just
        liked to play games, like polo.
        Now you play politics. Well, I
        am nothing if not a realist. The
        people like you rich boys. They
        think you got so much money of
        your own you won't go stealin'
        theirs. Also, they kind of hope
        one of those Rockefellers or Kennedys
        might get a notion to pay off the
        national debt out of their own
        pocket. You know -- just to be
        nice.

                    RUSSELL
        That "poor-but-honest" line of Joe
        Cantwell's doesn't hurt him.

                    HOCKSTADER
Ah, Joe Cantwell. He doesn't have
your money and he doesn't have your
brains, either. But then, very
few of us are as bright as you.

                    RUSSELL
Come off it, Art.

                    HOCKSTADER
No, I mean it. You were a superior
man of the sort we don't get very
often in politics. While Joe's
just another of the mediocre boys,
like me . . . only smoother, of course.

                    RUSSELL
No, he's <u>not</u> like you. He'll do
anything to win. And that makes
him dangerous.

                    HOCKSTADER
Now I wouldn't go that far.
          (the first turn
          of the screw)
At least he knows his own mind.

                    RUSSELL
And you think I don't?

                    HOCKSTADER
          (equably)
Well, son, you got such a good
mind that sometimes you're so busy
thinkin' how complex everything
is, important problems don't get
solved.

                    RUSSELL
Look, suppose the Chinese were to
attack India. Now that is the
kind of thing you and I understand
and I think we could handle it
without starting an atomic war
and without losing India. But
what would Joe do? He would look
at the Gallup Poll. And what would
the Gallup Poll tell him? Well,
ask the average American do you

                    RUSSELL (Cont.)
want to run the risk of being blown
up to save India? And he'll say,
hell no! Joe would do the popular
thing: to hell with India, and we
would be the weaker for it, and
that day we're all afraid of would
be closer.

Hockstader finishes his drink and rises.

                    HOCKSTADER
Son, you've been reading too much
of that Joe Alsop fellow. Things
are never <u>that</u> bad!
                    (a long beat;
                    thoughtfully suddenly)
Bill, do you believe in God?

                    RUSSELL
                    (startled)
Do I . . . ? Well, I was confirmed
in the Episcopal Church.

                    HOCKSTADER
And I'm a Methodist, but I'm still
askin': do you believe there's a
God and a Day of Judgment and a
Hereafter?

                    RUSSELL
No. I believe in us. In man.

                    HOCKSTADER
                    (nods)
I've often pretended I thought
there was a God, for political
purposes.

                    RUSSELL
                    (smiles)
So far I haven't told a lie in
this campaign. I've never used
the word "God" in a speech.

                    HOCKSTADER
Well, the world's changed since I
was politickin'. In those days

                    HOCKSTADER (Cont.)
you had to pour God over everything,
like ketchup.
                    (he sits on the bench)
No, I don't believe there's a Hereafter.
We pass this way just once. And
then . . . nothing. Bill, I am dying.

                    RUSSELL
               (stunned)
What?

                    HOCKSTADER
That thing about the hernia was
just another lie, I'm afraid.
               (drily)
I hope you don't disapprove . . . I
got cancer and they tell me I may
last just long enough to attend
the next inaugural.

                    RUSSELL
Art, I'm . . . !

                    HOCKSTADER
I tell you, son, I am scared to
death.
               (laughs)
That's a phrase for you. "Scared
to death" is exactly right.

                    RUSSELL
I wish I could say something
reassuring but you wouldn't fall
for it, anyway.

                    HOCKSTADER
The only thing I find is that
the rest of you * * * so-and-so's
are going to join me. There's some
consolation, I reckon, in that.

                    RUSSELL
There should be something more than
consolation, Art, in knowing * * * how much
you've accomplished in your lifetime.

                    HOCKSTADER
                 (drily)
     I suggest you tell yourself that
     when <u>you</u> finally have to face a
     whole pile of nothin' up ahead.

Jensen enters.

                    JENSEN
     Bill, you've got to talk to those
     Texans . . .
                 (sees Hockstader)
     Oh, hello, Mister . . .

Hockstader motions to Jensen to say nothing. Jensen
nods and shuts the door.

                    HOCKSTADER
     Bill, don't tell anybody what I told
     you.

                    RUSSELL
     Of course not.

                    HOCKSTADER
     Meanwhile, I am going to keep you in
     suspense until tonight at dinner.

                    RUSSELL
     And then?

                    HOCKSTADER
     I will throw my support like a bridal
     bouquet to the lucky man.

Hockstader beams; he starts to cross to bedroom; he pauses.

                    HOCKSTADER
     Oh, these rumors about you and your
     lady friends . . . won't do you a bit of
     harm.
                 (grimaces with pain)
     Oh, that upper plate of mine pinches!
     I was going to get a new one but they
     said it would take a couple of months
     to make. So I figured I could hold
     out with what I got.

                        RUSSELL
Art . . .

                        HOCKSTADER
You go on and talk to those crazy
Texans.
            (chuckles)
I sure wish I was a fly on that wall,
listening to you tell the whole truth
about what you really think of the
depletion of oil resources allowance!

                        RUSSELL
            (laughs)
Get out of here, you old bum . . .

14. INT. BEDROOM -- MED. SHOT

They go into the bedroom. Alice is at the closet, hanging
up clothes. She turns to them. Hockstader gives her an
airy wave and opens the bathroom door.

                        HOCKSTADER
            Now is that a respectful way to talk
            to the end of an era? The last of
            the Great Hicks as he shuffles off
            the stage? By way of the privy.

Hockstader is gone. Russell turns to Alice, his smile
fading.

                        ALICE
            What did he say?

Jensen is now at the bedroom door.

                        JENSEN
            Yes, what did he say?

                        RUSSELL
It's what he didn't say. He's going
to support Joe Cantwell.

                        ALICE
            He couldn't!

                        JENSEN
I don't believe it.

                    RUSSELL
        He thinks Joe's tough, and I'm not.
        I was afraid of this.

                    ALICE
        Are you sure you understood him . . . you
        know how politicians are: they talk
        in Morse code.

                    RUSSELL
        I decoded it.
                (to Jensen)
        We've got to head him off before
        tonight.

                    JENSEN
        How?

Telephone rings. Jensen answers it.

                    JENSEN
        Jensen. Yes.
                (turns to Alice)
        The Volunteer Women for Russell are
        on the mezzanine. They want to know
        if you can join them.

                    ALICE
        Of course.

                    JENSEN
        She'll be right down.

He hangs up.

                    ALICE
        Do I look all right for the Volunteer
        Women for Russell?

                    JENSEN
        You do!

                    ALICE
                (to Russell)
        I ought to. I'm a founding member of
        that considerable body.

Sudden uproar at the door; a nervous Janet enters, buffeted
by newsmen.

                        JANET
        Mr. Secretary, she's here.

Alice comprehends Janet; Alice looks at Russell; he comprehends
Alice; he looks away quickly, all business.

                        RUSSELL
                (to Janet)
        Who's here?

                        JANET
        Mrs. Gamadge.

                        RUSSELL
        Oh, God!
                (beams as Mrs. Gamadge
                enters)
        Oh, Mrs. Gamadge!

Mrs. Gamadge bears down on Alice.

                        MRS. GAMADGE
        So she's really here after all!

                        RUSSELL
        Alice, you remember Mrs. Gamadge.

                        ALICE
        Of course. Could I ever forget?
        How wonderful to see you . . . looking
        so well.

Mrs. Gamadge examines Alice as though she were a monument;
finally she breaks into a broad smile.

                        MRS. GAMADGE
        Love it! Absolutely love it! You . . .
        couldn't . . . look . . . better. I mean it.
        I like the whole thing. Especially
        the natural hair, that is such an
        important point with the women. Of
        course, Mabel Cantwell dyes her hair
        but she does such a bad job, the
        women feel sorry for her.

                        ALICE
                (softly)
        Thank you so much.

                         MRS. GAMADGE
             (cozily)
When you're the First Lady just
remember this: don't do too much . . .
like Mrs. Roosevelt. The women
didn't like that. On the other hand,
don't do too little . . . like Mrs.
Eisenhower. The women didn't like
that, either. All in all, Grace
Coolidge was really the best, bless
her heart. My husband had such a
crush on her . . .

                         ALICE
Oh? And what did Mr. Coolidge feel
about that?

                         MRS. GAMADGE
He never said. Now the important
thing . . .

During the foregoing Alice and Russell have exchanged looks,
his saying: You take care of Mrs. Gamadge. I've got other
things to do. He slowly backs out, leaving Alice to the
mercy of Mrs. Gamadge.

                                 CUT TO:

14A.   INT. HALL

Russell has almost made it to the nerve center when he is set
upon by the Spastic, copy of National Review clutched in his
hand.

                         SPASTIC
Mr. Russell . . . Mr. Russell . . .

                         RUSSELL
Yes, sir?

                         SPASTIC
Do you favor impeaching the Chief
Justice?

                         RUSSELL
Not immediately, no, sir . . .

                    SPASTIC
Are you aware that five members of
the Supreme Court are card-carrying
Communists . . . ?

                    RUSSELL
Well . . . well . . .

                    SPASTIC
Do you deny that you yourself, while
at Harvard, belonged to a cell of
Communists . . . ?

                    RUSSELL
That was no cell, that was the Hasty
Pudding Show.

Russell darts into nerve center; Spastic is stopped by
a guard.

                    SPASTIC
We'll get you Commies. Never fear!

15. <u>INT. NERVE CENTER</u>

Surrounded by the bustle of activity and noise from the
television sets, Jensen is talking to an AIDE.

                    JENSEN
His name is Bascomb. Sheldon. With
a "D." Get him on a jet. I don't
care if he doesn't want to come.
Then put him in a bag. I want him
here first thing tomorrow morning.

Russell enters with two AIDES. They go to television sets'.
One shows convention. The other, news.

                    AIDE A
We got an extra three minutes on the
demonstration.

                    AIDE B
Cantwell's demonstration just started.

                    RUSSELL
How does it look?

                    AIDE A
They spent money.

                    RUSSELL
              (suddenly)
So did we. Ah, there's Joe Cantwell!
Public enemy number one.

Russell turns up the sound. We see Cantwell being interviewed
in his ballroom headquarters. He is a handsome, vigorous man
with a profoundly sincere voice.

                    CANTWELL'S VOICE
Don't get me wrong. I gotta lot of
respect for William Russell . . .

                    RUSSELL
Thank you, Joe . . .

                    CANTWELL'S VOICE
But I don't think he's got the people's
touch . . .

                    RUSSELL
Never met a payroll.

                    CANTWELL'S VOICE
I think we need a real man of the
people for President, somebody like
Art Hockstader who has been my ideal
all my life.

Russell turns the sound off.

                    RUSSELL
No, I would not buy a used car from
that man.

                                        CUT TO:

16. <u>INT. CANTWELL HEADQUARTERS -- LONG SHOT</u>

This headquarters is a ballroom on the second floor of the
hotel.

There are banners "Go with Joe," "The Fighting Candidate,"
"You'll Do Well With Cantwell." The ballroom is crowded.
At display tables around the room, literature is being given

                    CANTWELL (Cont.)
agitation that's going on. I think
the colored people are often used by
the Commies who are all around us,
everywhere, high and low.

                    ANNOUNCER
On tax reform . . .

                    CANTWELL
I favor tax reform. I believe that
by cutting down government spending
we can eventually eliminate the income
tax entirely.

                    ANNOUNCER
As for Cuba . . .

                    CANTWELL
We got to get tough. That's all those
people really appreciate. We got to
get us a lot more military hardware.
Because when it comes to defense, we're
being sold down the river by the so-
called liberals . . .

                    ANNOUNCER
So you feel that we can increase
military spending <u>while</u> eliminating
the income tax . . . ?

Cantwell ignores this hay-maker.

                    CANTWELL
And I think it a pretty swell thing
that in a country like this, somebody
like me, who started from scratch,
can be here today, able to speak for
the real people of this country.
Where else but in America could
somebody from a poor family be running
for the greatest job in the world? I
guess I'm pretty proud, no matter what
happens tomorrow; pretty proud to be
an American.

Applause, cheers; Cantwell starts off. TV men hold him
back for one last word. Confused sound.

away; also, buttons, free coffee, the works. On one table there is a pile of books! "The Enemy Around Us" by Joseph R. Cantwell. At one end of the room a section has been roped off. Here there are lights, a sound boom, TV cameras. Cantwell is just finishing a TV appearance. An ANNOUNCER is winding up.

                    ANNOUNCER
          So you feel, sir, with your pledged
          candidates and the endorsement . . . if
          you get it . . . of the former President,
          you'll be ahead on the first ballot . . .

                    CANTWELL
          We certainly hope so. We're doing
          our best. And I got a hunch we're
          going to make it because there are
          a lot of people in this country who
          feel like we do, who are against all
          this government spending, and this
          knuckling under to the communists . . .

                    ANNOUNCER
          Senator, during the primaries, you
          and Mr. Russell disagreed over
          integration . . .

                    CANTWELL
          Now, we didn't disagree over the
          <u>moral</u> issue involved. I personally
          find any kind of segregation wrong.
          I've said that before. I'll say that
          again. But I <u>don't</u> think it's up to
          the federal government to decide
          something which is a local matter. I
          may not like what they do in
          Mississippi, but I will fight for
          their right to run their state the
          way they want to, and I think that's
          what our Founding Fathers intended.

                    ANNOUNCER
          At the moment you have all the Southern
          delegates . . .

                    CANTWELL
          Look, I think we're all concerned --
          North and South -- about this Communist

> CANTWELL
> Only hope the best man wins.

> PHOTOGRAPHER
> Senator . . . again . . . didn't get it . . .

> CANTWELL
> May the best man win.

He stands a moment, frozen smile as the photographers finish.
Then he is joined by DON CANTWELL, older brother and campaign
manager. Together they make their way through crowded
ballroom. Cantwell is manic with good fellowship. "Hiya,
fella!" Halfway they are stopped by a lean Spastic sort with
a copy of The National Review.

> SPASTIC
> Senator, we're with you . . .

> CANTWELL
> Thank you . . .

> SPASTIC
> Conservatism has found its voice . . .

> CANTWELL
> Yes . . .

> SPASTIC
> We must stop Communism now. Eliminate
> Social Security.

> CANTWELL
> Well . . .

> SPASTIC
> The closed shop.

Cantwell tries to pull away.

> SPASTIC
> And the flourine, we must keep flourine
> out of the water. Flourine is a
> Communist trick to weaken the fibre . . .

Cantwell and Don break away.

17. INT. KITCHEN -- DAY

They enter kitchen. The kitchen is deserted except for
guards, troopers, an aged charwoman. The smile drops from
Cantwell's face, like a light switched off. Don is grim.

                    CANTWELL
          Don, I want you to get to Hockstader
          right now. Tell him we have to see
          him before that dinner tonight.

                    DON
                (dubiously)
          You think you ought to tell him about
          Russell now?

                    CANTWELL
          I do. It's now or never.

A CLEANING WOMAN passes them. She pauses; her face breaks
into a smile of ecstasy.

                    CLEANING WOMAN
          Joe Cantwell!

                    CANTWELL
                (warmly)
          And how are you, ma'am?

                    CLEANING WOMAN
          I just want you to know I'm for you.
          Because you're not rich.

                    CANTWELL
          May the good Lord increase your kind.

                    CLEANING WOMAN
                (to Don)
          And your big brother. Oh, I like
          him, too. I always hoped you'd be
          President, Mr. Cantwell.

                    DON
          Thank you.

                    CANTWELL
          We all did. Thank you, ma'am. And
          don't forget us in November.

Cantwell, in a neat maneuver, takes her hand warmly, also
her elbow and in a near-embrace, moves her along.

DON

See? I still have my followers.

CANTWELL

Sure.

DON

Joe, that stuff on Russell, threaten,
but don't use it . . .

CANTWELL

Don, it's right what I'm doing. Some
things are right and some things are
wrong. It is wrong to let a man like
Bill Russell be nominated.
(points upstairs)
Hockstader.

CUT TO:

18. <u>INT. THE LIVING ROOM OF THE CANTWELL SUITE -- MED. SHOT</u>

MABEL CANTWELL, a blonde, pretty woman of forty, in a
dressing gown, lies on a sofa watching television and
drinking a martini. Around the room, placards and posters
implore us to vote for SENATOR JOE CANTWELL. On the set,
we see the CANTWELL demonstration.

* * * H. K. SMITH
That's a pretty frenzied demonstration
for Joe Cantwell. He's the darling
of the conservative element, only
they're not so conservative today.
Look at them!

On the screen appears a CANTWELL BANNER.

MABEL

Yea, team!

VOICE OVER
Now here are some scenes from the
candidate's life.

On the set, we see a still of JOE CANTWELL: he is about

       [VOICE OVER]

seven years old; beside him is his older brother, about ten.
Parents, tacky.

> VOICE OVER
> There he is as a boy, back in
> Tracy Junction. Son of a * * *
> store owner.

Picture changes to shot of Joe Cantwell quizzing a dark,
nervous man on television: a Senate hearing. Room full
of noises.

> * * * H. K. SMITH
> From this small town background Joe Cantwell
> rose through several low offices to the
> United States Senate. He became nationally
> known a few years ago * * * during the famous
> Mafia hearings, when * * * he sought to prove
> that the Mafia was really a part of the
> Communist conspiracy. That was the beginning
> of his historic rise.

> CANTWELL
> Do you deny . . .

> MAFIATYPE
> I refuse to answer on the grounds . . .

> CANTWELL
> That the Communists instructed
> your group . . .

> MAFIATYPE
> (doggedly)
> On the grounds that . . .

> CANTWELL
> To infiltrate the seven legitimate
> businesses whose names I have here
> in my hand . . .

---

18.   [small]

[There's the Senator] [he proved]

                         MAFIATYPE
          Might incriminate me . . .

                          CANTWELL
          What is your name, sir?

                         MAFIATYPE
                    (begins again,
                    laboriously)
          I refuse to answer on the grounds
          that . . .

                          CANTWELL
                    (dramatically)
          What could be more clear?   There
          sits the enemy around us!

Applause in committee room.   Much gaveling.

                         VOICE OVER
          Now a network exclusive, an interview
          with Joe Cantwell's mother, back
          in Tracy Junction.

The Mother is a large, bland woman, with spectacles
(transparent rims, hearing aid; youngish hair-do; glistening
dentures).

                         INTERVIEWER
          You must be a very proud woman,
          Mrs. Cantwell, today, with your
          son nominated for President . . .

                        MRS. CANTWELL
                    (as though rehearsed)
          He was always a fine boy, so ambitious.
          Oh, I remember when he said to me
          one day, I have met this fine girl
          who is just like my Mom, and it was
          Mabel who he married and this is her
          picture right here . . .

Holds up photograph of Mabel.

                           MABEL
          Yea, Mom!

19. INT. LIVING ROOM -- MED. SHOT

There is a noise of reporters as the hall door opens. Joe
Cantwell enters. He poses for one more photograph at door, arms
victoriously raised. Then Cantwell relaxes full length on the
sofa.

                    CANTWELL
                 (calls)
          Mabel, honey! Come on out. It's
          just me.

Mabel appears. She throws herself on him. They embrace warmly.

                    CANTWELL
                 (laughing)
          Hey, come on! You better get
          dressed. The reception for the
          press is in . . .
                 (looks at watch)
          . . . thirty minutes.

                    MABEL
          I'll be ready . . . don't you worry,
          baby.
                 (concern)
          Oh, Joe, you look so tired.

                    CANTWELL
                 (automatically)
          Never felt better.

Cantwell picks up a newspaper and reads, frowning.

                    MABEL
          We got awful nice coverage on the
          TV. And look, there's Mom.

                    MOM
          . . . hope he does like he says when
          he says the best man will win.

                    INTERVIEWER
          Thank you, Mrs. Cantwell.

                    MABEL
          Good old Mom.

                    CANTWELL
          Yeah.

He picks up a pile of newspapers.

                  * * * H. K. SMITH   voice only
So that's it for now. William   or see
Russell, Joe Cantwell, Governor   Smith
T. T. Claypoole, Governor John   briefly
Merwin and Senator Oscar Anderson
have all been nominated. Tomorrow
the balloting will begin. At the
moment William Russell is in the
lead. * * * But to the best of our
knowledge he is still at least 50
or 60 votes short of the 761 needed
to nominate.

Mabel turns the set off. Cantwell throws himself on couch.

                  CANTWELL
            (shuts his eyes)
I am tired.
            (then he sits up,
            abruptly, seeing
            Mabel at bar)
Mabel, come on, get dressed!

                  MABEL
I'll be ready, Joe, stop worryin' . . .
Don't get all het up.
            (embraces him)
Why is big Poppa Bear so mean to
poor little Momma Bear?

                  CANTWELL
Baby, I'm sorry.
            (goes into their
            private baby talk)
Poppa Bear is never mean to his
Momma Bear, never, ever. But you've
got to get dressed.

                  MABEL
I will. I will. Joe, when are

---

19.   [TV ANNOUNCER]

[With twenty-five pledged delegates.
But he needs 761 to be nominated . . .]

                    MABEL (Cont.)
you going to spring that . . . stuff
on Russell?

                    CANTWELL
Tomorrow: Pow!

                    MABEL
And then Poppa Bear and Momma
Bear and all the baby bears are
on their way to the White House.

                    CANTWELL
Where's my electric razor?

                    MABEL
I'll get it!
         (goes quickly
         into bedroom)
I'll just start putting on my
clothes and . . .

She finds razor and gives it to him.

                    CANTWELL
Where's the last Gallup poll?

                    MABEL
Russell 35%, Cantwell 28%, Merwin
12%, Claypoole 10%, Anderson 5% and
8% don't know.

Mabel removes her dressing gown and gets into her dress.

                    MABEL
Joe, do you think I've gained weight?
Around the hips? Honey, you listenin'
to me?

Realizing he is in the other room, Mabel, pouting, crosses
to living room door, the back of her dress unzipped.

                    MABEL
No, I guess you're not . . . You never
listen to poor Momma Bear any more.
         (pause)
Joe? Have you ever been unfaithful
to me?

                    CANTWELL
                (turns off razor)
No. Did you see Walter Lippmann
this morning? Listen to what that
guy says: "The country's affairs
will be in good hands should William
Russell be our next President."
                (slaps the paper down)
I don't know why I don't appeal to
those would-be intellectuals. My
image just doesn't project to them
like his does.
                (notices Mabel at last)
Well, look at you! Just good enough
to eat . . .
                (starts to nuzzle her
                in a bearish way)
Mmmm -- mmm --

                    MABEL
                (happily nuzzled)
Now what are you doing to me? Don't
muss my hair! Now come on! Stop
it! And zip me up!

She turns around; as Joe zips her dress, she returns to
her theme.

                    MABEL
Joe, are you sure you haven't been
unfaithful to me maybe just one
little time? On one of those junkets?
Like that awful one to Paris you
took, where the Senators got so
drunk and Clarence Wetlaw contracted
a social disease and Helen Wetlaw
was fit to be tied?

                    CANTWELL
Mabel, honey, there's nobody else.
And even if there was, how would
I have the time? I operate on a
tight schedule.
                (kisses her briefly)
You know that.

Don enters from corridor door.

                          CANTWELL
         O.K.?

                          DON
                     (nodding)
         Hockstader's waiting for you.

                          CANTWELL
         Good. Get me that file on Russell.

He starts to go.

                          MABEL
         Joe . . . play it cool, like the kids
         say.

                          CANTWELL
         I will.

Don gives him a manila folder and they exit.

                                              CUT TO:

19A.   INT. HOCKSTADER SUITE

HOCKSTADER * * * at window. TOM enters.

                          TOM
         They're on their way.

Hockstader nods. Tom goes into living room of suite.
* * * He rises.

20.   INT. HALLWAY OUTSIDE HOCKSTADER'S SUITE

                          CANTWELL
                     (warningly)
         Don: Remember . . . flatter him!

                          DON
                     (smiles)
         I taught you that!

_____

19A.   [sits wearily on bed.]

       [Hockstader takes a pill.]

They knock and enter.

21.   INT. HOCKSTADER'S SUITE

                    CANTWELL
        Mr. President!

Cantwell beams and crosses to Hockstader.

                    HOCKSTADER
        Hi, Joe! Well, we're getting near
        that time.
                (taps coat pocket)
        Get my speech right here. My
        teeth are in and I'm rarin' to
        go.
                (crosses to bar)
        Would you join me in striking a
        blow for liberty?

                    CANTWELL
        No, thank you, sir.

                    HOCKSTADER
                (to Don)
        That's right. Joe doesn't have
        the habit.

                    DON
        I do, however.

                    HOCKSTADER
                (chuckling)
        People who don't drink never realize
        how thirsty we old bucks get long
        'round sundown.
                (turns thoughtfully
                to Cantwell)
        No, sir, you don't drink, you don't
        smoke, you don't philander; fact,
        you are about the purest young
        man I have ever known in public
        life.

                    CANTWELL
        I try to be.

                    HOCKSTADER
I must say you've done a remarkable
job in the Senate. Most of the time.

                    CANTWELL
          (quickly)
<u>Most</u> of the time?

                    HOCKSTADER
          (nods)
There <u>have</u> been moments when I
have questioned your methods.

                    CANTWELL
Well, you have to fight fire with
fire, Mr. President.

                    HOCKSTADER
And the end justifies the means?

                    CANTWELL
Well, yes, sir. Yes. That is
what I believe.

                    HOCKSTADER
Well, son, I have news for you
about both politics and life . . .
and may I say the two are <u>exactly</u>
the same thing . . . There are no
ends, Joe. Only means . . .

                    HOCKSTADER
          (amused)
Now! None of them two-bit words
on poor old Art Hockstader. I'm
just an ignorant country boy. All
I'm saying is that what matters in
our profession . . . which is really
life . . . is <u>how</u> you do things and
<u>how</u> you treat people and what you
really feel about 'em, <u>not</u> some
ideal goal for society, or for
yourself.

                    CANTWELL
          (his District-Attorney
          voice)
Then am I to assume, Mr. President,
from the statement you have just

                    CANTWELL (Cont.)
made, that you are against planning
anything?

                    HOCKSTADER
          (laughs)
Oh, here it comes! I know that
voice! Senator Cantwell, boy
crusader, up there on the TV . . .

                    CANTWELL
I realize some of my methods upset
a lot of people, especially criminals
and Communists . . .

Hockstader smiles during this.

                    CANTWELL
          (tersely)
Just what do you find so funny?

                    HOCKSTADER
Nothing, only you know and I know
and everybody knows . . . except, I'm
afraid, the TV audience . . . that there
never was a Communist Mafia like
you said. There was no such thing.
You just cooked it up.

                    * * *

                    HOCKSTADER
Look, I don't object to your headline-
grabbing and crying 'wolf' all the
time, that's standard stuff in
politics, but it disturbs me that
you take your own phony stuff so
seriously. It's par for the course

---

21.   [CANTWELL
                    (dangerously)
          So we're going to get that number,
          are we? Well, my figures prove . . .]

                        HOCKSTADER (Cont.)
trying to fool the people but it's
downright dangerous when you start
fooling yourself.

                    CANTWELL
                (carefully)
Mr. President, I take myself seriously.
Because I am serious. This is
important to me. To all of us.
Which is why I don't want any little
lectures from you on how to be
a statesman.

                    DON
                (warningly)
Joe!

                    CANTWELL
And if you really want to know,
I think the record of your
administration is one of the
heaviest loads our party has to
carry.

Hockstader is suddenly furious.

                    HOCKSTADER
Now look here, you little . . .

                    DON
He's pretty tense, Mr. President.
It's the old pre-convention nerves.

                    HOCKSTADER
                (smiles, relaxing)
Yes, of course it is. We've all
gone through it. I must say I
had 'em when you almost knocked
me off.

                    DON
Almost is not enough.

                    HOCKSTADER
You were a good opponent, Don.

                        CANTWELL
          I'm sorry, sir, flying off the
          handle like that. Don, would you
          excuse us?

There is an awkward moment.

                        DON
          See you later, Mr. President.

Don leaves the room.

                        HOCKSTADER
          Well?

                        CANTWELL
          I know you don't like me . . .

                        HOCKSTADER
          Now that you mention it, I don't.
          I never have.

                        CANTWELL
          And I don't expect you to come
          out for me tonight . . .

Hockstader crosses to the bar. He fixes himself another
drink.

                        HOCKSTADER
          I've often endorsed men I disliked
          because I thought they'd do the
          job.

Cantwell picks up the file. Hockstader suffers a spasm
of pain at the bar. He clutches his stomach. Cantwell
does not notice this.

                        CANTWELL
          So I have something to show you
          about your friend William Russell.
          It's all here, in this file. I
          want you to look at it and . . .
                    (looks at Hockstader;
                    realizes something
                    is wrong)
          What's the matter with you?

                         HOCKSTADER
                    (with difficulty)
          Just . . . had to take one of my pills.
                    (takes a pill)
          Pep me up.

Hockstader looks at him thoughtfully.

                         HOCKSTADER
          Joe, you believe in God, don't
          you?

                         CANTWELL
                    (promptly)
          Yes, I do.

                         HOCKSTADER
          And you believe there's a Hereafter?
          A Day of Judgment?

                         CANTWELL
                    (sincerely)
          I do. If I didn't think there
          was some meaning to all of this
          I wouldn't be able to go on. I'm
          a very religious guy, in a funny
          way.

Cantwell spreads the contents of the folder on a coffee
table.

                         HOCKSTADER
          I'm sure you are.
                    (sighs)
          Times like this I wish I was.
          Dying is no fun, let me tell you.
          And that's what I'm doing.

Cantwell has not been listening.

                         CANTWELL
                    (briskly)
          Now it's all here. Psychiatrist
          reports . . . everything. And don't
          ask how I got it. My "means"
          might've been ruthless but for
          once I think you'll agree the end
          was worth it.

Hockstader is taken aback at being ignored. He indicates the
papers contemptuously.

> HOCKSTADER
> What is all this . . . crap?

> CANTWELL
> Several years ago your candidate,
> William Russell, had what is known
> as a nervous breakdown.

> HOCKSTADER
> I know that.

> CANTWELL
> He was raving mad for almost a
> year.

> HOCKSTADER
> He was not raving mad. It was
> exhaustion from overwork . . .

> CANTWELL
> That was the press release. The
> real story's right here . . .

> HOCKSTADER
> I know the real story.

> CANTWELL
> Then you know it's political
> dynamite. A full report on his
> mental state. How he deserted
> his wife, how their marriage has
> always been a phony, a political
> front . . .

> HOCKSTADER
> I won't begin to speculate on how
> you got hold of this.

> CANTWELL
> And all the big words are there,
> manic depressive, paranoid pattern,
> attempted suicide . . .

> HOCKSTADER
> He never attempted suicide . . .

                    CANTWELL
I'm sorry. It says right here
that he did. See?
          (points to page)
There. Suicidal tendencies . . .

                    HOCKSTADER
Everybody's got suicidal <u>tendencies</u>.
But he never tried to kill himself.

                    CANTWELL
But the point is he <u>could</u>.

                    HOCKSTADER
I thought you said he <u>did</u> try.

                    CANTWELL
I did not say he did. I said he
could. And then all that combined
with playing around with women . . .

                    HOCKSTADER
So what?

                    CANTWELL
I suppose you find promiscuity
admirable?

                    HOCKSTADER
I couldn't care less. I was brought
up on a farm and the lesson of the
rooster was not entirely lost on
me. A lot of men need a lot of
women and there are worse faults,
let me tell you.

                    CANTWELL
          (suspiciously)
What do you mean by that?

                    HOCKSTADER
Just that there are rumors about
every public man. Why, when I
was in the White House they used
to say . . . well, it gave a lot of
people a lot of pleasure talkin'
about me. You know, when that
Kinsey fellow wrote that book about

                        HOCKSTADER (Cont.)
how many men were doin' this and
how many men were doin' that, I
couldn't help but think how right
along with all this peculiar activity,
there was a hell of a lot of <u>nothin'</u>
goin' on!

                        CANTWELL
All right, leaving the moral issue
out, do you think it a good idea
to elect a man President who is
mentally unstable?

                        HOCKSTADER
He is not mentally unstable and you
know it.

                        CANTWELL
            (inexorably)
A manic depressive? Apt to crack
up under stress?

Hockstader gets the point.

                        HOCKSTADER
So that's your little number,
is it?

                        CANTWELL
If you support Russell tonight,
I am going to see that every
delegate gets a copy of this
psychiatric report.

                        HOCKSTADER
            (stunned)
Are you giving <u>me</u> orders?

                        CANTWELL
            (through him)
And then I am going to challenge
Russell openly. I'm going to ask
him if he really feels that a man
with his mental record should be
President of the United States.
Frankly, if I were he, I'd pull
out before this . . .

                    CANTWELL (Cont.)
                 (indicates papers)
. . . hits the fan.

                    HOCKSTADER
You sure play rough, don't you?

                    CANTWELL
I regard this as a public service.
So I suggest you think twice
before endorsing this neurotic.

                    HOCKSTADER
Thank you for the suggestion.
Well, you have changed my mind,
Joe. I am now going to get your
political scalp.

Cantwell starts to door.

                    CANTWELL
                 (dangerously)
Don't mix with me, Hockstader.

                    HOCKSTADER
You can't touch me. But I can
send you right back to the insurance
business.
                 (removes his speech
                 from his pocket,
                 almost sadly)
And just think! I was going to
endorse you for President!

                    CANTWELL
I don't believe you.

                    HOCKSTADER
It's not that I mind your bein'
a bastard, don't get me wrong there
. . . it's your bein' such a stupid
bastard I object to!

                                        DISSOLVE TO:

22. INT. BALLROOM -- LONG SHOT

The ballroom is crowded with tables crowded with people.
A long table on a dais faces the diners. American flags

are draped behind the head table. The atmosphere is festive
but hectic. At the center of the head table sits a party
chairman type; on his right is Alice Russell; on his left,
Mabel Cantwell. On Alice's right, President Hockstader;
on Mabel's left sits GOVERNOR CLAYPOOLE, a trumpeting
politician from the South, a favorite son. Then Joe Cantwell.
On Hockstader's right sits Mrs. Gamadge; then William Russell.
Then CELEBRITY 1. Then John Merwin. Then CELEBRITY 2. Then
Oscar Anderson. Then Mrs. Claypoole. The rest of the table
is filled with dignitaries unfamiliar to us, and celebrities
too familiar. Still photographers are busy snapping pictures.

The chairman is on his feet, droning in the background. In
the foreground the CAMERA CUTS to Hockstader and Alice.

> CHAIRMAN'S VOICE
> (behind scene)
> A wonderful turnout for this fund-
> raising dinner. I want particularly
> to thank those stars who have given
> so generously of their time to be with
> us tonight.

He then names the celebrities; applause after each name.

Hockstader is turned away from Alice, talking to Tom, who
is just behind him. We cannot hear what Hockstader says,
nor can Alice, who is smiling and blinking rather nervously
at the battery of still photographers. Tom goes. Hockstader
turns to Alice.

> ALICE
> It's awfully hard to eat, with all
> these flasbulbs . . .

> HOCKSTADER
> Who eats? I never touch the swill at
> these banquets.

WAITER deals him a plate.

> HOCKSTADER
> Thank you, young man. You tell the
> cook, now, that that was a fine spread.

> WAITER
> Yes, sir . . . I will, sir.

.

                        HOCKSTADER
                    (muttered aside)
            Go on, Miss Alice, tell him you
            liked it.

                        ALICE
                    (gamely)
            I thought! . . . Waiter, I thought
            the dinner . . .

But the waiter has gone; Alice sighs.

                        HOCKSTADER
            Gotta be quicker than that.

                        ALICE
            I have the feeling that my smile
            has been hooked on, you know,
            just above the ears.. . .

Alice reaches for the highball glass in front of her.
Hockstader restrains her; a fresh set of flashbulbs goes
off.

                        HOCKSTADER
            Never let 'em catch you with a
            cup of the sinful grape . . .

                        ALICE
            But Bill says we're going to lose
            the South anyway . . .

                        HOCKSTADER
            Even so, keep your booze hid.
                    (motions to flower arrangement
                     in which he has secreted glass)
            Those vultures are just dyin' to catch
            you in the act.

                        ALICE
            What a lot of hypocrites we are!

                        HOCKSTADER
            When you play tennis you use a net,
            don't you?

                        ALICE
            Oh? Yes, I see what you mean.

                          ALICE (Cont.)
                     (CAMERA approaches)
          Your serve.

23.   MABEL AND CLAYPOOLE

                          CHAIRMAN'S VOICE
                        (background)
               Now we take great pleasure in
               presenting to this distinguished
               audience one of the most famous of
               living Americans, the leader of our
               party, the former President of the
               United States, Art Hockstader!

Tumultuous cheering. Hockstader makes his way to center
table and microphone; poses for still cameras. While this
is in the background, Mabel and Claypoole ignore it in
foreground.

                          MABEL
               Governor Claypoole, you are just
               an old meanie the way you're holding
               out on my Joe, who admires you more
               than any man in public life today,
               and that is no lie.

                          CLAYPOOLE
               Honey, I am all for Joe, all the way,
               but I am also a favorite son . . .

Mabel catches the waiter's hand as it snakes in for the
plate.

                          MABEL
               That was just the best dinner so
               far, so prompt and so hot. You
               vote for my Joe, now, come November . . .

                          WAITER
               Well, sure, yes, ma'am . . .

Mabel thrusts a button on him.

                          MABEL
               You wear that, now.

                              CLAYPOOLE
            You are the ideal wife, and if divorce
            was not a thing unheard of in politics,
            I would chuck Narcissa and run away with
            you.

                              MABEL
            It's a promise. But first you give
            my Joe your votes on the second ballot.

Claypoole laughs.

                                                    CUT TO:

24. HOCKSTADER

     beaming. Applause continues.

                              HOCKSTADER
            Thank you, thank you. I'm sort
            of like a clock; I only talk when
            I'm running.
                    (pleasant murmur)
            But I've been invited to say a few
            words tonight, and I've never been
            able to resist the sound of my own
            voice. Not that anybody ever pays
            me the slightest mind.
                    (laughter)

                                                    CUT TO:

25. RUSSELL AND MRS. GAMADGE

     Tom leans over and talks into Russell's ear. Mrs. Gamadge
     tries valiantly to hear what is said. Tom goes.

                              MRS. GAMADGE
            That was Art Hockstader's secretary,
            wasn't it?

     Russell nods. He is busy writing a note.

                              MRS. GAMADGE
            Secrets?

     Russell motions for waiter.

                        RUSSELL
                  (to waiter)
            Give this to Dick Jensen.   Table
            forty-one.

Waiter goes.

                        RUSSELL
                  (to Mrs. Gamadge)
            Just a little bird, telling me
            something.

He smiles pleasantly, despite tension.

                                          CUT TO:

26. <u>HOCKSTADER</u>

now at the microphone.

                        HOCKSTADER
            Now we are all of us going into that
            big convention and we are going to
            start voting and when we finish we
            are going to vote ourselves a President!

Huge applause.

CAMERA PANS ALONG table: the presidentials are tense,
expectant.

                        HOCKSTADER
            That is a great responsibility.
            For all of us. Luckily we have
            some fine men to choose from.
            There's my old friend and Attorney
            General . . . Now Senator Oscar Anderson.

                                          CUT TO:

27. <u>ANDERSON AND MRS. CLAYPOOLE</u>

She is a lean, dour Southern type.

                        MRS. CLAYPOOLE
            What very <u>warm</u> applause, Mr. Anderson.

                         ANDERSON
          Art Hockstader is a great American,
          Mrs. Claypoole.

                         MRS. CLAYPOOLE
          And a warm human being. I just hope
          he sees the light and supports my T. T.

Anderson gives her a look: <u>What?</u>

                                                   CUT TO:

28.   <u>HOCKSTADER</u>

                         HOCKSTADER
          And there's another old friend, the
          last flower of the Confederacy, and
          yet also a progressive liberal.
          Everybody's favorite son, Governor
          T. T. Claypoole.

                                                   CUT TO:

28A. <u>CLAYPOOLE</u>

                         CLAYPOOLE
                   (beams)
          Thank you . . . thank you, friends . . .

                         MRS. MERWIN
          Can you give a Rebel yell? . . .

                         CLAYPOOLE
          I can, Mrs. Merwin, but I'm not
          gonna. I am now a national statesman,
          not a mere regional politician.

                                                   CUT TO:

28B. <u>HOCKSTADER</u>

                         HOCKSTADER
          Then there's a fine young Westerner
          with a good record of minding his own
          business, unlike some of us (I name
          no names) -- Governor John Merwin.

                                                   CUT TO:

29. MERWIN AND CELEBRITY 2

                    CELEBRITY 2
          Well, get up, say something, do
          something! Make a speech. <u>I'll</u>
          make a speech.

                    MERWIN
          Later, _____. Right
          now we <u>just sit and smile</u> . . .

                    CELEBRITY 2
          Who needs it?

                                        CUT TO:

29A. HOCKSTADER

                    HOCKSTADER
          Now, we've had some bad old customs
          in this country; one was if you were
          a Jew or a Negro or a Catholic you
          couldn't get to be President. Well,
          as you've probably all heard, a
          Catholic can now be elected President.
          And soon we'll have a Jewish President,
          a Negro President, and then after all
          the minorities have been heard from,
          we'll do something for the downtrodden
          <u>majority</u> of this country -- I mean the
          ladies, and if there is ever a woman
          President, I see no reason why it
          shouldn't be the beautiful and energetic
          Sue-Ellen Gamadge!

     Mrs. Gamadge for one mad moment sees herself as President;
     dream fades; all applaud her.

                    MRS. GAMADGE
          What a tease Art is!

                    RUSSELL
          But you <u>are</u> the ideal President for
          the women. No, I really mean it,
          Sue-Ellen.

     Mrs. Gamadge -- on her face a plot is writ.

                        HOCKSTADER
        Now we come to what they call the
        front-runners. The two fellows who
        got the most pledged votes.

                                              CUT TO:

29B.   CANTWELL

       He watches with a fixed smile, like an animal ready to strike.

                        HOCKSTADER
                     (very straight)
        One of them, while in the Senate,
        alerted the nation to the dangers
        of the Mafia. As President, he'd
        be able to see to it that the leaders
        of the Mafia who have so far escaped
        the law will be rought to justice.
        This young man is also known for his
        profound sense of right and wrong.
        Of course, sometimes that means they're
        wrong and we're right.
                     (beginning laughter)
        But that's true. They are wrong. We
        are right. Joe Cantwell!

       Storm of applause. Joe waves to the crowd.

                        HOCKSTADER
        Finally, there's my old friend and
        comrade in arms. One of this country's
        great Secretaries of State. He's a lot
        smarter than me -- and that's sayin'
        quite a lot despite what you sometimes
        read in the papers!
                     (laughter)
        Bill Russell, you and Alice take a bow!

       Great applause. Russell and Alice bow.

                        HOCKSTADER
        And now one last word . . .

                                              CUT TO:

29C.   MABEL

MABEL
(excitedly)
Here it comes, T. T. This is it!

CUT TO:

29D. <u>HOCKSTADER</u>

HOCKSTADER
So tomorrow we're going to nominate
one of these men and the one we
nominate is going to get the full
support of every man and woman here,
so that come November, we win, for
the good of this country!

Hockstader sits down; a startled silence, then applause.
Chairman tries to silence crowd.

CUT TO:

30. <u>MRS. GAMADGE AND RUSSELL</u>

MRS. GAMADGE
(looks at Russell sharply)
Well! Well!

RUSSELL
(wanly)
Not what I would call a <u>hearty</u>
endorsement . . .

MRS. GAMADGE
(grimly)
That's no endorsement at all. He's
not for either one of you. Oh, this
means an open convention!
(rises)
How the women hate open conventions!

She goes.
* * *

[30A. *CELEBRITY 1*
She is now singing "I Could Go On Singing" but no one is
listening. Newsmen are dashing out of the banquet room.
Hockstader has vanished. The presidentials are trying
to escape from the table.]

CUT TO:

31. <u>CANTWELL</u>

Mabel has crossed to him; she leans across him. Cameras
start to flash. Both grin and pose for cameras while
talking under their breath.

                    MABEL
          What do we do now?

                    CANTWELL
          Just the break we needed.
                    (smiling to cameras)
          How's this?

                    MABEL
          But Hockstader's still against you.

                    CANTWELL
          Yes. But he isn't <u>for</u> Russell.
          That's the point. Keep smiling.

                                        CUT TO:

31A. <u>RUSSELL AND ALICE</u>

They are trying to leave the room. Reporters questioning.

                    REPORTER
          Mr. Russell, why didn't President
          Hockstader . . .

                    RUSSELL
          Sorry . . .

                    REPORTER
          Will you get his endorsement?

Russell does not answer.

Celebrity 1 has finished her song to applause. The chairman is
speaking.

                    CHAIRMAN
          Wonderful evening . . . an inspiring
          occasion . . . all of us renewed . . . by
          the democratic process . . . great
          country . . . malice toward none . . .

While we hear these bits of his speech, CAMERA REVEALS
Hockstader has gone. Russell is on his feet, mechanically
smiling as he starts away from table. Cantwell and Mabel
are also on their feet, smiling for cameras. A melee.
T. T. Claypoole embraces Mrs. Gamadge for cameras.

>   CLAYPOOLE
>   I'm here to say to the people
>   of this country that I am in this
>   race to the end! The field is now
>   wide open. Anybody can win!

                                        CUT TO:

32. <u>INT. HOCKSTADER SUITE</u>

Hockstader is seated. Russell stands. Tom is in the
bedroom.

>   RUSSELL
>   Why?

A long moment.

>   HOCKSTADER
>   (awkwardly)
>   Bill, this isn't easy to say, but
>   I came here to nominate Cantwell
>   for President.

>   RUSSELL
>   I knew that this morning.

>   HOCKSTADER
>   Did you now?

>   RUSSELL
>   (drily)
>   I have <u>some</u> gift for politics.

>   HOCKSTADER
>   I never said you didn't.

>   RUSSELL
>   But tonight you warned me about
>   Cantwell's smear. So that means
>   you've changed your mind about
>   him . . . doesn't it? . . .

                    HOCKSTADER
Yes . . . I have changed my mind. About
him. He lost me because he wasn't
smart. He made a mistake. He
figured I was goin' back to you when
I wasn't. You got my message. Joe
didn't. Now that's a serious error.
Shows he * * * doesn't understand character,
and a President, if he * * * doesn't understand
anything else, has got to understand people.
Then he got flustered when I needled him.
A President * * * doesn't get flustered when a
man gives him the needle. He keeps a
straight face, like poker.
          (smiles)
Like you're doin' right now. But
what does Joe do? He don't run
scared; he runs terrified. He fires
off a cannon to kill a bug. And that
is just plain dumb and I mean to
knock him off . . . which means that you,
I guess, are goin' to be our next
President.

                    RUSSELL
President . . . but by default. Because
you still have your doubts about me,
don't you?

                    HOCKSTADER
Yes. * * * I'm sorry.
          (pause)
Anyway, I'm sort of working for you
now and my advice is: start scrappin'.
You got to counteract this head-doctor
report . . .

---

32.   [don't] [don't] [don't]

[You're not decisive. You never were.

          RUSSELL
I may not shoot from the hip, but . . .

          HOCKSTADER
Sometimes you don't shoot at all.]

                    RUSSELL
My doctor's on his way here now.
He'll testify I'm . . . all right.

                    HOCKSTADER
You aren't crazy, are you?

                    RUSSELL
Anyone who wants to be President is
crazy.

                    HOCKSTADER
Speak for yourself, son.

                    RUSSELL
Jensen just found out that Don
Cantwell bribed a nurse to give him
my case history. The clinic plans
to sue for theft.

                    HOCKSTADER
That's the stuff!

                    RUSSELL
I think we can scare Joe off. I'm
not too worried. Right now I need
* * * votes.

                    HOCKSTADER
I can get you Claypoole. * * *

                    RUSSELL
How much?

                    HOCKSTADER
Vice President.

                    RUSSELL
Too high.

                    HOCKSTADER
Picky, aren't we?

---

32.   [thirty-six]

             [That's thirty-three.]

                          RUSSELL

Yes.
            (smiles)
And decisive. What about Merwin?

                       HOCKSTADER

Vice President?

                          RUSSELL

Yes.

                       HOCKSTADER

Okay. Anderson?

                         RUSSELL

If I have to.

                       HOCKSTADER

I'll see what I can do. Oh, I
tell you there is nothing like a
dirty, low-down political fight
to bring the roses to your cheeks.

                          RUSSELL

How do you feel?

                       HOCKSTADER

Immortal! Before the sunrise, Joe
Cantwell will be out of presidential
politics.

                          RUSSELL

And I will be . . . in?

                       HOCKSTADER
            (a beat)
Yes. You will be in. And I hope
I'm doin' the right thing.
            (shouts)
Come on, Tom! We're goin' into
battle.

A GENERAL SWIFT MONTAGE OF THE NIGHT'S PROGRESS

33. INT. ANDERSON HEADQUARTERS

"Anderson for President" signs. In a back room, Anderson and
Hockstader have their heads together. Anderson supporters
hurry about. Tom is in foreground with several Andersonites.

                    ANDERSONITE 1
What's this about Russell being
sick or something?

                    TOM
He looks okay to me.

                    ANDERSON
Who's the old boy supporting?

                    TOM
He's not supporting Cantwell.

                    ANDERSONITE 3
Oscar Anderson is perhaps the greatest
conservationist in the United States . . .

                    ANDERSONITE 2
His soil erosion control program . . .

                    ANDERSONITE 1
Old Art ought to come out for
somebody like Oscar.

                    ANDERSONITE 3
We had this dust bowl and now it is
a flowering garden . . .

Hockstader appears, beaming; takes Tom's arm.

                    HOCKSTADER
Good evening, gentlemen.

They proceed to door amid many handshakes: "Hi, Mr. President",
"You remember me, don't you?", etc.

34. EXT. ANDERSON SUITE

Hockstader and Tom are suddenly faced with Cantwell and Don.
The press is excited. Hockstader and Cantwell shake hands.

                    CANTWELL
Wonderful to see you, Mr. President.

                    HOCKSTADER
Nice to see <u>you</u>, Joe.

                    CANTWELL
How's my old buddy Oscar Anderson?

                              HOCKSTADER
          Just fine!
                    (under his voice, only
                    for Cantwell's ears)
          We got him.
                    (louder)
          Keep up the good work, Joe.

                              CANTWELL
          Thank you, Mr. President. I sure
          will.

Hockstader and Tom plunge into crowd of newsmen. Cantwell
enters suite.

35. EXT. AMBASSADOR SWIMMING POOL -- NIGHT

with a pool. Japanese lanterns. Claypoole and Hockstader
are here. Assorted politicians and rich laymen wander
about; the mood is very much that of a party. Tom has been
buttonholed by a T. T. supporter.

                              SUPPORTER
          You with the Prez?

                              TOM
          I'm his secretary.

                              SUPPORTER
          Well, you tell him ol' T. T. done
          more for civil rights in our state
          than anybody ever has before or
          since . . .

                              TOM
          Since what?

                              SUPPORTER
          T. T. would make a fine conservative
          President with a dynamic and progressive
          approach to real problems . . .

                              TOM
          Like integration?

                              SUPPORTER
          T. T. has done more for integration
          than any governor we ever had.

                          TOM
          How many integrated schools are
          there in your state?

                          SUPPORTER
          None, thank God, but we are making
          the most remarkable progress.

36. <u>OMITTED</u>

37. <u>EXT. MERWIN SUITE</u>

     Newsmen in corridor. Placard: "MERWIN HEADQUARTERS."
     Hockstader with Tom.

                          REPORTER 1
          Mr. President . . .

                          REPORTER 2
          You supporting Russell tomorrow . . . ?

                          HOCKSTADER
          Wait till tomorrow.

     Hockstader crosses to door, which suddenly opens: the
     Cantwell brothers emerge. Delight from the newsmen.
     Flashbulbs go off as Joe clasps Hockstader's hand.

                          CANTWELL
                     (jovially)
          You're up kind of late, Mr. President.

                          HOCKSTADER
          Just making my rounds, spreading
          sweetness and light.

                          CANTWELL
          Well, we don't have to worry about
          John Merwin, Mr. President. He's
          with us every inch of the way.

                          HOCKSTADER
          You don't say?

                          DON
          He's going to run with Joe.

                          HOCKSTADER
          Well, that's nice to know.

Hockstader slips into the room; Tom follows. Cantwell beams
at reporters.

                    CANTWELL
          We're over the top!

38. INT. MERWIN SUITE

The usual crowd of eager volunteers, campaign literature,
buttons. Hockstader and Merwin are glimpsed for a moment
in a large closet, talking intently among the coats.

Tom is again surrounded by PARTISANS.

                    PARTISAN 1
          Why doesn't Hockstader support our
          boy . . . ?

                    TOM
          For Vice President . . . ?

                    PARTISAN 2
          President.

                    PARTISAN 3
          New broom . . .

                    TOM
          What about Russell?

                    PARTISAN 2
          What about Cantwell? He just
          promised us the key to the
          Treasury.

                    PARTISAN 3
          You got to admit, we're in the
          best spot.
                    (gestures at Merwin)
          The man in the middle . . .

                    PARTISAN 1
          . . . who calls the turns.

39. INT. RUSSELL NERVE CENTER

Late as it is, the nerve center is half full. Jensen is
on the telephone.

                        AIDE
                     (on phone)
          Who's covering Minnesota?

                       JENSEN
          He's at the airport? Okay. Bring
          him straight here. But don't let
          anybody see him.

He hangs up. Turns to the ineluctable Janet.

                       JENSEN
          This is the end of Joe Cantwell.

                       JANET
          I hope so. Whatever it is: Jim
          Connor, California delegation, just
          called . . .

                       JENSEN
          Another split in the Golden State?
          Good news.

Janet crosses out of shot. Jensen picks up phone, humming
"California, Here I Come." Russell enters in shirtsleeves.

                      RUSSELL
          Anderson just called. He's agreed
          to run with me.

                       JENSEN
                     (hangs up)
          Anderson? Well, why not?
                    (checks board)
          With his sixty-eight votes on the
          first ballot, we're * * * nearly in.

                      RUSSELL
          Art made the deal. I wish he'd
          called me first.

                       JENSEN
          Anderson's not bad, you know.

Telephone rings. Jensen answers it.

                       JENSEN
                    (into phone)
          Yes. He's here.

Russell takes phone.

                    RUSSELL
               (into phone)
     Who? Oh, Governor Claypoole.
     Hello. You saw Art. Good. Good.
     Oh, he did. Yes.
               (frowns)
     You what? . . . Well, yes, of course
     I'm happy to have you on the same
     ticket with me -- if I'm nominated,
     of course. Look, let me call you
     back. I've got a meeting here . . .
     Oh, good, yes. Thank you. Yes.
               (hangs up, furious)
     Art promised the Vice Presidency
     to Claypoole.

                    JENSEN
     Well, why not have two Vice Presidents?
     It's never been done, but this is the
     party of progress . . .

                    RUSSELL
     I don't find that very funny.

                    JENSEN
     Listen, play along with the old
     buzzard.

The phone rings again. Jensen answers.

                    JENSEN
               (into phone)
     Yes. Who? Oh, hello, Mrs. Gamadge . . .

                    RUSSELL
               (bellows)
     No! No! I'm not here.

Russell storms from the room.

                    JENSEN
               (into phone)
     A little bird told you T. T. is
     going to be Vice President? Well,
     we had sort of counted on you, Mrs.
     Gamadge. Why not? The hand that
     rocks the cradle, and all that . . .

Eyes to heaven as the blurred voice of Mrs. Gamadge continues
into the receiver.

                                          DISSOLVE:

40. EXT. AMBASSADOR HOTEL -- DAY

The front door. Jensen is coming in. Senator Lazarus is
going out. A few newsmen record their meeting.

                    JENSEN
          Oh, Senator Lazarus . . .

                    LAZARUS
          Hi, Dick. On my way to the
          convention.
                    (lowers voice)
          What's this about Bill not being
          all right?

                    JENSEN
          The usual Cantwell smear.

                    LAZARUS
          Will it hurt?

                    JENSEN
          Not as much as what we've got
          on Joe.

                    LAZARUS
          Well, you better get busy. I'm
          having a tough time holding my
          boys in line.

                    JENSEN
          We'll make it on the second ballot.
          That's a promise.

Lazarus gets into car. Jensen goes inside.

41. INT. CANTWELL NERVE CENTER

Much activity; especially the walkie-talkies. On the TV set
we can see Howard K. Smith. Cantwell, in shirtsleeves, watches.

                    SMITH
          Today is the big day. At noon the
          balloting will start for President.

                         SMITH (Cont.)
          William Russell remains in the lead.
          But he does not have the 761 votes
          needed for nomination on the first
          ballot, assuming that all the favorite
          sons hold tight, which they are expected
          to do . . .

Cantwell turns away from the set, scowling. Don joins him,
carrying a list of states.

                         DON
          We're okay on the first.

                         CANTWELL
          Okay? We don't have Merwin. We
          don't have Anderson. Even that ape
          Claypoole is sitting tight . . .

                         AIDE 1
                    (walkie-talkie)
          This the Maryland delegation?

                         DON
          But they have to * * * hold on the first.
          On the second we'll get T. T. . . . .

                         CANTWELL
          I don't trust him.

Aide crosses to brothers.

                         AIDE 2
          Oscar Anderson just announced he's
          in the race to the end.

Cantwell mutters an obscenity. Aide begins moving away.
Don looks miserable.

                         AIDE 1
          Just testing.

                         DON
          Anyway, there's still Merwin.
          * * * Maybe we can still make a
          deal for Vice President.

                        CANTWELL
        We didn't get anywhere last night.

                        DON
        Neither did Hockstader. Everybody's
        sitting tight.

                        CANTWELL
        What've we got in the file on
        Merwin?

        DON

        Nothing.

                        CANTWELL
        There must be something we could
        use to shake up that little . . . Don,
        we've got to release that psychiatrist's
        report.

                        DON
        I wouldn't, Joe . . .

                        CANTWELL
                (snarls)
        Of course you wouldn't. That's why
        you're a loser and I'm not.

                        DON
                (patiently)
        At least wait till after the first
        ballot . . .

Mabel joins them, dressed to the teeth.

                        MABEL
        Honey, I am on my way to a
        rendezvous with Alice Russell.

                        CANTWELL
                (vaguely)
        Oh, swell . . .

                        MABEL
        There's going to be a joint press
        conference for all the wives in
        the Baroque Room, downstairs.

                        CANTWELL
          Swell. You look swell, too.

                         MABEL
          Oh, I feel today is <u>the</u> day!

Cantwell gives her a quick kiss. She goes.

                        CANTWELL
                      (to Don)
          Okay. We sweat out the first ballot.
          But have the stuff ready.

                          DON
          It's ready. One mimeographed copy
          for each delegate, neatly bound.

                        CANTWELL
          I'm sorry what I said, Don, about
          your being a loser.

                          DON
          It's true.

                        CANTWELL
                      (sighs)
          Nothing's easy, is it?

                          DON
                      (smiles)
          Nothing good.

42. <u>INT. BAROQUE ROOM -- HOTEL</u>

      The wives of the candidates are meeting in the hotel nightclub.
      The room is crowded with newsmen; Alice and Mabel together
      with the other candidates' wives (Mrs. Anderson, Mrs.
      Claypoole, Mrs. Merwin and Mrs. Gamadge) have been sitting
      side by side. The meeting is breaking up.

                         MABEL
          Well, as for me, I just hope the best
          man wins . . . I mean, for the country
          and everything.

Reporters go.

                     MRS. GAMADGE
          Amen to that.

                    MRS. GAMADGE (Cont.)
                  (to Mrs. Claypoole)
Narcissa Claypoole, I've never seen
you more radiant.

                    MRS. CLAYPOOLE
Oh, thank you, Sue-Ellen. 'Bye now.

She leaves.

                    MRS. GAMADGE
                  (turning to Mabel)
I must say Narcissa Claypoole has
never looked more sickly.

                    MABEL
It's that awful hat.
                  (she turns to Mrs.
                  Anderson)
Oh, Mrs. Anderson, I love that color
blue.

                    MRS. GAMADGE
Yes, dear, it's the blue for you.

                    MRS. ANDERSON
Thank you very much, ladies.
Goodbye.

Mrs. Anderson goes. Murmured goodbyes from the others.

                    MRS. GAMADGE
                  (to Mabel)
What taste!

                    MABEL
                  (turning to Mrs. Merwin)
As for Mrs. Merwin, well, I must say
she is the most decorative of all us
girls.

                    MRS. MERWIN
I wish I were.

                    MABEL
Especially with all those votes that
husband of hers is sitting on this
very moment . . .

Mabel pats Mrs. Merwin fondly and charges after Alice Russell, who has started to leave.

                    MRS. MERWIN
               (to no one in particular)
          I'd better be going.
               (she tries to get Mrs.
               Gamadge's attention)
          Oh, Mrs. Gamadge, I was so looking
          forward to chatting with you. My
          husband . . .

                    MRS. GAMADGE
               (giving her the brush)
          Yes, dear.
               (she also rushes after Alice)
          Oh, Mrs. Russell . . . just a minute . . .

Thoroughly ignored by all, the crestfallen Mrs. Merwin turns and leaves. Mabel has now trapped Alice Russell near the bar.

                    MABEL
          I must say that was an ordeal,
          wasn't it?

                    ALICE
          I'm sure it wasn't for you. I
          mean, you've done so much of this
          sort of thing. I'd better go.

                    MABEL
          Oh, come on, let's visit a minute.

She leads Alice to the bar and starts pouring as Mrs. Gamadge arrives.

                    MABEL
          You know, I have always said, haven't
          I, Sue-Ellen, that of all the women
          in public life, Alice Russell is the
          most courageous.

                    ALICE
               (curiously)
          In what way, courageous?

                    MABEL
          Why, that committee you were on!

                    MRS. GAMADGE
                (suddenly alert)
Committee? What committee?

                    MABEL
                (ready for the kill)
You know -- in New York City, the
one where you did all that work for
birth control.

                    MRS. GAMADGE
Birth control! I didn't know that.

                    ALICE
Well, it was twenty years ago. And
of course I'm not supposed to mention
it now . . .
                (to Mabel)
as you know.

                    MRS. GAMADGE
I should hope not! You'll have the
Catholics down on us like a ton of
bricks. The rhythm cycle, yes . . .
                (makes a vague circular
                motion with her hand)
but anything else . . . is out.

                    MABEL
Of course, I guess you didn't know
then your husband would be running
for President one day and when you
do that, you just can't afford to
offend a lot of nice people who vote.

                    ALICE
I realize that. We must offend no
one. Of course, if you offend no
one, you don't please anyone very
much either, do you?

There is a pause.

                    MRS. GAMADGE
Well, now!

                    MABEL
                (overlapping)
Well, hooray for Mrs. Russell! Do

                              MABEL (Cont.)
                    you know, you sounded just like your
                    husband then?

                              ALICE
                    I should like to think intelligence
                    is contagious. But I'm afraid it
                    isn't -- at least, in my case. * * *
                    I'm not awfully quick.

                              MABEL
                    Oh, yes, you are, honey!

GIRL enters.

                              GIRL
                    Mrs. Russell. The photographers
                    are waiting.

                              ALICE
                    Thank you.

                              MABEL
                    Oh, this must be one of the Volunteer
                    Girls for Russell. They're so good-
                    looking! Everybody's remarked on
                    them.

Alice gives her a look intended to kill. She and girl
start to leave.

                              MABEL
                         (one last shot)
                    Oh, by the way, how is Mr. Russell's
                    health? I mean really? I thought
                    he looked so peaked last night at the
                    dinner and someone did say . . .

                              ALICE
                         (grimly)
                    The reporters are gone, Mrs. Cantwell.
                    You know as well as I do he's perfectly
                    all right. Goodbye.

                              MRS. GAMADGE
                    'Bye.

_____

42.   [Bill has the brains.]

Alice goes.

>   MABEL
> Well . . . listen to her!   "The reporters
> are gone, Mrs. Cantwell"!

Mabel and Mrs. Gamadge start to door.

>   MRS. GAMADGE
> She's not cozy, I'm afraid. Not
> cozy at all.

43. <u>INT. HOTEL LOBBY</u>

Together, CAMERA WITH THEM, Mabel and Mrs. Gamadge make their
way to elevators; politicians wave to them, greet them.

>   MABEL
>   (gaily)
> How you, Senator? You vote for
> my Joe, now!

>   SENATOR
> Your wish is my command. What
> are you up to, Sue-Ellen?

>   MRS. GAMADGE
> I'm just chaperoning the girls.
>   (to Mabel)
> I don't like what Joe's doing.
> It's just plain dirty.

>   MABEL
> <u>It</u> <u>is</u> <u>a</u> <u>public</u> <u>service</u>. I read
> that report on him.
>   (to group)
> Hiya, boys!

>   BOYS
> Hello, Mabel.
> Good luck today.
> We're with you.

>   MRS. GAMADGE
> Well, I'm a loyal Party worker and
> the women are solidly behind Bill
> Russell.

238 The Best Man

> MABEL

Under him is more their usual
position.

It's just sex, sex, sex morning,
noon and night with Bill Russell,
and that is just plain immature . . .
> (to group at elevator)

"Go with Joe!"

They cheer her good-naturedly.

> MABEL
> (to Mrs. Gamadge)

And we don't want an immature
President, now, do we?

They enter elevator.

44. INT. RUSSELL SUITE -- BATHROOM

Russell is in the bathtub. T. T. Claypoole is sitting on
the commode.

> CLAYPOOLE

I'm with you, Bill. I just wanted
to tell you that myself. I talked
to Art last night, and he told me
about your high hopes for me and
the country.

> RUSSELL

I appreciate that, T. T.

> CLAYPOOLE

Now, first ballot I got to hold on.
My people back home sent me here as
a favorite son and I cannot betray
their trust. But second ballot, I
switch to you. That is a promise.
A solemn promise.

> * * *RUSSELL

Thanks, T. T.

T. T. takes Russell's hand, which is covered with soap:
a disastrous, slimy handshake.

                    CLAYPOOLE
By the way, there's a rumor makin'
the rounds that Joe's got something
on you that can knock you off.

                    RUSSELL
I'm not worried.

                    CLAYPOOLE
No? Well, keep out of trouble and
try not to make too many inflammatory
statements about integration . . .

                    RUSSELL
I promise only to quote Abraham
Lincoln.

                    CLAYPOOLE
         (flatly)
Well, he started the Civil War --
I hope you are less ambitious.
'Bye now.

Claypoole goes. Jensen enters.

                    JENSEN
You got him?

                    RUSSELL
Second ballot. So he says.

Russell reaches for towel. Jensen goes into bedroom,
studies newspapers.

44A.   INT. BEDROOM

                    JENSEN
Bill, you may have to pull a Nixon.

Russell dresses behind half-open door.

                    RUSSELL'S VOICE
And what does 'pull a Nixon' mean?

                    JENSEN
Go on television and cry on the
nation's shoulder. With two cocker
spaniels.

                         RUSSELL'S VOICE
          And tell them I'm not crazy? No.

Russell enters, shirt inside jacket, tie in place, buttons
still to be done.

                         RUSSELL
          I admit it's possible to look directly
          into a camera and persuade the people
          I won't steal their money, but I
          promise you, Dick, you can't look a
          camera in the face and say, "Honest,
          I'm not crazy, I just had a nervous
          breakdown like any regular fellow
          might." No, it won't work.

                         JENSEN
          Why not?

                         RUSSELL
          Because it won't. And even if it
          did, I couldn't do it.
                    (chuckles)
          I might laugh. It's too idiotic.

                         JENSEN
                    (looks at watch)
          Eighty seconds to dress.

                         RUSSELL
          The record still stands -- it's
          forty seconds.

Hockstader enters.

                         HOCKSTADER
                    (cheerily)
          Well, there he is -- our candidate . . .

                         JENSEN
                    (sourly)
          On the fiftieth ballot . . .

                         HOCKSTADER
                    (soothingly)
          Now, things don't look that black.
          T. T. come to see you?

RUSSELL
Yes. We agreed that all colored
people are highly musical, with
wonderful white teeth, but essentially
children who never telephone when
they aren't coming to work.

HOCKSTADER
(to Jensen)
Who wound him up this morning?

JENSEN
Not I, said the campaign manager.

Russell starts to eat breakfast and read papers at the same
time.

HOCKSTADER
I just heard the head doctor was here.

JENSEN
(nods)
He's preparing a statement to the
effect that we're not crazy.

HOCKSTADER
Even so, those big words like manic-
mania sound pretty scary to the
average person.

JENSEN
Anybody's case history sounds scary.

Russell looks up from paper.

RUSSELL
In the South a candidate for sheriff
once got elected by claiming that
his opponent's wife was a thespian.

During this thunderclap of laughter, aide crosses to Jensen,
gives him a note; Jensen goes. Russell then turns to
Hockstader.

RUSSELL
I must thank you for the three Vice
Presidents you got me last night.

HOCKSTADER
Two and a half. Merwin's on the
fence. He's holding tight.
          (sighs)
They all are, waiting . . .

RUSSELL
Waiting for Joe and me to bleed to
death. What are we going to do?

HOCKSTADER
Stop the rumors. That's the first
thing. Now, I got it figured . . .

Jensen enters with plump man of forty-five (SHELDON BASCOMB).

JENSEN
This is Sheldon Bascomb.

HOCKSTADER
          (irritably)
Who the hell is Sheldon Bascomb?

Hockstader turns, realizes that the man is already in the
room. He flashes his presidential smile, crosses to Bascomb,
hand outstretched.

HOCKSTADER
If you'll excuse me, sir.

BASCOMB
That's all right. I . . . I never thought
I'd meet a President.

Bascomb runs his shake hand against his trouser leg.

BASCOMB
My hands sweat. I . . . I'm nervous,
I guess. You see, I just now came
in from Wilmington, where I live --
outside Wilmington's actually where
I live, a suburb you never heard of
called . . .

RUSSELL
          (suspiciously)
Dick, what have you been up to?

                    JENSEN
              (quickly)
Mr. Bascomb served in the army with
Joe Cantwell . . .

                    HOCKSTADER
In the army?
              (starts to beam with
              anticipation)
Ah . . . ah . . . Now we're getting somewhere.
Well, what was it? Was he a member
of the Ku Klux Klan? The Communist
Party? Or did he run away when the
guns went off?

                    BASCOMB
Well, sir, Mr. President, sir, uh,
we weren't anywheres around where
there were guns . . .

                    JENSEN
They were both in the Aleutians.
On the island of Adak. The
Quartermaster Corps.

                    BASCOMB
              (nods)
We were there for a year -- well,
maybe more like eighteen months for
me, and, oh, maybe sixteen, seventeen
months for Joe -- he came there
February '43 and I got there . . .

                    RUSSELL
I'm sorry, Mr. Bascomb, but I'm
afraid we're not interested . . .

                    HOCKSTADER
Now shush, Bill. And let's hear
the dirt, whatever it is.

                    BASCOMB
Well . . . Joe . . .
              (pauses in an agony
              of embarrassment)
Oh, I sure hate talking about him,
telling something so awful . . .

JENSEN
I had a lead on this months ago.
I finally tracked it down . . . Tell
them, Mr. Bascomb.

BASCOMB
Well, Joe Cantwell was a captain
and I was a captain and Joe Cantwell
was . . . you know how it is sometimes
when there's all those men together
and . . . and . . .

JENSEN
And no female companionship . . .

BASCOMB
That's right, though we had some
nurses later on, but not enough to
make much difference. I mean, there
were all those men . . .

JENSEN
(helpfully)
And no women.

RUSSELL
(irritated)
Oh, come on, Dick, stop it, will
you?

HOCKSTADER
(soothingly)
Now . . . now, let's not get ahead of
ourselves.

RUSSELL
You know Joe isn't that . . .

HOCKSTADER
I find this very interesting.
Mr. Bascomb . . . Captain Bascomb, I
should say . . .

BASCOMB
(gabbling)
I was a major, actually, promoted
just before my discharge in '46.
I'm in the Reserve . . . the <u>inactive</u>

                    BASCOMB (Cont.)
Reserve . . . but if there was another
war I would be . . .

                    HOCKSTADER
                (through him)
Major Bascomb, am I to understand
by the way you are beating slowly
around the bush that Joe Cantwell
is what . . . when I was a boy . . . we
called a degenerate?

                    BASCOMB
                (relieved to have
                the word said)
Yes, sir, Mr. President, sir, that's
just what I mean . . .

                    RUSSELL
                (amused in spite of
                himself)
I don't believe it! Nobody with
that awful wife and those ugly
children could be anything but
normal!

                    HOCKSTADER
Bill! Patience. Whether you
believe it or not is beside the
point.

                    RUSSELL
But even if it is true, so what?

                    HOCKSTADER
                (patiently and slowly)
Bill, I too am a tolerant man. I
personally do not care if Joe Cantwell
enjoys deflowering sheep by the light
of the full moon. But I am interested
in finding a way to stop him cold.

                    RUSSELL
Look here, Art. I am the one running
for President, not you.
                (to Jensen, grimly)
And as for you, Dick . . .

                    JENSEN
               (growing desperate)
     Bill, at least <u>listen</u> to the man.

                    RUSSELL
     No!

                    HOCKSTADER
     I'm beginnin' to wonder if maybe
     I'm tryin' to help the wrong team.

                    RUSSELL
               (losing control)
     Perhaps you are. Perhaps you'd
     be happier with Cantwell, helping
     him throw his mud!

A tense silence. Hockstader remains impassive. Russell
recovers himself quickly. He is contrite.

                    RUSSELL
     Sorry.

                    HOCKSTADER
               (wheedling)
     No, Bill, as a favor to an old
     man in his . . . sunset years, will
     you just listen to Major Bascomb?
     That's all. Just listen.

                    RUSSELL
     All right, Art. I'll listen.
     But only as a favor . . . to a friend.

Hockstader crosses to the dazed Bascomb.

                    HOCKSTADER
     After all, how often does a million
     dollars . . .
               (pats Bascomb)
     . . . drop in your lap? Not to mention
     the Presidency.
               (propels Bascomb to a
               chair as Jensen goes
               into bedroom)
     Sit down, Major Bascomb, sit down.
     Please. Make yourself comfortable.
     Fact, I will mix you a drink myself

>   HOCKSTADER (Cont.)
> with these old skilled fingers, and
> while I do you will tell us your story.
>   (crosses to bar)
> Omitting no details, no matter how
> sordid.

45. <u>OMITTED</u>

46. <u>INT. CANTWELL SUITE</u>

Cantwell is at TV set. Claypoole studies dossier. A
walkie-talkie is close at hand.

>   CANTWELL
>   (scowls)
> There goes * * * Delaware. <u>And</u> the
> first ballot.
>   (to Claypoole)
> Now we start to play rough.
>   (indicates dossier)

Cantwell picks up walkie-talkie.

>   CANTWELL
> Don? Yeah, * * * I'm watching the
> vote. Get ready to pass the stuff
> out. Soon as the ballot's over.
> During the recess. Swell.
>   (hang up)

>   CLAYPOOLE
> That does it for me. I'm with you,
> Joe. I'm going right down to the
> Arena and switch my delegation.

>   CANTWELL
> You won't regret it, T. T.

>   CLAYPOOLE
> I look forward to running with you.

---

46.   [Pennsylvania]

           [I saw]

                    CANTWELL
I think we're a pretty darn swell
team . . .

                    CLAYPOOLE
But on this integration issue . . .

                    CANTWELL
You don't have to worry about me.
That's a promise.

                    CLAYPOOLE
          (sighs)
Nice thing about you, Joe, is you
can <u>sound</u> like a liberal, but at
heart you're an American. That's
a rare gift. Not since Dick Nixon
has there been anybody like you . . .

Telephone rings. Mabel appears from bedroom.

                    MABEL
I'll answer it, honey. Hi, T. T.

                    CLAYPOOLE
How you?

                    MABEL
I had the nicest chat with your
lovely wife Narcissa.
          (on phone)
Who? <u>Dick Jensen</u>! Why, yes!
          (to Cantwell, who
          has leapt for phone)
This is it! They're givin' up!

                    CLAYPOOLE
          (at door)
I'm on my way. See you in the
White House, Joe.

Claypoole exits.

                    CANTWELL
          (into phone)
Hi, Dick. Howsa boy? Fine . . . Well,
gosh, I don't see how I can delay
much longer. I've told everybody:

                    CANTWELL (Cont.)
    right after the first ballot. Which
    won't be long.
                    (squints at set)
    * * * Of course, I'd sort of hoped Bill
    would be helpful. You know, for the
    Party's sake. He could back out so
    easily now, on this health issue . . .
    Yeah? Well, frankly, I don't see
    any point of postponing . . . Do I know
    who? Sheldon Bascomb? No, I don't
    think so . . . Where?
                    (harshly)
    I want to see Russell. Right now!
    Okay. After the first ballot, during
    the recess . . . I'll meet him there.

He hangs up, frowning.

                    MABEL
    Well, honey, what did he say? Come
    on now . . . give with the T. L.!

Cantwell picks up walkie-talkie connection.

                    CANTWELL
    Don. Hold that stuff. I said:
    Hold it! And get back here. Fast.

Cantwell hangs up.

Cantwell sits down, thinking hard. Mabel approaches,
panic beginning.

                    MABEL
    Joe, what did Russell say to you?
    What's he doing to you?

Cantwell looks at her blankly. Mabel begins to understand.

                    MABEL
    It's not . . . it's not . . .

Mabel stops. Slowly, Cantwell nods. Mabel, horrified,
sits beside him on the bed, her arm around him.

---

46.   [We're almost up to South Dakota now.]

                              MABEL
                            (softly)
                    Oh, my God!

47.   INT. RUSSELL SUITE -- MED. SHOT

Bascomb has just finished his story. Russell stands, back
to Bascomb. Hockstader starts to rise from sofa to give
Bascomb some papers he's been studying. He sits back
suddenly. Bascomb takes the papers from him as Jensen
enters from next room.

                              JENSEN
                    The first ballot's almost over.
                    The vote will be Russell 725,
                    Cantwell 602, Merwin 84, Claypoole
                    33, Anderson 68. And then there's
                    a recess. And . . .

Russell turns and crosses to Bascomb, who rises.

                              RUSSELL
                    Mr. Bascomb, I want to thank you.
                    I know that all this must be as . . .
                    distasteful to you as it is to us.

Russell shakes Bascomb's hand.

                              BASCOMB
                    Well, yes, it is . . . Peggy, my wife,
                    oh, she was fit to be tied when I
                    said I'd talked to Mr. Jensen and
                    was going to come here and see you.
                    She knew the whole story of course.
                    I tell her everything, we have no
                    secrets, Mrs. Bascomb and me . . .

Russell talks through him as he tries to get him to leave.

                              RUSSELL
                    Yes . . . yes . . . well, many thanks.

                              JENSEN
                            (to Bascomb)
                    Would you wait . . . please? In my
                    office? That's the second room,
                    across the hall.

                    BASCOMB
         Yes, sir, Mr. Jensen.
                 (to Hockstader)
         I guess this is the biggest moment
         of my life, meeting you, Mr.
         President, sir.

Hockstader, seated, shakes his head.

                    HOCKSTADER
         I expect this is the biggest
         moment of your life, Major. You
         may have changed history. Excuse
         me for not getting up.

Bascomb is now beginning to enjoy the situation.

                    BASCOMB
         I'll say one thing, I certainly
         never thought back in '44 when
         Joe Cantwell and I were on Adak
         that twenty years later we'd be
         here in this hotel with him running
         for President and me talking to you,
         sir, who I always admired --

Jensen starts to maneuver him out of the room.

                    BASCOMB
         -- though I didn't vote for you
         the second time. You see,
         Mrs. Bascomb felt that . . .

                    HOCKSTADER
         Let your vote, Major Bascomb,
         remain between you and your God.

                    JENSEN
         Many thanks, Mr. Bascomb. I'll
         see you in a few minutes.

Jensen gets him through the door at last.

                    JENSEN
                 (to Russell)
         Bill, we've done it! We've stopped
         Joe Cantwell! I just spoke to
         him. He wants to see you during
         the recess.

                              RUSSELL
                          (dangerously)
          And you said I would see him?

                              JENSEN
          Bill, I . . . I had to.

                              RUSSELL
          Then you talk to him. I won't.
                          (turns to Hockstader)
          This is exactly the kind of thing
          I went into politics to stop!
          The business of gossip instead of
          issues, personalities instead of
          policies . . . We've got enough on
          Cantwell's public life to defeat
          him without going into his private
          life which is nobody's business!

                              HOCKSTADER
                          (sharply)
          Any more than yours is?

                              RUSSELL
          Any more than mine is.

                              HOCKSTADER
          But Cantwell is using your private
          life . . .

                              RUSSELL
          All the more reason for my not
          using his. I'm not Cantwell.

                              HOCKSTADER
                          (reasonably)
          But nobody's used anything yet.
          Now, Jensen, you go to see if you
          can arrange a meeting where nobody
          can see them.

Jensen pauses.

                              HOCKSTADER
          Go on now.

Jensen goes.

                    RUSSELL
              (to Hockstader)
I won't do it.

                    HOCKSTADER
You have to.

Alice enters.

                    ALICE
Do what?

                    HOCKSTADER
He's got the stuff to knock off
Cantwell. Only your lily-livered
husband won't go through with it.

                    ALICE
              (to Russell)
You can keep them from bringing
up all that . . . mental business?

                    RUSSELL
Maybe . . .

                    HOCKSTADER
Definitely.

                    ALICE
Then do it!

                    RUSSELL
You don't know what it is.

                    ALICE
And I don't care. I should be
quite happy to take a gun to both
of them.

                    HOCKSTADER
Atta girl! Listen to her, Bill.
She don't run from a fight.

                    RUSSELL
You know I'm not afraid.

                    HOCKSTADER
              (exasperation)
Then what is wrong with you? Why

                              HOCKSTADER (Cont.)
        are you hesitatin' <u>this</u> time?

                              RUSSELL
        Look, I'm not being righteous and
        I do want to win, but how can I,
        in all conscience, use . . . <u>this</u>,
        even against Cantwell!

                              HOCKSTADER
                         (furiously)
        My God, what would happen if you
        had to make a quick decision in
        the White House, when maybe all
        our lives depended on whether you
        could act fast . . . and you just sat
        there, the way you're doin' now,
        having a high old time with your
        divided conscience.

                              RUSSELL
                         (hotly)
        I am <u>not</u> divided! I know what
        I should do and this is <u>not</u> it.

                              HOCKSTADER
        Then you don't want to be king
        of the castle. So stay away from
        us. Be a saint in your own time.
        Because you aren't fit to lead
        anybody.

                              RUSSELL
                         (stung)
        Why? Because I don't fire off a
        cannon to kill a bug? Because I
        don't have that mindless reflex
        you confuse with strength? Don't
        you understand, if I start to fight
        like Cantwell I lose all meaning . . .

                              HOCKSTADER
                         (evenly)
        If you don't start to fight, you
        are finished. Now I am here to
        tell you this: power is not a toy
        we give to good children; it is a
        weapon and the strong man takes it

                    HOCKSTADER (Cont.)
and he uses it. * * * Now if you
don't go down there and beat Cantwell
to the floor with this very dirty
stick, then you got no business in
this big league, and bastard or not,
I'll help Joe Cantwell . . . that's
right. I'll say you were mentally
unstable. Yes, I'll do even that.
I'll lie my head off because if
you don't fight, this job's not
for you and never will be.

A long moment, broken by the return of Jensen. He studies
Hockstader, Russell and Alice, trying to divine their
moods. He nods imperceptibly to Hockstader, indicating
that a meeting has been arranged.

                    RUSSELL
               (half to himself)
And so, one by one, these compromises,
these small corruptions destroy
character.

                    HOCKSTADER
To want power is corruption already.
Dear God, you hate yourself for
being human.

                    RUSSELL
No. I only want to be human . . . and
it's not easy . * * *

---

47.   [and I can assure you he don't
           turn it on himself nor let another
           man come at him with a knife that
           he don't fight back. Well, that
           knife is at your throat and]

           [Once this sort of thing starts,
           there is no end to it, which is
           why it should never begin. And
           if *I* start . . . well, Art, how does
           it end, this sort of thing? *Where*
           does it end?

* * *

Russell looks first at Hockstader; then at Alice. He goes
into the bedroom. Alice follows him; she pauses at the
door and watches as Russell exits to the bathroom, where
Jensen and Don are waiting.

                    ALICE
              (slowly)
      You are a good man, Mr. President.
      Only I wonder . . .

                    HOCKSTADER
      I reckon I am, when all's said
      and done.

Hockstader, in pain, tries to take one of his pills; he
cannot get his hand to his mouth.

Alice continues to look after Russell, unaware of Hockstader's
pain.

                    HOCKSTADER
      At least I put a fire under the
      candidate. I just hope it don't
      go out . . . Now don't you get alarmed.

Alice turns on this, startled.

                    HOCKSTADER
      But I want you to go over and pick
      up that phone and ask for Dr. Latham,
      he's in the hotel. Tell him I'm
      in here . . . tell him to come quick,
      through the back way. Tell him
      to bring a stretcher because I
      can't move. I'm afraid the old
      man's just about dead.

Alice, horrified, goes quickly to the telephone.

                                        DISSOLVE TO:

---

47. *(Cont'd)*   **HOCKSTADER**
      In the grave, son, where the dust
      is neither good nor bad, but just
      nothing.]

48. INT. CANTWELL SUITE -- MED. SHOT

A moment later, Cantwell is on the telephone in the living room. Mabel is beside him. Both wait, nervously. TV recess.

> CANTWELL
> (at last)
> Yes, that's right. The name is
> Conyers, General Conyers . . .
> C-o-n-y-e-r-s . . . Yes, this is
> Senator Cantwell. Yes, it's an
> emergency. You . . . what? Oh, no!
> (to Mabel)
> They can't find him!

> MABEL
> But he has to be there!

> CANTWELL
> (into telephone)
> Try his quarters, then.
> (softly, to himself)
> Dammit, dammit, dammit.

> MABEL
> Are you sure General Conyers will
> back you up?

> CANTWELL
> He better.
> (into telephone)
> Well, isn't there a phone anywhere
> near there?
> (to Mabel)
> He's playing golf!
> (into telephone)
> O.K. Tell him as soon as you find
> him to call Senator Cantwell, in
> Los Angeles. The number is
> Dunkirk 7-7011.

> MABEL
> Joe, I am scared to death . . .

> CANTWELL
> Well, don't be.
> (soothingly)
> Come here, poor Momma Bear.
> (embraces her)

                              CANTWELL (Cont.)
          And don't worry. Poppa Bear
          isn't going to get shot down this
          close to the honey tree.

                              MABEL
          I just don't know how they can use
          something like that which is so
          untrue, which is a dirty lie and
          everybody knew it was a lie even
          at the time . . . Oh, how I hate politics!

                              CANTWELL
          We're going to make it, honey. Don't
          you worry.

     A final kiss. He starts to go.

                              MABEL
          Joe . . . be careful.

48A. INT. HALL

     Cantwell walks.

49.   INT. LINEN ROOM

     Cantwell enters. Russell is waiting for him amidst the stacks
     of towels and sheets. There is a long moment as the two
     men stare at one another. Cantwell, finally breaks the
     silence.

                              CANTWELL
          Well, Bill, here we are . . . the main
          event like they say.

                              RUSSELL
          The main event. And here we stand,
          as Martin Luther said . . .

                              CANTWELL
                    (misunderstanding)
          Oh, I'm sorry . . . sit down, please . . .

                              RUSSELL
          And it is not safe to move.

                              CANTWELL
          Who said that?

                    RUSSELL
Martin Luther said: it is not safe
to move.
          (explaining)
Luther was . . .

                    CANTWELL
          (irritably)
You don't have to tell me who Martin
Luther was. I happen to be a
Protestant. I'm a very religious
kind of guy . . . Bill.

                    RUSSELL
          (ironically)
You don't need to tell <u>me</u>, Joe.

Cantwell, through him.

                    CANTWELL
Bill, it's time for the party to
unite behind a candidate . . .

                    RUSSELL
You?

Cantwell nods.

                    RUSSELL
What makes you so sure?

                    CANTWELL
          (as to a child)
Because I expect you to withdraw . . .
because you've got no choice,
considering your medical history.

                    RUSSELL
          (thoughtfully)
Never defend, always attack. You're
very good at this, Joe, I mean that.

                    CANTWELL
          (passionately)
Of course I am! I understand the
people of this country because I'm
one of them. Because I think like
they do. And I'm not afraid to fight

                    CANTWELL (Cont.)
hard for what I believe. Nothing was
ever given <u>me</u> on a silver platter.

                    RUSSELL
A self-made man . . . With a self-made
issue, your imaginary Communist Mafia.

                    CANTWELL
               (coldly)
<u>How</u> I was made is not the question.
What matters is, I'm here. I'm going
to question Sheldon Bascomb now and
you're going to get the surprise of
your life.

                    RUSSELL
Nothing <u>you</u> do ever surprises me,
Joe. But what <u>I</u> do is beginning to
surprise me.

He touches the folder.

                    CANTWELL
Then what are you doing down here?
What have you got this joker Bascomb
standing by for except to smear me
as a homosexual, which I'm not.

                    RUSSELL
<u>I</u> never said you were . . .

                    CANTWELL
               (triumphantly)
You realize you've practically admitted
that you don't believe this accusation
against me. That you are openly
confessing collusion . . .

                    RUSSELL
Mr. Chairman, Mr. Chairman, point of
order. Oh, how're you going to keep
them down in the Senate, after they've
been on TV?

                    CANTWELL
Very funny. Very cute. Now . . .

                    RUSSELL
Art Hockstader was right when he said
you're not very sensitive to people.
                    (pause)
Well, let's get this dirty business
over with. I won't throw my mud if
you won't throw your mud.

                    CANTWELLL
And you get nominated on the next
ballot? No.

                    RUSSELL
Well, then . . . good luck. And may
"the best man" win, assuming we
don't knock each other off and the
Party.

                    CANTWELL
Where's Bascomb?

                    RUSSELL
In the basement.

                    CANTWELL
Is that the court-martial testimony?

Russell gives it to him. He glances at it.

                    CANTWELL
Okay. Let's go.

                                        DISSOLVE TO:

50. OMITTED

51. INT. BOMB SHELTER

Cantwell studies document. The terrified Sheldon Bascomb is
there. Cantwell continues to study paper while he talks.
He does not look at Bascomb.

                    CANTWELL
Hi, Shelly, how's the boy? Long
time no see.

                    BASCOMB
Yeah . . . Joe . . . long time . . .
Hello again, Mr. Russell.

                        RUSSELL
    Joe wants to ask you some questions . . .

                        BASCOMB
    Well, I really ought to be getting
    back to Wilmington, you see, my wife . . .

                        CANTWELL
    You live in Wilmington, eh? Great
    town . . . used to have some cousins
    there named Everly, Jack and Helen
    Everly, maybe you know them, in real
    estate . . .

                        BASCOMB
    Well, it's not Wilmington proper,
    actually, it's a suburb where Peggy
    and I live. I don't think I know
    anybody named . . .

For the first time, Cantwell looks at Bascomb, who steps
back in alarm.

                        BASCOMB
        Everly . . .

                        CANTWELL
            (smiles)
    Shelly, you look fine, just fine . . .

                        BASCOMB
    So do you, Joe. I thought, Mr.
    Russell, I wouldn't have to . . . to . . .

                        CANTWELL
    To see your old buddy? Now you know
    I would've been fit to be tied if
    I had known Shelly Bascomb from Adak
    was in town and hadn't come to see me.

                        BASCOMB
    Well, I . . . I know how busy you are . . .
    <u>both</u> you men are . . . running for this
    President thing, and I was just . . .
    well, passing by.

                         CANTWELL
                      (pleasantly)
         And you thought you would pause long
         enough to smear your old buddy?

                         BASCOMB
         Now, Joe, don't get mad at me . . .
         it was . . . it was my duty!

                         CANTWELL
         To get even with me for seeing you
         were passed over for promotion
         because of incompetence?
                      (to Russell)
         Always a good idea to start with
         the motive.

                         RUSSELL
                      (to Bascomb)
         Is this true?

                         BASCOMB
                      (taken aback)
         Well, no, not really . . . I mean my
         efficiency report was . . .

                         CANTWELL
                      (in for the death)
         Can be found in army records!
         Unsatisfactory! I was adjutant and
         I personally stopped his promotion
         and his transfer and he knew it.

Cantwell refers to the documents.

                         CANTWELL
         Now, on 6 April, 1944, into my quonset
         hut at the army base on Adak there
         moved a Lieutenant Fenn . . .

                         BASCOMB
         That was the one, like I told you . . .
         that was the one . . . we all knew . . .

                         CANTWELL
         We shared the same hut for three
         months.

                    BASCOMB
Just the two of them. Like I told
you. It's all in the record there . . .
they were, you know . . . they were . . .

                    CANTWELL
               (inexorably)
Fenn was caught with an enlisted man
<u>in flagrante delicto</u> on the afternoon
of 14 June, 1944, in the back of the
post church. The MP's caught him . . .

                    BASCOMB
               (rapidly)
That's right. And that's when he
broke down and told about everything
and everybody . . . The MP's laid this
trap for him . . . they'd been tipped off.

                    CANTWELL
By the Advocate General . . .

                    BASCOMB
That's right. By Colonel Conyers, he
was the one finally broke up this whole
ring of degenerates . . . And Fenn, when
he was caught, gave oh, maybe twenty,
thirty names and one of those names was
Joe Cantwell, his roommate . . .

                    CANTWELL
Correct. Now: what happened to those
twenty-eight officers and men who were
named at the court-martial?

                    BASCOMB
They were all separated from the service . . .
Section 8 we called it . . . for the good of
the service, they were all kicked out . . .

                    CANTWELL
All except one.

                    BASCOMB
That's right . . . all except you.

                    CANTWELL
               (smiles at Russell)
And why wasn't I?

                    BASCOMB
I . . . well.. . . I don't know. I suppose
it's in the records or something.
But I know I thought then what a
lot of people thought: how Joe
must've pulled some pretty fancy
wires to save his neck. Yes, sir,
he was a real operator, he could get
out of <u>anything</u>, and that's the truth.
. . . Anyway, it's all there in the
court-martial; how he was one of them,
named under oath by Lieutenant Fenn.

                    RUSSELL
          (to Bascomb)
Where is Lieutenant Fenn now?

                    CANTWELL
He's dead.

                    BASCOMB
That's right, he died after the war
in that plane crash, you remember the
one? Out in Detroit, that freak one
where the lightning hit the engine,
and . . .

                    RUSSELL
          (to Cantwell)
If you were innocent, why did Fenn
name you?

                    CANTWELL
          (coldly, carefully)
Because I was the one who turned him
in.

                    BASCOMB
          (stunned)
<u>You</u> turned him in?

Cantwell turns on Bascomb, who retreats before him.

                    CANTWELL
That's right, Shelly, when I found out
what was going on, I went to Conyers
and told him what I had discovered
about my roommate. We laid a trap for

                              CANTWELL (Cont.)
          Fenn and he fell into it. At the
          trial I gave secret evidence against
          him and that's why he named me; <u>in
          revenge</u>, and that's why no action was
          ever or could ever be taken against
          me.
                         (to Russell)
          I even got promoted on the strength
          of having helped clear those types
          out of our command.

                              BASCOMB
          Oh, I bet that isn't so . . . I bet you'll
          find he sneaked out of it like he did
          everything else . . .

                              RUSSELL
                         (to Cantwell)
          Can you prove this?

Cantwell nods.

                              CANTWELL
          This clown wouldn't know, but I'm
          ashamed of <u>you</u>, Bill, for not doing
          your homework, for not checking with
          a certain Colonel, now Major General
          Conyers, who was the Advocate General
          up there. I talked with him a few
          minutes ago in Colorado. He told me
          he would back me up. In every way.

Cantwell gives Russell the telephone number.

                              CANTWELL
          Here's the name and phone number.
          He's expecting a call from you, Bill.

Like a carnivore, Cantwell stalks the terrified Bascomb
to the door.

                              CANTWELL
          And now, Shelly Bascomb, if you ever
          say one word about this to anybody, I
          will have you up for libel, <u>criminal</u>
          libel . . .

                    BASCOMB
          Now, look here, Joe, don't you
          threaten me . . .

Bascomb grabs his briefcase and raincoat and tries to get
to the corridor door before Cantwell reaches him.

                    CANTWELL
          In fact, I will involve you personally
          in the whole mess at Adak and by the
          time I finish with you . . .

                    BASCOMB
          Don't you bully me, Joe, don't you
          try to intimidate me . . .

                    CANTWELL
          I'll make you wish you'd never been
          born!

Just as Cantwell seems about to seize him, Bascomb bolts
into corridor. But to his horror, NEWSMEN and PHOTOGRAPHERS
are waiting. He is borne straight back to Cantwell, who
smiles and straightens Bascomb's jacket. Then he turns him
about for the photographers, who want a picture.

52. INT. CORRIDOR -- CANTWELL'S POV

                    CANTWELL
          Just one second . . .

Cantwell puts an arm about Bascomb's shoulder.

                    CANTWELL
          Sure was swell to see you, Shelly.
          Next time when you drop by, bring the
          wife . . . uh, bring Peggy. Mabel and I'd
          love to meet her. Love to see you both.
          You come see us now in Washington.

Poses again with Bascomb.

                    CANTWELL
          How's that?

                    PHOTOGRAPHER
          Hold it!

Bascomb goes.

                              REPORTER
          Senator . . . Is William Russell in there
          with you?

                              CANTWELL
          Here? But this is a bomb shelter.

                              REPORTER
          So what are you doing in there?

                              CANTWELL
          I'm counting the bombs.

On this amiable laugh, Cantwell shuts the door.

53.   INT. BOMB SHELTER

Cantwell pauses a moment, unobserved by Russell. He passes
his hand wearily across his face. Then he pulls himself
together.

                              CANTWELL
          I'm sorry to disappoint you, Bill,
          but this won't work. I'm covered
          on every side.

Russell stares at him with a fascinated revulsion.

                              CANTWELL
          Well, go on. If you don't believe me,
          you got General Conyer's number in your
          hand. Call him.

                              RUSSELL
          True? False? We've both gone beyond
          the "truth" now. We're in dangerous
          country.

RUSSELL drops the paper with the telephone number on a
counter.

                              CANTWELL
                    (begins)
          Every word I said was true . . .

                              RUSSELL
          You are worse than a liar. You
          have no sense of right or wrong.
          Only what will work.

Russell picks up court-martial testimony.

> RUSSELL
>
> Well, this is going to work.

> CANTWELL
>
> But you're not going to use that
> now!

> RUSSELL
>
> Oh, yes! Yes! I'll use anything
> against you. I can't let you be
> President.

Russell crosses to back door. Cantwell tries to block his
way. Russell pushes him aside.

> CANTWELL
>
> Okay, Russell, go ahead, it's your
> funeral. Against me, you haven't
> got a chance.

Cantwell sits down on a bench. For the first time, he
seems exhausted, played out. Don enters.

> DON
>
> What was that all about?

Cantwell ignores him.

> DON
>
> Joe?
> (sudden alarm)
> Hey, Joe?

Cantwell is recalled from some private reverie. He looks
at Don, smiles suddenly; his tone is casual.

> CANTWELL
>
> Oh, Don, hi.

> DON
>
> What's Russell up to? What's this
> all about? What's he got on you?

> CANTWELL
> (thoughtfully)
> You know what that guy said just now?
> He said I wasn't very sensitive about

                    CANTWELL (Cont.)
other people. He said I didn't
understand character . . .

                    DON
Is that why he wanted to see us?
To give you a lecture?

                    CANTWELL
Yeah. Pretty much.

Cantwell sees the paper with General Conyers' telephone
number on it. He picks it up. He smiles.

                    CANTWELL
Well, I have news for him. I am
a very good judge of character.
                (abruptly)
You can release that stuff on Russell
now. One copy to every delegate.
                (excitement)
Don, we're home free.
                (he rolls the paper
                into a tight wad)
And I'll make you a bet: Russell
quits before the third ballot.

Cantwell flicks the wad across the room.

53A.   <u>INT. FISHBOWL AT CONVENTION HALL</u>

The second ballot has ended. Howard K. Smith looks into
camera. Behind him, through the window, the floor of the
convention can be seen. The delegates are seated and
fairly quiet as the Chairman bangs his gavel.

                    HOWARD K. SMITH
The third ballot is about to begin.
As you know, the second ballot saw
a shift in votes. Because of rumors
about William Russell's health,
112 Russell votes were lost between
the first and second ballot. Also,
as a result, the favorite sons are
still holding fast. On the second
ballot the vote was Cantwell 654,
Russell 613, Merwin 126, Anderson
86, Claypoole 33. At the moment,

> HOWARD K. SMITH (Cont.)
> no one is budging and this convention
> may be headed for a deadlock.

Smith glances off screen at his own monitor, or, perhaps,
is informed by an Aide sitting next to him.

> HOWARD K. SMITH
> We take you now to the floor and
> Robert Gopelin . . . How does it look
> down there to you, Bob?

> CUT TO:

54. INT. CONVENTION HALL

A TV Newscaster is on the floor with a hand mike. In the
background, the Chairman speaks, simultaneously.

> CHAIRMAN
> We will now begin the roll of the
> States . . .

> NEWSCASTER
> (excited)
> It certainly looks like a stand-off
> from down here, Howard . . .

> CHAIRMAN
> Alabama?

> NEWSCASTER
> There's Dick Jensen, Mr. Russell's
> campaign manager. Mr. Jensen, Mr.
> Jensen. How's it going?

> CLERK
> Alabama, 29 votes for Joe Cantwell.

Jensen is dashing past, with a clipboard and a worried
expression.

> JENSEN
> (angrily)
> How do you think it's . . . ?
> (sees camera)
> We're holding our own.

                    NEWSCASTER
          And Senator Cantwell . . . ?

                    JENSEN
          He can't get it on this ballot.
          Excuse me.

                    CHAIRMAN
          Alaska?

                    NEWSCASTER
          Do you expect any Anderson or Merwin
          votes?

                    JENSEN
          Yes, I do.

                    NEWSCASTER
          Has the health issue hurt, would
          you say?

                    JENSEN
          Mr. Russell is in excellent health.

                    DELEGATE   off-screen
          Alaska casts 9 votes for William
          Russell.

                    NEWSCASTER
          There's a rumor Pennsylvania may
          go for Cantwell on this ballot.
          If that happens, he can win.

                    CLERK
          Alaska, 9 votes for William Russell.

                    JENSEN
          Pennsylvania is still pledged to us . . .
          excuse me . . .

          Jensen is gone into crowd.

                    NEWSCASTER
          That was William Russell's campaign
          manager. As you can see, Pennsylvania
          is the key -- the Keystone State --
          to this ballot. Who wins Pennsylvania
          . . . Governor Crespi . . . over here . . . !

                        CHAIRMAN
        Arizona?

                                            * * * CUT TO:

Russell & Cantwell, typical silent scenes -- Cantwell writing
acceptance speech -- Russell?

55. PENNSYLVANIA DELEGATION

     Lazarus stands by statemarker, fiercely arguing with delegates.
     Don Cantwell is busy exhorting all of them. We cannot hear
     dialogue in the general din. Jensen joins them. All
     gesticulate, argue, heads together.

                        DON
        Look, we've already won. We're
        in the bag.

                        JENSEN
        You're not.

                        LAZARUS
        I know they're not, but . . .

                        DELEGATE 1
                   (nervously)
        We got to do the right thing here,
        I mean this thing on Russell . . .

                        CHAIRMAN   off-screen
        Oklahoma?

                        JENSEN
        The dirtiest bit of politics since . . .

                        DON
        A public service . . .

                        DELEGATE
        Oklahoma -- the Sooner State --
        casts its 29 votes for Joe Cantwell!

                        DELEGATE 2
        Don't care what it is. If those
        things about Russell are true . . .

                        JENSEN
        They're not . . .

                         CLERK
Oklahoma, 29 votes for Cantwell.   off-screen

                         DELEGATE 3
                    (pragmatic)
Point is people think they are . . .

                         DELEGATE 4
                    (activist)
Point is, Cantwell's winning. I'm
for switching . . .

                         LAZARUS
We have to caucus first . . .

                         DELEGATE 4
So we do it right now.

                         DON
Yes. After all, we've got Merwin's
support on the next ballot . . .

                         JENSEN
They're lying.

                         LAZARUS
You don't have Merwin . . .

                         CHAIRMAN
Oregon?

                         JENSEN
                    (fast)
The delegates ought to know we're
filing suit against Joe Cantwell
for theft. And we've also got
something in reserve, Don. Something
which won't be in reserve if you
don't get out of here.

This has its effect.

                         DON
                    (sadly)
You guys can never play it straight,
can you?

Don goes.

                    LAZARUS
               (to quarreling
               delegation)
     Okay. We stick for this ballot.
     Then we caucus.

                    DELEGATE
     Oregon casts its 17 votes for that
     patriotic American and next President,
     Joe Cantwell.

The rebellion is momentarily put down. Lazarus turns
fiercely to Jensen.

                    LAZARUS
     What the hell's wrong with Russell?
     I've got copies of that court-martial
     all ready to go . . .

                    DELEGATE
     Oregon, 17 votes for Russell.

                    JENSEN
     Bill says to hold it. He's trying
     to see Hockstader right now. If
     he can get a statement from the old
     man, he thinks . . .

                    LAZARUS
     A statement from God won't help
     after this ballot. What's the
     matter with him?

                    CHAIRMAN
     Pennsylvania?

                    JENSEN
     He feels . . .

                    LAZARUS
               (furiously)
     He feels . . . he thinks . . . he sits!
     Keen, aggressive leadership . . .

Lazarus grabs microphone.

                    LAZARUS
     State of Pennsylvania casts its
     81 votes for William Russell!

CUT TO:

56. <u>ANOTHER DELEGATION</u>

Don on walkie-talkie telephone.

>   DON
>   Joe? You watching? Yeah, we're
>   a little ahead. And Pennsylvania
>   wants to split. But Lazarus won't
>   let them. We've got momentum but
>   we can't win on this ballot.

CUT TO:

57. <u>INT. CANTWELL NERVE CENTER</u>

While talking on phone, Cantwell is watching the three
TV sets. Don is unaware that he -- Don -- is visible
on one of the sets. There are only two aides in the room.
The place is deserted: all action has transferred to the
convention hall.

>   CANTWELL
>   Okay, Don, I'm coming down there.
>   Yes, I know it's not done, but I'm
>   doing it. Now you line up the
>   Merwin people and I will personally
>   sew them up. What about Russell?
>   Not a peep?
>   (laughs)
>   See? I was right! He hasn't got
>   the guts of a flea!

Joe hangs up. Turns to aides.

>   CANTWELL
>   We got it made! Now get the files
>   on the Merwin, the Anderson, and
>   the Claypoole delegates. We're
>   going to twist a few arms . . .

CUT TO:

58. <u>INT. CONVENTION HALL</u>

Jensen is on telephone.

                    JENSEN
          Alice? Where's Bill? On his way
          up to Hockstader? Okay. Tell
          him this place is about to fall
          apart. Get up there and call me
          back and put the phone in his
          hand. I've got to get him.

58A. EXT. AMBASSADOR HELIPORT

Cantwell and aide run to board helicopter which is already
warmed up. Cantwell carries a cardboard file case. They
clamber aboard.

58B. INT. HELICOPTER

Cantwell is running through file, talking on walkie-talkie.
Aide takes notes.

                    CANTWELL
          Okay, Don. This guy Warren. He's in
          debt to International Tool and Die.
          Put the pressure on. Copeland, got an
          ex-wife. She's willing to make trouble,
          cost us maybe a thousand. Get to her.
          Ruger . . . R-u-g-e-r. Wants a Federal
          Judgeship, promise it. No. Not in
          writing. Congressman Maynard, got a
          defense contract for his brother-in-
          law. His cut was two hundred twelve
          thousand dollars, 9 August 61.
          Right. Halliday, accused of malpractice,
          Kansas City, 7 January 42. The
          presiding judge made the following
          statement . . .

59. INT. HOCKSTADER SUITE

Hospital-ward appearance. Oxygen tanks, plasma bottles, two
nurses, doctor, intern, in and out.

Russell sits very still in the living room of the suite.
Tom joins him.

                    RUSSELL
          How is he?

                              TOM
                         (low voice)
          Still unconscious. He's been
          hemorrhaging badly. We've
          told the press it wasn't serious.
          He doesn't want to upset the
          convention.

                            RUSSELL
          How long has he got?

Tom gestures: It's all over.

60. EXT. CONVENTION HELIPORT -- DAY

Helicopter has just landed. Cantwell and aide dart into
car.

61. INT. CAR

They barrel through tunnel to convention hall. Cantwell is
on the car phone, still at work.

                            CANTWELL
               O'Malley, arrested for car theft
               in 1927, suspended sentence.
               Myer, named in liquor commission
               scandal, New York City, Autumn 1949.
               Turn the heat on. Okay. I'll see
               the Merwin people first. Then the
               Anderson people. Keep pushing!
               Go, go, go!!

62. INT. HOCKSTADER SUITE

Doctor comes out of bedroom; he nods to Russell, who rises
and follows him into bedroom. Hockstader is being fed
intravenously.

                            HOCKSTADER
               How's it going?

                            RUSSELL
               Don't talk.

                            HOCKSTADER
          You . . . do like I say?

                         RUSSELL
          I talked to him.

                         HOCKSTADER
          That's the ticket.

Tom enters with a sheet of paper.

                         TOM
          Mr. President, here's the * * * third
          ballot. You wanted to know the ‾ ‾ ‾
          votes.

A glance between Russell and Tom. Russell: Don't. But
it is too late.

                         HOCKSTADER
          What's the score?

                         TOM
          Cantwell 664, Russell 597, Merwin
          133 . . .

A long, ominous pause.

                         HOCKSTADER
          You didn't do it, did you?

                         RUSSELL
          I couldn't, Art. I tried to. I
          wanted to. I couldn't.

                         HOCKSTADER
          Then to hell with both of you.

                         RUSSELL
          Art . . .

But the strain has been too much for Hockstader; with a
sigh, he slips into a coma. Doctor appears.

                         DOCTOR
          I'm sorry, Mr. Russell. You'd
          better go.

Russell takes one last look at the old man, then he goes.

63.   INT. HOCKSTADER LIVING ROOM

Alice is there, telephone receiver in hand.

                    ALICE
          Is he any . . . better?

Russell shakes his head.

                    ALICE
          Dick Jensen.

Russell picks up telephone.

63A1. INT. CONVENTION HALL

Jensen is near the floor at the edge of the tunnel, with two
aides, and the convent   delegates can be seen in the
background.

                    JENSEN
               (into walkie-talkie)
          Cantwell's here. I know it's
          impossible, but he's here. He's
          strong-arming everybody in sight.
          The Merwin people are ready to fold.
          The fourth ballot's just beginning.
          Yes, we're holding our own . . . barely.
          Wait a minute . . .

Jensen hands walkie-talkie to an aide and dashes up ramp,
just in time to watch a moment's balloting.

63A2. INT. CONVENTION FLOOR

                    DELEGATE
          Arkansas casts its 27 votes for
          that great American and next
          President, William Russell.

63A3. CLOSE -- JENSEN

His face expresses relief. He dashes back to the aides and
grabs the walkie-talkie.

                    JENSEN
          Bill? We held Arkansas. But listen,
          you've lost more than 120 votes.

The Best Man 281

                              JENSEN (Cont.)
          Pennsylvania's caucused and Lazarus
          barely managed to hold it for you.
          * * * They'll split next time & then
          you're finished. * * * You've got to
          hit Cantwell. Hard. Now.
                    (pause; he brightens
                    visibly)
          Wonderful!
                    (turns to two aides)
          Spread the word. Our boy is on his
          way here. We are about to fight.

Jensen plunges into the crowd.

                         DELEGATE'S VOICE
          California casts its 81 votes for the
          great American and next President,
          William Russell!

                         * * *

64.   INT. LIMOUSINE

Alice and Russell sit in the back seat, both thoughtful, as
car moves along freeway to Sports Arena.

63A3.   [he says]

63B. [INT. LIVING ROOM SUITE
      Russell hangs up. He turns to Alice.

                         RUSSELL
          I'm going to the convention hall.

                         ALICE
          Now? But . . .

                         RUSSELL
          It's usually not done. But Cantwell's
          already there.
                    (dryly)
          The great innovator. Do you want to
          come with me?

                         ALICE
          I wouldn't miss it for the world.]

RUSSELL
It's a strange sort of power to have . . .

ALICE
To be able to end Mr. Cantwell's
career?

RUSSELL
(nods)
One word from me and Joe Cantwell
retires from politics.

ALICE
* * * Will you say the word ?

* * *

64.

[I hope]

[RUSSELL
This morning I almost did.
I almost did a little while ago.

ALICE
But now?

RUSSELL
I'm not sure. I don't know.

ALICE
Cantwell did what *he* said he would.

RUSSELL
Yes, and even so, I'm still in the
race. To my surprise.

ALICE
You've lost a good many votes.

RUSSELL
But not all to Cantwell. Anderson
and Merwin picked up quite a few.
That proves something.

ALICE
Yes, that you can disgust some of the
people some of the time . . .]

                          RUSSELL
            What would you do if you were me?

                          ALICE
            I'm not very good at other people's
            conscience.
                          (smiles)
            I have a hard enough time with my
            own. But whatever you do, I'm sure
            it will be right.
                          (pauses)
            * * *

                          RUSSELL
            Thank you.

Unconsciously, his hand covers hers; she smiles.

                          ALICE
            Do you realize that's the first time
            you've touched me when there wasn't
            a camera or someone watching?
                          * * *

_____

64.   [Yes, pious as that sounds, I mean it.]

[Russell immediately removes his hand. He laughs nervously.

                          RUSSELL
            Well . . . here we are.

64A.   EXT. ARENA—DAY

The car is stopped outside the Sports Arena by two
troopers. Russell speaks to driver on car-phone.

                          RUSSELL
            Gate Seven.

The troopers wave the car on. Russell pulls down his hat
over his eyes as they swing into the main driveway, filled
with partisans carrying Cantwell and Russell signs.]

65. INT. HALL

Cantwell emerges from a room and he carries a list. Don
waits for him in the hall, receiving reports from various
men who come up with messages.

>   DON
>   Well?
>
>   CANTWELL
>   Picked up * * * nine votes. You?
>
>   DON
>   Five . . . one on the fence. Listen . . .
>
>   CANTWELL
>   (scowls)
>   Not enough. If only we had more time.
>
>   DON
>   (overlaps)
>   Russell's here.
>
>   CANTWELL
>   (stunned)
>   Russell? Here? At the convention?
>   But that's impossible! Candidates
>   aren't supposed to.
>
>   DON
>   (drily)
>   I know.
>
>   CANTWELL
>   (gets the point;
>   springs to his feet)
>   Oh, yeah. Okay. Come on.

66.-
67. OMITTED

68. INT. CONVENTION ROOM 2

Jensen, Alice, Russell. The television set is going.

                        JENSEN
                (on telephone, speaks
                to Russell)
        Lazarus is all set to let fly. We
        can ask for a recess, then . . .

Russell crosses to set and turns up sound. Jensen hangs
up.

                        RUSSELL
        There's my old friend T. T. Claypoole,
        faithful to the end!

Claypoole's voice and face fill the screen.

                        CLAYPOOLE
        . . . sovereign state casts its 33 votes
        for the next President, fightin' Joe
        Cantwell.

Russell turns down the sound.

                        RUSSELL
                (thoughtfully)
        T. T. Claypoole has every characteristic
        of a dog except loyalty.

There is a knock at the door. Jensen opens it. Don and
Joe Cantwell enter.

                        DON
        Gentlemen . . .

                        CANTWELL
        Hello, Bill.

Aide gives Cantwell a note; he glances at it perfunctorily.

                        RUSSELL
                (gaily)
        Hi, Joe! Long time no see!

                        CANTWELL
        Yes . . . Mrs. Russell, I'm Joe Cantwell . . .
        I don't think we've met.

Cantwell shakes Alice's hand.

                        ALICE
How do you do.

                        RUSSELL
I thought you would be busy working
on your acceptance speech. Or is it
already written?

                        CANTWELL
          (begins)
Now, Bill, as I see the picture . . .

                        RUSSELL
I've been working for months on my
acceptance speech, trying to strike
that delicate balance between humility
and confidence.

                        CANTWELL
Yes. Now as I see this convention . . .

                        RUSSELL
You of course have a gift for hitting
the right note.

                        CANTWELL
Yes . . .

                        RUSSELL
I like the way you always manage to
state the obvious with a sense of
real discovery.

                        CANTWELL
Yes. Now, Bill . . .

                        RUSSELL
And that wonderful trick you have of . . .

                        CANTWELL
          (exploding)
Bill, at least let me get one word in
edgewise!

                        RUSSELL
          (laughs)
I'm sorry, Joe. I couldn't resist it.
          (to the others)
I was using Joe's technique: never let

                    RUSSELL (Cont.)
the other man get started. Talk right
through him. Also, whenever Joe starts
a sentence with "Now Bill" . . . you know
he's up to no good.

                    CANTWELL
          (quickly)
Now, Bill . . .

                    RUSSELL
See?

Cantwell controls himself with some difficulty.

                    CANTWELL
Very cute. Bill, this convention is
really hung up and the way things are
going we may never nominate anybody.

                    DON
And who wants to spend the next four
years in L.A.?

                    CANTWELL
Believe me when I say I have given
the whole thing a lot of thought; and
I want you to be on my ticket.

                    RUSSELL
Well, that's very generous of you,
Joe. But tell me, how can I possibly
run for Vice President when I am at
this very moment suffering from one
of my frequent nervous breakdowns?

                    CANTWELL
There was no way of keeping a report
like that secret.

                    DON
"The truth will out" as old Art
Hockstader would say.

                    CANTWELL
Yes.
          (pulls note from pocket)
By the way, he just died, right after
you left him. Now your support . . .

                    RUSSELL
Will you two please get out?

                    JENSEN

Bill!

                    CANTWELL
                (drily)
We can hold the wake later. Look,
Russell, for a lot of reasons we want
you on the ticket, and, frankly, if I
were you, I'd show a little . . . well,
gratitude.

Russell wheels about, fiercely.

                    RUSSELL
Gratitude! Do you realize all I have
to do is call Senator Lazarus . . .

                    CANTWELL
Bill, I solemnly promise before these
witnesses that I will give you anything
you want . . . the Vice Presidency, Secretary
of State . . . it's yours if you throw me
your votes on the next ballot.

                    JENSEN
                (delighted)
Bill, come on, they're scared. Look
at them sweat.

                    DON
                (angrily)
We're not sweating.

                    CANTWELL
I want a united front, for the sake
of the party.

                    JENSEN
Bill, we've got them. We've really
got them. Let me call Lazarus.

                    CANTWELL
I wish you would. And tell him you'll
support me, in the interest of Party
unity, and that you'll accept the
second spot on the ticket.

JENSEN
(overlaps)
And tell him you're ready to lower
the boom on Cantwell?

RUSSELL
All right, Dick, get me Senator Lazarus.

68A. <u>MED. SHOT</u>

Ecstatic, Jensen goes to the telephone, dials.

JENSEN
Senator? This is it. Brace yourself.

Russell comes to the telephone.

DON
(pleads)
Bill, don't. You <u>can't</u> use that stuff.
Joe's our only hope. He's the Party's
only hope.

CANTWELL
Shut up, Don. We don't have to worry
about Mr. Russell. He always does
the right thing.

RUSSELL
(to Cantwell)
Thank you.
(into telephone)
Senator? This is William Russell.
I want you to get to the chairman
of the next delegation pledged to
me . . . Wisconsin. All right. Tell
the chairman to announce to the
convention that I have withdrawn
from the race.

JENSEN
(aghast)
Bill! * * * <u>No!</u>

DON
Mr. Secretary, I swear you won't
regret . . .

                              RUSSELL.
          And that I am releasing my pledged
          delegates with instructions to
          support Governor John Merwin.

Russell hangs up.

                              JENSEN
          Merwin!

                              DON
          But . . . you can't . . .

                              RUSSELL
          I can. And I have.

                              JENSEN
          Merwin's nobody.

                              RUSSELL
          Well, he is now somebody.

                                        CUT TO:

69.   INT. CONVENTION HALL FLOOR

     We see Lazarus fighting his way to the Chairman of the
     Wisconsin delegation. In the background the roll-call
     is proceeding, with the states called upon being those
     just prior to Wisconsin: Vermont, Virginia, Washington,
     West Virginia. Lazarus whispers heatedly into the Chairman's
     ear, then, as Wisconsin is called upon, the Chairman grabs
     the microphone and stands up.

                              WISCONSIN CHAIRMAN
          Mr. Chairman, Wisconsin had expected
          to cast its 30 votes for William
          Russell, but I have just been advised
          by Mr. Russell himself that he would
          like his name withdrawn from nomination
          and further consideration in the
          ballotting.

     A roar breaks loose on the convention floor and the Convention
     Chairman gavels fiercely for order as the Wisconsin Chairman
     struggles to make his voice heard.

                          WISCONSIN CHAIRMAN
                In the light of the position, and at
                the explicit request of Mr. Russell,
                who urges all his delegates to do the
                same, Wisconsin casts its 31 votes for
                that great American and the next
                President of the United States . . .
                John Merwin.

                                                       CUT TO:

70.   INT. TV BOOTH   * * * Russell -- silent

       Newscasters hastily reconstructing what has happened.

                          HOWARD K. SMITH
                The deadlock is broken. All Russell's
                delegations are trying to get the
                floor to change their votes, and in a
                few minutes Governor Merwin will be
                nominated. Everyone's getting on the
                bandwagon . . .

                                                       CUT TO:

71.   CHAIRMAN OF WYOMING DELEGATION   * * * Russell -- silent

                          WYOMING CHAIRMAN
                State of Wyoming casts its 15 votes
                for John Merwin.

       Another great roar.

                                                       CUT TO:

71A.   CONVENTION CHAIRMAN   * * * Russell -- silent

                          CONVENTION CHAIRMAN
                The Chair recognizes the State of New
                York for the purpose of changing its
                vote . . .

72.   NEW YORK DELEGATION

                          NEW YORK CHAIRMAN
                New York casts all of its 114 votes
                for the next . . .

The rest is lost in an explosion of sound. Delegates are on their feet. Merwin banners appear in a sudden demonstration.

                                                              CUT TO:

73.   CHAIRMAN OF CONVENTION

He is gaveling happily but ineffectively for order as the demonstration starts in earnest. Show MONTAGE of demonstrators: delegates ecstatic, glum, eager.

                                                              CUT TO:

74.   TV BOOTH

                         HOWARD K. SMITH
                 That's it. Because of William Russell's
                 extraordinary action, Governor John
                 Merwin has been nominated for President
                 of the United States. The governor is
                 not expected to make a speech. That
                 will be for tomorrow. But he will make
                 a brief appearance here in the hall.

75.-
77.   OMITTED

78.   INT. CONVENTION ROOM 2

                         RUSSELL
                     (turning to Cantwell)
                 I meant it, Joe, when I said I could
                 never let you be President.

                         CANTWELL
                 I don't understand you.

                         RUSSELL
                 I know you don't. Because you have
                 no sense of responsibility toward
                 anybody or anything and that is a
                 tragedy in a man and it is a disaster
                 in a President! * * *

---

78.   [You said you were religious. Well,
                     I'm not. But I believe profoundly
                     in *this* life and what we do to one
                     another and how this monstrous "I,"
                     the self, must become "we" and
                     draw the line at murder in the games
                     we play with one another, and try
                     to be good even when there is no
                     one to force us to be good.]

> CANTWELL
> You don't understand me. You don't
> understand politics. You don't
> understand this country and the way
> it is and the way we are. You are
> a fool.

Cantwell goes, shutting the corridor door after him.

> JENSEN
> You don't even know Merwin. Nobody
> knows him. He's a man without a
> face.

> RUSSELL
> So was Art when he was nominated.
> Men without faces tend to get elected
> President, and power or responsibility
> or personal honor fill in the features,
> usually pretty well.

> JENSEN
> I'm afraid, Bill, your conscience is
> my enemy.

Jensen goes to his briefcase and starts to load it with
documents he has had scattered around the room. After a
long moment, Russell takes Alice's arm and exits.

CUT TO:

78A. THE CORRIDOR

The Merwin limousine moves down the ramp, stops, and Merwin
and his wife get out. The Merwin party makes its way out
of limousine, dazzled by TV lights and flashbulbs, as they
are hurried toward the back of the convention stage. Mrs.
Gamadge darts forward and takes Mrs. Merwin's arm firmly
in her own.

CUT TO:

79. CORRIDOR

The Russells walk toward the same staging area at which the
Merwins have just arrived. The throng around the Merwins
engulfs them and for a brief instant the Merwins and the
Russells are face to face. Merwin grabs Russell as if to

say, "Come with me," but Russell motions him on and continues
in the other direction with Alice. Once again, he and Alice
are alone as the tidal wave bearing Merwin clusters at the
foot of an escalator. Russell pauses briefly and watches
Merwin ascend the escalator. Then he turns to go down the
empty corridor with Alice. On the wall is a poster, "Hustle
with Russell."

                    RUSSELL
          Everybody hustled except Russell.

They walk down the empty corridor.

                    RUSSELL
          Disappointed?

                    ALICE
          Yes.

                    RUSSELL
          Seriously?

                    ALICE
          No. * * * I wish you'd been nominated
          but I like the way you really won.

                    RUSSELL
          * * * Thank you.

                    * * *

                    RUSSELL
          The Treaty of Suite 1101?
          Abrogated? Or renewed? You don't
          have to stay with me, you know.

_____

79.   [You did the right thing.

                    RUSSELL
          I think so.

Alice indicates the convention behind them.

                    ALICE
          It's what you might call *American*
          Roulette . . .

                    RUSSELL
          There are worse games . . . And]

ALICE

I know.

RUSSELL

But would you like to? Even without
the Lincoln bedroom?

ALICE

Yes.

RUSSELL

I'm glad. But I warn you, the fires
of autumn burn notoriously low.

ALICE
(smiles)
Well, I've been cold such a long time.

RUSSELL
(takes her arm)
Let's get out of here.

By this time they have arrived at their limousine, whose
chauffeur has opened the door. At this moment, a cluster
of newsmen overtakes them. All at once:

REPORTER #1
Your choice for Vice President?

REPORTER #2
You for Anderson?

REPORTER #3
What about Cantwell?

REPORTER #4
Will you campaign?

REPORTER #5
Back to New York?

While Alice enters car, Russell stands alone and makes one
last statement.

RUSSELL

I think Governor Merwin will make a fine
candidate. And I will do everything
possible to see that he's elected in
November.

                    RUSSELL (Cont.)
               (starts to get into
               car, pauses; second
               thought; smiles)
          And I am of course happy that the best
          man won.

     Russell gets into car. As car drives away . . .

                                        CUT TO:

80.- OMITTED
83.

84. INT. CONVENTION HALL

     Merwin is now coming out on the stage. To ear-splitting
     cheers, he takes his place in the center of the stage;
     for the moment he is quite alone. CAMERA DRAWS BACK until
     it HOLDS the whole SCENE in a single frame, whose center is
     the small figure in the blaze of light.

                                        FADE OUT

                         THE END

DARLING

1965—An Embassy Picture
Director John Schlesinger
Script—Frederick Raphael
Source Original screenplay
Stars Julie Christie, Dirk Bogarde, Laurence Harvey

In his *Sex in the Movies,* Alexander Walker writes: *"Darling* was meant to expose the English *dolce vita* set through the corrupt rise of a cover girl who uses sex to procure herself wealth and status till she finally gets her come-uppance in the shape of that modish twentieth-century malaise—boredom with it all." Whatever his intention might be, Producer Joseph Janni assembled some of the outstanding talent in Britain for his film. He had an original screenplay by Frederic Raphael; John Schlesinger, one of the new young British film directors of the sixties with the experience of a TV actor and director behind him and two feature films, *A Kind of Loving* (1962) and *Billy Liar* (1963), to his credit; Dirk Bogarde, an old pro, Laurence Harvey, a star since *Room at the Top,* and Julie Christie, who had captured attention in *Billy Liar* and was now destined to become a star in her own right.

The story line, if not the "message," described by Alexander Walker is substantially correct, a reversal, then (what old Hollywood called the "switcheroo") in different terms upon the story line of *Room at the Top.* But by 1965 new influences at home and from abroad were already working to change the style of British films. Generally, *Darling* is now viewed by the historians of cinema as either one of the last of the films of what Roger Manvell calls "direct realism," beginning with the successes of *Room at the Top* and *Saturday Night and Sunday Morning,* or the precursor of the new, less "realistic" British film that has followed very recently.

In any event *Darling* made its mark here and abroad. Its initial reception by the establishment critics was not so much mixed as it was contradictory. The film was either liked and highly praised or disliked and well-damned. Philip Hartung's review in *Commonweal* (August 20) is representative of the approving stance. "Everyone who worked on *Darling,"* he wrote, "contributed to its success; and it is obvious that scriptwriter Frederic Raphael, whose dialogue and character delineations are penetrating, Joseph Janni, who gave the picture its handsome production, and John Schlesinger, whose first-rate direction is a cinematic flow that rises above the mundane subject matter, worked together in close harmony. . . ." *Newsweek*'s earlier notice (August 16) said pretty much the same thing, that everyone connected with this Joseph Janni production "delivers the finest kind of goods." The screenplay was highly praised and characterized as making "the sort of deep, clean and bloodless incisions that Evelyn Waugh's best satire used to." Schlesinger's direction of *Darling* "gave it more cutting edges than a diamond saw."

Representative of the negative position are Dwight Macdonald of *Esquire*, Stanley Kauffmann of *The New Republic*, and Brendan Gill of *The New Yorker*. The latter admitted to enjoying the first two-thirds of it, but thoroughly disliked the last third. "What they couldn't get around was the script," he explained, "which is oddly uncertain of what it intends to convey." Stanley Kauffmann expressed his mixed feelings somewhat differently, saying that "*Darling*'s first effect is dazzling; its net effect is something else." With praise for the writer and the actors he blamed the director, "who feels the need to deck his work in borrowed finery." He noted analogies to (and thefts from) *La Dolce Vita*, then compared the two, to the disadvantage of *Darling*.

Speaking *ex cathedra* from his place on *Esquire* a couple of months later (November), with time to weigh and sift his own reactions (as well as to see the reviews of the others), Dwight Macdonald decided *Darling* was "an interesting failure." Its direction was "brilliant," and the acting was "uniformly good." By implication, then, difficulty arose from the script. Macdonald liked the first two-thirds and not the last, which he called "an indeterminate, bastard form of *Kitsch*." He concluded that the film "sometimes provokes satire and sometimes sentimentality." In passing he noticed an influence of Fellini.

Pauline Kael hit at the picture from a woman's point of view (in *Kiss Kiss Bang Bang*). "We (women) know what we're *supposed* to think: that this girl has no direction in life. . . . She even spells it out for us: 'If I could just feel complete.' But since she was empty and pushing at the beginning and is still empty at the end, all we can really feel is, 'Well, if she's going to be unhappy, rich is better.'"

All those involved in this production have continued to produce good work, to change and grow. And in the short time since it appeared on the scene, *Darling* has already become, if not a benchmark, then at least a standard point of comparison with other films in the file cards of the critics. Writing of the Polish director Roman Polanski's film *Repulsion*, John Simon was moved to call it "superficial—say, on the level of *Darling*'s investigation of the psyche of a cocotte." And here is Pauline Kael writing of *Two for the Road* in *The New Republic* (reprinted in *Film 67/68*): "It's too bad that the ways in which this couple is shown to be ideal are so falsely romantic or silly-cute, that the movie would be far more true to itself if they *were* shown to be ideally happy. *Funny Face* and *Darling* don't mix."

When John Simon drops your name in passing, when Pauline Kael uses your name, even for a one-line joke, you are finally *established*.

The Script This is the first script in this series of film scripts with a section labeled "Title Sequence" and offering a detailed description of the titles and credits as an inherent part of the script. Similarly, this script contains more camera directions, and editorial directions as well, than is usual. In that sense it is almost the opposite of scripts like those of *The Apartment* or *A Hard Day's Night*. Though there are differences between the script and the finished film, the detail of the script indicates a high degree of *pre*-planning. Also, the many shots and editorial directions seem designed to place an emphasis upon the *style* in which the film must be made; that is, because of the subject matter and the fragmentation of conventional story line, style was a major part of the experience of the film, here beginning with the written script.

Credits Producer, Joseph Janni; Director, John Schlesinger; Screenplay, Frederic Raphael; Art Direction, Ray Simm; Music, John Dankworth; Photography, Kenneth Higgins; Editor, James Clark.

Cast		
Diana Scott:	Julie Christie
Robert Gold:	Dirk Bogarde
Miles Brand:	Lawrence Harvey
Malcolm:	Ronald Curran
Prince Cesare:	Jose Louis de Vilallonga
Tony Bridges:	Trevor Bowen
Sean Martin:	Alex Scott
Estelle Gold:	Pauline Yates
Alec Prosser:	Basil Henson
Felicity:	Helen Lindsay
Lord Grant:	Peter Bayliss
Kent:	Ernest Walder
Allie:	Lucille Soong
Gillian:	Sidonie Bond
Lady Brentwood:	Lydia Sherwood
Charles Glass:	David Harrison
Sybil:	Ann Firbank
Governess:	Helen Stirling

Awards *Darling* received three Academy Awards in 1965: Julie Christie, for "Best Actress"; Frederic Raphael, for "Best Story and Screenplay Written Directly for the Screen"; and Julie Harris, for "Costume Design—Black and White."

DARLING

1. TITLE SEQUENCE

A large poster hoarding bearing the evidence of a last poster torn
off but leaving fragments that show an advertisement for War on
Want. A ladder rests against the hoarding and a bill poster climbs
to put up a fresh poster. In pieces a vast blow-up of DIANA SCOTT
obliterates what was left of the old image. We see DIANA's huge
face and at the top of the poster the words 'MY STORY BEGINNING
TODAY' -- at the bottom 'IN IDEAL WOMAN.'

CREDITS are played over sections of the poster going up, her eyes,
nose, mouth, earrings, and so forth: a true Princess!

> MAN'S VOICE: Well I do want our
> readers to see that this is really
> your story so I thought that I'd
> start by putting * * * a few questions,
> and if you just answer in your own
> words.

> DIANA: (over) Yes, I see. All
> right, ask away.

> MAN'S VOICE: Well let's start at
> the beginning, shall we?

> DIANA: (over) Well, I had a terribly
> ordinary childhood, I'm afraid.

CUT TO

2. EXT. ROEHAMPTON LANE. DAY.

A crocodile of YOUNG GIRLS (6-11) issuing from the gate of a strict
private day school and walking placidly along the brick wall which
fences off the school. They are escorted by two severe TEACHERS.

> DIANA: (over) Born at an early age
> and all that -- fell off lots of
> bicycles -- ate too many cream cakes --
> quite an ordinary childhood, you know.
> Oh, this is me aged six. Probably a
> piece of chewing gum stuck under my
> hat only you can't see.

The CAMERA swings along the line and zooms in to pick up a single
smudge-faced little GIRL. The frame freezes.

                                                    CUT TO

3. INT. SCHOOL HALL. STAGE. NIGHT.

A Nativity scene. DIANA is dressed as the Virgin, the star. She
advances with studied piety to the centre of the stage and gazes
at the manger in which she stiffly lays the pink doll she has been
holding in her arms. Animals, kings, etc.

                         DIANA: (over) I do remember I was
                         always the sort of child who got
                         picked on for doing things.

                                                    CUT TO

4. INT. THE HALL. NIGHT.

MRS SCOTT, DIANA's mother, sitting prim-proud in the audience.

                         JOSEPH: What a darling little baby
                         this is, but he feels cold. I'll
                         hang my coat across the entrance to
                         keep out the wind.

                         DIANA: (over) Joseph was actually
                         my eldest sister, Felicity. I'm
                         afraid I told everyone she had grown
                         the beard specially for the part.
                         Felicity was <u>not</u> amused.

                         MARY: That is kind of you, Joseph.

CAMERA on MRS SCOTT and her NEIGHBOUR.

                         JOSEPH: (o.s.) Why, there are some
                         men coming this way. I think they're
                         shepherds.

                         NEIGHBOUR: You must be very proud of
                         her, Mrs Scott.

                         MARY: (o.s.) Perhaps they've come to
                         see the baby.

                         JOSEPH: (o.s.) Do you think we should
                         let them in?

NEIGHBOUR: * * * (gush_es_) Darling!

MARY: (o.s.) Hurry up then.

M.C.S. JOSEPH and MARY

1st King: (o.s.) I bring gold to show
the world you are King.

2nd King: (o.s.) I bring frankincense
to show the world that you will bring
the word of God.

NEIGHBOUR: (o.s.) She's going to go
a long way. You can see.

MRS SCOTT: Yes, I think she is.

CUT TO

5.   EXT.   VICTORIA & ALBERT MUSEUM.   DAY.

DIANA is swinging her bag as she walks along wearing a smart new
trouser suit.

DIANA: (over) Me aged 20! I don't
know what I thought I was wearing.
Terribly Chelsea I thought I was --
and really I suppose I was as square
as an ice cube.

A TELEVISION DIRECTOR and his ASSISTANT are standing outside the
museum.   The DIRECTOR, whom we shall later know as ROBERT GOLD,
points with his clipboard.

ROBERT: Try that one over there.

ASSISTANT: Right you are.

The ASSISTANT crosses over and goes up to DIANA.

DIANA: What, me on the telly?

ASSISTANT: Won't take a minute.

DIANA: Oh, but how fascinating. You
must tell me what to do though.

> ASSISTANT: Er -- could you come this way please, then.

DIANA has reached ROBERT who is now interviewing her.

> DIANA: (laughs) Oh yes, I hate convention. You can't breathe. You have to break away.

> ROBERT: But isn't the breakaway of yesterday, the convention of today?

> DIANA: (nervous giggle) Well then you have to break away again.

> CUT TO

6. INT. TV MONITOR GALLERY. DAY.

Six monitor screens of ROBERT and then the same six screens filled with the faces of ROBERT and DIANA together. ROBERT himself is seen editing the programme.

> ROBERT: (on screen) Just for the sake of it -- isn't that conventional? And the way young people live today -- I mean the way -- eh -- they dress -- the way they dance -- the way they talk even -- that's more conventional than what they're trying to get away from.

> DIANA: (o.s.) And you say the way I dress is conventional?

> ROBERT: Well, you're dressed in the height of fashion and your hair is . . .

> DIANA: Oh, I just wash and comb it.

> DIRECTOR: She's fine. We'll use that. Very good.

> ROBERT: Conventional enough. How conventional are we in matters of public taste, the London skyline is constantly altering and yet young architects . . .

CUT TO

7. EXT. BBC TV CENTRE. DAY.

DIANA and ROBERT have come out of the studio.

> DIANA: Thank you so much for letting me see the finished product. It was a very good programme.
>
> ROBERT: You really think so?
>
> DIANA: * * * I thought I looked ghastly, but it was a <u>super</u> programme.
>
> ROBERT: But I thought you looked super and the programme was ghastly. What's more I'm right, too.
>
> DIANA: No, I thought you looked frightfully lean and intelligent.
>
> ROBERT: (laughs) I . . . I am frightfully lean and intelligent.

DIANA laughs. They go down towards car park.

> DIANA: You must lead such an interesting life.
>
> ROBERT: Being a professional question mark?
>
> DIANA: Oh it's better than being a professional bosom.
>
> ROBERT: (laughs) What's that?
>
> DIANA: You should try posing for bra ads some time.
>
> ROBERT: I did once -- ghastly . . . completely ghastly.
>
> DIANA: (laughs) Oh is this yours?

---

7.   [Hm.]

She is looking at a large Jaguar.

              ROBERT: Why yes -- as a matter of
              fact it is.

              DIANA: Oh.

              ROBERT: This one.

ROBERT is now seen to have opened the door of a run-of-the-mill
Mini.

ROBERT and DIANA get into the car. He offers DIANA some sweets.

              ROBERT: There's so much junk in this
              place. I keep chucking things out.

              DIANA: Yes.

              ROBERT: But the more I chuck out the
              more I chuck in. Have an acid drop?

              DIANA: Oh yes, I'd love one, thank you.

              ROBERT: One.

              DIANA: Thank you.

              ROBERT: Two.

              DIANA: Oh thank you.

              ROBERT: Here, have the lot.

DIANA laughs.

We cut down to a high angle shot of the car leaving the car park on
a fine day when the whole of London seems spread out in front of
us.

              DIANA: (over) Oh we -- er -- just sort
              of began to meet, you know. He had
              tickets for this -- or he thought I
              might be interested in that. It was
              really mostly mental to start with --
              there was nothing deliberate about it.
              We didn't know what we were doing at all.

                        CUT TO

8. EXT. CHISWICK. DAY.

There is a railway bridge in the background. ROBERT and DIANA
are casually throwing stones into the Thames. It is low tide.

> ROBERT: That's your lot.

> DIANA: I never could hit anything.

A coin is lying on the foreshore: ROBERT picks it up.

> ROBERT: Hmm . . . buried treasure.

> DIANA: Oh.

> ROBERT: Heads we do, tails we don't.

ROBERT spins coin.

> ROBERT: We do.

DIANA gives him a kind of bold nervous look. They move away up
towards where a row of derelict cottages is about to be renovated.
DIANA peers in through a shattered window.

> DIANA: Oh how I'd love to live here.
> Phoo . . . Phoo . . . Phoo . . .

ROBERT laughs.

> CUT TO

9. INT. EMPTY COTTAGE. DAY.

DIANA and ROBERT on the outside looking in.

> ROBERT: Well we'd have to do an awful
> lot to it.

> DIANA: We'd have to do everything to it.

> ROBERT: (through broken glass of window)
> Yes, you're right.

> CUT TO

10. EXT. COTTAGE. DAY.

ROBERT and DIANA outside the cottage walk towards CAMERA looking
at poster. They cross to the river and lean on a rail.

> ROBERT: Do you know these cottages
> are being carefully rehabilitated?
>
> DIANA: At great expense.
>
> ROBERT: Only to emerge as cottage-type
> homes of distinction. Do you want to
> live in a cottage-type home of
> distinction?
>
> DIANA: I wouldn't mind.
>
> ROBERT: With a yellow front door and
> a carriage lamp to match.
>
> DIANA: Absolutely lovely.
>
> ROBERT: (laughs) You are ghastly. I
> really believe you would.
>
> DIANA: I would.
>
> ROBERT: (laughs) You are a fantastic
> girl.
>
> DIANA: Why?
>
> ROBERT: I don't know, you just are.
>
> DIANA: Oh it should be so easy to be
> happy, shouldn't it? Should be the
> easiest thing in the world.
>
> ROBERT: It should be.
>
> DIANA: I wonder why it isn't? Maybe
> it is.

ROBERT lights a cigarette.

> DIANA: Is it all right for Wednesday?
>
> ROBERT: Yes, it's all right for
> Wednesday. I hate this furtiveness --
> it's so corny . . . And so
> embarrassing. (Laughs)

        DIANA: What do you want to do then?

        ROBERT: I don't know. (Pause) I do
        know . . . I don't know.

DIANA looks off at sound of train.

        DIANA: I know.

An underground train crosses the bridge behind them. ROBERT looks
at his watch.

        ROBERT: Wife.

        DIANA: Husband. (She mock-shoots
        herself) Poom!

                        CUT TO

11. INT. BRIDGES' FLAT. NIGHT.

DIANA is watching TONY doing a linguaphone course. She has two or
three books on her lap.

        LINGUAPHONE: Gianni, vuoi farci trovare
        un tè pronto nel salone fra un mezz'ora
        circa.

        TONY: Gianni vuoi farci trovare un tè
        pronto nel salone fra un mezz'ora circa.
        Come on darling, Fra un mezz'ora circa.

        DIANA: (looking down at the book) Oh,
        it's so boring.

        TONY: But darling, you started it.
        You said -- Let's plan, let's go to
        Italy for our holiday . . . let's learn
        the language.

        DIANA: (throwing her arms out) We'd
        never be able to <u>say</u> anything.

        TONY: Well, I'm getting on with it.

        DIANA: Well, you get on with it.

TONY lifts the needle back on the record.

LINGUAPHONE: Gianni, vuoi * * * farci
trovare un tè pronto . . .

Over this we see DIANA as she examines the book, its binding, its
title page. A thing she would not have done before.

> DIANA: (over) Of course I loved him
> dearly -- he was one of the nicest boys
> in the world . . . * * * Only he was * * *
> desperately immature and marriage had * * *
> been * * * foisted * * * upon him -- poor
> lamb -- and he just wasn't ready for the
> responsibility. He tried nobly, but
> you know he hadn't really got the faintest
> idea what it was all about.

CUT TO

12. INT. SOUTHGATE'S COTTAGE. DAY.

WALTER SOUTHGATE is an old man of 70, but his face is still mobile,
if lined, full of vitality.

C.U. of tape recorder spools running backwards at speed. ROBERT's
hand stops them, then switches recorder on.

> ROBERT: (o.s.) Now --

ROBERT and SOUTHGATE are sitting on the settee -- ROBERT holding
microphone.

> ROBERT: Mr. Southgate, you have the
> reputation of being something of a . . .
> lone wolf . . .

DIANA is sitting in an armchair under a Matthew Smith which adorns
the simple cottage. There are a couple of Johns as well, some
other drawings. Many books. The whole place has the cosy neatness
you find in the homes of retired sailors.

> ROBERT: (o.s.) Is this a protest
> against the Establishment?

---

11.   [proglari di]

                       [It was just that] [just] [just] [sort of]

SOUTHGATE: (o.s.) It's true I have always preferred . . . to be a mouse that walks by itself rather than being a member of a group of literary lions -- always licking each other, washing each other behind the ears, and biting each other; and as you well know, they're behind bars in a cultural zoo.

ROBERT and SOUTHGATE laugh.

SOUTHGATE: They won't let you print that.

ROBERT: Oh yes they will, if I fight.

SOUTHGATE: And will you fight?

DIANA: He fights.

ROBERT: Now there is something else. Now that you've moved down here into the country, into virtual isolation . . .

DIANA: (over) Robert has a marvellous tact . . .

The conversation between ROBERT and SOUTHGATE continues inaudibly in the background.

DIANA: (over) . . . incredible maturity, sensitivity. He'd got this funny old bloke spouting his head off -- fascinating. I've never met anyone like old Southgate --

She gets up and walks slowly to the mantelpiece.

DIANA: (over) Suddenly one felt madly -- oh you know . . . I mean, to think . . . this is one of the great writers of the century and here I am -- oh it was extraordinary. I don't really remember much anyone said . . . but I can remember the thing -- the thing was they accepted me.

DIANA: I'm just dying to read your books.

ROBERT starts to go out of the room to fetch a drink.

SOUTHGATE: They're mostly out of print.

ROBERT: Do you mind if I help myself?

SOUTHGATE: Please do.

DIANA: (off) No thank you. (To SOUTHGATE) It's been fabulous meeting you.

SOUTHGATE: Are you a truth teller?

DIANA: (o.s.) Yes . . . I think so.

SOUTHGATE: Is she?

ROBERT: Er . . . yes, she is with me.

SOUTHGATE: You consider yourself a very lucky man.

ROBERT: Oh yes, I do.

DIANA is looking at a painting on the mantelpiece.

DIANA: Gosh, that's marvellous.

SOUTHGATE: I'm glad you like it.

He gets up from the settee and walks across to look at the picture.

SOUTHGATE: I'd rather have done it than written half my stories. It probably only took him half an hour, you know. I should like you to have it.

DIANA: Oh no.

SOUTHGATE: Both of you.

ROBERT: No, really.

DIANA: We couldn't possibly -- absolutely not.

        SOUTHGATE: Please.

        DIANA: But it's yours -- it belongs to you.

        SOUTHGATE: I'm 78 years old more or less. And anyway I'd sooner you left this place with this under your arm than that antique birdsong . . .

DIANA takes the picture and kisses SOUTHGATE on his cheek.

        DIANA: Thank you.

                CUT TO

13. EXT. COUNTRY STATION (MAIN LINE). DAY.

A train coming slowly into a station. We track back to keep pace with it and see DIANA and ROBERT silhouetted against the skyline on the high platform as the train steams in. We are outside the station and pull back to disclose a Black Maria from which a PRISONER and his two PRISON OFFICER escorts are descending.

                CUT TO

14. EXT. THE TRAIN AND PLATFORM. DAY.

DIANA and ROBERT already in the train. DIANA watches with fascination as the PRISONER handcuffed to the OFFICERS is led through the booking hall and boards a reserved compartment. She turns to ROBERT and says something. He looks uneasy. The train begins to move out.

                CUT TO

15. INT. TRAIN COMPARTMENT. DAY.

ROBERT leans back, tiredly. DIANA cocks her head.

        ROBERT: Headache, suddenly.

        DIANA: No! I've got some aspirin.

He takes them. They are sitting opposite each other, alone. He leans back and closes his eyes, opens them and smiles at her. He dozes off. His face falls into a serious expression, vaguely pained. She feels a deep, urgent desire for him.

She sees he is asleep and gets up and goes and sits beside him and studies his face very intently. She takes the mirror from her bag and studies her own face.

On impulse, she holds the mirror in front of his nostrils. It mists over. She makes a noughts-and-crosses board on the face of it and then puts it away. She touches his lips with her finger. They pucker like a baby's on a bottle. She pushes the finger between his lips, smiling. He slowly becomes conscious. He opens his eyes; he sees her. They fall passionately together.

                                                    CUT TO

16. EXT. RAILWAY. DAY.

Place boards on a station blurred by speed. A signal twitches up.

                                                    CUT TO

17. INT. THE TRAIN. DAY.

The train is stopping. The PRISONER and his GUARDS ready to get off, are edging along the corridor. They look in at ROBERT and DIANA embracing with the same curiosity that DIANA looked in at them.

                                                    CUT TO

18. INT/EXT. TELEPHONE BOOTH. LIVERPOOR STREET STATION. EVG.

DIANA and ROBERT squeezed inside. DIANA with receiver.

                        DIANA: Just one moment please. I
                        have a call for you -- go ahead Ipswich.

                        ROBERT: Estelle?

                                                    CUT TO

19. INT. GOLD HOUSE. SITTING ROOM. EVENING.

                        ROBERT: (o.s.) How are the children?

                        ESTELLE: Oh fine.

                        ROBERT: (o.s.) I shall have to stay
                        overnight.

                                                    CUT TO

20. INT/EXT. TELEPHONE BOOTH. LIVERPOOL STREET STATION. EVG.

DIANA and ROBERT in the telephone booth.

                        ROBERT: I'm staying with him actually.

                                                    CUT TO

21. INT. GOLD HOUSE. SITTING ROOM. EVENING.

        ESTELLE: Oh, all right.

        ROBERT: (o.s.) Tell them I'm sorry --
        but give them my love, will you --

                            CUT TO

22. INT/EXT. TELEPHONE BOOTH. LIVERPOOL STREET STATION. EVG.

        ROBERT: And tell them I'll see them
        tomorrow.

        ESTELLE: Mm. Bye.

Robert replaces the receiver.

               * * *

        ROBERT: * * * Your turn now. Wait
        while I get some money.

               * * *

                            CUT TO

23. INT. BRIDGES' FLAT. EVENING

TONY lifts receiver.

        TONY: Euston 4614.

        ROBERT: (o.s.) Go ahead Southampton.

        DIANA: (o.s.) Hello Tony -- Hello love,
        I'm still in Southampton.

        TONY: Oh hell -- what a bore.

        DIANA: (o.s.) I know darling, but it's
        just as much * * * of a bore for me.

---

22.   [DIANA: Yes, you've done well.]

                     [It's]

[Ad lib chattering by DIANA in background.]

CUT TO

24. INT./EXT. TELEPHONE BOOTH. EVENING.

>   DIANA: Okay then, I'll see you
>   tomorrow -- bye bye darling -- mmm -- bye.

DIANA replaces the receiver. She and ROBERT laugh together and
embrace deliriously. An impatient GENTLEMAN punches hand into hand
and glares at them.

CUT TO

25. EXT. LONDON STREET. PICCADILLY. EVENING.

ROBERT and DIANA swinging along, looking into shop windows, seen
across moving traffic and late shoppers.

>   ROBERT: We can't turn up at a hotel
>   with just this.

He holds up his small briefcase and portable tape recorder.

They reach a luggage shop and go into it as a moving vehicle obliterates
our view of them.

CUT TO

26. EXT. STREET. EVENING.

ROBERT and DIANA emerge from the shop. ROBERT is now carrying a
large but obviously very light suitcase. DIANA takes over and
swings it easily on her little finger.

They reach a paper stand.

The placard advertises: MINERS -- NOW HOPES FADE. ROBERT stops to
speak to the NEWSVENDOR who looks startled as ROBERT takes out money
and buys two large stacks of Evening papers which he packs into the
suitcase. He judges the weight and nods to DIANA.

CUT TO

27. INT. SMARTISH HOTEL BEDROOM. NIGHT.

A BELLHOP opens the door of the room and shows them in. He hefts the
suitcase, obviously heavy, onto the luggage rack.

ROBERT tips the BELLHOP who goes.

ROBERT opens the lid of the suitcase. It is filled with two piles of evening papers. He throws a copy onto each pillow and grins.

> ROBERT: Wait till we get these on.

DIANA is sitting on the bed. She laughs.

> DIANA: (mimicks BELLHOP) Funny pair that Mr and Mrs Gold in 409.

ROBERT goes and checks the radiator heat. He looks out of the window. It opens onto a well, blank white brick-tile wall opposite. He pulls the curtains and turns.

> DIANA: I suppose you've done this kind of thing hundreds of times before.
>
> ROBERT: Well -- you're wrong.
>
> DIANA: I haven't ever . . .
>
> ROBERT: It's not exactly my line either. I just happen to love you.

They kiss.

> ROBERT: I told you.
>
> DIANA: It is for real then?
>
> ROBERT: It's the first time I've felt real for a long time.
>
> DIANA: Me too.
>
> ROBERT: You what? Go on.
>
> DIANA: Ooh look -- isn't that jazzy -- every two or three hours we can call for refreshments. Well -- (she smiles as he comes towards her). Welcome!

He kisses her. Gently and then with growing passion.

DIANA's bare feet impatiently kick the bedclothes off the bed.

> DIANA: (over) The thought of breaking up somebody's family was absolutely repellent to me, honestly.

CUT TO

28. EXT. GOLDS' HOUSE. DAY.

> DIANA: (over) If anyone had told me
> that I was doing anything like that I
> would have been horrified. I have
> always regarded families as -- well --
> unbustable, you know.

Under this we see as if from a slight rise the garden of the GOLDS'
house and a boy on a swing. We see ESTELLE GOLD calling him. We
pull back slowly to include DIANA in a telephone booth, holding
the phone in her hand but obviously not using it. She puts down
the receiver and looks through binoculars. ROBERT GOLD comes out
of his house into the garden. He has a girl of about three in his
arms. He has obviously just lifted her out of bed from her afternoon
sleep. She is resting her cheek against his and his hand is on her
thigh, lovingly. DIANA draws back, shocked, piqued.

CUT TO

29. EXT. SOUTH KENSINGTON. MANSION BLOCK. DAY.

Across the square we see DIANA and an AGENT through the window of
DIANA's flat.

ZOOM into flat where DIANA is contemplating her new surroundings.

CUT TO

30. INT. FURNISHED FLAT. HALL. STUDIO. DAY.

The AGENT comes with DIANA out of the sitting room into the hall.

> AGENT: And through here, you've got
> your hall. You've got -- hall table,
> vase, picture -- reproduction of clown.

> DIANA: Glass is cracked.

> AGENT: Yes. A mirror with gilt ormolu
> frame, one clock -- it seems to have
> stopped. I'm sure it only needs winding.
> And through here, of course, you've got
> your hall. Ah, the Gas Meter's there.
> And through there's the kitchen and
> three steps up here to the bathroom.

                                                                CUT TO

31. EXT. GOLD HOUSE. DAY.

L.S. through Living Room window. ROBERT walking away from CAMERA
towards the gate, with luggage. PAN down to letter on table addressed
to ESTELLE.

                         AGENT: (o.s.) Large cupboard there --
                         very useful for leaving one's coats.
                         And -- er -- in the kitchen here we
                         have the gas cooker which was put in
                         by the last tenant. It is relatively
                         new.

                         DIANA: (o.s.) Hm. Hm.

                                                                CUT TO

32. INT. HALL. LIVING ROOM. DIANA'S FLAT. DAY.

ROBERT standing in the doorway. He is carrying his case. DIANA
is looking at him from the bedroom. Between him and DIANA stretch
piles and piles of books. They look at each other.

                         DIANA: Your books have arrived.

ROBERT looks around slowly.

                         ROBERT: And your records.

From ROBERT's P.O.V.: the hall and through the hall, the living
room where sprawled out like a pack of upset cards on the empty
table and floor lie masses of records. A record player, playing
loudly, also lies on the floor, and near it a goldfish bowl.

ROBERT comes into the room from the hall. He finds the goldfish
bowl at his feet.

DIANA has walked in from the bedroom. She is nervously holding a
photo-cutting of herself in her hand.

ROBERT picks up the goldfish bowl.

                         ROBERT: (slightly surprised) Is this
                         yours?

He looks at her -- there is a silence.

DIANA: Yes.

ROBERT looks at them. DIANA looks at him. For one moment she does not know how he is going to react. He smiles indulgently.

CUT TO

33. CLOSE ON MIRROR

DIANA's hand comes into picture and sticks the cutting in the side of the mirror. A stylised collage now begins to build up. Invitations, cuttings, messages, postcards, etc. All the trivial incidentals of living together. Some messages are scribbled in lipstick:

PHONE THE BBC
MIKE? PHONED
HAPPY BIRTHDAY DARLING XXX
YOUR MOTHER RANG!!!

Eventually Christmas cards are being put up on the mantelpiece as well.

CUT TO

34. INT. SITTING ROOM. NIGHT.

DIANA draws in another berry on the holly on the mirror and then walks to where ROBERT is toying with his eternal tape recorder.

ROBERT: Hello my darling.

TAPE RECORDER: Rome doesn't intrude on you because it's been dead for so long. It has the property of a sort of beautifully laid out corpse. You know, you don't worry about it. It is always there when you look out the window. Much the same as it was the last time you looked out.

DIANA: Oh darling.

C.U. tape recorder -- ROBERT's hand comes in and switches it off.

DIANA: Sorry -- are Liz and Willie on or off at the moment?

ROBERT: Oh I don't know Di -- I've no idea at all.

DIANA: What shall I put?

ROBERT: Well, just put 'With best wishes' and leave out 'to you both'.

C.U. DIANA writing on card 'Love, Robert. . . .

DIANA: (o.s.) Love . . .

DIANA writing. She looks up towards ceiling for noise upstairs.

DIANA: Robert and Diana. Kiss, Kiss!

CUT TO

35. EXT. FRONT DOOR. DIANA'S FLAT

DIANA comes out of front door and speaks to two NEGROES.

FIRST NEGRO: Happy Christmas, baby.

SECOND NEGRO: Happy Christmas.

DIANA: Happy Christmas.

CUT TO

36. INT. LIVING ROOM. DIANA'S FLAT

DIANA: Darling, two of the most gorgeous Negroes you have ever seen have * * * just gone up the stairs. What on earth's going on up there?

ROBERT: They're having a Diplomatic Reception.

DIANA: Oh.

ROBERT: Would you like to have a Diplomatic Reception?

DIANA: What a good idea!

CUT TO

37. INT. BEDROOM. THE FLAT. NIGHT.

We start on a large pile of coats on the bed where DIANA is sitting disconsolately. ROBERT comes in looking rueful.

> DIANA: (moans) Oh!
>
> ROBERT: I can't get them to go.
>
> DIANA: Oh well make them, <u>force</u> them to go.
>
> ROBERT: But I don't know half of them.
>
> DIANA: Oh dear, I just wish they'd all go <u>away</u>.
>
> ROBERT: Why did we ever have this party?
>
> DIANA: Oh I wish they'd all go.

We cut back to the bed and all the coats have gone.

DIANA and ROBERT are lying on the bed.

> DIANA: Well, my friends seemed to get on very well with your friends.
>
> ROBERT: Hmm. Your friends are so pretty.
>
> DIANA: Darling, yours were so intelligent.
>
> CUT TO

38. EXT. GOLDS' HOUSE. DAY.

ROBERT and his two CHILDREN walking round the corner and up to the gate.

> DIANA: (over) I couldn't have been happy if I had kept Robert from his children. I was absolutely insistent rain or shine that he saw them. I couldn't have forgiven myself if he hadn't done that, you see. I've never really been the jealous type.
>
> CUT TO

39. INT. DIANA'S FLAT. LIVING ROOM AND BEDROOM.

DIANA: Where the hell have you been?

ROBERT: I told you I was going to see the children.

DIANA: Until this hour? Did you see her?

ROBERT closes the wardrobe and turns to DIANA.

ROBERT: Her?

DIANA: Her.

ROBERT: No.

DIANA: I don't know whether I believe you.

ROBERT: What makes you think she wants to see me?

DIANA: Perhaps you want to see her.

ROBERT: Perhaps I do.

DIANA: Well why don't you tell me if you want to see her -- if you're still in love with her?

They sit on the bed and embrace.

ROBERT: Oh Lor. Look here. Now listen (laughs) I love you. Honestly.

DIANA: Oh Robert, you won't leave me, will you?

ROBERT: Leave you? Leave you -- heavens -- if only you knew.

DIANA: I'm so . . . I'm so frightened sometimes.

ROBERT: What do you mean, so frightened sometimes? Why? What are you frightened of?

> DIANA: Because I'm so happy.
>
> ROBERT: (laughing) Listen, shall we get married? Get married and finish all this?
>
> DIANA: Oh darling, I'm so happy as we are. I don't want anything to change. If we got married there'd be so much bitterness and unhappiness, Robert, wouldn't there? Oh Robert, darling.

They begin to make love. As they embrace, DIANA continues to watch herself in the mirror, enchanted with the movement of her arm and breast. ROBERT's eyes are shut, but hers -- despite her passionate return of his embrace -- stay on herself, curious, almost anxious. CLOSE ON the mirror image of DIANA looking at herself.

CUT TO

40. EXT. RAILWAY LINE. DAY

A huge poster of DIANA fills the whole screen. She is advertising a product of the Glass Group of Companies -- Honeyglow, a new kind of Shampoo.

The hoarding now begins to pull away and swing from us slightly and we realise that it is a rail-side site.

CUT TO

41. INT. TRAIN. DAY.

ROBERT is sitting in the train on its journey to the Provinces. He looks at the poster until the train has moved away.

CUT TO

42. EXT. PROVINCIAL CITY STREET. DAY.

On the corner of the street we find ROBERT with a four man sound/camera unit. ROBERT is stopping PASSERSBY in the street.

> ROBERT: Good evening. An American statesman recently said that Britain was a country which had lost pride in itself. Have we so much to be ashamed of, I wonder? Let's find out.

ROBERT (Cont.): (To YOUTH with fringe) What are you ashamed of in Britain today?

YOUTH: Eer. I'm not sure -- I can't think of nothing.

ROBERT: Nothing?

YOUTH: Well -- er -- the traffic and that. It's a bit congested? Mmmmmm.

ROBERT: It's worse here is it?

MAN: Well, some people don't work hard enough. I work hard in Bristol for one person -- I do it for one person.

ROBERT: Mmmmmm.

MAN: Her name is Margaret Robertson -- I've got the photograph on me . . .

ROBERT: Mmmmm.

POLICEMAN: Well everyone these days wants something for nothing. They don't want to put anything out for what they are striving to get out of it.

ROBERT: Mmmmm.

SECOND MAN: Ahm -- talking as a Londoner I think in London itself the amount of -- ahm -- how rife homosexuality has become -- in London itself. And I would say again in that respect, a few years back that -- er -- again two or three years ago -- that you were very badly sort of approached by different people in different places.

ROBERT: Were you?

SECOND MAN: Ahm.

ROBERT: And it does -- do you -- do you think get worse?

SECOND MAN: I think in actual fact it has
become worse over a period of time.
It's just one of those things you
have to live with.

ROBERT: Yes, I suppose so.

                                        CUT TO

43. INT. HOTEL BEDROOM. NIGHT.

ROBERT is sitting on the bed of the obviously provincial hotel
bedroom, typing on his suitcase on the bed. He picks up the
telephone.

VOICE ON PHONE: Night porter.

ROBERT: Try my London number again,
will you?

VOICE: (on phone) What was that
number again, sir?

ROBERT: Flaxman 2249.

VOICE ON PHONE: One moment please.

                                        CUT TO

44. INT. LIVING ROOM. DIANA'S FLAT. NIGHT.

The telephone ringing in the empty flat.

                                        CUT TO

45. INT. HOTEL BEDROOM. NICHT.

ROBERT listening to the telephone ringing.

                                        CUT TO

46. INT. PLAQUE D'OR. CLUB ROOM. NIGHT.

It is a very smart gambling club indeed. DIANA is drawing a Charity
Tombola. She looks like a million dollars, standing on a rostrum
overlooking the smart crowd who are attending the draw, a mink
draped over her shoulders. Behind her, on the wall, is hung a big
board with "World Hunger Draw" stencilled on it and the prizes

listed underneath. The best ones are very lavish and we see "Donated by Charles Glass Esq." next to the most lavish.

It is said that £100,000 has been spent on refurnishing the club and it looks like it. Negro pageboys in Regency costume are handing round great heart-shaped boxes of chocolates.

DIANA draws a number. A counterfoil is handed her by JOHN BASILDON, managing director of the club, a smooth ex-naval type, 47, very establishment.

> DIANA: Morphy Richards Refrigerator, gift of Mr Charles Glass -- No. 81.
>
> BASILDON: Yours -- Mr. David Rodney Barnett.
>
> DIANA: Holiday for two in the Bahamas -- gift of Mr Samuel Goldstone. No. 68.
>
> LADY ISABEL McLAREN: Yes, me . . . But I've only just come back . . .
>
> BASILDON: (o.s.) Lady Isabel McLaren.
>
> DIANA: (over) Normally I never did charity work. It's usually terribly draggy . . . but, you know -- er -- Robert was away and Miles Brand happened to phone the same day . . .

We move on, taking a look at the fashionable crowd. MILES BRAND stands looking at himself in a wall mirror.

MILES is 28, lean, handsome, with a kind of self-consciously mysterious "cool" air about him. His hair is as well clipped as an Oxford lawn, but he has no interest in lost causes. His clothes are immaculate, but not showy, his face powdered, but not pampered, his hands manicured but not effeminate.

> DIANA: (over) After all, he had chosen me for the 'Honeyglow Girl.'
>
> MAN: Hello Miles.
>
> MILES: Hello.

DIANA: (over) Miles didn't mean a
thing, you know, in my private life;
and I didn't attach any importance to it.

An attractive woman in her early forties, CARLOTTA HALE, comes up
to MILES, and looks at him too.

CARLOTTA: Still admire yourself as
much as ever, Miles?

MILES: Carlotta . . .

CARLOTTA: How lucky it is that you're
a man after your own heart.

MILES: Darling. I thought I could
smell prussic acid. I put it down to
the weather.

CARLOTTA: Must make a change from
putting it down to expenses.

MILES: How savage we are tonight.
Somebody's husband gone back to his
wife?

CARLOTTA: If he had, you'd have been
there to greet him.

MILES: Leftovers aren't exactly my
diet, my dear.

CARLOTTA: Oh, I thought you were
always in the market.

MILES: That remark was young when
you were . . .

They are interrupted by DEREK, an associate of MILES.

DEREK: Miles -- Mr. Glass.

MILES: Oh, excuse me . . .

He moves towards GLASS's table. He smiles and bows.
CARLOTTA makes a face.

> DIANA: (over) I suppose the main
> attraction really was Charles Glass --
> you know. Mr. Honeyglow himself.

MILES BRAND is now talking to CHARLES GLASS, the tycoon who heads
the Glass Group (which makes, among other things, * * * Honeyglow
Products). GLASS is a short man, inconspicuous, but very alert without
seeming sharp, 56. He has an air of relaxedness about him. He sits
with a small drink in front of him, with his WIFE, and some FRIENDS.

> DIANA: (over) He was a terrible sweety.
> Do you know Charles? He's a terrible
> sweety.

DIANA draws the next number out of the Tombola.

> DIANA: Eighty-two.

LADY ZINNIA SHARPE stands up, showing ticket, and smiles.

> BASILDON: (o.s.) Eighty-two. Lady
> Zinnia Sharpe --

MILES has now moved away towards the door with a smile and a wave.
He meets SEAN MARTIN and leads him through into the hallway.

> CUT TO

47. INT. HALLWAY. PLAQUE D'OR. NIGHT.

SEAN is a man of 37, surly with a kind of bottled sensuality.

> MILES: Ah, Sean, my dear fellow.
> I hear you're making a new movie.

> SEAN: How the hell do you know that?

> MILES: I take a great interest in
> your squalid career. I have to.

In the background, we can hear DIANA at the Tombola.

> DIANA: (o.s.) And the final prize is
> an Austin Cooper -- a gift of Charles
> Glass Esquire -- No. 72.

46.   [Cordex]

> MILES: If you're shooting full-length
> epics, you won't want to do commercials
> for the Glass Group.
>
> SEAN: Sez who? I always say a lie
> can be shot with integrity just like
> everything else.

They smile and MILES puts his hand on SEAN's shoulder.

> SEAN: Who's the crumpet?

>> CUT TO

48. INT. HALL AND MAIN ROOM. PLAQUE D'OR. NIGHT.

They have turned and we can see into the room. The applause is
now for DIANA who is coming down off the platform, smiling and
waving, the perfectly poised Miss!

She comes through the polite clapping crowd.

> BASILDON: You have been most kind --
> thank you so much.
>
> DIANA: Thank you.

DIANA walks down from BASILDON towards CAMERA. She is greeted by
various guests.

> BASILDON: Now, ladies and gentlemen,
> a few words from the President of the
> charity we've all been assisting
> tonight. Pray silence for the Right
> Honourable Basil Willett, M.P.

DIANA has joined MILES and SEAN.

> MILES: A man of few words but all
> of them long ones. Ah, you were
> splendid, Diana. Now I want you to
> meet Sean Martin. This is Diana
> Scott . . .
>
> DIANA: How do you do?
>
> SEAN: How do you do?

BASILDON: Would Mr. Glass say a few
words?

MILES: I doubt it but I'll ask him.
Will you excuse me?

He moves over towards GLASS.

WILLETT: Now I want to say just this . . .
that no matter how much public money
we, the Government, devote to good
causes, there will always be a place
for private generosity like yours,
ladies and gentlemen, tonight.

AUDIENCE: Hear . . . hear . . . hear . . .

MILES is now with GLASS who is shaking his head, quite firm. MILES
looks at BASILDON and does the same.

WILLETT: Never have I seen so many
hearts so obviously in the right places.
I'm sure I've no need to bring this to
your attention -- the plight of our
brothers of every creed, race and
colour, in every far-flung corner of
the earth . . .

L.S. over a roulette wheel on to a BARONESS and other GUESTS.
A WAITER brings the BARONESS a plate of sandwiches.

WILLETT: . . . and at this very moment
are suffering the humiliation, degradation
and shame of the agonies of malnutrition.

We see the BARONESS eating * * * the meat out of the sandwiches,
leaving the bread.

                                                    CUT TO

49. INT. HALLWAY & STAIRS. PLAQUE D'OR. NIGHT.

DIANA: Oh well, of course I'd love to
make a film some day, but so much is
important . . .

DIANA and SEAN are standing at the foot of the stairs.

                              DIANA: . . . the right Director . . . the
                              right script.

                              SEAN: Ah, you think the Director makes
                              a difference, do you?

DIANA smiles and touches SEAN's arm, embarrassedly unsure if he's
joking. He keeps a straight face.

                              DIANA: Well, it has been known.

SEAN's wife, SYBIL, comes up to him and puts his arm round her
waist, with a dampening effect on DIANA.

                              SEAN: Oh, this is my wife Sybil --
                              Diana Scott.

                              DIANA: Hello.

                              SYBIL: Hello.

MR and MRS GLASS, MILES and WILLETT come out of the Main Room and
join DIANA, SYBIL and SEAN. They all start to walk upstairs.

                              MRS GLASS: I think he managed that
                              very well indeed, don't you?

                              MILES: Ah, here she is -- Diana.

                              WILLETT: Oh -- I was afraid you'd
                              walked out, you know, in protest
                              against my speechifying.

                              DIANA: (laughs) Not at all.

                              MILES: They've got something for us
                              upstairs. Crisps and Pepsi-cola.

                              WILLETT: (to DIANA, as they go away
                              from us) I'm afraid I've not seen
                              one of your films -- so little time
                              when one's in politics to do anything
                              except try and stay in --

MILES drops back now to join GLASS and MRS GLASS, with BASILDON.
As they continue up the stairs, MEMBERS are descending.

DUCHESS: Someone said that Bruce
Romford lost twenty-seven thousand
pounds last week -- absolutely ridiculous
exaggeration. Good evening.

MRS GLASS: Good evening.

DUCHESS: It was only twenty-one
thousand.

DUKE: Oh, is that all.

DUCHESS: Miles! How are you?

MILES: Well, your Grace . . . and you?

DUCHESS: Absolutely splendid.

She continues on down the stairs.

MILES: I am delighted. It was said
of her great-grandmother that the only
members of the cabinet who weren't her
lovers were the ones who had reason to
think they might be her father.

WILLETT: (to DIANA, amiably) Yes, poor
Elspeth, she's got a lot to live up to.

MILES: Well, if it isn't the Lord
Grant.

LORD GRANT: My dear Miles . . .
I like your black boys, John. I
suppose I can't wrap one up and take
him home?

BASILDON: I wouldn't advise you to try.

MILES: They're all numbered, Alex,
and I wouldn't try to change your luck
if I were you. I think everything's
laid on here.

WILLETT has taken DIANA's arm, paternally, on the landing and opens
a door.

WILLETT: Would you like to see the
Library?

DIANA: Oh . . .

WILLETT: Only one way to preserve an
old library these days and that's to
build a gambling hall round it.

They have come level with a huge, dominating equestrian portrait
of Royalty on which we now close and hold.

CUT TO

50. INT. THE LIBRARY. NIGHT.

An elegant book-lined room, filled with bridge tables. WILLETT
and DIANA alone. WILLETT is sitting with his feet up and a rapt
expression on his face. We first hear DIANA's voice and then PAN
round to pick her up sitting in an armchair declaiming from a
volume of Shakespeare.

DIANA: (reading) "This royal throne of
kings, this scepter'd isle,
This earth of majesty, this seat of Mars,
This other Eden, demi-paradise,
This fortress built by nature for herself
Against infection and the hand of war;
This happy breed of men, this little
world;
This precious stone set in the silver
sea . . .
Which serves it in the office of a wall
Or as a moat defensive to a house,
Against the envy of less happier lands,
This blessed plot, this earth, this
realm, this England."

DIANA reads with the honest monotony of an eager auditionist.
WILLETT, without opening his eyes, claps solemnly. DIANA
meanwhile has been running her free hand nervously along the seat
cushion lining. She has found something. She fetches it up and
looks at it. It is a plaque used in gambling at the club. It is
stamped with the face value £25.

CUT TO

51. INT. GAMBLING ROOM. PLAQUE D'OR. NIGHT.

A Greek Millionaire, ARTEMIS STAVROPOULOS, is betting heavily at
Baccarat. He shows no emotion, but loses impassively. Below the
table line he toys cautiously with a string of amber 'worry beads.'

GLASS comes in, with BASILDON, and nods to ARTEMIS, a small, ugly, tubby man, with a certain dignity. The DUCHESS looks at GLASS, but is not acknowledged.

MEMBERS and GUESTS at the tables. An atmosphere of important ritual. Divine service. A new bank is being laid out, rows of rich plaques, before play at a new table. DIANA watching. LORD GRANT is now with CARLOTTA.

DIANA steps forward. She is still nursing her £25 plaque.

Play going on. LADY BRENTWOOD is now next to DIANA, putting on a bet.

> LADY BRENTWOOD: I do want to see your new film.

She puts a £5 plaque on a sixieme. DIANA with apparent coolness puts her £25 next to it. They win. A casual CROUPIER chucks her her winnings. She takes them, inwardly shaken. But no one seems interested or impressed. Shattering!

> CUT TO

52. EXT. GLASS HOUSE. NIGHT.

DIANA and MILES walk towards the Glass House. As they climb the shallow steps through the central courtyard we ZOOM BACK. They shrivel into dwarfs against the huge buildings.

> MILES: That's the Glass House.

They stop and look at the modern statue which towers over them.

> DIANA: What's this supposed to be?

> MILES: Oh, it's known familiarly in the Group as three couples taking their pleasure with a fourth looking on.

> DIANA: Charming.

They walk on towards the Glass House.

> DIANA: Won't it be locked?

> MILES: One has a key.

> DIANA: One would.

They walk up the steps and reach the main door which MILES unlocks.

                                                        CUT TO

53. INT. MILES' OFFICE. NIGHT.

It is very luxurious indeed. A de Kooning hangs on the wall in the
outer office.

                    DIANA: (o.s.) Is this you?

                    MILES: (flatly) My secretary.

DIANA advances into SHOT, barefoot, luxuriating in the thick carpet
as in snow.

                    DIANA: Do you go winter sporting?

                    MILES: (o.s.) Yes, I do. Do you?

                    DIANA: (shakes her head) No, I don't
                    do anything.

She looks at him.

                    MILES: What is it?

                    DIANA: Do you have parents? I can't
                    imagine you with parents.

                    MILES: Yes, I have. Two of them.

                    DIANA: (smiles) Imagine . . .

MILES opens a shelf of books and reveals drinks.

                    MILES: What?

                    DIANA: If it took three.

                    MILES: Took three?

                    DIANA: Sexes to make a child.

                    MILES: Very entertaining.

                    DIANA: Everything would be different,
                    wouldn't it? Quite different. With
                    three sexes.

MILES: Haven't we got enough problems
with two?

CUT TO

54. INT. BOARDROOM. GLASS HOUSE. NIGHT.

The great boardroom table with pads and pencils and crystal pen
sets, ink holders. A very modern room lined with fine paintings.
DIANA looking. She discovers a small safe behind a sculpture on a
pedestal in a corner.

DIANA: Ooh . . . Is this where the
Glass millions are stored?

MILES: Millions? No.

DIANA: Oh, don't tell me it only
contains a pint of milk and a four
and sixpenny book of stamps! Leave
me my illusions, please!

MILES: It's mainly papers.

DIANA: Oh . . . Important papers?

MILES: Very.

DIANA: Do open it. I should love to
see an important paper.

MILES shakes his head.

DIANA: I never have. Wouldn't you?
Under any circumstances?

He shakes his head.

DIANA: If someone made it worth your
while? <u>Really</u> worth your while?

MILES has taken a battery electric shaver out of a drawer in his
desk and begins, casually, to shave.

DIANA: Have you ever been afraid?

Miles finishes shaving.

DIANA: Really afraid?

DIANA gets up on the boardroom table and starts to walk towards
the CAMERA.

MILES puts down his razor and takes up a drink.

                DIANA: What's an important paper about?

                MILES: All sorts of things.

                DIANA: People you're about to take over?

                MILES: It could be. The people we're
interested in. One reason or another.

                DIANA: Don't people . . . know when you're
interested in them?

                MILES: They know. Sometimes.

                DIANA: Well, then --

MILES put his drink down on the table.

                MILES: But they don't know how
interested.

                DIANA: No, I suppose not.

She walks on down the table and stops as she reaches MILES.

                DIANA: That's not so easy to tell,
I suppose.

                MILES: No. One hopes not.

                DIANA: I wish you'd open up.

                MILES: I can't do that.

                          CUT TO

55. EXT. TRAFALGAR SQUARE. DAWN.

The squeal of tyres. We pick up the Lotus going round the Square
and away from us. DIANA is at the wheel. Squeal of tyres again.
It comes round for another go.

                DIANA: (laughs) Sorry.

>MILES: What for?

>DIANA: Oh, I just seem to be leaving most of your tyres on the road.

>MILES: Enjoy yourself. With the compliments of the Glass Organization.

>DIANA: (irritably impressed) Don't you possess <u>anything</u> of your own?

>MILES: Only the things I can't replace.

The car going round the corner and along the road past the National Gallery.

>DIANA: (over) Of course I told Robert about Miles. Huh -- he didn't mean anything, after all. I was always -- always absolutely honest with Robert. I always had to be --

>CUT TO

56. INT. DIANA'S BEDROOM. DAY.

Down by the side of the bed is a row of elegant shoes from which DIANA selects, with her feet, a pair.

>DIANA: (over) -- always -- Well, there's nothing wrong with someone helping you with your career after all -- is there?

CLOSE on a long pair of gloves which lie amongst a clutter of stuffed animals on DIANA's bed. DIANA's hands come into the picture and she slowly slips the gloves on. PAN up to reveal DIANA in front of the mirror. She pats her hair.

>DIANA: (over) Miles was just that madly helpful. He knew absolutely everyone.

>CUT TO

57. INT. PRODUCER'S OFFICE. DAY.

SEAN is sitting behind a desk. Two OTHER MEN at either side of him. One seems dazed and asleep, the other is writing as he talks.

DIANA is at the opposite side of the desk. She is very pretty, face over made-up, a mad hat on.

> SEAN: We just wanted to have a look at you.
>
> PRODUCER: Yes, we just wanted to take a look at you.
>
> DIANA: Well, have a look.

Although she is pretending to be casual she is a little nervous.

> MAN: Would you look towards the street?

She turns her head.

> MAN: (looks at her) That's right. Now . . . (he unwinds paper clip and puts it in his ear) . . . the door. That's right, now I want you to look at me . . . but keep your neck at the same angle.

SHOT of DIANA doing that.

> MAN: Well, what do you think?
>
> SEAN: Yes, she's all right -- um -- fine, fine.
>
> PRODUCER: Has she enough profile?
>
> SEAN: Yes, sure -- she'll be standing up most of the time.
>
> DIANA: Excuse me, but I don't even know what the film is called.
>
> SEAN: Jacqueline.

The PRODUCER picks up a paperback book. Waves it at her.

> DIANA: Oh -- the book.
>
> SEAN: Yes.
>
> DIANA: And what part would it be?

> SEAN: Jacqueline.

DIANA is astonished.

> DIANA: Oh . . .

CUT TO

58. EXT. MANSION. NIGHT. (FILM SEQUENCE).

The terrace of a large country house. All is dark and still but
for the hoot of an owl. Suddenly light comes on in the house.
DRAMATIC MUSIC surges up as DIANA, wearing black underwear and a
black negligee, runs from the front of the house onto the terrace.
She is in a state of agitation.

She comes into CLOSE UP and stops. She hears a noise, sees something
and lets out a wild scream. A pistol shot. She begins to fall.
STOP ACTION 1. STOP ACTION 2 as she falls to the ground, and lies
prostrate and motionless.

SUPERIMPOSE lurid Chinese-print overpowering Credits:

> "JACQUELINE, JACQUELINE . . . . ."

As the Credits disappear we hear a well-echoed voice.

> VOICE: (o.s.) Who was Jacqueline?
> Who knew Jacqueline?

CUT TO

59. INT. CINEMA. NIGHT.

DIANA is sitting in the audience with ROBERT who stares at the
screen. She looks at him and making an apologetic face takes his
hand.

> DIANA: So much for me. That's me lot.

> ROBERT: (amazed, turning and looking at
> her) What?

> DIANA: There was a bit at the end when
> I was picked up by the ambulance, but
> that's been cut.

> ROBERT: Tough.

                    DIANA: From now on it's just about who
                    did me and why.

DIANA sighs and looks round, as if the picture were over. DIANA's
P.O.V.: MILES sitting with another GIRL a few seats away. He
adjusts a fur around the GIRL's shoulders, whispers down her ear
and looks back over his shoulder. He removes his arm.

C.U. DIANA looking towards MILES.

ROBERT looks at DIANA and then follows her gaze to MILES.

                                                    CUT TO

60. INT. DIANA'S FLAT. LIVING ROOM/KITCHEN. NIGHT.

The room is in darkness.   ROBERT and DIANA switch on the lights as
they reel into the flat.   DIANA lies down on the settee. ROBERT
goes into the kitchen.

                    DIANA: Wheeeee! What a party! What
                    a wake!

                    ROBERT: What a bunch of Zombies.

                    DIANA: (rather high) Did you hate that
                    movie? You did, didn't you? If you
                    did, say you did.

                    ROBERT: I did.

                    DIANA: (shocked) You didn't!

                    ROBERT: All right, I didn't.

                    DIANA: You did. Well, I must say
                    I 'ave never bin so hinsulted in all
                    me days. Me first taitle role.

ROBERT, in the kitchen, walks over to the fridge.

                    DIANA: (from settee) Robert . . .
                    (kicks off her shoes) What did you
                    think of Miles?

                    ROBERT: I'm absolutely crazy about him.

                    DIANA: No -- seriously -- what did you?

ROBERT: Well -- what can I say?

DIANA: Do you think I've been a fool?

ROBERT: No. People do what they want to.

DIANA: You are jealous.

ROBERT: Who knows what I am.

DIANA: Well -- you're the one I bed with.

ROBERT: At present.

DIANA: (clouds with tears) I hate you. What a thing to say --

ROBERT: Well, what do you want me to say? You know as well as I do what you're doing.

He walks into the living room and over to the fireplace.

DIANA: Don't be jealous. There's no need.

ROBERT: No.

DIANA: Anyway this is the finish.

ROBERT: Of what?

DIANA: Me and showbiz.

ROBERT: Oh -- why?

DIANA: (oh well, here goes) Well -- it so happens I'm * * * preggers.

ROBERT: Oh.

DIANA: Are you angry?

ROBERT shakes his head.

DIANA: Are you pleased?

[pregnant]

He comes over to her and puts his head in her lap.

> ROBERT: I'm pleased. You should have told me sooner. I'd have carried you. I can't hear it ticking.
>
> DIANA: It won't for months.
>
> ROBERT: No, I know that.
>
> DIANA: Of course, you would.
>
> ROBERT: Are you pleased?
>
> DIANA: If you are. What shall we call it?
>
> ROBERT: Jacqueline.
>
> DIANA: Oh, but of course. Jacqueline.
>
> CUT TO

61. INT. MATERNALLY YOURS. DEPARTMENT STORE. DAY.

DIANA and JULIE having a shopping spree to get maternity clothes for DIANA. It is only a few days later. But we start on a gorgeous baby's rattle being shaken in C.U. Has she had the child? No, she is simply toying with the idea. She and JULIE twitter over the floppy toys and chinking rattle-type things on the counter. An ASSISTANT is bringing pretty you'll-never-guess maternity clothes. DIANA holds a dress up against herself.

> DIANA: Shall I wear it at Pat and Margie's tomorrow night?
>
> JULIE: But darling it's much too soon for that.
>
> DIANA: Oh, yes, * * * just for a giggle! * * * (to Assistant) I'll have this.

Behind them a very pregnant WOMAN is talking to another ASSISTANT.

> CUT TO

___

[but] [Hmm.]

62. INT/EXT. THE LIFT. DEPARTMENT STORE. DAY.

DIANA and JULIE stand in the crowded lift. DIANA is very silent
as the lift falls, floor by floor, back to earth.

                                                   CUT TO

63. EXT. STREET. DAY.

DIANA and JULIE walking towards CAMERA on the crowded pavement.

                         DIANA: (over) I hadn't really thought
                         about what it meant, you know. It
                         seemed lovely, then I realised it was
                         going to be the ruination of my career.
                         Disrupt people's lives, you know --
                         mine, Robert's, everybody's. I just
                         began to realise I couldn't go through
                         with it. * * * Julie was lovely. She's
                         terribly nice because you know she --
                         she had a miscarriage herself recently
                         and -- er -- well -- er -- she sort of
                         knew the ropes and that.

                                                   CUT TO

64. INT. DOCTOR'S OFFICE. DAY.

DIANA is sitting facing the DOCTOR over the desk. A pile of
five-pound notes is put by DIANA's hand on the edge of the very
elegant hand-tooled desk. All we can see of the DOCTOR is a framed
photograph of his wife and children.

                         DOCTOR: (o.s.) Oh thank you. If you
                         can be here Friday at eleven that would
                         be best. Bring overnight things and,
                         oh, better skip breakfast that morning,
                         would you?

                         DIANA: Thank you.

                                                   CUT TO

65. INT. PRIVATE NURSING HOME. DAY.

DIANA is lying quite still in a white room. A NURSE comes in with a tray-lunch. Chicken.

The NURSE puts down the tray and pats DIANA's pillows, then leans forward to take the cover off the dish.

> NURSE: How do you feel?

> DIANA: I'm never going to have anything to do with sex again as long as I live.

The NURSE gives a * * * tight little smile and goes. DIANA looks at the chicken. Oddly babylike! She leans over very suddenly and heaves up, choking with tears. No one comes.

She closes her eyes. She opens them again. ROBERT is there with a bunch of flowers.

> ROBERT: Hello. How do you feel?

> DIANA: Empty.

He smiles * * * bleakly.

> ROBERT: When're they going to let you out?

> DIANA: (shrugs) Any time. Lots of eager ladies queuing for the bed, it seems.

> ROBERT: (smiles wanly) I can believe that.

> DIANA: I'm not going back to the flat.

> ROBERT: I see.

> DIANA: You don't -- but it doesn't matter.

> ROBERT: All right. I don't.

---

65.   [wan]

   [wanly]

> DIANA: My sister came to see me.
> I'm going down there. The country.
> I need. . . .

The tears roll down her cheeks.

> ROBERT: (comes to her) What?
> Jesus . . . I --
>
> DIANA: Don't touch me.
>
> ROBERT: I just wish that . . .
>
> DIANA: No good wishing.
>
> ROBERT: No. I'll probably stay on at
> the flat for a bit. If you want me
> that's where I'll be --
>
> DIANA: Don't forget to feed the fishes.
>
> ROBERT: Mmmm.
>
> DIANA: Poor little things!

She makes herself unhappy with the skill of a child.

Clash of dustbin lids below. ROBERT turns and walks miserably to the window.

> CUT TO

66. EXT. PROSSER JONES' GARDEN. DAY.

It is Sunday. ALEC and FELICITY are sitting in deck chairs after lunch with the newspapers, doing the crossword puzzles. A third chair is empty beside them. At the bottom of the garden, DIANA is playing with WILLIAM who is wearing a Wild-Man-From-Borneo mask on his head, a gun in his hand. Their dog is scampering around with them.

> WILLIAM: Bang, bang.

DIANA falls on the grass.

> DIANA: Ooh, ooh, ooh.
>
> WILLIAM: Are you really dead?

        DIANA: Deading.

        WILLIAM: I bet you can't catch me --
        I run very fast.

        FELICITY: * * * (not looking up from her
        paper) I've got trouble at Number Ten --
        what have you got?

        ALEC: * * * (the same) I've got 'Morality
        in the test tube.' Don't point guns,
        William. I've told you that before.

        FELICITY: I don't want her to get too
        tired, Alec.

        ALEC: No.

DIANA is chasing WILLIAM with the gun.

        ALEC: Come on William -- that's enough --
        leave Auntie Diana alone.

        FELICITY: Come on, darling -- don't be
        tiresome.

WILLIAM and DIANA stop playing and join FELICITY and ALEC.

        ALEC: Come on -- come and sit down
        here -- and play with your comics.

        FELICITY: Darling, come and sit down.
        You don't want to get too tired out,
        you know. Come and relax. * * * (Indicates
        Sunday papers) Have a comic, help yourself.
        A pity you missed the daffodils this year,
        darling. They were absolutely lovely.

                             CUT TO

67. INT. PROSSER JONES' DINING ROOM. NIGHT.

CLOSE on a side table where ALEC is carving the beef, FELICITY serving
the vegetables. There is a mirror above the table and as she turns
to bring a plate to the table FELICITY catches sight of herself in
the mirror and touches her hair.

PULL BACK to reveal the table where DR IVOR DAWLISH, his wife HELEN,
RUPERT CRABTREE, a young officer from the nearby garrison and DIANA

next to him are sitting. FELICITY puts the plate down in front of
HELEN and goes back to the serving table.

> ALEC: Ivor, do you like crispie?
>
> IVOR: Just a bit Alec, but no fat.
>
> FELICITY: Here you are, Ivor.
>
> IVOR: Changed your hair style, I see,
> Felicity.
>
> FELICITY: Oh, I'm glad you like it.
> Yes, they've got a new Hungarian -- a
> refugee, who does it nicely -- gives it
> volume which is what I like. Now do
> start please, Rupert. Don't stand on
> ceremony, dear. (to ALEC) Is that
> mine, darling?
>
> ALEC: Yes.
>
> FELICITY: Thank you.
>
> IVOR: Lawn looks good, Alec; how do
> you do it?

RUPERT passes the gravy to DIANA.

> ALEC: It's that new Staygreen.
>
> IVOR: What about that plastic sprinkler
> I recommended?
>
> ALEC: It's absolutely useless. Can't
> get the stuff through the holes.
>
> IVOR: Oh, really? I'm awfully sorry.

FELICITY walks to the table and comes and sits down between IVOR
and RUPERT.

> FELICITY: It's going to be one of
> those frightful gardening conversations
> -- gardening's very therapeutic, but you
> really must stop it.
>
> IVOR: Yes, all right. (To DIANA) Saw
> your film at the local fleapit.

FELICITY: Oh yes.

IVOR: I'm sorry we didn't see more of you.

HELEN: Unfortunately we missed the beginning.

RUPERT, silent until now, bursts forth.

RUPERT: Best part. You were stunning.

DIANA: Liked my black lingerie, did you?

Ahahahahahaha! FELICITY smiles uneasily, but DIANA seems to be going down well.

HELEN: Ivor's been after me to buy some.

IVOR: Really, Helen, is nothing sacred?

HELEN: Not much!

IVOR: See what you do to our suburban morals? Your type of picture?

RUPERT: No, honestly, you were jolly good.

DIANA: Thank you.

FELICITY serves RUPERT.

FELICITY: Um -- Rupert makes films too, you know.

DIANA: Oh, how fascinating.

RUPERT: Honestly, Felicity, I thought we had made a solemn pact --

DIANA: No. You must tell me about it.

RUPERT: Well -- um -- It's something I had to do for the War House actually -- er -- training film. . . . .

FELICITY: Oh -- a training film?

> RUPERT: Hmm. Umm. How to service an
> armoured car.
>
> DIANA: A star vehicle, no less!
>
> RUPERT: Hadn't thought of that.
> Nothing like yours, of course.
>
> FELICITY: (To ALEC) Darling, could I
> have -- Alec -- * * * pass the horseradish.

ALEC looks up.

WILLIAM appears at the door in his pyjamas. ALEC is the first
to see him.

> WILLIAM: Mummy . . .
>
> ALEC: What <u>are</u> you doing up at this
> hour?
>
> WILLIAM: I haven't had my chocolate
> or anything.
>
> FELICITY: Oh William, you are being so
> boring. Darling, I thought we had
> discussed all this before.

WILLIAM feels his parents' reaction and is about to weep.

> ALEC: Now don't start your snivelling.
>
> DIANA: Don't worry, Felicity, I'll
> find him his chocolate.
>
> FELICITY: Oh, would you, Di darling.
> Thank you so much.

DIANA jumps up and goes out with WILLIAM. RUPERT rises and looks
longingly after DIANA as she goes out.

> FELICITY: Yes . . . yes.

RUPERT sits down.

---

67.   [may I have a little ketchup.]

FELICITY: Absolutely brilliant with children -- quite quite marvellous. I hope -- I do apologise. * * * So sorry.

CUT TO

68. INT. PROSSER JONES' BEDROOM. NIGHT.

They are considering the problem of DIANA as they settle for the night in their big double bed with headboard and fitted bedside tables. They rotate and shuffle like a pair of dogs in a twin basket.

ALEC: What was actually wrong with Diana's original husband?

FELICITY: * * * Tony Bridges? * * * Too young.

ALEC: Rupert's the right age.

FELICITY: And steady.

ALEC: Well, Bridges was steady.

FELICITY: But he was too young. Rupert's the right age.

ALEC: Yes. Do you think he . . . um . . . ?

FELICITY: I think he did . . .

ALEC: Do you think she . . . ?

FELICITY: I think she did, yes. Alec, you've got your elbow somehow.

ALEC: I wasn't aware of it. Sorry dear.

CUT TO

69. INT. LONDON EXPRESS. EARLY MORNING.

TRACKING SHOT through train window on to passing countryside, DIANA

---

68.   [Oh] [Oh]

sitting in a corner seat, forlorn. She is wearing a coat down over her knees and sitting very sedately. Unusual for her.

> ALEC: (over) I shall never understand this -- how you and she -- same parents, same background --
>
> FELICITY: (over) Yes, I know it is odd.

CUT TO

70. INT. DIANA'S FLAT. HALL & BEDROOM. EARLY MORNING.

DIANA comes in through the front door and goes into the bedroom.

> ALEC: (over) This chap of hers in London . . . Is that all finished now?
>
> FELICITY: (over) Oh yes, there's no more of that at all -- completely finished.

CUT TO

71. INT. DIANA'S FLAT. BEDROOM. EARLY MORNING.

DIANA'S P.O.V.: ROBERT tossing in bed, asleep.

> DIANA: I'm back.

ROBERT just waking up.

DIANA opens her coat. She is still in her nightie.

ROBERT blinks.

> ROBERT: Like that?

DIANA gets on to the bed beside ROBERT. They kiss.

> DIANA: I had to. It was so boring I could have screamed.
>
> ROBERT: You mean you came in a train dressed like that?
>
> DIANA: No one noticed.
>
> ROBERT: You funny girl, aren't you?

* * *

* * * He cannot resist embracing her joyfully, though with a kind
of melancholy foreboding.

                                                      CUT TO

72. INT. SITTING ROOM. DAY.

ROBERT is typing an article. DIANA wanders in. She looks over his
shoulder. He looks questioningly. She shrugs, wanders off. He
watches her, uneasy, types a little.

She sprinkles food on the goldfish bowl. And sighs. And files
at her nails, then starts to clean the polish off them. The
noise of the file sets ROBERT's teeth on edge. He stops typing.
She stops. He types. She starts again. He stops. She stops
and goes over to the window. He types. She taps on the window.
She clicks her teeth.

ROBERT pulls out the paper from the machine and crumples it.
DIANA whistles through her teeth. She looks at a print they've
stuck on the wall and wrinkles her nose.

ROBERT inserts more paper. He looks round. DIANA is on the floor
doing bicycling in the air. The moulding round the light fitting
is of little cupids playing naughtily with the flex holder.
DIANA pedals on.

DIANA gets up and ambles around. She looks out of the window.
She goes out of one terrace door, in the next, out of the next,
back through the second. She hangs onto the doorpost and leans
at ROBERT.

          DIANA: Do you want some coffee?

          ROBERT: No, I don't think so.

She goes on ambling in and out. She comes in the door nearest
him. A silence.

          DIANA: Sorry. Sorry I spoke.

ROBERT types a bit more and then stops.

---

71.   [One day I'm going to have to bail you out of
                       the clink . . . for indecent exposure.

                       DIANA: Will you?

                       ROBERT: Umm . . . course I will.]

                    ROBERT: Would you rather I went up to
                    the office and worked?

DIANA .shrugs and scuffs her foot. She goes to the mirror and starts
doing funny things with her hair. He looks at her for a moment or
two and then starts typing again.

                    DIANA: Oh, I don't know -- there's
                    something about a typewriter.

                    ROBERT: (laughs) I'm sorry. Here,
                    quick, come on. Look, why don't you
                    do something, eh? Why not that
                    audition? It's your sort of thing.
                    Go on, have a try -- just go on and have
                    a go -- take the car, and don't crash it.

He takes out his car keys and holds them out to her.

                    DIANA: (sarcastically) Si, señor.
                    Gracias, señor.

She gives him a look and goes towards the door. He starts typing.
She jerks out.

                                                        CUT TO

73. INT. WEST END THEATRE. DAY.

An audition in progress. A pretty young GIRL, very neat and pro,
is reading a scene for the feet (all that is visible of the PRODUCERS)
in the stalls.

                    GIRL: I want to dance. I want to
                    dance. That's what you'll never
                    understand. I don't want to think.
                    I want to dance.

She says these lines with some conviction, her body moving as if
trapped but wanting to burst out.

DIANA is talking to the ASSISTANT STAGE MANAGER. She watches the
GIRL nervously from the wings.

                    A.S.M.: Your name please.

                    DIANA: Diana Scott.

A.S.M.: (ticking it on a list) Diana Scott . . . Would you like to wait over there, please.

DIANA: Thank you.

PRODUCER: (to GIRL on stage) Tell me about yourself. What you've been up to recently.

GIRL: Well, I've done six months at Bournemouth rep, playing leads and things. In television, Z Cars, the Avengers, a season at Worthing rep, a couple of Edgar Wallaces at Merton Park.

PRODUCER: (o.s.) That's fine. Thank you. Thank you very much. Next, please.

The PRODUCER, SECRETARY and MANAGER shake their heads.

A.S.M.: Miss Joyce Green, please. Miss Joyce Green, thank you.

PRODUCER: (o.s.) Miss Green.

SECOND GIRL: (o.s.) Yes.

PRODUCER: (o.s.) You have that speech?

SECOND GIRL: (o.s.) Yes, yes I have. Right, thank you. I want to dance. I want to dance. That's what you'll never understand. I don't want to think. I want to dance.

Other GIRLS wait with DIANA, for their turn. They are all quiet and assured, check make-up and books. DIANA feels hopelessly inadequate. The feet are quite impersonal -- she doesn't know who's in the stalls and there's no way of jumping the queue. She turns and walks away.

CUT TO

74. EXT. STREET. PARKING METER. DAY.

A car drives towards us and stops. It prepares to back into parking space. DIANA drives in forwards behind him. The DRIVER shouts at her.

> DRIVER: Hey -- that's my meter.
>
> DIANA: Sorry.
>
> DRIVER: Sorry -- I should think you are sorry! Go on, get out of it.

DIANA gets out of her car and puts 6d in the parking meter.

> DRIVER: Women drivers . . .

> CUT TO

75.   INT. GYMNASIUM. DAY.

DIANA enters. A strange, unreal atmosphere. Noises.

MILES is fencing. He performs with exceptional ease. Even when the poise is against him he is unruffled, always balanced. What is conveyed here, is the attraction of facelessness, of a contest without personal commitment on either side.

MILES scores a conclusive hit, removes his mask and comes with a look of mild surprise over to DIANA. He salutes her with his weapon.

> MILES: Well . . . look who's here!
>
> DIANA: Your secretary told me you'd be here. I hope you don't mind.
>
> MILES: Mind? Not at all. How're things?
>
> DIANA: (pats her tummy) Flat.

> CUT TO

76.   INT. MILES' FLAT. SITTING ROOM. DAY.

DIANA and MILES are facing each other. They raise glasses of milk to each other, catching exactly the salute two fencers give each other before the bout begins.

The flat is elegant, even sumptuous, without being ostentatious.
Subtly, there is an echo here of the gymnasium, an air of functional
strangeness. The parallel bars are echoed by a small gridiron
abstract, the sporting prints by small erotic drawings of a delicate
order, etc.

           MILES: Skol.

           DIANA: Skol.

They drink.

           DIANA: (looks round) Nice place. Had
           it long?

           MILES: Not too long. It's convenient.
           The firm owns it. Came to us by
           mistake.

           DIANA: (at the window now) Nice
           mistake.

           MILES: One tries to see that one's
           mistakes usually are.

There is an Adolphe Gottlieb on the wall. Beside it, a * * *
de Kooning, with dribbles.

DIANA turns and leans against a metal bookcase and drinks.

They put their glasses, empty, side by side on the shelf. The
glasses stay.

           CUT TO

77. INT. MILES' BEDROOM. DAY.

Small change, all silver, being stacked with great care on the top
of the chest of drawers. The money graded through half crowns to
sixpence.

MILES takes a hanger out of the wardrobe where his suits hang in
neat rows like executed gentlemen. He takes out a hanger and holds
it out.

---

76.   [small]

DIANA's bare arm takes it. The essence of this scene is that the
two are never seen embracing or in two-shot. They undress and seduce
each other very coolly, in ritual, never as part of a relationship,
never in mutual joy.

> DIANA: I always feel as if there's one
> more corner to turn . . . and I'll be
> there.
>
> MILES: (sitting on a chair, taking
> off his shoes) And so you will.

DIANA raises a stocking over her head.

> DIANA: And there'll be another.
>
> MILES: (taking off his sweater) That's
> the attraction of corners.

The coverlet is pulled off the bed and neatly folded.

> DIANA: I do love Robert, you know.
>
> MILES: Why not?

CUT TO

78. EXT. STREET. DAY.

DIANA's (and ROBERT's) Mini parked at the meter. It clicks up,
donk! -- to excess time.

CUT TO

79. INT. MILES' BEDROOM. DAY.

MILES walks slowly forward.

DIANA lying on the bed. She turns over on to her front.

MILES takes the cigarette out of his mouth. DIANA smiles. MILES
bends forward, and DIANA closes her eyes.

CUT TO

80. EXT. STREET. DAY.

Penalty! The red warning flicks up.

DIANA and MILES walking along the pavement to her car. She gets
into it.

> DIANA: My goodness, what a bit of luck.

> MILES: You're a clever girl.

> DIANA: My lucky day.

> CUT TO

81. INT. HALL AND SITTING ROOM. DIANA'S FLAT. NIGHT.

It is dark. DIANA comes in the front door. She turns on the hall
light. She looks puzzled.

> DIANA: Robert?

She comes into the sitting room. She turns on the light.

ROBERT is sitting in a chair by the window.

> DIANA: What the hell are you doing?

> ROBERT: What the hell am I doing?

> DIANA: Sitting in the dark.

> ROBERT: Admiring the view.

> DIANA: Oh. Good for you.

He looks at her.

> DIANA: Sorry I'm so late. The car
> got towed away.

> ROBERT: It did?

> DIANA: Bloody meters. I had to go
> miles to get it back.

> ROBERT: Poor you.

> DIANA: So I'd have been back sooner if
> it hadn't been for that.

> ROBERT: Where did you have to go?

DIANA: I don't know. Taxi took me.
I didn't know. It took hours.

ROBERT: Didn't you have to pay?
I mean to get it out?

DIANA: Yes, of course. You always
have to pay to get your car out, don't
you? What sort of day have you had?

ROBERT: Quiet. What kept you?

DIANA: I told you, I had to get the car.

ROBERT: I mean so that you overshot
the meter.

DIANA: Oh. Well . . . I didn't go to
my audition. I went to my agent
instead, and I think I've got a job
coming up in Paris soon.

ROBERT has taken two pounds out of his wallet, and looks straight
at her. DIANA looks amazed and puzzled.

DIANA: What's that for?

ROBERT: * * * Getting the car out.

She smiles and puts her arm round his neck and sits in his lap.

DIANA: Where would I be without you?

CUT TO

82. EXT. PARIS. DAY.

Despite all of her affectations of worldly knowledge, it is the
first time that DIANA has ever been to Paris. MILES drives her
around in an open car, showing her all the sights of the town.

DIANA: (over) Of course, Miles was a
perfect guide because he knew Paris on
every possible level. He knew the
tourist level . . .

                                    CUT TO

83. EXT. PARIS. NIGHT.

                      DIANA: (over) . . . and then he could
                      take one inside and show one how
                      sophisticated people live. Oh, we
                      went to a fabulous wedding, I remember . . .

The tone is now slightly different. DIANA and MILES and their
party have dined at a smart restaurant and are now on their way
to a slightly less banal rendezvous.

                                    CUT TO

84. INT. HOTEL CORRIDOR/BEDROOM.

DIANA and MILES and their party coming down the hotel corridor
and entering a bedroom where they are greeted by MADAME.

                      DIANA: (over) Chloe Calmen the film
                      actress had remarried Toto Daniarno,
                      you know, the American Magazine heir,
                      and afterwards we went on to the most
                      extraordinary place with them. They
                      were astonishing people -- terribly
                      sophisticated and sort of emotionally
                      inquisitive; but it was a marvellous
                      feeling. Raoul Maxim, the Nouvelle
                      Vague film director, was our guide --

RAOUL is embracing the hotel proprietress who is pouring champagne
for the guests: * * * LUMUMBA, the African writer who had recently
settled in Paris, BILLIE CASTIGLIONE the American sculptress, and
a whole group of fascinating people.

                      MADAME: Naughty Miles! * * * Comme c'est
                      * * * exquis de te voir -- comment ça va?

MILES introduces DIANA to MADAME.

                      MADAME: Are you English?

                      DIANA: Yes.

---

84. [MAMBO]

                      [Ah] [bon]

        MADAME: Ah, she is beautiful. You
        live in England?

        DIANA: Yes.

        MADAME: Yes.

Sitting on a bed a bit isolated from the group is a * * * WOMAN
wearing only a * * * white plastic macintosh. She is given champagne
by RAOUL. The MADAME excuses herself and leaves. Laughter and
chatter. They look at the * * * WOMAN. MILES whispers to BILLIE
as he touches a medallion which hangs round her neck and admires it.

        MILES: Ah Billie. One of yours?

She laughs.

        MILES: I thought I recognised the
        rivets. You're improving.

        BILLIE: Miles, I love you. You're
        such a . . .

She whispers in his ear, eyeing DIANA as she does so.

        MILES: Come, Billie, if I didn't know
        you were a man, I'd be very shocked.

DIANA, who has been drinking and talking to RAOUL, moves towards
MILES.

        MILES: Diana darling . . . I want you to
        meet the Billie Castiglione. He's one
        of the greatest sculptresses in Paris
        and he's dying to do your bust.

        BILLIE: I'm going to kill that man, I
        am . . . You've got a beautiful head.
        Wonderful bones. Truly.

        DIANA: (flattered) Thank you.

---

84.   [GIRL]

      [GIRL]

The WOMAN on the bed indicates the chairs and invites them to sit
down. She apologises in French that the young man is late, she
cannot understand why, but he will be arriving any moment. The
chatter of the party subsides as they sit down in a semi-circle
facing the bed.

> WOMAN: Asseyez-vous, messieurdames.
> Soyez comme chez vous. Le jeune homme
> arrive tout de suite. Je ne sais pas
> qu'il lui arrive . . . Fumez, si vous
> voulez.

DIANA studies the young WOMAN intently. MILES offers her a cigarette
which she refuses.

> WOMAN: Merci, Monsieur, mais moi,
> je préfère des "menthole."

> BILLIE: It's very hot in here.

She takes off her coat.

> BILLIE: She's got an interesting head.

Suddenly the door is flung open and a personable YOUNG MAN who has
obviously been hurrying makes his appearance.

> YOUNG MAN: Mille pardons -- mais c'est
> absoluement impossible de parquer la
> voiture . . .

There is a polite murmur and then an abrupt silence as, loyal to his
metier, he begins to take off his tie and shirt. The WOMAN starts to
undress. We move in close to the SPECTATORS as they begin to watch
the performance.

> DIANA: (over) It was a great experience
> to be among genuinely adult people who
> were concerned above all with the fullest
> possible expression of their personalities.

The party watch.

85. EXT. 16^e ARRONDISSEMENT. NIGHT.

The PARTY getting out of two cars. DIANA wearing the white
mackintosh which she has bought from the PROSTITUTE. She parades
in it, showing her outrageousness.

RAOUL has unlocked the iron grille of the smart apartment building where he lives. This is living! DIANA surveys the street.

                                                           CUT TO

86. INT. RAOUL'S FLAT. NIGHT.

It is luxuriously furnished, what we can see of it, full of self-conscious "effects" -- lighting, outré furniture, etc.

A ciné projector has been rigged up. A white screen erects itself against the far wall and the projector runs wild white light onto it. Musique-concrète from a tape recorder.

> RAOUL: Alors, mes amis, nous jouerons le spécialité de la maison.
>
> TOTO: Qu'est-ce que c'est?
>
> RAOUL: C'est une espèce existentielle du cinéma-vérité! André, music please.
>
> MILES: This is going to be fun.
>
> DIANA: What is it?
>
> MILES: Well, it's a -- kind of truth game -- sort of.
>
> BILLIE: Come, will you play with me?
>
> DIANA: Oh -- no -- I don't know how to do this.

DIANA is alarmed, she doesn't panic but she feels uneasy, the low lights, the laughter of the others, LUMUMBA camping round in the white mackintosh which he has picked up, prancing into the light, all these things cause her a deep unease which show themselves in an almost brutal acceptance of what is happening, cheap grins, pulling up of skirts, etc. The music gets more frenetic.

BILLIE has put on LUMUMBA's leather jacket. It's all very weird.

> BILLIE: Diana, come on, play -- it's fun.
>
> DIANA: But I've never played it.
>
> BILLIE: Come on. I'll show you.

BILLIE pulls DIANA up off her chair while MILES watches.

The PARTY is now tramping round and round the room through the white light. LUMUMBA swings past in the mac.

> LUMUMBA: (American accent) Huh --
> when the music stops the cradle will
> rock.

Laughter. They parade around. Several people in other people's clothes, following LUMUMBA's lead.

The music stops. LUMUMBA is in the spot. He curtsies, looks coy.

> BILLIE: Why, Diana Scott, how you've
> changed.

> LUMUMBA: (touches his black face)
> Why, darling, it's only because I've
> got a little too much sunray.

> DIANA: I don't understand. Is he
> pretending to be me?

> BILLIE: You're home and dry.

DIANA looks at LUMUMBA and gives a dreadful sort of snigger. She turns and sees CHLOE resolutely changing clothes with RAOUL.

> CHLOE: Combien de fois --

> LUMUMBA: I don't understand français,
> je.

DIANA is alarmed. Does he hate her? She turns again.

> CHLOE: How many times --

Boos and catcalls. Not that old question! DIANA going.

> BILLIE: (puts an arm round DIANA) Diana,
> relax, relax, don't be frightened. It's
> fun. (Calls out) Will you come on a
> cruise with me to --

She grins at DIANA next to her.

> LUMUMBA: (cuts in) Only if I can have
> the top berth.

> RAOUL: What would you do to be in my
> next film, Diana?

> LUMUMBA: I don't know the name of it,
> but I'll definitely do it.

He makes big eyes. Laughter.

> DIANA: Why is he doing * * * <u>this?</u>

> BILLIE: It's * * * <u>fun.</u>

The music starts again. DIANA breaks away from BILLIE. But she
finds no MILES. He's with BABS. She shrugs and falls in behind
LUMUMBA as the game recommences.

As they go round now, there is a constant jump forward, and we
see that now everyone is wearing a piece of costume, at least,
belonging to someone else. Identities are completely swapped.
DIANA has MILES' shirt and jacket and tie. She is getting high
on the whole deal.

The music stops. She is in the light.

> MILES: Ah Miles, my dear fellow, I'd
> know you anywhere. Tell me, do you
> love Diana?

> DIANA: No.

> CHLOE: Is she good in bed, Miles?

> DIANA: I haven't noticed. I am.

.Laughter, some applause. DIANA, excited at this, sticks out her
tongue vindictively at MILES.

> BILLIE: Does she love you?

> DIANA: Like a prisoner loves the
> jailer. Because I carry a big bunch
> of keys.

> BABS: Oh shut up!

---

86.   [it?]

                            [all]

Oh la la! DIANA is playing with confidence.

MILES is amused, sort of.

> MILES: Miles, my love, have you ever been in love?
>
> DIANA: Yes, for as long as I can remember. With myself.
>
> LUMUMBA: Tell me Miles, if you could be anything in the world -- what would you most want to be?
>
>   * * *
>
> DIANA: A pimp in a royal whorehouse.

The music begins again. DIANA reels out of the light into MILES.

> MILES: Well, well?

She puts her arms round his neck and kisses him passionately, looks sad and serious at him.

> CUT   CUT TO

87. INT. LONDON AIRPORT. CUSTOMS LOUNGE. DAY.

> ANNOUNCER ON TANNOY: Will Mr and Mrs Parker please come straight to General Enquiry -- Mr and Mrs Parker.

PASSENGERS coming through. We pick up MILES and DIANA. DIANA is carrying a shopping basket full of French provisions, a long loaf of bread, some salad, pâté, etc. She puts her arm through MILES', puts the provisions on the counter.

> PORTER: All right sir?
>
> MILES: Thank you.
>
> CUSTOMS MAN: Is this all your luggage?
>
> MILES: Yes, it is.
>
> CUSTOMS MAN: (holds up regulations board) Have you read this before?

---

86.   [MILES: I wanted to be a dancer.]

CUSTOMS MAN: Have you anything to declare?

MILES: Only her lunch . . .

DIANA: (over) The experience which I had had with Miles was something so new and so important to me that I couldn't, in fairness to everyone, let it end too abruptly.

CUT TO

88. TELEPHONE BOOTH. LONDON AIRPORT. DAY.

DIANA and MILES are both inside the phone booth. Outside on the ground are their cases and the basket of provisions.

MILES: (speaking in French accent) I have a personal call from Paris for a Mr Robert Gold, Western 7655. Mr Gold. Ne quittez pas. Ne quittez pas.

DIANA: Robert. Hello. I'm -- I'm ringing from . . .

DIANA: (over) I just couldn't help myself . . . I mean, all I wanted to do really was not hurt Robert -- you know -- that was the main thing.

CUT TO

89. INT. LIVING ROOM. DIANA'S FLAT. DAY.

ROBERT on the telephone.

DIANA: (over) I kept thinking to myself -- you know -- Miles'd sort of burn itself out . . . And that meanwhile all that mattered was trying to make sure that nobody got hurt -- that was the main thing.

CUT TO

90. INT. LIVING ROOM. MILES' FLAT. NIGHT.

DIANA and MILES are sitting on the floor eating the French provisions and drinking wine from the tile-topped coffee table. They are listening with great attentiveness to some * * * Jacques Brel records * * *. DIANA nods gravely at MILES.

                                                      CUT TO

91. EXT. MILES' FLAT. MAYFAIR STREET. DAY.

L.S. DIANA saying goodbye to MILES. They walk into the road as a taxi pulls up. DIANA gets into the taxi -- MILES into his car to go to the office. Bye!

                                                      CUT TO

92. INT. DIANA'S BEDROOM. DAY.

ROBERT is heard coming in the front door. He comes into the bedroom and finds DIANA's things strewn all over the room. He looks. There is a message written in lipstick on the dressing table mirror: "C.U. THERE! LOVE -- D." A red arrow points to an invitation card stuck in the corner of the mirror. Close on it. It reads: The Directors of the Brandini Gallery, etc., etc., Private View of the new paintings of RALPHIE RIGGS. The noise of the Private View starts immediately, chatter, chatter:

> TELEPUNDIT: He's spent more time in gaol than any other painter of his age. It gives him a tremendous edge, one can't help feeling.

ROBERT has gone to the bed and sees DIANA's passport and tickets. He turns them over ruefully.

                                                      CUT TO

93. INT. ART GALLERY. BOND STREET. NIGHT.

RALPHIE RIGGS' paintings are nearly all compositions involving bars, executions, floggings, etc. RALPHIE himself is 34, a tall, thin, grinning cockney who carries his new fame with almost cynical assurance.

> LADY: Is he really a crook?

---

90.   [French] [of a smart Chansonnier.]

TELEPUNDIT: (almost offended) Most
certainly he is. He's just served
five years. I've done an interview
with him for the programme on Sunday.
It's already in the can.

PSEUDO GREAT WRITER: . . . and No 24
"Man's Head in Bucket" are strongly
influenced by Grünewald.

LADY: He's got a fantastically lean
and hungry look. (Whispers) Is it
true he's tremendous in bed?

TELEPUNDIT: I'm afraid I didn't get
round to asking him.

Behind this we see RALPHIE signing autographs, etc.

Now DIANA has come in and we see LORD GRANT greet her and kiss her
famously.

DIANA: Alex darling!

LORD GRANT: Diana! Sweetie! It's
terribly to see you!

DIANA: Terribly to see you, Alex!
Isn't this awfully?

LORD GRANT: Hm, yes -- come and meet
Ralphie before he disappears.

DIANA: Oh, my dear . . .

LADY: For another five years.

PSEUDO GREAT WRITER: (to TELEPUNDIT)
In the great tradition of silent
screams. Goya, Gogol, Guernica, that
tradition --

TELEPUNDIT: Roughly what I said in
the interview I did with him for the
programme on Sunday.

P.G.W.: Yes, tremendous fire.

        TELEPUNDIT: I'm with you. Tremendous
        fire!

        P.G.W.: A sort of purist lyricism one
        seldom finds in Whitechapel these days.

        TELEPUNDIT: Quite so, quite so.

RALPHIE RIGG surrounded by people. LORD GRANT brings DIANA towards
him to introduce her.

        RALPHIE: Ah, it's a load of cobblers,
        all that. Ain't no one man responsible . . .

        LORD GRANT: Ralphie dear! Ralphie dear,
        I've got someone here who is dying to
        meet you. Ralphie Rigg meet Miss Diana
        Scott.

        DIANA: How do you do.

        RALPHIE: How do you do.

        DIANA: I do so much admire your work.
        I think it's wonderful.

        RALPHIE: Thank you so much, I'm sure.

ROBERT has now come in and approaches.

        LORD GRANT: Ralphie, come and meet the
        agent for Stavropoulos.

        ROBERT: (to DIANA) Hi.

        DIANA: (flinging her arms round him)
        Darling, you got here. I'm so glad.

        ROBERT: (looking around at the people)
        Yes, alas.

        DIANA: (coyly) Don't say that. He's
        tremendously talented, Ralphie.

        ROBERT: When did you get in?

        DIANA: This afternoon. I'm exhausted.

        ROBERT: This afternoon.

DIANA: Yes, naturally, of course.

ROBERT: (mimicking her) Yes, naturally, of course.

DIANA: (looking round at the pictures) Well, look at them. I mean, don't you think he's tremendously talented?

ROBERT: How's the job? How did it go?

DIANA: Tremendous fire. What job?

ROBERT: (coldly) The job you went to Paris to see about.

DIANA: Oh, I had to do a test for Raoul Maxim. He's a tremendous talent, Raoul. There's no one in England to beat these new French directors.

ROBERT: Tremendous fire?

DIANA: Yes, I think so -- tremendous.

ROBERT: And you went down well?

DIANA: Like a dozen oysters . . . I <u>think</u>.

CUT TO

94. EXT. BOND STREET. NIGHT.

ROBERT and DIANA walking along. DIANA quite gay and smiling.

DIANA: Taxi!

CUT in CLOSE now to ROBERT.

ROBERT: (casually almost) We're not taking a taxi.

DIANA: (blinks at him) Why not?

ROBERT: I don't take whores in taxis.

DIANA: What do you mean?

ROBERT: That's what you are, isn't it?
A little whore, isn't it? You've been
back from Paris two days already. Well,
if you don't want me to find out what
you're doing don't leave your tickets
and passport lying all over the place.

DIANA: Robert. I knew you'd get the
wrong end of the stick.

ROBERT: Your idea of fidelity is not
having more than one man in the bed at
the same time. You're a whore, baby,
that's all. Just a whore . . . And I
don't take whores in taxis.

CUT TO

95. INT. UNDERGROUND STATION. BOOKING HALL AND ESCALATOR. NIGHT.

ROBERT is putting some notes in his wallet, change from the tickets.
As they step onto the escalator, DIANA's hand comes across and
quietly filches a pound from him.

ROBERT: Now what?

DIANA: (in a sudden, shrill nasal voice)
A pound's not enough.

ROBERT: What do you mean?

DIANA: A pound's not enough.

PASSENGERS stare curiously. It is as if DIANA were a whore, ROBERT
her customer, but otherwise a complete stranger.

ROBERT: Now, wait a minute. Don't . . .

DIANA: Don't you give me "wait a
minute". A pound's not enough.

ROBERT: Diana, don't be a . . .

DIANA: Don't you Diana me. It was
Kiki before and it's Kiki now. And
a pound's not enough.

ROBERT accelerates down the steps. DIANA points after him, cackling.

                    DIANA: Makes a lot of promises,
                    typical, but when he's had his whack
                    he's . . .

ROBERT turns and looks up the escalator.

                    ROBERT: You're not <u>worth</u> more than a
                    bloody quid anyway.

                    DIANA: I'm an honest working girl.

                    ROBERT: Five bob in the Walworth Road,
                    that's about your bloody mark!

                    DIANA: You crumb . . . You creepy crumb
                    . . . * * * <u>yo</u>u crumby <u>cree</u>p . . . don't
                    touch me . . . I'll teach you to call me
                    a bloody whore.

                                        CUT TO

96. INT. DIANA'S FLAT. NIGHT.

ROBERT catches her by the arm and drags her into the bedroom and
flings her on the bed.

                    DIANA: Five bob in the Walworth Road,
                    eh?

                    ROBERT: What were you doing in Paris,
                    anyway -- ?

                    DIANA: Working.

                    ROBERT: Well, I hope you got more than
                    five bob that time.

                    DIANA: I should think I did. I wasn't
                    with you, was I?

                    ROBERT: Fine. (Takes out his wallet
                    and throws the contents at her) Help
                    yourself.

                    DIANA: Huh -- quel largesse! I'm
                    impressed.

ROBERT: You bitch. You * * * f̲i̲l̲t̲h̲y̲
little bitch.

DIANA: Enjoy yourself. You've got no
right to call me a̲n̲y̲t̲h̲i̲n̲g̲.

ROBERT: I have every right to call you
e̲v̲e̲r̲y̲t̲h̲i̲n̲g̲.

DIANA: Oh have you! We're not married,
you know.

She walks out of the room. He follows her.

CUT TO

97. INT. SITTING ROOM. DIANA'S FLAT. NIGHT.

DIANA: At least, not to each other.

ROBERT: I'd never have believed that
anyone as trivial and shallow as you
could cause as much pain as you do.

DIANA: Oh, blameless Gold! Well, if
you really want to know, I've stuck it
out just about as long as I can.

ROBERT: Yes -- and just about as often
as you can.

DIANA: You're so faithful and so loving,
aren't you?

She opens a cupboard to get herself a drink. The door is off its
hinges.

DIANA: Look at this place. This rat
trap. I'm not going to be a prisoner
any longer.

ROBERT: So you're a prisoner, are you?

DIANA: Yes. Prying in my life.
Looking in my handbag. Spying on me.

ROBERT: It's the quickest way of getting to know you.

DIANA: You never intended to stay here or you'd have done something with this place -- look at it.

She starts kicking chair legs.

Then she chucks books off the shelves onto the floor.

DIANA: Books! God, how I hate books!

ROBERT: Stop that.

DIANA: That gets you, doesn't it? Anyone touching your books. They matter more to you than anybody.

She throws a book at ROBERT, who turns and walks into the bedroom, closing the door behind him.

DIANA: Oh, Robert . . . What the hell are you doing?

CUT TO

98. INT. BEDROOM. DIANA'S FLAT. NIGHT.

ROBERT packing his suitcase.

99. INT. THE HALL. DIANA'S FLAT. NIGHT.

ROBERT comes out of the bedroom with his suitcase and picks up his coat. He walks to the front door. DIANA is there.

DIANA: Don't be so melodramatic.

ROBERT: Excuse me.

She tries to stop him, but he opens the front door and goes out.

DIANA: Robert, where are you going?

DIANA: (over) * * * It just all seemed so unnecessary -- all these dramas --

Slowly she goes into the living room and goes to the mirror.
The lipstick message still remains and she rubs it off. She stares
at the blurry image of herself.

> DIANA: (over) I couldn't help feeling
> that Robert had been desperately
> unreasonable about it all. You see,
> after all, we were supposed to be adult
> people. Oh well, * * * one just * * * had
> to take a grip on oneself, that was all.
> This would mean the only possible hope
> was to fling oneself absolutely madly
> into one's work. It was either that,
> you know, or the old gas oven.

> CUT TO

100. INT. PHOTOGRAPHIC STUDIO. DAY.

DIANA is being photographed by MALCOLM, a pleasant young photographer
who spends all his time with young women and knows very well how to
get the best out of them, though his sexual interests lie elsewhere.

> MALCOLM: One . . . two . . . three . . .
> Happy . . . happy . . . turn round . . .
> that's it . . . a happy friendly mood now.

As he photographs relentlessly we see the various poses and positions
of DIANA in a hat and chiffon scarf FREEZE against the white background
of the studio backing.

> MALCOLM: Come on . . . that's it . . .
> good, good. Now over you go -- better.
> Brighter . . . happy . . . friendly mood
> now -- ah, good. Turn your head round
> suddenly. That's it -- good -- good --
> again -- good. That's it, darling.
> You've done it. That was lovely.
> * * * Lovely, darling.

DIANA tries her professional best to maintain the requisite joie de
vivre but her unhappiness bleeds through and her face begins to
crumple.

---

99.   [Now]
                           [have]

100.   [You've got something.]

MALCOLM claps his hands together.

>MALCOLM: Come on, ducky, forget it.
>We've all been through it. For
>Christ's sake smile, love. Come on
>then -- that's it -- come on -- that's it.

He puts down the camera and holds out his hands.

>MALCOLM: Come on. Stop.

He walks across to DIANA and helps her down from the stool. He offers her a drink.

>MALCOLM: Darling, you're marvellous.
>Come on then, now. I'll carry you.
>You're jolly good, marvellous. You
>really are. You really are. Come on.
>Take a drink of this. Drinkie, * * *
>ducks.
>
>DIANA: No.
>
>MALCOLM: Come on.
>
>DIANA: Oh Mal. (Sobs)
>
>MALCOLM: Do you have anywhere to go?
>Really, Diana, really, you're a very
>pretty girl, you know. Hmm . . . that's
>it.

He embraces her. He is powerless to give her any real comfort except that which comes from a joint sense of isolation and disappointment. He is wise in the knowledge of how often he has been in this situation himself.

>CUT TO

101. INT. GLASS HOUSE. BOARD ROOM. DAY.

The frozen image of DIANA has become a large blow-up on a display rack in the boardroom of the Glass House where Denton, Frith and Langley, advertising agents, have put on a display of a projected campaign for one of the Glass Group's German subsidiaries, Neumann,

Braun of Hamburg. KURT WASSERMANN, their rep, is sitting near MILES.
KURT is a serious, amiable young German of 33. Also with them is
LORD GRANT, representing the agency, and some other executives from
both sides, ART MEN, etc.

Big blow-ups of DIANA and other girls are being passed round like
a cattle market and murmurs of approval and disapproval are
thrown out.

MILES gets up with a MALCOLM photo of DIANA and holds it out to
KURT and the AGENCY PRODUCER.

> AGENCY PRODUCER: Oh, Gould, may we
> have a look at that again -- thank you
> so much. The question is, is she
> over-exposed?
>
> KURT: (puzzled) Sorry?
>
> MILES: Have the public seen too much
> of her face?
>
> KURT: How can you see too much of
> this face, I ask you?
>
> LORD GRANT: We do get continuity of
> image.
>
> GROUP HEAD: Good thinking.

There is a general murmur of approval.

> MILES: (with DIANA's photo) Buy her,
> then, do you, Kurt?
>
> KURT: Definitely.
>
> MILES: Yes, she's got a sort of Aryan
> quality, I think. She would go down
> extremely well in Germany.
>
> AGENCY PRODUCER: Hmmm.

During this a balloon -- rather crude in the shape of a naked
woman with a grinning face -- a novelty from a different campaign --
is being blown up, to many gigglements down the other end of the
room. A burst of approving laughter.

GERHARD: (another German) Kurt, how
about this for the Happiness Girl, eh?

He bats the balloon down the room.   MILES lights a cigarette.

The EXECUTIVES round the table are all laughing and patting the
balloon.

GERHARD: Let Kurt have a look at it.
Go on, Kurt, you have a look at it.
Oh, let Kurt have it.

KURT: Yes, for the German territory . . .
I am happy.

MILES: Well, there it is. We want
you to be the Happiness Boy, Kurt.

The balloon is still being patted backwards and forwards across
the table.

GROUP HEAD: Gentlemen, gentlemen,
please.

The balloon floats down on MILES who doesn't look up. He simply
holds up his cigarette. The balloon floats down onto the burning
end and pops!

MILES: Very well then, we are all
agreed . . . Diana Scott, hereinafter
known as the Happiness Girl.

They nod. Laughter.

                                                    CUT TO

102. EXT. WEST END FLORIST. DAY.

A luscious hydrangea is moved from the window. DIANA emerges from
the shop in a state of euphoria. She presents the plant which is
wrapped in a balloon of tissue paper to MALCOLM.

DIANA: For you! The Man who Turned
the Tide at Monte Carlo!

She feels rich. They go swinging along with the hydrangea, arms
round each other. They stop for big kissings! Ideal couple!

                                                    CUT TO

103. EXT. FORTNUM & MASON. DAY.

HIGH SHOT: We look down onto the front entrance in Piccadilly,
picking up DIANA and MALCOLM as they come down the street, the
balloon-shaped plant in MALCOLM's hand, and enter the shop.

                                                   CUT TO

104. INT. FORTNUM & MASON. DAY.

                    SALESMAN: Can I help you, madam?

DIANA points to some jars up on a top shelf.

                    DIANA: Yes, we would like to see
                    some peaches in brandy, please.

                    SALESMAN: Certainly, madam, if you
                    would just come this way.

As he goes to get the peaches, DIANA pops a tin of something choice
in among the tissue balloon on the hydrangea.

The ASSISTANT comes down with the jar, but DIANA rejects it.

                    DIANA: Have you got a large size I
                    could see?

                    SALESMAN: Yes, madam, just wait one
                    moment.

Up he goes again. And DIANA whips another something as MALCOLM
giggles and secretes it, too.

TWO WOMEN SHOPPERS appear round the corner, discussing the merits
of apricots in brandy or curaçao for an invalid friend. Have they
seen DIANA? She doesn't care, and whips something else. She
looks innocent, cheeky at MALCOLM who frowns, deliciously appalled.

                    MALCOLM: I -- I -- I'm not with you.
                    I have never seen you before in my
                    vie.

                    DIANA: (whispers) You're in this up
                    to your navel, Pawson.

The SALESMAN returns with a large bottle.

DIANA: Oh no, I didn't want them in
a bottle -- no, thank you very much
indeed, I think we'll forget it.

SALESMAN: Thank you madam.

DIANA: Thank you.

CUT TO

105. INT. THE HALL. DIANA'S FLAT. DAY.

The front door opens and they tumble into the flat, roaring and
gasping with excitement and relief at having got away with their
escapade.

MALCOLM: Outrageous behaviour.

DIANA: (laughs) I could have sworn
that man was following us.

MALCOLM: He was. Outrageous!

There are a couple of letters on the mat. DIANA grabs them up
on the way into the kitchen. One for ROBERT. Slight change of
expression.

CUT TO

106. INT. THE KITCHEN. DIANA'S FLAT. DAY.

MALCOLM: Rule Britannia, Britannia
up your flue!

They put the hydrangea on the table. Things fall out, prawns
in whiskey, plums in brandy, marrons glacés, etc., etc. More and
more. At last DIANA puts on the table the tin they bought, with
the bill. She reaches under her sweater and produces two avocadoes.
They fall about with laughter.

DIANA: Oh . . . Oh . . . darling, where
did I get them all -- my dear -- * * *
ringaling, the shop's open!

MALCOLM: Tingaling, the shop's <u>denuded</u>!
Diana, you are an outrageous girl, and
I would like you to know, dear, that we've
only paid for Smogins' Shrimps.

DIANA opens a fat letter from the post she's brought in.

MALCOLM: What's that? * * * Happiness
Girl contract already?

DIANA: (sad) My husband wants a
divorce. (Looks up at MALCOLM, who
seems puzzled) My husband Tony --
he wants a divorce.

MALCOLM looks dazed.

DIANA: (gaily now) Granted soon as
arsked, ai'm shu-er!

She is at the drinks cupboard. She opens it and the door comes
off its hinges.

DIANA: I hate this flat.

MALCOLM: (picking up the tin) Well,
you've got your Escargots, anyway.

CUT TO

107. INT. THE SITTING ROOM. DIANA'S FLAT. NIGHT.

DIANA and MALCOLM have drunk a good deal and they are now settling
down to the goodies. The food is spread out for eating on the
same table as the goldfish bowl.

DIANA: (laughs) Have * * * <u>an</u> avocado
strangled with prawns.

MALCOLM: Have a bit of smoked salmon
stuffed with caviare * * * and matured
in fine English gin. For wh<u>a</u>t we are
about to receive may the Lord make you
truly thankful.

They clink glasses.

---

106.   [The]

107.   [another]

DIANA: Cheers.

MALCOLM: Cheers.

They drink. DIANA spills whiskey into the fishes' bowl. She drops
a couple of grains of caviare in as well. She clinks glasses with
MALCOLM and then with the fish bowl and drinks again. They giggle
at each other and make small kissing faces. MALCOLM goes on looking
at her.

DIANA: Oh. Oh why is life such a
pisspot?

MALCOLM: Well, you see, I have the
answer to that.

DIANA: Oh, you have, have you?

MALCOLM: It's the bomb, lovey, it
must be.

DIANA: That's right. It's the great
big nasty bomb.

MALCOLM: Great big nasty bomb.

He throws a cherry into the goldfish bowl.

MALCOLM: Let's face it, darling,
life's a great big steaming mess.

DIANA: Never mind, darling, I
love you, if no one else does.

She gets up and puts her arms round MALCOLM's neck.

MALCOLM: * * * Well, no one else does.

DIANA: Oh, poor you. I'll tell you
what I'm going to do with you.

MALCOLM: Yes?

She spears a meat ball in marsala.

---

107.   [Hmm.]

DIANA: Well . . . (Grand voice) I may
be filming in Italy next month.

MALCOLM: It-lay?

DIANA: Yes.

MALCOLM: Oh, fascinating place. I
want to go there some day.

DIANA: And if I do . . .

MALCOLM: Hmmm . . .

DIANA: I'm going * * * to * * * take the
most wonderful holiday of my life and you
are coming with me.

MALCOLM: Ahh. I am?

DIANA: Yes. And to hell with them
all. We'll have a ball! (Offers the
meat ball) Have a ball!

She reaches and puts it in MALCOLM's mouth, from her fork.
He flinches slightly, but takes it.

MALCOLM: Oh, darling!

DIANA throws another meat ball into the goldfish bowl.

DIANA: Have a ball!

MALCOLM: Have a ball!

DIANA falls backwards onto the settee and passes out. MALCOLM
squirts soda from the siphon into the goldfish bowl. The two
goldfish float quietly dead in the bowl, bellies up.

CUT TO

108. EXT. ALBERT BRIDGE. DAY.

Funeral music.

DIANA: Ashes to ashes . . .

MALCOLM: Dust to dust . . .

Two small matchboxes wrapped in flowers are quietly dropped over the bridge into the water. The fish are dead.

DIANA turns away, stricken, and MALCOLM supports her.

As they turn away, the funeral bell seems to swell up, bong, bong, bong . . .

CUT TO

109. EXT. VILLA POGGIO CAIANO. DAY.

CLOSE on an image of a Renaissance statue.

PULL BACK to reveal that this is the top of a chocolate box with the trade mark "Cupid Chocolates" inlaid over it. The box is resting on a velvet cushion, carried by a PAGEBOY on the film set of a cinema commercial for chocolates. DIANA, dressed in full renaissance costume, sits on a balustrade, while a PRINCE, in a most chivalrous manner, gets off a white charger which is being held by another PAGEBOY and, taking the box of chocolates from the cushion, gives it to DIANA. On the other side of the staircase, HERALDS stand in full regalia.

COMMERCIAL JINGLE as DIANA receives the box and takes off the lid.

CONTINUITY GIRL: (over) Yes, there's nothing dreamier than . . .

DIANA puts her hand up to her face.

CONTINUITY GIRL: (over) . . . Cupid chocolates. Those fairy tale centres . . .

DIANA takes one from the box held by the PRINCE.

CONTINUITY GIRL: (over) . . . take you out of this world into a land . . .

C.U. DIANA eating chocolate.

CONTINUITY GIRL: (over) . . . of make-believe come true.

SEAN: (O.S.) Cut it.

ASSISTANT DIRECTOR: (O.S.) Cut it.

CUT TO

110. REVERSE TO WHERE THE UNIT IS SHOOTING.

The DIRECTOR, who is SEAN MARTIN, stands by the camera. He is momentarily still as he decides his next move.

>SEAN: How was it for you?

>CAMERA OPERATOR: Not bad -- could be better though.

>SEAN: How long did it run?

>CONTINUITY GIRL: Thirty-five seconds.

>SEAN: Oh lor . . . um . . .

>AGENCY PRODUCER? I -- I -- I'm a bit worried about the caress bit. Could he caress her this time? After all, the jingle does say the one you love to caress. It's talking about the girl.

>SEAN: Yeah . . . yeah . . . yeah. We'll try it that way this time. Darling, this time would . . . would you let him caress you?

DIANA is having her make-up adjusted, her hair retouched.

>SEAN: Would you let him touch your cheek?

>DIANA: All right. I see. I caress him.

>SEAN: No. He caresses you. All right. Now please don't break it up.

SEAN turns his head. Coming towards the unit are PRINCE CESARE DELLA ROMITA, a distinguished man of 54, and his son, CURZIO, a boy of 19, dark, handsome. SEAN waves to them.

CURZIO points to DIANA and CESARE nods, smiles at his son.

> AGENCY PRODUCER: Come on boys.
> Try a take for the Prince, shall we?
> Good afternoon, sir.
>
> CESARE: Good afternoon. Excuse me --
> er -- don't you think the angle of the
> house would look better from here.
>
> SEAN: (patiently) Ah -- er -- yes, sir,
> but it's a question of the light.
>
> CESARE: Oh -- the light.

A clapperboard comes in and snaps at DIANA's nose.

> CLAPPER BOY: Scene two, take three.
>
> SEAN: Action.
>
> CONTINUITY GIRL: (over) Yes, there's
> nothing dreamier than Cupid chocolates.
> Those fairy tale centres take you out
> of this world into a land of make-
> believe come true.

The PAGE hands the box of chocolates to the PRINCE who walks over
to DIANA. As he reaches up to touch her face, the box of chocolates
falls to the ground.

> CONTINUITY GIRL: (over) As those
> fairy tale centres melt in the mouth
> they'll melt the heart of the one you
> love to caress. Fairy tale
> chocolates . . .

The AGENCY PRODUCER claps his hand to his head.

> CUT TO

111. EXT. ARCHED TERRACE. THE VILLA. DAY.

DIANA walks across the arched terrace to a Roman bath and stands
looking at it while men carry modern bathroom equipment into the
house.

> CUT TO

112. INT. GRAND HALL. VILLA POGGIO CAIANO. DAY.

DIANA is looking up at the portrait of a POPE. CURZIO is with her.
She turns to him.

>   CURZIO: He is the Pope Urban. One
>   of my father's many ancestors.
>
>   DIANA: Should Popes be ancestors?
>
>   CURZIO: Yeah -- the call came late
>   in life. He was an ancestor before
>   becoming a Pope.
>
>   DIANA: (laughs) I don't see much
>   resemblance.
>
>   CURZIO: Er -- he was better looking
>   when he was younger.

DIANA laughs and they move on.

>   CUT TO

113. INT. PICTURE GALLERY. THE VILLA. DAY.

DIANA being shown the family portraits by CURZIO. He stands close
to her as they consider one of a woman.

>   DIANA: Who is she?
>
>   CURZIO: My mother. She was very
>   beautiful.
>
>   DIANA: Was . . . ?
>
>   CURZIO: She died two years ago.
>   In a car crash.
>
>   DIANA: Oh, how awful.
>
>   CURZIO: Very awful.

And they look up to see CESARE watching them, smiling and sad, from
the doorway.

>   CESARE: So there you are. I've
>   ordered some tea.
>
>   DIANA: How marvellous. Curzio's
>   been giving me some of the family
>   history.

She gestures sadly, speechless, at the portrait. CESARE and CURZIO look at each other affectionately and CESARE takes his son's arm for a moment. DIANA is genuinely affected.

> CESARE: Oh yes.
>
> CURZIO: (looks at watch, as they move off the portrait) If you'd excuse me, I must go. I have a long way to drive. But I hope we'll meet again.
>
> DIANA: I hope so.
>
> CURZIO: Goodbye. Till soon then.
>
> DIANA: (smiles) Till soon.

CURZIO runs off. CESARE watches him with warmth, smiles at DIANA.

> CESARE: He is a nice boy, Curzio.
>
> DIANA: Yes. Yes, very.

> CUT TO

114. EXT. THE TERRACE. THE VILLA. DAY.

DIANA is sitting in a basket chair next to CESARE at the tea table.

They get up and walk to the edge of the terrace together and stand looking at the view.

> DIANA: It's so beautiful.
>
> CESARE: I'm glad you like it.
>
> DIANA: There's nothing like this in England.
>
> CESARE: But you have in England the most beautiful country houses in the world. Have a chocolate.
>
> DIANA: No thank you. Yes, but it's different. Here, there's a sense of . . . eternity . . . sort of peacefulness. It's almost religious, if you know what I mean.

CESARE: Yes.

DIANA: It seems to make life easier
to bear.

CESARE: But you don't have any
problem in bearing the weight of life,
do you?

DIANA: I don't know about that.

CESARE: Then on you it must weigh
very lightly. For me it is different.

DIANA: I recently lost someone too.
Not like you did, but . . . Well, I don't
much care to go back to England just
now.

CESARE: You have a family?

DIANA: Not like yours. I mean, not
that supports one, gives one strength
-- you have God practically in the
family.

CESARE: Huh. Well, you know, every
man is alone in the last resolve. And
I more than most men. Well, perhaps
not . . . in some ways.

He smiles and waves, and across towards them come several of his
young CHILDREN waving towels above their heads.

DIANA: They're beautiful.

CESARE: Yes, like their mother.

DIANA: They really are. Lovely.

CESARE looks fixedly, smiling at DIANA.

The CHILDREN come racing up the stairs.

CHILDREN: Papa -- (they grab him)
Viene, viene -- bagno --

          CESARE: Va bene. Adesso . . . vengo.
          (To DIANA) So now you must excuse me.
          I swim with them every day, you know.

          DIANA: Oh.

          CESARE: It is a duty which is also
          a pleasure. Excuse me, will you?

          DIANA: Of course -- thank you so much.

          DIANA: (over) I don't think I have
          ever in my life needed a holiday . . .

                      CUT TO

115. EXT. THE SEA AND CAPRI. DAY.

          DIANA: (over) . . . quite so much as I
          did then, and Capri was ideal. I
          just wanted peace and quiet and just
          to get away from everything really.

                      CUT TO

116. EXT. PIAZZETTA. CAPRI. DAY.

A procession of every conceivable TOURIST in mad hats, PORTERS
with baggage, a PARTY of GERMANS, kept BOYS and kept WOMEN wander
backwards and forwards through the square.

PULL BACK to reveal DIANA and MALCOLM at a café table watching
the parade. The WAITER, GINO, comes up to them.

          MALCOLM: (to DIANA) Campari?

She nods.

          MALCOLM: (to GINO) Due campari, per
          favore.

GINO gives them a look and goes.

          DIANA: Hmmm. We are not complicating
          our holiday with any disgusting
          sexcapades.

          MALCOLM: Brother and sister till
          death do us part?

They shake hands solemnly.

> DIANA: Done! Share and share alike.

> MALCOLM: Everything split down the middle.

> DIANA: Absolutely . . . And now, tell us what's new in London.

> MALCOLM: Oh, nothing much. I tell you who I did bump into the other day. Robert.

> DIANA: My Robert?

> MALCOLM: The same.

> DIANA: And . . . ?

> MALCOLM: Seemed okay.

> DIANA: ·Alone?

> MALCOLM: Me or him?

> DIANA: Darling, do you think I care who <u>you</u> were with?

> MALCOLM: Oh charming. Do you care who <u>he</u> was with?

> DIANA: No, not particularly. (Pause) What was she like?

> MALCOLM: Blonde. 21. Extremely well-appointed, as they say.

The drinks come. DIANA looks lustrelessly at GINO. She looks at her drink.

> MALCOLM: Grazie. Okay -- he was alone.

> DIANA: He wasn't!

> MALCOLM: Swear.

                    DIANA: You rotten --

                    MALCOLM: -- thing. I know. (Raises
                    glass) Happy holiday!

                    DIANA: And you, principe! And you.

                                                CUT TO

117. EXT. STREET. CAPRI. DAY.

CLOSE on the head of an elaborately dressed-up horse.

PULL BACK to find that DIANA is holding the reins of a carrozza
while MALCOLM and the DRIVER relax behind.

                                                CUT TO

118. EXT. THE ISLAND. DAY.

MALCOLM and DIANA scramble up to unsophisticated countryside.
Ahead of them is a promontory on which stands a little hut
surrounded by a wall. They make towards it.

                    DIANA: Oh Mal, what a dream. Oh,
                    it's super. It really is fabulous.

                                                CUT TO

119. EXT. THE HUT. CAPRI. DAY.

They have come into a courtyard in the middle of which there is a
well. They look and listen, but there is no sign of life. DIANA
goes over to the well. MALCOLM follows. They both lean over and
peer down into the dark. DIANA calls and her sound is echoed
and re-echoed. She smiles and then turns and goes to the door of
the hut.

                                                CUT TO

120. INT. THE HUT. DAY.

It is plain, dusty, with rusty pots, wooden furniture. But
idyllic! Simple life!

                    DIANA: I was just thinking how nice
                    it would be if we could live here.

MALCOLM laughs.

DIANA: I could do without sex. I
don't really like it that much. If
I could just feel -- oh -- complete.
Oh Mal, let's buy this place -- it
can't cost much.

MALCOLM: Hmmm . . . be marvellous.

DIANA: Oh, I want it more than
anything in the whole world.

                                    CUT TO

121. EXT. ROOF OF HUT. DAY.

DIANA and MALCOLM are genuinely ecstatic. DIANA runs forward and
spins round. MALCOLM lifts his camera up to his eye.

                MALCOLM: Happy girl.

He sets the camera up and runs to pose with DIANA.

                                    CUT TO

122. EXT. CHURCH. CAPRI. DAY.

DIANA and MALCOLM wander hand in hand up the steps. They go into
the church.

123. INT. CHURCH. DAY.

Shadowy darkness. MALCOLM is admiring the frescoes.

DIANA wanders off, bored. MALCOLM turns to say something, but she
has gone. He scans the nave for her.

A row of PRAYING WOMEN. DIANA is disclosed with a scarf over her
head, at the end of the row. MALCOLM is slightly scandalised.
One of the WOMEN rises, so does DIANA, and they both cross themselves
to the altar. MALCOLM catches her and they pass the confession
stalls. They walk out of the church together as the CAMERA tracks
after them and holds on the confessional.

                                    CUT TO

124. EXT. CAPRI. NIGHT.

LONG SHOT of the Harbour.

                                              CUT TO

125. EXT. CAFÉ. CAPRI. NIGHT.

A WAITER stacking chairs. The neon sign goes out.

                                              CUT TO

126. INT. HOTEL BEDROOM. CAPRI. NIGHT.

DIANA is lying on her bed smoking, unable to sleep.

                         * * *

She switches on the light, gets out of bed and goes to the
bathroom. She takes two pills and then crosses to the window and
goes out into the balcony.

                                              CUT TO

127. EXT. HOTEL BEDROOM BALCONY. NIGHT.

DIANA comes out into the balcony and taps on MALCOLM's bedroom
window which is ajar next door.

                    DIANA: Mal? Are you asleep?

She smiles. Charming boy! Already dead to the world! She leans
over the balcony. Beyond the lights of the harbour twinkle.
Sound of a Vespa.

                                              CUT TO

128. EXT. MARINA GRANDE. CAPRI. NIGHT.

MALCOLM stands waiting below. GINO's Vespa appears and rides up to
MALCOLM who hops on the pillion and the machine roars away into the
night.

---

126.   [DIANA: (over) There is hardly a
                          terror that cannot be braved better
                          when a hand is clasped . . . Nature did
                          not intend that a woman should face
                          the world alone. Malcolm and I had
                          something that I do not hesitate to
                          call "beautiful". More beautiful
                          perhaps because of the underlying
                          pathos beneath it.]

CUT TO

129. EXT. DIANA'S BALCONY. NIGHT.

CLOSE UP on DIANA's reaction.

CUT TO

130. EXT. THE HOTEL TERRACE. DAY.

It is the next morning. A motor cruiser is making dramatic blue
exhaust as it careers round the point and heads in towards the
harbour.

DIANA comes down and out onto the terrace where MALCOLM is calmly
having breakfast. She comes and sits, not at the same table, as
he expects, but at the next.

> MALCOLM: Morning.

> DIANA: Morning.

She looks at him. The cruiser is now approaching the jetty. GINO
brings rolls, butter, jam, coffee, etc. She considers the pair of
them through stern dark glasses.

> DIANA: Traitor.

> MALCOLM: Why the harsh words?

> DIANA: Harsh <u>word</u>. One is
> sufficient.

GINO smiles at her. She looks severe.

> MALCOLM: Darling, really.

> DIANA: (slowly, sarcastically)
> Brother and sister till death do us
> part! Ha!

Her eyes bulge suddenly. She gasps.

CUT TO

131. EXT. THE JETTY. DAY.

A cruiser is moored on the jetty. A gangplank has been shot out and
along it in racy boating rig comes PRINCIPE CESARE DELLA ROMITA.
He waves.

CUT TO

132. EXT. THE COAST AND SEA. CRUISER. DAY.

MALCOLM lies sunbathing on the deck above the cabin. He looks along towards the stern. DIANA sitting against the bulkhead. He makes a face. She looks innocent.

> CESARE: (o.s.) Well, I happened to be passing so I thought -- why not drop in?

> DIANA: (ahead -- at MALCOLM, deadpan) Why not indeed?

MALCOLM makes a new face and lies back, stares upwards.

CESARE is now revealed, next to DIANA but masked till now by the roofing over the stern. They have iced drinks on the shelf in front of them, also CESARE's panama hat.

> CESARE: Diana -- I've been thinking about you a lot.

> DIANA: That's nice!

> CESARE: And -- er -- what you said --

> DIANA: Did I say something?

> CESARE: Yes. About Italy. How much you like it.

> DIANA: Oh yes. I simply adore it.

CESARE's bare head is gleaming with his efforts. He wipes his handkerchief over it. She touches it with her hand and makes to wring her burnt fingers. She puts his hat on his head.

> CESARE: Curzio is very taken with you, you know.

> DIANA: (is this what the visit is about?) Oh . . . he's very young.

> CESARE: He recognises a certain -- quality in you.

> DIANA: I expect he'll get over it.

CESARE: I don't think so. He was
very much in favour of my coming here.
As a matter of fact he persuaded me.

He takes his hat off again.

DIANA: Why? I'm afraid I don't
understand.

CESARE: To propose to you.

DIANA: But -- er -- why couldn't he
propose himself? I mean, it's all
ridiculously childish, but . . .

DIANA looks to MALCOLM for help. MALCOLM stares up into the sky
and closes his eyes contentedly.

CESARE: (amusement in his eyes)
Curzio approved that I should propose
to you . . . since -- er -- it is I who
wish to marry you.

She looks at him. MALCOLM, chin dug into chest, is looking at her.

DIANA: I see . . .

CESARE: There is no point in not
saying what is in one's heart.

DIANA: No, really, Principe.

He takes her hand and kisses it.

CESARE: Cesare.

DIANA: Cesare.

MALCOLM is lying on his back eating grapes.

CESARE: I'll stay here until
tomorrow. Will you think it over?

She stares at him, lost in thought. She looks at him and
shakes her head slowly, smiles. He turns away. She looks over
at MALCOLM and makes a "Phew! -- golly!" face.

The cruiser accelerates fiercely and races, skidding, across the
water.

CUT TO

133. EXT. HARBOUR CAFÉ. DUSK.

DIANA sitting at a table, looking out at the cruiser which bobs at anchor in the harbour. Romantic decision being made? Ah, the problems of the heart!

She turns and walks up and down. Ooook-oook of a Vespa hooter behind, and up rides GINO.

        DIANA: Ciao.

        GINO: I was late finishing.

She shakes her head: no matter. She gets on the back of the Vespa. GINO wears a striped T-shirt, very matelot. They start up and whizz round a corner of the road, out of sight.

CUT TO

134. EXT. ZIG-ZAG ROAD. DUSK.

CLOSE on the Vespa as it zig-zags along the road.

ZOOM back until it becomes a small dot below.

CUT TO

135. EXT. HARBOUR CAFÉ. DAWN.

Same set as 132. The cafés are now closed, the shutters down, the chairs piled up. The scooter is coming back. DIANA has her arms around GINO very closely and she is wearing his T-shirt, he her luminously orange sweater.

CUT TO

136. EXT. THE CRUISER. PORT. DAY.

DIANA and CESARE. The SAILORS making ready for sea. DIANA is shaking her head. CESARE speaks with passion.

                    DIANA: I thought about it all last
                    night. I hardly slept at all,
                    Cesare, thinking. I know I can't --
                    I can't give up my life -- you
                    understand.

CESARE: Well . . . if you ever change your mind, I shall not have changed mine. I am very sorry I gave you a sleepless night. I too had one. Goodbye.

DIANA: Goodbye, Cesare.

She shakes his hand, he kisses her. She walks off the boat.

SAILOR: Principe, posso . . .

CESARE: Si, si. Adesso.

The gangplank is lifted.

CUT TO

137. EXT. THE HARBOUR AND SEA. DAY.

The cruiser pulls away. CESARE, in the stern, waving.

CUT TO

138. EXT. THE QUAYSIDE. DAY.

DIANA waving.

CUT TO

139. EXT. THE SEA. DAY.

The cruiser sailing further away.

CUT TO

140. EXT. THE BEACH. MARINA PICCOLA. THE SEA. DAY.

Row of sunbathers lying on the beach. DIANA in a bikini comes and flings herself between MALCOLM and GINO who lie spread out to fry.

The cruiser splutters and moves off across the bay.

DIANA sits up and waves.

DIANA: Bye bye, Principe.

A lone figure waves back.

MALCOLM: Arrivederci Roma.

DIANA laughs and lies back among the sunbathers.

CLOSE UP of a timer on a tray of drinks. It goes off.

The men all turn over onto their stomachs. CAMERA TILTS UP to the
sky. Sound of romantic Italian music.

* * *

CUT TO

141. INT. TV STUDIO. NIGHT.

CLOSE on a big blow-up photograph of WALTER SOUTHGATE.

PULL back to the studio set where ROBERT is doing an obituary memoir
of Walter Southgate, who has died. There are other big blow-ups
of the great writer on placards round the studio. ROBERT is with
two other LIT GENTS, but now turns, solo, to the CAMERA.

> ROBERT: When they bury Walter
> Southgate tomorrow there will be
> buried with him something of the
> regional tradition of English literature.
> Nowadays it is London which more
> and more devours the talent, London,
> that damn jam factory boiling out
> the goodness from writers, as
> Southgate once described it to me.
> A certain kind of flinty integrity has
> gone, perhaps for ever. Goodnight.

As he finishes, a roller caption comes in. It is a literary
pot-pourri programme. We see: IN MEMORIAM WALTER SOUTHGATE --
Robert Gold . . . on the Fade Out. ROBERT stares sadly at a
blow up.

> TV INTERVIEWER: And that's all from
> us * * * this * * * time. We'll be back

---

140.   [EXT. PICCADILLY CIRCUS. NIGHT.

SOUND of sweet Italian music continues over the lights of
Piccadilly Circus sparkling and suggesting the night life
of London.]

141.   [for] [week]

TV INTERVIEWER (Cont.): with you
again with another programme in
a * * * fortnight. * * * . . . Till
then, goodnight. * * * (On the FADEOUT,
to ROBERT) * * * Coming down for a drink?

ROBERT: No, I don't think I will . . .

                                        CUT TO

142. INT. NIGHTCLUB. NIGHT.

MILES and DIANA dancing very close and sexy. With them are ALLIE,
KURT WASSERMANN, LORD GRANT and another girl, GILLIAN.

DIANA and MILES seem quite an item again.

The atmosphere is very Charles of the Ritzy -- all soft lights, glam
hairdos, the high life. DIANA and MILES whisper and smile, and kiss
with delicious restraint.

                                        CUT TO

143. INT. DIANA'S FLAT. SITTING ROOM. NIGHT.

The dancing continues. DIANA is slightly drunk, so are the others.
MILES moves deftly to where his drink is and raises it -- makes a
face.

                    MILES: Ice?

                    DIANA: Kitchen.

There is about this occasion a strange melancholy, yet an air also
of suave sophistication, as if they were all figures in some glossy
dance routine.

MILES ducks out of the room, taking ALLIE with him and leaving KURT
smiling at DIANA.

                                        CUT TO

144. INT. HALL & KITCHEN. DIANA'S FLAT. NIGHT.

DIANA comes out of the sitting room.

DIANA: Find it OK?

She pushes open the kitchen door.

The kitchen is empty. DIANA looks across at the bedroom door. There is a light under it. She stands looking at it, sniggers rather chillingly.

Behind her now we see GRANT and GILLIAN creeping across and going into the carpeted bathroom. The door shuts. DIANA wheels. She feels alarmed and lonely. She goes back, the last sardine, into the sitting room.

CUT TO

145. INT. THE SITTING ROOM. DIANA'S FLAT. NIGHT.

KURT looks up and smiles. He is looking at a book of ROBERT's which was left behind on the shelves. DIANA smiles -- not hurt, not she! -- and slips off her shoes.

DIANA: Well, well. Where did all the young flowers go?

She comes up and looks closely at him. She puts her arms round him. She turns him round and puts her face up.

DIANA: Well? Proceed . . . Amuse me.

CUT TO

146. EXT. DIANA'S STREET. NIGHT.

ROBERT standing at the end of the street looking up towards the entrance to the flats. He moves slowly forward, stops, moves forward again and stops.

CUT TO

147. INT. DIANA'S APARTMENT HOUSE. NIGHT.

ROBERT coming up the stairs.

CUT TO

148. INT. THE HALL. DIANA'S FLAT. NIGHT.

The door bell is ringing. DIANA comes out of the sitting room, buttoning up her dress. She goes to the front door and puts the chain on it before opening it.

She opens it. ROBERT's face in the gap.

> ROBERT: It's me.

DIANA is speechless.

> ROBERT: Could I . . . ?

She shakes her head, bewildered.

> ROBERT: I wondered if you knew
> Southgate had died.

Her face seems hard and wild with grief at the same time. A door
opens behind her.

CUT TO ROBERT's P.O.V.: MILES comes out of the bedroom.

DIANA's P.O.V.: ROBERT gone. Footsteps hurrying downstairs.

> MILES: What's going on?

DIANA lowers her eyes and shuts the door. She pushes past MILES,
goes into the bedroom where ALLIE sits at the dressing table
re-doing her make up.

> DIANA: I think you had better go.
> Get out of here, will you.

She pushes past MILES in the doorway, knocks on the bathroom door,
shouting to the other occupants.

> DIANA: Get -- get out of here.

> CUT TO

149. INT. LIVING ROOM. DIANA'S FLAT. NIGHT.

DIANA is picking up glasses, rather automatically, from the tables.
She stops by the window with one in each hand and then turns and
sees: MILES is in the door of the room.

> DIANA: I thought you'd gone too.

He shakes his head.

> DIANA: You bastard -- you really
> are, aren't you? A bastard.

MILES: Would you like some tea?

DIANA: <u>Tea</u>?

MILES: To calm you down. You seem
a bit hysterical.

DIANA: I asked you to go. Why
haven't you?

MILES: Because I * * * <u>stayed</u><u>.</u>

MILES shrugs slightly and goes over and looks at the books of
ROBERT's still on the shelves. He glances at DIANA -- somehow
suspicious, anxious.

DIANA: (puzzled) What is it?

MILES: Nothing.

DIANA: You afraid of something?

MILES: Afraid?

DIANA: I get the feeling you're
afraid of something. What's wrong?

MILES: Wrong? Nothing.

She goes up and looks at him closely. His face in C.U. holds
the camera's stare unflinchingly, yet isn't there a flicker of
uneasiness somewhere behind his professionally certain, confident
eyes?

MILES: I didn't ask you to leave
Robert, you know.

DIANA: You never asked me to do
anything.

MILES: As long as you realise --

DIANA: As long as <u>you</u> realise -- I
hate your guts. As long as you
realise Robert's the only person I

[I'm staying]

DIANA (Cont.): ever remotely loved --
as long as you realise <u>that</u> --

MILES takes all this on the chin, almost relishing, needing it,
like an expert boxer who for some self-destructive reason no
longer bothers to defend himself.

MILES: (quietly) When you've
finished. As long as you're convinced,
you don't have to persuade me, my
darling.

DIANA: You're afraid I'd kill
myself.

There is a silence. MILES nods and smiles with a sort of
sarcastic acknowledgment. But there is something forced in his
manner and DIANA, almost appalled, almost touched, is onto it.

DIANA: Has that ever happened to
you? (She comes round to confront
him) Who was she, Miles?

He doesn't answer. We move in on his studiedly composed face.

MILES: Put away your Penguin Freud,
Diana --

DIANA: Who was she?

MILES: -- <u>and</u> your crystal ball. It's
late.

He goes out of the room.

CUT TO

150. INT. THE HALL. DIANA'S FLAT. NIGHT.

DIANA: (following) Poor Miles! You
can't risk feeling anything, can you?

MILES: I shall survive.

DIANA: Of course. As long as you
remain impotent.

MILES: My impotence, my darling,
makes a pair with your virginity.

DIANA: Impotent in every way except in bed.

MILES: Don't underestimate me, my dear. I can also be very effective on the telephone.

He opens the front door.

MILES: I'll say goodnight.

He goes out. She shuts the door and puts the chain across. She takes a step forward and stands still.

DIANA: (over) Life's full of 'if onlys', isn't it? You know -- 'if only . . .' 'if only . . .' If only Robert had come half an hour later I suppose the whole thing might have been completely different. Oh yes -- I sort of felt that it wasn't any good, you know -- I just had to go and try and find him again. I remember thinking 'I'll bet he'll be at that funeral'.

CUT TO

151. EXT. COUNTRY CHURCHYARD. DAY.

WALTER SOUTHGATE's funeral. We follow the cortege as it winds slowly between the antique graves under the little church. We have already seen DIANA and ROBERT walk through here in the happy days when they first came down to see the great man.

The coffin is being lowered into the grave. A number of mourners. With surprise effect we discover DIANA, alone, among them, anxiously scanning the faces as she goes through a ritual show of grief. Is ROBERT there? What a great moment to begin a reconciliation! But ROBERT, as we see face after face, is clearly not there.

People begin to move away, DIANA among them.

A VOICE: Miss Scott?

DIANA turns -- for a moment hope and the intonation deceive her -- and sees a reporter, LESLIE PAGE, coming towards her.

PAGE: Leslie Page -- Evening Standard.

DIANA: Oh yes.

PAGE: I didn't know you knew Walter Southgate, Miss Scott.

DIANA: Oh yes. (Sniffs) We were considerable friends, actually.

PAGE: When was this?

DIANA: Oh about -- er -- two years ago. He found out how much I admired his work and -- er -- sweet man -- he invited me down to see him.

PAGE: Which was your favourite book?

DIANA: Oh, all of them. As a matter of fact, I may be filming one of his books in Paris.

PAGE: Really?

DIANA: . Yes, I was talking to Raoul Maxim, you know, the French film director who . . .

PAGE: Hmmmm. Hmmmm.

                                        CUT TO

152. EXT. PICCADILLY CIRCUS. DAY.

DIANA comes up to a paper stand and buys an Evening Standard. She smiles and buys six more copies. As the VENDOR hands her the bundle, close on her: she remembers buying the many papers with ROBERT. And her quick triumph begins to wane.

                                        CUT TO

153. EXT. SHAFTESBURY AVENUE. DAY.

DIANA marches with vain pride down the street, with the neon and the posters echoing her own empty success. She has this big bundle of papers. She stops and stares at the entrance of a hotel. She feels lost. She sees two lovers meet. She walks on and stops. A couple of GIRLS stop and look at her. She's famous! A MAN stops and looks from his paper to her and back. He raises his hat. She walks on, smiling uneasily.

CUT TO

154. INT. DIANA'S FLAT. EVENING.

The telephone is ringing as DIANA unlocks the door hurriedly and comes in to answer it. The idea of a friend, someone she knows. What joy!

Thump -- she flings the bundle of Evening Standards on to the hall chair. And runs to answer the phone.

                         DIANA: Hullo!

                         VOICE: Diana?

                         DIANA: Yes! Robert?

                         VOICE: Robert? Who's Robert?

                         DIANA: Who is that? Malcolm, is that you?

                         VOICE: I rang to congratulate you -- I read the piece about the film.

                         DIANA: Who is that?

                         VOICE: Are you Diana Scott?

                         DIANA: Yes, it is, will you tell me who's speaking, please.

                         VOICE: I sure wish I was Robert, whoever he is.

                         DIANA: Please, who is that speaking?

                         VOICE: Oh come on now, Diana, we met a coupla times at Charlie's.

                         DIANA: For god's sake, who is it?

                         VOICE: All I wanted to say was <u>bonne chance</u> and all that jazz. This could be it for you.

                         DIANA: For Christ's sake stop mucking around. Tell me who's speaking. Hello? Oh.

She is left holding the empty telephone.

>   DIANA: (over) Oh, I got so fed up
>   with absolutely no one to turn to.

                                                    CUT TO

155. EXT. CHURCH. DAY.

DIANA and a PRIEST walking along a path, towards the church.

>   DIANA: (over) No one to turn to,
>   nothing to fall back on, you know.
>   Then suddenly there was someone
>   who really understood, who really
>   cared about me. Didn't want anything
>   out of me. He was so terribly
>   understanding. Father Chapman.
>   Do you know him? He's Monsignor
>   Chapman now. Oh, he's a terrible
>   sweetie, terribly <u>human</u>, you know.

                                                    CUT TO

156. INT. DIANA'S BEDROOM. DAY.

DIANA kneeling in front of a crucifix.

>   DIANA: (over) I suppose I've always
>   believed in God. There has to be a
>   God, doesn't there? -- someone who
>   understands? There has to be. I
>   really took it very seriously, you
>   know. I knew I couldn't go ahead
>   with my marriage unless I was really
>   serious about it.

                                                    CUT TO

157. EXT. TERRACE. VILLA. DAY.

A great range of PHOTOGRAPHERS jostling and signalling. At first
we are not clear where we are or whom DIANA has married. We only
know that it is all a great sensation.

And then we see: DIANA and the PRINCIPE himself sitting as for
some great court portrait, with the CHILDREN (excepting CURZIO)
all ranged round them.

> NEWSREEL COMMENTATOR: (over) It
> isn't every day that we have a new
> English princess, but it happened
> last week at the ancient home of the
> Prince Della Romita to our own Diana
> Scott who became the bride of this
> famous Italian Prince and bobsleigh
> enthusiast.

The PHOTOGRAPHERS flash away, while DIANA smiles regally in a
family group, all of whom look very uncomfortable.

> NEWSREEL COMMENTATOR: (over) Everyone
> was there, old family friends, the
> people from the estate, and my
> goodness, how happy they were to
> find themselves in the midst of it
> all. The Prince, who stems from one
> of Italy's oldest families, has been
> married before and has seven children.
> It isn't every Princess who finds
> herself the mother of seven on her
> wedding day.

CUT TO

158. INT. THE DINING ROOM. THE VILLA. DAY.

> NEWSREEL COMMENTATOR: (over) Simple
> family meals are something the
> Princess is determined to maintain.

DIANA is seen solemnly feeding spaghetti to an unwilling STEPSON.

CUT TO

159. INT. THE KITCHENS. THE VILLA. DAY.

> NEWSREEL COMMENTATOR: (over) She
> intends to supervise all of the
> family cooking, and she is a
> regular and welcome visitor to
> the kitchen.

DIANA is seen tasting sauces in the kitchen, watched with barely
concealed hostility by an anxiously servile COOK.

CUT TO

160. EXT. THE FARM OF THE VILLA. DAY.

> NEWSREEL COMMENTATOR: (over) The
> Princess has always loved country
> life. She herself comes from Sussex
> and she and the Prince aim to
> spend plenty of time in the open air.

DIANA in hunting hat and tweed plus fours is posing with a
GAMEKEEPER who arranges a gun on her shoulder and several hares
in her hand.

                                                    CUT TO

161. EXT. THE VILLA. DAY.

> NEWSREEL COMMENTATOR: (over) The
> Princess hopes to be of service to
> all sorts and conditions of men, not
> least those less fortunate and less
> gifted than herself.

DIANA, very much the lady of the manor in swathed chiffon dress,
is posing with a group of INVALIDS ·from the local hospital with
their escort of NURSES. They are being entertained by the PRINCIPE
and PRINCIPESSA for the day and six NUNS are chanting devotional
songs through microphones on the terrace conducted with great energy
by a PRIEST. The INVALIDS join in the chorus but DIANA is evidently
less than at home.

> NEWSREEL COMMENTATOR: (over) Princess
> Diana is regally confident that she
> can make a real and meaningful
> contribution to her new family and to
> her new country. We all join in
> wishing "auguri" -- good wishes in
> her new language -- to a new Italian
> Princess who will for us always
> remain a British one as well.

                                                    CUT TO

162. EXT. THE VILLA TERRACE. DAY.

DIANA is on the terrace alone, dwarfed by the villa. She sees the
younger CHILDREN with their GOVERNESS walking across the grass.
They turn and bow rather stiffly. She waves and smiles. But the
GOVERNESS, after a stiff bow, seats them with their backs to her
and begins to give them some lesson.

DIANA sighs and walks along. She is watched by a FOOTMAN, who opens
a door for her to go in. She goes in. She walks back and he opens
it for her to come out. She makes half a step back again. He half
opens the door. She smiles and walks along the terrace again.

A luxurious Mercedes now drives round the palace and pulls up at
the bottom of the many flights of stone steps which lead up to the
terrace where DIANA is standing. The CHAUFFEUR opens the door and
CESARE gets out. He comes up the steps toward her. She waits,
superb. CESARE reaches the terrace and DIANA goes a step towards
him. But at the same moment, his secretary, PALUCCI, comes out of
the house with a briefcase.

> PALUCCI: Ah, principe, scusi . . .

CESARE has come up to get his briefcase (oh, and to say goodbye
to DIANA!).

> CESARE: Si, si, le dimenticava.
> Andiamo adesso a Roma.

> PALUCCI: Si, si, principe.

They chat briskly. CESARE turns now to DIANA with a warm smile.

> CESARE: Are you all right, my
> darling?

> DIANA: I'm fine.

> CESARE: Have you understood what
> I said to Palucci?

> DIANA: (shrugs) Enough.

> CESARE: Well I'm sorry, but I must
> go to Rome. The Bank meeting is
> tomorrow morning.

> DIANA: And tonight?

> CESARE: Oh tonight . . . I'll go and
> see my mother -- you know I must go
> and see my mother.

> DIANA: Yes.

> CESARE: Next time you must come with
> me. But just now Rome is not amusing.

DIANA: Yes, I know.

CESARE: If you need anything,
Palucci will . . .

PALUCCI bows.

DIANA: All right. I'll have plenty
to do.

CESARE: Look, I will be back on
Thursday -- probably Friday. So
take care of yourself. Bye darling.
Bye Bye.

DIANA: Bye bye.

He bends and kisses her hand. She is full of sadness as he goes
down the steps, swiftly. Is he actually deceiving her already
with someone in Rome?

She looks at PALUCCI. He smiles flutteringly, like a eunuch.

Suddenly we hear the prattle of CESARE's CHILDREN and the stern
admonitions of their GOVERNESS (Scots, of course) who is
marshalling them to bed. The CHILDREN run up and say goodnight
to DIANA with less affection than she attempts to show them.

DIANA is left alone once more as the GOVERNESS bows curtly and
goes indoors. DIANA hesitates and then follows. The FOOTMAN
courteously opens the door as she goes in.

CUT TO

163. INT. THE DINING ROOM. NIGHT.

DIANA is dining alone with many SERVANTS attending her.

The door opens and PALUCCI comes in, obviously sent for.

PALUCCI: Principessa?

DIANA: Oh, Signor Palucci, my
husband's mother --

PALUCCI: Yes, Principessa.

DIANA: Do you have her telephone
number?

> PALUCCI: The Principessa had the instrument removed some years ago, Principessa.

The SERVANTS exchange looks.

> DIANA: My husband isn't obtainable tonight at all, then?

> PALUCCI: One could send a telegram, Principessa.

> DIANA: And that's the only means whereby you could get in touch?

> PALUCCI: That is so, Principessa.

> DIANA: Thank you.

She reaches for some water. A FOOTMAN gets there and pours it for her.

> DIANA: Thank you, Signor Palucci.

> PALUCCI: Principessa.

He bows and withdraws.

DIANA looks up at the great portraits on the walls. They seem to stare her down as she tries to rise. A FOOTMAN comes forward and withdraws her chair. Another opens the door. She walks out.

> CUT TO

164. INT. THE VILLA. NIGHT.

DIANA walks along corridors and up stairs echoing emptiness.

> CUT TO

165. INT. DIANA'S BEDROOM. NIGHT.

She stands in front of a huge mirror and slowly undresses, watching herself. Her jewellery, her fine gown, her exquisite lingerie, all are removed. She stands quite naked in front of the mirror. She slumps on her heels and stands there, less a symbol of sexuality than of glum loneliness. She stares at herself contemptuously enough to bring tears to her eyes. Then she turns and walks slowly to the bed and sits down heavily on it with her head in her hands. Again

she catches sight of herself and begins to cry harder. Over this we
begin to hear the sound of a jet plane screaming in flight.

                                                    CUT TO

166. INT. CUSTOMS HALL. LONDON AIRPORT. DAY.

DIANA is standing alone by her luggage watching the door which
leads out into the main concourse. She is obviously looking for
somebody to meet her.

                    CUSTOMS MAN: (o.s.) Is this all
                    your luggage?

                    DIANA: (without taking her eyes off
                    the door) Yes. Yes.

                    CUSTOMS MAN: (o.s.) Have you seen
                    one of these before?

                    DIANA: (as before) Yes.

                    CUSTOMS MAN: (o.s.) What have you
                    bought while you were abroad?

                    DIANA: I am not resident here. I
                    am resident abroad. I have got
                    practically nothing with me. Only
                    personal things.

Suddenly her face lights up. ROBERT is standing there in the
doorway.

                    CUSTOMS MAN: (o.s.) No cigarettes
                    or spirits?

ROBERT waves to DIANA, a weary, amused wave.

                    DIANA: I've got nothing to declare
                    at all.

                                                    CUT TO

167. INT. LONDON AIRPORT MAIN CONCOURSE. DAY.

DIANA walks slowly up to ROBERT.

                    DIANA: Hullo.

                    ROBERT: Hullo.

                    DIANA: I didn't know whether you'd
                    come.

                    ROBERT: I was always easily seduced.
                    Especially by telegram.

                    DIANA: I hoped you would be. You
                    look older.

                    ROBERT: You don't. Come on, I hate
                    this ant heap.

                                                    DISSOLVE TO

168. INT. PUB BEDROOM. DAY.

DIANA is lying on the bed with an unmistakably satisfied smile on
her face.

                    DIANA: Well!

                    ROBERT: (o.s.) Well.

                    DIANA: Isn't it a miracle? We're
                    still a couple. I thought maybe
                    after all this time something
                    would've changed, but it hasn't.
                    We're still a couple.

                    ROBERT: We are?

                    DIANA: Aren't we? Oh, thank God
                    it's never too late. Two people
                    who really belong to each other --
                    it doesn't matter what happens.

DIANA is lost in a reverie of her own sentimental contentment. She
scarcely notices that ROBERT is sitting with his back turned to her.

                    DIANA: (rapturously) This time,
                    darling, let's go somewhere in the
                    country, right away from all this
                    London racket -- somewhere quiet
                    where you can write. We've both
                    learnt our lesson and we won't make
                    any more mistakes. I know we can be
                    so happy.

ROBERT: We're not going back to
anything, you know. This was just
for old times' sake. (Into telephone)
Porter, please.

DIANA: What are you doing?

ROBERT: (into telephone) Oh,
Porter, will you get on to London
Airport, and reserve me one seat on
any flight this afternoon to Rome.

DIANA rushes at ROBERT and tries to grab the phone from him. He
flings her away and shoves her clothes at her.

ROBERT: (into phone) Yes, that's
right.

DIANA: What the hell are you doing?

ROBERT: (still into phone) For the
Princess Della Romita. First class.
R, O, M, I.

DIANA: Robert, put down that phone.
What are you doing? Stop it.

ROBERT: You're going back to Rome.

DIANA: I'm not going back to Rome --
give me that phone --

ROBERT: Now get dressed.

DIANA: You bastard. You just used
me.

ROBERT: You used me. Now get
dressed.

DIANA: (bitterly) God, I hate you.
(Pleadingly) No, it's not true,
Robert. I love you. You know I
love you. What are you doing,
Robert? Please. Please, I've
come all this way.

ROBERT: (implacably) Get dressed and
I'll take you to the airport.

DIANA: Robert, I've come all this way because I love you. I can't say goodbye. I need you. Please.

ROBERT: Get dressed.

DIANA: Robert, just give us one more chance, I beg of you.

ROBERT: We haven't got a chance.

DIANA: Let's spend a week together. It won't hurt to try a week.

ROBERT: I don't have a week.

DIANA: (breaking down) I don't know how -- I don't know how you can throw away something that's meant so much to us. (She grabs at him fiercely) It doesn't put me off, you know, being vile to me. It doesn't put me off.

ROBERT: It puts me off. It disgusts me.

DIANA: What does?

ROBERT: To hear myself. To hear the way I want to treat you. I don't want to feel this way a moment longer than I have to.

DIANA: We can't just go like this.

ROBERT: (laughs harshly) You'd be surprised.

CUT TO

169. INT. ROBERT'S CAR. DAY.

They are on their way to the airport.

DIANA: (sobbing) You're in love with someone else -- is that it?

ROBERT: No.

DIANA: You've gone back to your wife?

ROBERT: On the contrary. She wants to divorce me. She's found someone else she wants to marry.

DIANA: Well --

ROBERT: (savagely) Now isn't that good news?

DIANA sits there.

DIANA: Well, if there isn't anyone else, what are you going to do?

ROBERT: I'm going to America.

DIANA: What are you going to do in America?

ROBERT: Teach, kid, what else? Now I know all the answers.

DIANA: Robert, stop the car.

ROBERT: No.

DIANA: (hysterical) I won't go back to Rome.

ROBERT: You're going back to Rome.

DIANA: (screams at him) I'll kill myself.

ROBERT: Then kill yourself.

DIANA: I will, I swear I will.

ROBERT: So do.

She wrenches open the door of the car. The car swerves as ROBERT hauls the door shut and wrenches her back into the car.

ROBERT: I didn't say I wanted to come with you.

DIANA: (sobbing) If I can't be with you, I don't want to be alive.

ROBERT: Like hell.

DIANA: It's true.

ROBERT: All your lies are true at the time.

DIANA sits there while the inevitable becomes plain to her. She reaches to the back seat for her hat and puts it on, her sobs slowly diminishing. Finally she has to take out her mirror and make sure that she looks all right. She puts on dark glasses. The car moves down into the tunnel which leads to the main airport building.

                                                            CUT TO

170. EXT. MAIN BUILDING. LONDON AIRPORT.

The car stops outside the main building and ROBERT leans across and opens the passenger door. The two of them sit silently beside each other for a few seconds and then DIANA swings her feet out onto the ground.

                        DIANA: Porter.

A PORTER comes and takes her bag. She follows him into the building.

ROBERT pulls the door shut and watches DIANA go. Abruptly he clenches his fist on the rim of the steering wheel and lets his head fall forward in despair. The car hooter obediently honks.

                                                            CUT TO

171. EMBARKING CORRIDOR. LONDON AIRPORT. DAY.

DIANA is walking towards CAMERA haunted by the inevitable REPORTER with his notebook.

                        REPORTER: What actually is the
                        purpose of your visit here?

                        DIANA: (laughs shortly) I don't
                        even know how you found out I was
                        in England.

                        REPORTER: Any special reason?

DIANA: For one thing, my mother hasn't been well. I came over to see her.

REPORTER: What else?

DIANA: Surely one's mother is reason enough?

REPORTER: Are you happy in Italy, Principessa?

DIANA: As happy as anyone could possibly be.

REPORTER: Are you likely to resume your career soon, Principessa?

DIANA: I have a family now and that gives me all I could possibly want.

                                        CUT TO

172. EXT. TARMAC. LONDON AIRPORT. DAY.

DIANA climbs the steps into her plane and pauses at the top to give the ritual wave of those who suppose that their arrivals and departures are of some importance to the world. As she does so, we close on her face and FREEZE.

The face becomes petalled with paint and turns into one of those pseudo-academic portraits in which the expert flatterers of rich femininity specialise.

                                        CUT TO

173. INT. DINING ROOM. THE VILLA. NIGHT.

We track back from the portrait which we now see to be hanging on the wall of the great hall alongside the petty princes and pretty princesses. At the head of the table sits CESARE presiding over a great dinner party. We track past innumerable GUESTS until finally we come again to DIANA sitting embalmed between two courtly and cynical BANKERS.

                                        CUT TO

174. INT. HAIRDRESSER'S SALON. DAY.

The tracking continues but now we are passing middle-class WOMEN
and SHOPGIRLS in the process of being done. We track in close to
the shoulder of one WOMAN and then tilt down to see that on her
knees is a copy of Ideal Woman, with the last instalment of DIANA's
story in it.

The WOMAN sighs: Ah, to live such a life! She closes the magazine
and on the front of it we see a reproduction of the classy oil
painting and across it the words: "Inside: A DOUBLE PAGE PORTRAIT
of the PRINCESS DELLA ROMITA for YOU to keep".

                                                    FADE OUT

                          THE END

Something of the complexity of modern filmmaking, of the hard and carefully coordinated labor that goes into any production, is suggested by the following two documents.

The first is the initial and closing pages of the final shooting schedule for *The Best Man* (1963). The usual shooting schedule, unless the production is very elaborate, is based on thirty working days. Note that the film is not shot in order of the sequence of scenes. The large number of extras and minor cast numbers needed and the specific days when a location is available and accessible to film equipment are a few factors that help to determine the production sequence as actually drawn up. The problem of the production manager is to arrange the shooting in such a way as to keep costs down efficiently, yet at the same time to permit the director, the principals, and the crew to create the best possible work.

The second item supplements the first. It is a sample from the daily call sheets for Samuel Goldwyn, Jr.'s production of *The Young Lovers* (1963), a low-budget picture with a small cast and limited crew. Note that for the ten numbered scenes only two actors, Peter Fonda and Sharon Hugueny, are involved and only two exterior settings, both on location at the U.C.L.A. campus, which is in Westwood, not far from Hollywood. Yet, including stand-ins, a technical crew of 45 is required, together with 15 vehicles, and a catered lunch for 77. In case of inclement weather, or some other necessity, a cover set—"Schwartz' Classroom"—is indicated. Note that this same studio interior is listed on the advance schedule as the set for the next two working days, September 9 and 10; also given for those two days are the scenes to be shot and their order.

PROD. NO. __914-83__ TITLE __THE BEST MAN(MILLAR/TURMAN PROD)__

DIRECTOR __F SCHAFFNER__ PRODUCER __MILLAR/TURMAN__ ART DIR. __L WHEELER__

PROD BREAKDOWN ASST. __D.MODER__ SCRIPT DATED __8-30-63__

DAYS __30 PLUS__ START DATE __9-16-63__ FINISH DATE __10-25-63__ TYPED __9-3-63__
9 DAYS REHEARSAL

FINAL SHOOTING SCHEDULE

DATE	SET	PAGES	SEQ	SC'NS	CAST
1st DAY 9-16	STAGE #8 INT. RUSSELL SUITE(D) SCS: 11,12 Meet Alice-Jensen enters. Hockstader appears	5			Russell #1,Alice #7,Jensen #2 Hockstader #3
	TOTAL PAGES	5			
2nd DAY 9-17	LOCATION: AMBASSADOR HOTEL INT. CANTWELL HQTRS(D) SC: 16 Cantwell on TV. He & Don exit. Pickup TV for Sc 15A	3			Cantwell #8, Announcer,Don Cantwell #9, bit photographer, Spastic,announc-er #2, 60 extras (attendants,re-porters,photog-raphers, men, women, tv crew, guards, 10 Cantwell girls) tv cameras,news-reel camera, tv boom,big sign "Go with Joe" Books,coffee
	INT. KITCHEN(D) SC: 17 Cantwell & Don meet cleaning woman	1 2/8			Cantwell #8,Don #9,cleaning wo-man bit,3 police etc,4 Russell girls,5 kitchen help

PROD. NO. __914-83__ TITLE __THE BEST MAN__

DATE	SET	PAGES	SEQ	SC'NS	CAST
2nd DAY CONT'D	INT. HOTEL LOBBY(D) SC: 43 After lunch 2 ladies thru lobby to elevator	1			Mrs. Gamadge #5, Mabel #10, Senator bit,boys(men 2)bits,5ad libs, extras from int (men,women, elev operator, desk clerk,bell hops) posters, pictures
	TOTAL PAGES	5 2/8			
3rd DAY 9-18	LOCATION: AMBASSADOR HOTEL INT. BAROQUE ROOM(D) SC: 42 Ladies luncheon.Alice & Mabel do best to knife each other	6 2/8			Alice #7,Mabel #10,Mrs.Gamadge #5,Janet #6,Mrs. Claypoole bit #19, Reporters #1 & #3(35),Mrs. Anderson #77, Mrs.Merwin #20, 32 extras(4 bus-boys,photograph-ers,20 women,8 men)drinks
	TOTAL PAGES	6 2/8			
4th & 5th DAYS 9-19 & 9-20	LOCATION: AMBASSADOR HOTEL INT. BALLROOM(N) SCS: 22,23,24,25,26,27,28,28A 28B,29,29A,29B,29C,29D,30,30A 31,31A Dinner party.Hockstader introduces candidates & wives. Celebrity sings.	9 1/8			Russel #1,Jensen #2,Hockstader #3,Tom #4,Mrs. Gamadge #5,Alice #7,Cantwell #8, Don #9,Mabel #10 Claypoole #11, John Merwin #12 Celebrity #1 & #2,Oscar Anderson #13,Mrs.Claypool #19,Mrs.Merwin #20,Chairman #17 Reporter #51, waiter bit, wives at table dignitaries,men.

PROD. NO. <u>914-83</u> TITLE <u>THE BEST MAN</u>

DATE	SET	PAGES	SEQ	SC'NS	CAST
4th & 5th DAYS CONT'D					women, 3 waiters orchestra,newsmen,photographers
	TOTAL PAGES	9 1/8			
6th & 7th DAYS 9-23 & 9-24	<u>STAGE #8</u> INT. RUSSELL SUITE(D) SCS: 13,14 Hockstader talks politics with Bill & tells him of his cancer condition. Mrs. Gamadge enters, passes advice to Alice. Bill exits.	9 4/8			Russell #1,Mrs. Russell #7, Hockstader sc 12 #3,Jensen,#2 Mrs. Gamadge sc 14 #5,Janet reporters in hall,man Luggage clothes,bar set-up
	TOTAL PAGES	9 4/8			
8th & 9th DAYS 9-25 & 9-26	<u>STAGE #8</u> INT. RUSSELL SUITE(D) SCS: 44,44A Russell bathes as Claypoole pledges support. Hockstader enters. Jensen brings in Bascomb who tells about Cantwell's past in army.	8			Russell #1, Claypoole #11, Jensen #2, Hockstader #3, Bascomb #15,aide (sb)1 valet,1 room service
	INT. CANTWELL HOME(FOR TV SET SC) SC: 18C Mother Cantwell interviewed.	2/8			Interviewer,Mrs. Cantwell, T.V. announcer
	INT. SENATE RM(D)(FOR TV SET SC) SC: 18B Cantwell questions Mafia man	4/8			Cantwell,Mafia man,voice over, Extras?
	TOTAL PAGES	8 6/8			
10th DAY 9-27	<u>STAGE #8</u> INT. RUSSELL SUITE SC: 47 Bascomb finishes story. Jensen says he has arranged meeting.	6			Russell #1, Hockstader #3, Jensen #2, Bascomb #15, Alice #7

PROD. NO. __914-83__ TITLE _____THE BEST MAN_____

DATE	SET	PAGES	SEQ	SC'NS	CAST
10th DAY CONT'D	As Russell leaves Hockstader has attack,asks for doctor TOTAL PAGES	 6			
11th DAY 9-30	LOCATION: BASEMENT BOMB SHELTER INT. BOMB SHELTER(D) SC: 51 Cantwell reads document,greets Marcus & explains his innocence. Marcus rushes out door into newsmen TOTAL PAGES	5 5/8 5 5/8			Russell #1, Cantwell #8, Bascomb #15, 6 newsmen & photographers
12th DAY 10-1	LOCATION: BASEMENT BOMB SHELTER INT. CORRIDOR OUTSIDE BOMB SC: 52 SHELTER(D) Cantwell poses w/Marcus for photographers	7/8			Cantwell #8,Don #9,Bascomb #15 Jensen #2,photographer bit, reporter bit,6 reporters & newsmen
27th DAY 10-22	INT. LIMO(PROCESS)(D) SC: 64 Russell 7 Alice riding to arena INT. LINEN CLOSET(D) sc; 49 Russell & Cantwell meet. Big discussion as Cantwell asks Russell to withdraw from race. 2 exit to hall TOTAL PAGES	1 4/8 4 4/8 6 6/8			Russell #1,Alice #7,driver?, mockup limo,process plates to cover Russell #1, Jensen #2, Cantwell #8,Don #9
28th DAY 10-23	LOCATION: AMBASSADOR HOTEL INT. PALM COURT(D) SCS: 1,2 Russell talks to press	5 1/8			Russell #1, Jensen #2, reporters #1,#2, #3,#4,#5,fan,35 extras(reporters men,women,1

PROD. NO. ___914-83___ TITLE _____THE BEST MAN_____

DATE	SET	PAGES	SEQ	SC'NS	CAST
28th DAY CONT'D					bartender,1 guard,2 waiters) no tv camera
	EXT. PALM COURT(D) SC: 3 Russell tries to call wife on phone. No luck	6/8			Russell #1, Jensen #2,5 reporters,fan, from sc 1, re-porters,man Indian,men, women,elderly lady(SB)6yr old boy(SB)3 Russell girl w.worker, banners,bass drum,mixed but-tons
	TOTAL PAGES	5 7/8			
29th DAY 10-24	LOCATION: AMBASSADOR HOTEL EXT. POOL AREA(D) SCS: 4,5,6,7 Two at pool meet Mrs. Gamadge. They talk, she exits	4 5/8			Russell #1, Jensen #2,Mrs. Gamadge #5,girl bit sc 7,tv in-terviewer sc 7 100 extras (husky woman golfer(SB)men bathers,women bathers,men, women,waiters, tv crew, photogs newsmen,5 Cantwell girls) tv camera tran-sistor radios, private cameras
	INT. HOTEL LOBBY(D) SC: 8 Continuation of pool seq 2 men to elevator	6/8			Mrs. Gamadge, Russell,Jensen, men,women,2 bellhops,from 100 in scs 4-7
	TOTAL PAGES	5 3/8			

PROD. NO. ___914-83___ TITLE _____THE BEST MAN_____

DATE	SET	PAGES	SEQ	SC'NS	CAST
30th DAY	LOCATION: AMBASSADOR HOTEL EXT. AMBASSADOR(D) SC: 40 Jensen entering,meets Lazarus	6/8			Jensen,Lazarus, 45 extras(15 picket line (some colored)5 Cantwell girls, man on stilts,2 attendants,men, women,photogs, newsmen,doorman) cars,Jensen's car,Lazarus car
	EXT. AMBASSADOR HELIPORT(D) SC: 58A Cantwell & Aide board copter	1/8			Cantwell #8, Aide bit,men, women,pilot, copter
	EXT. AMBASSADOR SWIM POOL(N) SC: 35 Hockstader asks Claypoole to be VP. Supporter talks to him	7/8			Hockstader #3, Tom #4,Claypoole #11,supporter bit,40 extras (men,women, servers,see colored help)
	TOTAL PAGES	1 6/8			
POST LAST PRODUCTION	INT. COPTER(D) SC: 58B Cantwell on walkie-talkie	3/8			Cantwell,Aide, Pilot,shoot in flight,copter
	TOTAL SCRIPT PAGES	134 7/8			
		****			

TIGERTAIL PROD., INC.

4th day of shooting   CALL SHEET   Prod. No. 5000

PICTURE: "THE YOUNG LOVERS"   DIRECTOR: SAMUEL GOLDWYN, JR.

SHOOTING CALL: 8:00 A.M.   DATE: FRIDAY, SEPT.6, 1963

SET AND SCENE NO.

     EXT. CAMPUS PARKING ENT. (D) U.C.L.A.
         Scs. 189, 190

     EXT. SMALL PARKING LOT (D) U.C.L.A.
         Scs. 214, 215, 216, 217, 218, 219, 220, 221

COVER SET: INT. SCHWARTZ' CLASSROOM

- -

CAST & BITS	CHARACTER & WARDROBE	HAIRDRESSING	MAKEUP	ON SET
PETER FONDA	EDDIE		7:15	8:00
SHARON HUGUENY	PAM	6:00		8:00

STANDINS: THRU GATE

T. CONNERS	MR. FONDA w/car	7:00
1 WOMAN	MISS HUGUENY w/car	7:00

- -

ADVANCE SCHEDULE

MON. 9/9 & TUES.	INT. SCHWARTZ' CLASSROOM (D)	Scs. 68, 69, 70, 71, 72, 73, 74, 75, 76, 77, 78, 79, 80.	STAGE 4
	INT. SCHWARTZ' CLASSROOM (D)	Scs. 262, 263, 264, 265, 266, 267, 268, 269, 270, 271, 272, 273.	STAGE 4
	INT. SCHWARTZ' CLASSROOM (D)	Scs. 103, 104, 105 188C	STAGE 4
	INT. CLASSROOM	Sc. 188D	STAGE 4

CAMERA	TIME:
1 Camera	6:30
1 Cameraman	6:42
1 Operator	6:42
2 Assistants	6:30

TECHNICAL

1 Key & 2nd Grip	6:30
4 Co Grips	6:30
1 Greensman	6:30
1 Laborer	6:30

ELECTRICAL

1 Gaffer & Best Boy	6:30
8 Lamp Opers	6:30
1 Generator	6:30
1 Gen Operator	6:30
1 Booster Lights	6:30

WARDROBE

1 Ward Man	6:30
1 Ward Girl	6:30

MAKEUP

1 Makeup Man	6:00
1 Hairstylist	6:00

SOUND

1 Mixer	6:42
1 Recorder	6:30
1 Mikeman	6:30
1 Cableman	6:30

STILL

1 Still Man	7:00

PROPERTY	TIME:
1 Property Master	6:30
2 Asst Prop Man	6:30
Tarragoo's car	6:30
Eddie's Motorcycle	6:30
Pam's Car	7:00

RESTAURANT

77 Lunches	11:30
1 Gals Coffee Box donuts	7:00

HOSPITAL

1 1st Aid Man	6:30

TRANSPORTATION

1 Standby Car	6:42
1 Car	7:00
1 Car	7:30
1 Bus (41)	6:30
1 Grip Trk	ON LOC
1 Prop Trk	ON LOC
1 Ward Trk	ON LOC
1 Sound Jeep	ON LOC
1 Elec Trk	ON LOC
1 Generator Trk	ON LOC
P.U. trk	ON LOC
1 LU Driver	6:30

Above the line expenses (cost)   cost of staff, talent, and story in preparation and production of a motion picture.

Absolute film (also **abstract film**)   a nonrepresentative film whose parts are composed of moving visual patterns.

Abstract music   musical accompaniment to a scene or scenes which aims at more than **crutch music;** based upon correspondence or juxtaposition with the structure and rhythm of the images on the screen.   .

Abstract set   a nonrepresentational setting without a definite period or locale.

Academy players directory (casting bible)   several volumes listing professional actors available for American film productions; includes photographs.

Accelerated motion (also **fast motion** and **speedup motion**)   by slowing down the camera mechanism during shooting, the resulting projection of action at standard rate (24 frames per second) will appear to be taking place at greater speed; often used for farce or comic effect, also to emphasize mechanistic order; opposite of **slow motion.**

Accent light   a small spotlight focused on a specific detail of a subject; usually placed to one side of the subject or used as backlighting.

Action   anything recorded by the camera in a shot; the command, "Action!" beginning a shot, may be given only by the director.

Action director (also **second unit director**)   a supplementary director for action scenes and scenes without dialogue which do not require the presence of the director.

Action still   a still photograph taken of a scene as it appears in the film, distinguished from other types of still photographs taken during production, such as **art stills, production stills, publicity stills.** See also **Unit still photographer.**

Ad lib extemporaneous dialogue and action not in a prepared script; or working without a script.

Adapt to translate and to change a story, novel, play, or other property for the purpose of making a film.

Aerial shot photograph taken from helicopter, airplane, balloon.

Against the grain (opposite of **on the nose**) any artistic technique in any aspect of the filmmaking process in which one element is used unconventionally, in contrast to audience experience and expectation, to create a sense of conflict, "mixed feelings," and to comment upon the convention violated.

Allusion as in literature, an explicit or implicit reference to another film or films achieved by dialogue, impersonation, music, visual style of shots.

Angle see **Camera angle.**

Animation process by which drawings or objects are photographed so that when shown there will be the illusion of movement.

Answer print (also **first-trial print**) first combined print received from the laboratory and approved as representing the standard for all subsequent prints.

Aperture lens opening admitting light to film; also opening in the camera permitting lens to project images onto the film.

Arc (also **brute**) a large, high-powered carbon light used to illuminate a set for filming.

Arrange to adapt the music created by the *composer* for various voices and instruments.

Art director designs and supervises all sets, exterior and interior, in studio and on location. See also **Production designer.**

Art film used to describe any film, foreign or domestic, ostensibly not intended for large-scale commercial release and distribution.

Art house (or **theater**) a theater specializing in the presentation of art films.

Art still a photograph made of a film actor, not taken from the context of actual filming.

Assemble to begin the editing process by collecting separate shots and arranging them in order.

Assistant cameraman member of camera crew, charged with loading the camera with raw stock and with focusing of lenses.

Assistant director doubles as an assistant to the director and to the unit production manager; generally serves as foreman of the set; specifically charged with handling all bit players and extras, with presence of all players for their shots, notification of all players of their calls, also transportation and set discipline.

Associate producer an immediate assistant to the producer; when the producer is involved in the making of more than one film, he may be charged with the making of one film.

Atmosphere details of setting, costumes, extras, properties which establish verisimilitude; or aspects of lighting, photography, direction, editing which contribute to convey an emotional mood.

Attitude the use of **objective** and **subjective** shots by the filmmaker to reveal a meaning or to make a point or statement.

Audience participation shots any shots in a film in which actors seem to speak to, act, and react to the theater audience or the camera *as camera;* or any scenes or shots in which the audience is explicitly introduced to the process of making the film being seen.

Auteur (French for author) the filmmaker, in particular, the director, viewed as analogous to the author of a book in the sense that he has authority and control over the creation of the film and responsibility for the finished work, and each work becomes part of his canon; assumes that the director is a responsible artist with a recognizable cinematic manner and style and an artist's concern for specific subjects and areas of experience.

Avant garde used loosely to describe any films in which form or content or both are experimental.

B & W abbreviation for black-and-white film.

Back lighting light directed into the subject and towards the camera from a point behind the subject.

Back projection (also **rear projection**) projection of a film of an action or setting through a transparent screen, in front of which another action or scene may be filmed. See also **Process shot.**

Background (bg) that portion of the setting or frame farthest, in real or apparent distance, from the camera.

Background light light placed on the background to create a visual separation of the subject of a shot from the background.

Background music music composed and arranged to accompany particular action or dialogue in a film; sometimes prerecorded.

Background players (crowd) see **Extra.**

Backing a flat background, which can be a photograph or painting, against which actors are filmed.

Backup schedule an alternate to the scenes to be shot in regular shooting schedule in the event that, for any reason, the regular schedule cannot be followed.

Balance when the process of **dubbing** has been completed and the film is a single unit with a single sound track, the editor balances it, equalizing, insofar as possible, the footage in each reel, prior to any preview showing.

Barndoor a black flap used to block light from shining into the camera lens.

Below the line expenses (cost) all production expenses involved in filmmaking, including technical facilities, staging and studio costs.

Benshi (Japanese)   live narrator and commentator for silent films.

Big closeup   see **Closeup**.

Bit (player)   an actor with a small speaking part.

Bits (of business)   miscellaneous movements, actions, gestures created by the director and actors for dramatic purposes and for characterization.

Blimp   soundproof camera housing used to eliminate the noise of the camera.

Blocking (also to **block in**)   rehearsal preparation by the director, assistants, actors, and crew in arranging the composition of a scene, with special emphasis on positions, movements, and gesture of the actors; may involve the use of diagrams or sketches or marking the set with chalk lines or tape; also the initial arrangement of lights. See also **Rough in.**

Blowup   an enlargement of a photograph or a particular part of a photograph, or an enlargement of any printed material.

Body makeup woman   a woman charged with all makeup used for female members of the cast, except those specifically reserved for the makeup artist under union regulations.

Bold   a take which has not been printed, has been put aside, and held in reserve for possible use.

Boom   a mobile suspended microphone, held near actors but out of camera range, to record dialogue. See also **Camera boom.**

Bounce light   creation of soft, diffused, general and almost shadowless illumination by reflecting ("bouncing") light off the ceiling.

Breakdown   an estimated budget for the making of a film, derived from analysis of the script, and subdivided according to estimates of necessary shooting time required, cast and crew, technical resources, and materials.

Bridge music   music designed to accompany and support visual transitions in the film.

Bridging shot   any shot inserted during editing to cover a break in continuity. See also **Insert.**

Broad (also **broadside**)   a reflector light containing two powerful bulbs, creating an even flood covering an angle of roughly sixty degrees.

Brute   see **Arc.**

Budget   the overall estimated and allocated expense for the making of a film, or for any particular aspect of the process; also a daily sheet, issued to cast and crew, indicating which scenes are to be shot on the following day and which people will be required. See also **Call sheet.**

Burnt up   scenes in which set or actors are overlighted.

Busy   anything in action or setting which distracts from the intended focus of interest.

Butterfly lighting   light is placed in front of the subject and shadow reduced to a delicate minimum; used chiefly in closeups, for glamor.

Call sheet a mimeographed list, prepared by the assistant director and the unit production manager, indicating the requirements and calls for the next day's shooting; includes cast, crew, and equipment required.

Calls estimated time for various members of cast and crew to report for work.

Cameo part a bit part in a picture for which a star is cast.

Camera motion picture camera designed to take photographic images on cinematographic film; conventionally a 35 MM camera for commercial filming, but 16 MM cameras, and, occasionally, 8 MM cameras, are also used; capable of using a wide variety of lenses.

Camera angle the position or standpoint of the camera in terms of the scene and the subject being filmed; unless otherwise specified, is usually assumed to be eye level. See also **High angle shot** and **Low angle shot.**

Camera boom (also **crane**) a mobile crane with a platform for the camera which can be used for either fixed or moving shots, and allows for movement horizontally and vertically, backward and forward.

Camera operator second man of the camera crew; operates the camera physically, responsible for frame and focus.

Cameraman (also **cinematographer** and **director of photography**) senior member of the camera crew; supervises all operations of the camera and the lighting of sets and actors; with director creates the composition of the shots.

Cant (**frame** or **shot**; also **oblique angle, slant frame**) a shot made with the camera slightly tilted, to create a special effect or to exaggerate normal angles.

Cast the actors participating in a film, including **stars, featured players, bit players,** and **extras.**

Casting director responsible for keeping records of actors suitable for parts and available for work on a film.

Changing gag canvas or rubber bag, enclosed in a black cover, used for handling film in darkness when no darkroom is available.

Cheat shot a shot in which a portion of a subject or part of an action is excluded from view to create an illusion or suggest a special effect.

Cinéaste (French for filmmaker) the ordering mind of the director.

Cinema of ideas as in theater of ideas, filmmaking for ideological or social purpose, or films which probe and question intellectual concepts in the context of fiction as well as in the documentary.

Cinéma vérité (also **direct cinema**) deriving from technique of newsreels and documentary filming; deliberate imitation of style and manner of a happening; a conscious attempt to represent an unplanned, accidental filming.

Cinematography the art of recording motion photographically and reproducing it for audiences.

Cinemobile Mark IV   a single, 35-foot, bus-like vehicle, created and designed by Fouad Said, containing all necessary equipment, bathrooms, dressing rooms, and space for a staff and crew of fifty, which is rapidly replacing the huge caravans of trucks and vehicles necessary for filming on location; a self-contained unit, this vehicle has been widely and successfully used in filming recent American pictures at a variety of locations.

Clapper (also **number board** and **slate**)   a pair of hinged boards which are clapped together at the beginning of each numbered take so that sound and picture can be synchronized in editing; a slate on which the scene number and take number are written and photographed.

Clip   a short section or sequence from a film.

Close medium shot (also **close middle shot, MCS**)   a shot of indefinite distance between a medium shot and a close shot; a close medium shot of a human subject is usually a bust shot.

Closeup (CU, also **close shot, CS, tight shot**)   shot in which the camera, actually or apparently, is close to the subject; in terms of an actor, it usually includes area from shoulders to top of head or face only; variations are the large closeup or big closeup, focused on one part of an object or part of the face or anatomy of an actor.

Color correction   use of color filters to restrain one or more subject tones so that film will record the scene as if seen by the naked eye.

Combined continuity   a complete verbal and numerical record of the finished film, including action, dialogue, sounds, camera angles, footage, and frames, prepared by the **script supervisor.**

Commentary (also **voice over narration**)   descriptive or narrative talk in accompaniment with the film.

Composer   creates music for a film.

Composite print (British: **combined print**)   an edited, completed, positive print of the film, or strip of film, containing all sound tracks.

Composition   the arrangement and real or apparent movement of subjects in frame, shot, scene, or sequence, together with qualities of perspective, lighting, photography. The composition of a single shot is often analyzed analogously to the composition of a painting.

Comprehensive shot   a complete shot of a large area or large-scale action. See also **Establishing shot.**

Continuity   the editorial organization of shots and sequences, with transitions between them, in a film.

Continuity editing   editing which is tied to establishing definite story points; distinguished from **dynamic editing.**

Contrast   the relationship of the elements of brightness in a picture.

Contrast ratio (also **contrast range**)   range of contrast between the darkest and lightest elements of a frame.

"Cookies"   black opaque screens used to cut off light from one or more parts of the set or to shield the camera from direct light.

Costume designer   designs and creates wardrobe for a film.

Costumers   maintain clothing and wardrobe during production, assist players in dressing, and stand by on set.

Cover   the number of **setups** and **takes** used in filming a scene.

Cover set   a set in readiness for filming in the event that, for any reason, the regular filming schedule cannot be followed.

Coverage   the amount of film, the number of takes and footage, from various angles, allotted by the director in the filming of a scene or sequence.

Crab dolly   a small wheeled platform mount for the camera, which may be moved on level ground by hand; is moved by **grips**; used for easy movement over level ground or on studio sound stage floors; may be moved in any direction (crabbed). See also **Dolly.**

Crane shot (also **boom shot**)   a shot taken by a camera from a camera boom.

Credits (also **screen credits**)   the names of members of staff, cast, and crew who are officially credited, that is, recognized according to custom, contracts, and union regulations, in the film.

Critical focus   distance between subject and the camera.

Cross-cut (also **parallel editing**)   juxtaposition of two or more separate shots or scenes with parts of each presented alternately so that separate actions are represented as simultaneous.

Crutch music   mood pieces supporting scenes; principal problem is timing to end simultaneously with the scene.

Cut   (1) an individual strip of film; (2) a transition between two separate shots joined together so that the first shot is instantaneously replaced by the second; (3) as a verb, to trim and join shots together, to edit a film; (4) a shot; (5) an instruction to terminate a shot, given only by the director.

Cutaway   a shot apparently taking place at the same time as the main action of a scene; most commonly a **reaction shot.**

Cut-in (also **insert shot**)   a shot of some detail of the main action other than the faces of actors involved.

Cut-in scene   a scene taken separately and inserted into a film.

Cutout   parts of film discarded by the film editor.

Cutter   the **film editor**; also refers to his assistants.

Cutting bench   a special, vinyl-surfaced table used by film editors.

Cutting on movement   a method associated with the **match cut**; when cutting between shots of the same subject in an apparently continuous time sequence, the cut is made on the motion of the subject to reduce audience awareness of the cut.

Cutting piece   an illusory blending of widely separated locations or sets into an apparent whole.

Cutting room   room or space assigned to the editor and his assistants for editing the film.

Dailies (also **rushes**)   film photographed on the previous working day, developed, printed, **rough cut**, and screened on the following day for the benefit of the director and his staff; also daily progress reports on the production.

Day for night   shooting night scenes in daylight, using filters and other technical devices to simulate darkness.

Deep focus   sharp focus for a **long shot** or **far shot.**

Deep focus lens   a lens permitting simultaneous focus for a closeup and a long shot background in the same shot.

Depth of field   the distance to and from the camera in which an actor can move or an object can be moved without becoming out of focus.

Depth of focus   the extent to which a lens can focus on near and distant objects at the same time.

Detail shots   shots of details, cut into the action of a sequence, usually with the effect of expanding the *time* of a sequence; for example, in a race sequence, cutting to feet of runners, crowd reactions, faces, etc., while maintaining master sequence of race.

Development (also **processing**)   laboratory process for developing and fixing exposed film.

Dialing   control of the sound during filming by the **mixer;** unwanted sounds can be dialed out.

Dialogue (also **lines, words**)   all spoken words in a film.

Dialogue director (also **coach**)   assigned to rehearsal of lines and prompting of players.

Diaphragm   an adjustable ring on the aperture of the camera serving to control the amount of light entering the lens.

Differential focus   photographing an object in sharp focus with rest of the shot out of focus.

Diffusion screens   screens used to control light and shadow on a set. See also **Reflectors.**

Diffusor   material which is used to soften a beam of light.

Direct cut   a cut, but stipulated direct cut in script directions to emphasize this particular form of transition rather than to leave it optional; often used at a place where, conventionally, the editor might use another transition.

Directional movement   real or apparent movement of the subjects of a shot or scene as blocked and arranged by the director as a part of his composition and **structured rhythm;** movement, within a frame, may be left (**l**) or right (**r**), towards the background (**bg**) or foreground (**fg**) of the shot; also applied to arrangements of static objects on a set which may be photographed in such a way, by moving the camera, by lens adjustment, or by changing the angle, as to make objects seem to move, as, for example, when the camera imitates the **point of view** of a moving character; also applied to the relationship of movements and motion in separate shots and scenes linked together in editing.

Director responsible for all aspects of filmmaking from the beginning of production to release.

Dissolve (also **lap dissolve** and **mix**) the merging of one shot into the next, produced by superimposition of the two shots and a fade out of the first and a fade in of the second; usually a laboratory process, but can be done in the camera while shooting.

Documentary film a nonfiction film on subjects of general interest.

Dolly a wheeled platform serving as a camera mount which can be man-handled in any direction; sometimes called **trolley** when mounted on tracks.

Dolly in (also **track in**) moving the camera towards the subject, decreasing the distance of the shot.

Dolly out (also **track out**) moving the camera backwards, away from the subject, increasing the distance of the shot.

Dolly shot (also **travelling shot, tracking shot**) a moving shot, usually made of a moving subject. See also **Following shot, Running shot, Trucking shot.**

Domestic release commercial release of a film to be shown in theaters in the U.S. and Canada.

Double see **Stunt double.**

Double-exposure use of the same film strip for two or more exposures to create superimposed images on developed film.

Dress extra an **extra** reporting for work in his own tuxedo or full dress, her own evening gown.

Dubbing (also **mixing** and **rerecording**) process of combining all sound tracks, including music, sound effects, and dialogue, into one synchronized sound track for the film; also the process of synchronizing foreign language dialogue for foreign language versions of a completed film.

Dupe negative a negative made from a positive print.

Dynamic editing a style of editing suitable to action scenes and characteristic of documentary filmmaking where the film is "made" in editing; its quality is rapid pace and maximum visual impact in combinations of shots.

Dynamic frame any device or technique which serves to make the screen itself appear either to enlarge or decrease in size.

Editor (also **cutter**) responsible to the director for entire process of editing and assembling the film, from first takes to final **work print**, including all technical aspects, optical and sound.

Effect shot a cut made within context of a scene or sequence to another scene or shot, to comment on original scene or to establish a relationship between the two contexts.

Electric eye light meter built into camera to set the lens opening automatically.

Emulsion chemicals on the film's acetate base which, being sensitive to light, receive the image during filming.

Establishing shot   a shot which serves to locate the action for the scene to follow.

Exciter lamp   projector lamp which, in coordination with the amplifier, produces sound for a projected sound film.

Expressionism   in cinema refers to a filmmaking movement in post-World War I Germany; characterized by deliberate artifice in lighting, costumes, and sets, by symbolic or mime-like acting, by fantasy or strong elements of the fantastic.

Extended image   an image in which persons or objects overlap the limits of the frame, suggesting the larger context beyond the frame.

Exterior (EXT.)   shooting done outdoors, on location, or on the lot of the studio.

Extra (also screen extra)   a member of the cast used for background purposes and authenticity; if the extra acts or reacts in a scene, a silent bit, he receives additional pay. See also **Stand-in.**

Extreme closeup (also **extreme close shot**)   close shot of a very small detail.

Extreme long shot   shot made with the lens of the camera focused on infinity.

Eye level (also **horizontal**)   the standard camera angle, assumed unless otherwise specified by the director or the script.

Eyelight   small light used near camera to cause actor's eyes to "sparkle."

Eyepiece   viewing lens attachment to camera permitting the operator to see exactly what the camera lens will record. See also **Viewer.**

FPS   abbreviation for **frames per second.**

FX track   the sound-effects tracks.

Fade   the screen is blank (dark) with no image projected; a fade, in context of a film, usually serves as a distinct break in continuity, clearly setting off one sequence of shots from another; a slow fade calls for a very gradual diminishment of light and the image until the screen is blank.

Fade in   the gradual appearance of a picture on the screen.

Fade out   the gradual disappearance (fading) of picture and images from the screen, ending with a blank screen.

Far shot (also **very long shot, extreme long shot, distance shot**)   a shot which includes not only the entire setting, but also the details of a distant background.

Fast film   type of film with high sensitivity to light, able to record images with less light than is required by slower films.

Fast motion (effect)   see **Accelerated motion.**

Fast tempo   the overall sense of timing, of "fast and slow" scenes and sequences in a film, is determined not by the speed of photography or by the physical speed or movement of subjects filmed, but by narrative and visual context and, chiefly, by the editorial craft in cutting. The effect of fast tempo might be achieved through cross-cutting or by dynamic editing.

Favoring (also **featuring** and **centering on**)   in any two shot or group shot, this direction calls for photography which will stress the significance of one or more of the characters involved.

Featured player   an actor with a major part who receives screen credit (billing), but who is ranked below the stars.

Feeler print   a print made from the edited negative of the work print with all effects inserted, but before final mixing.

Fill light   light placed so as to control the shadows cast by the **key light**.

Film grain   the size of the particles composing the light-sensitive layer of a film; a shot or print is said to be grainy when these particles are clearly visible in projection.

Film gauge   the width of film measured in millimeters, as, for example, 70 MM, 35 MM, 16 MM, 8 MM.

Filters   transparent glass or gelatin placed in front of or behind the camera lens to alter the light qualities or, in color filming, the tone relationships; among the standard filters used are *neutral density filters*, a gray filter uniformly cutting down on the light hitting the lens; *polarizing filters*, used especially to decrease sunlight and reflections on glass and water; *diffusion filters*, which serve to soften hard lines and are used for facial closeups; *fog filters*, which create a foggy effect; for black-and-white films, a *color filter*, which lightens its own color and darkens its compliment; and *color-compensating filters*, used to control illumination and give good color rendition.

Final negative   the edited negative from which the composite print is made.

Fine cut   editor's best complete version of an unfinished film, lacking **supportive elements** (see below).

Fine grains   duplicate negatives of the film ordered from the laboratory for technical and editorial use.

Fish-eye lens   very wide-angle lenses which, because of distortion, are sometimes used for dream sequences, fantasy and other devices of **subjective camera** (see below).

Fixed (also **static**) **camera**   shooting from any angle or distance when the camera remains in a fixed position throughout the shot; distinguished from **mobile** or **moving camera.**

Fixed frame   a shot in which the camera is fixed (static) and in which there is no background movement.

Fixed-focus lens   a lens without focus adjustment.

Flare check   a cameraman's test to determine if light is shining into the lens.

Flash cutting   insertion of extremely brief fragments between direct cuts from shot to shot or scene to scene.

Flash forward   shot, scene, or sequence interrupting the ongoing time sequence of a film by introducing action or events to come; it may refer forward to scenes which will be viewed or may imply future time and events outside the chronology of the film.

Flash shot   a shot of very few frames and short duration, therefore almost subliminal in effect; often used as an insert within the context of an ongoing shot or scene to represent a fragment of subjective memory or an intimation or intuition of future time.

Flashback   a shot, scene, or sequence, introduced into the chronological sequence of a film and breaking that sequence by referring to time past; it may refer back to action already seen or may introduce narrative elements or subjective memory of the past into the imagined present of the film.

Flip (also **flipover wipe** and **flip frame**)   a transitional device in which the frame of one shot revolves 360 degrees, and flips over, ending its revolution with the frame of the next shot.

Floor   any part of a studio where shooting is in progress; the ground level of any set, exterior or interior.

Focus   to adjust the lens of a camera (or projector) in order to keep a sharply defined image.

Follow focus   adjustment of the lens during filming to keep a moving subject in focus.

Following shot   a shot in which the camera moves or seems to move to follow a moving actor or object. See also **Running shot.**

Footage   a length of film measured in feet; often used loosely to refer to a shot, scene, or sequence of a film.

Foreground (fg)   that part of the scene immediately in front of the camera.

Foreshadowing   cinematic or narrative (or both) means of preparing the audience to accept as probable some future action or event.

Form cutting   the framing in a following shot of a subject or compositional arrangement which has a shape or contour in some way similar to an image in the shot preceding it; the relationship and juxtaposition of the two can serve as a simple comparison (as in a simile in poetry), or, by association, within the context of the film, or by allusion, can be raised to the higher power of metaphor and symbol.

Frame (sometimes **still**)   a single photograph in the series printed on a length of cinematographic film; in photographing a scene or shot the frame of the shot, seen through the eyepiece of the camera, or the **viewer,** determines the staging areas (background and foreground, left and right) and the composition of the shot or scene; anything which can be seen is said to be *in frame;* anything in the scene or shot which cannot be seen is *out-of-frame* or *off-frame* (of); see also **Off-camera** and **On-camera;** the average ninety-minute feature film is made up of 129,000 separate frames or 8,100 feet of film.

Frame line   the dividing line separating each single frame from the next.

Frame slant   a shot in which the camera is slightly tilted on its axis so that the image appears on the screen off center, in a tilted position. See also **Cant.**

Freeze shot   the repetition of a single frame for an extended time, done either in camera while photographing or by editing, so that, when seen in projection, the shot appears to freeze, to be a still photograph. See also **Zoom freeze.**

Front lighting (also **pancake lighting**)   the light source is from approximately the same position and angle as the camera; serves to flatten out planes and angles.

Full shot   a shot of indeterminate distance, from any angle, but fully including the subject of the shot; when applied to actors, the shot calls for the full body to be in frame.

Gaffer   the electrical foreman of the set; also may be used, loosely, to designate any foreman of any production department or crew.

Gendai-geki (Japanese)   films set in time from mid-nineteenth century to the present time.

General shot   any shot from any angle in which a complete action or a large part of the set is visible.

Ghost and glare   optical effects caused by rays from improperly placed lamps; *ghosting* occurs when faint images of the light source appear in the picture; *glare* is general veiling caused by scattered light which flattens the contrast.

Glass shot   a shot in which part of the background or setting is painted or photographed on glass or other transparent material, which is placed between the camera and the subject so that it will merge with the full-size set being photographed.

Gobo (also **nigger**)   a black screen, mounted adjustably, used to control light falling on the camera.

Goose   any vehicle designed especially to transport camera and sound equipment.

Grain   dot patterns on projected film; *fine grain* is characteristic of slow film; fast film creates *coarse grain.*

Greensman (also **nurseryman**)   charged with all trees, plants, shrubbery, and flowers not in vases on exterior or interior sets; responsible for required seasonal changes.

Grip   a skilled set laborer, general, all-purpose set assistant; the foreman is known as the **key grip** or **head grip.**

Group shot   a shot of unspecified distance and angle, concentrating upon three or more characters.

Hair check   test for line, dust, etc., in the camera aperture, made after film stock has been threaded in the camera.

Hand-held camera (HH)   use of a camera—a 16 MM camera whose film will subsequently be blown up to 35 MM—without any conventional fixed or mobile mounting; characteristic of documentary and direct cinema filming; *effect* of hand-held camera can be imitated with conventional camera mounting; though held by hand, the camera can be firmly controlled by means of body braces, shoulder rests.

Hard light   artificial lights (arcs) used to represent sunlight on a set.

Hatchet lighting   light source placed ninety degrees from the camera to create a half-shadow effect on the subject.

Head-on shot   a shot in which the action appears to come directly towards the camera; most often used in relation to **trucking shot.**

Heavy   a movie villain.

Hi hat   a small, low mount for the camera for very **low angle** shooting, or for shooting a few inches off the floor.

High angle shot (also **high shot**)   a shot taken by any means from an elevated angle in terms of the subject; sometimes referred to as **shooting down** or **looking down.**

Implicit music   music for film which, in addition to supporting the physical sense of action (see also **Kinetic music**), also serves to fit with visual image and dialogue to convey a parallel or corresponding mood, and likewise to accentuate visual techniques and transitions.

In-depth movement   movement from the foreground in a direction away from the camera or vice versa, resulting in a sense of the depth and dimension of the image.

In sequence   shooting on a schedule which follows the sequence and order of the shooting script; this is very seldom done, for reasons of economy and efficiency.

Insert slate   pocket-size identification board without a clapstick used in filming without sound.

Incidental music   music apparently coming from a real sound source in the scene, as for example, radio, jukebox, musical instrument.

Inkie   an intensely bright incandescent lamp.

Insert   (1) a shot, usually a closeup, used to reveal a **title** or any subject in detail; (2) any material cut into a scene, though not shot in the making of the scene, by the editor; (3) also a camera car used for mobile photography.

Intercut   a short cut used within a larger sequence. See also **Cross-cut.**

Interior (INT.)   any set which represents an indoor situation; distinguished from **exterior.**

Interpolated shots   see **Insert.**

Intertitles (also **titles**, distinguished from the **main title** or **titles and credits**) any shot of any written or printed material inserted in any scene or sequence of a film.

Invisible cutting (also **invisible editing**)   unobtrusive cutting by means of **match cuts** or by **motivation**, intended to distract audience attention from awareness of editing.

Iris in to open up the photographed image from a pinpoint or small portion of the frame until the whole frame is filled with the picture.

Iris out to close down the photographed image to a pinpoint or small portion of the frame.

Irising a gradual opening up or closing down of the photographed image from or to a pinpoint; can be done in camera by means of an *iris diaphragm* or by **masking;** can be accomplished in laboratory by optical or chemical means; a transitional device for linking one scene to another.

Jidai-geki (Japanese) historical and costume films.

Juicer any electrician working on the set.

Jump cut (distinguished from a **match cut**) in perjorative sense, refers to any poorly made match cut; used as a deliberate artistic device, it represents the cutting out of footage which would give the sequence a conventional continuity; also a cut in which the camera angle changes slightly on the cut, giving an impression of a jump in action.

Key light the main source of light illuminating the subject of a shot.

Kinesthetic involvement the result of artistic techniques designed to involve the audience in sharing physical and psychological feelings of the film.

Kinetic music music designed to accompany and express the actions shown in a scene or sequence.

l left; stage left or frame left.

Lap dissolve see **Dissolve.** See also **Overlap shot.**

Lay behind musical term; music to be subdued and unobtrusive in accompaniment to a scene.

Lens hood camera fitting designed to shield camera lens and film from light.

Lens turret a rotating device on the camera which carries two or more lenses which may be turned swiftly into position during shooting.

Library score a musical score created from pre-recorded music purchased from a music library.

Library shot any shot taken from a film library for use in a film; a shot not taken for a particular film, but used in it. See also **Stock shot.**

Light meter instrument used to measure intensity of light on the subject or scene being photographed; unit of measurement is *foot candles.*

Lighting the set with very few exceptions all sets, exterior and interior, in studio and on location, must be **lit,** that is, illuminated by lights and controlled by reflectors, diffusion screens.

Lip sync the synchronization of lip movements and the sound of voices.

Location any place outside a studio and its lot where exterior or interior shooting takes place; such shooting is said to be *on location; local* location is within easy driving distance of the studio; any other location is classified as *distant.*

Long lens a lens with a focal length greater than normal, therefore including a narrow angle of a scene; incorrectly called a **telephoto lens.**

Long shot (ls)   shot taken at a distance from the action or subject, conventionally not less than fifty yards and often at a greater distance; a long shot need *not* be a **full shot** including a complete setting or action.

Loop film (also **cyclic film**)   a short film with its ends joined together which can be run through a projector without interruption in continuous repetition.

Looping   process by which actors replace lines made on the original sound track, for purposes of clarity and inflection, in a studio sound recording room; a loop film is prepared and projected and the actor repeats his lines, timing (**synchronizing**) his words with his filmed lip movements; frequently used, wrongly, for **dubbing.**

Lot   any land owned by a studio and situated near sound stages where shooting may take place; also a term for the entire studio; something is located as happening *on the lot* or *off the lot*.

Low angle shot (also **camera looking up**)   the camera is situated below the subject of the shot, shooting upward.

Low key   (1) when only a few highlights are used to illuminate the subject and a large portion of the set is shadowy, the lighting is called *low key;* (2) similarly the subject may be shot in low key by stopping down the lens opening of the camera; (3) finally, a dark print, in color or black and white, is low key.

Low truck shot   a moving shot taken from a low angle.

Main title (also **title and credits**)   the title of the film; usually shown in combination with the screen credits.

Makeup artist   responsible for all makeup; except, when making up female players, union regulations confine the makeup artist's activities to area from top of head to apex of breastbone, from fingertips to elbows; also responsible for creation of all character effects, as, for example, wounds, scars, aging; and responsible for mustaches, beards, and male wigs.

Map location   convention, established by earliest filmmakers and followed ever since, in which the frame is viewed as analogous to a map; thus right-to-left movement indicates movement east to west and vice versa, and the top of the frame may suggest north, the bottom, south; from this beginning developed more sophisticated means of directional cutting, using a rhythm of lines of movement within a shot, scene, and sequence.

Married print   see **Combined print.**

Mask   a shield or shape placed in front of the camera lens to eliminate (that is, mask out) some part of the shot.

Mask shot   shot made with lens covered to limit what can be filmed; most often used (analogous to insert shot) to simulate a shot seen through an object, as, for example, a keyhole or crack, telescope, gun sight, binoculars, or camera.

Master film the final edited negative from which all theatrical prints are made.

Master scene the overall scene, as indicated in the shooting script and by the director, considered as a unit, without regard to the breakdown of the scene into separate shots and takes or the cutting within the scene by the editor.

Master shot a single shooting or take of an entire piece of dramatic action.

Match cut a carefully unobtrusive cut designed to blend the action of two shots so closely together that the effect of cutting is minimized.

Matte shot a special effects process whereby two separately shot sequences are combined harmoniously into one print, giving the effect of being done at one time and in one location; related to **process shot.**

Meal penalty a union regulation requiring that on all location shooting the entire film company must be fed at precisely specified hours and with high quality food; failure to meet this regulation requires that the producer must pay a penalty to all workers.

Medium (or middle) close shot (MCS) or closeup (MCU) a shot of indeterminate distance between a medium shot and a close shot; basically a close shot in which a larger part of the subject than usual is visible.

Medium long shot (MLS) shot of indefinite distance between medium and long, tending towards the long shot but retaining the medium shot's characteristics of clear identity of persons and at least part of the immediate setting.

Medium shot by convention a shot made from between five and fifteen yards' apparent distance and including a subject or group in entirety.

Metteur en scène (French; also *réalisateur*) director, filmmaker.

Middle shot (mid-shot; also American shot) a medium shot which focuses on the subject from the knees up.

Minitheater a complex of two or more small, fully automated motion-picture theaters, sharing a box office, refreshment stand, and projection booth, and showing more than one motion picture.

Mirror wipe a wipe made by sliding a 45-degree mirror across the lens.

Mise en scène (French) scenery, setting, and staging; involves, for the director, direction of actors in delivery of lines and in blocking (planning) their movements; also includes planning individual camera shots.

Mixer on the set, a member of the sound crew who operates a sound console in conjunction with the camera; charged with obtaining clear and distinct sound recording during shooting; during dubbing, any one of several sound men who dial in and dial out sounds from the various tracks, creating the sound track for the film.

Mobile (also motion) camera the capacity of the camera to be changed in distance and angle between shots, or to move or seem to move during a single shot.

Model shot any shot in which a model or an object or objects is photographed.

Montage (1) term used by Sergei Eisenstein to describe rhetorical arrangement of shots (sometimes single frames) in juxtaposition with each other in order to produce or imply another unit independent of the separate elements forming it; defined by Ernest Lindgren in *The Art of the Film* as "the combination in art of representative fragments of nature to form an imaginative whole which has no counterpart in nature"; (2) French term for the editing process; (3) American term for an assembly of short shots used to indicate a passage of time and events within that time span.

MOS (also **wild picture**) any shots, scenes, or sequences taken without sound; when used in script directions it calls for a silent unit.

Motivation establishing probability or causality for anything in the film whether in narrative of script, action, and characterization of actors, or in the editing cuts and transitions.

Moving shot (also **running shot**) any shot in which the camera, by any means, follows with actors or objects moving in that scene.

Moviola originally a trade name, now used for all brands of the special projection machine used by film editors; machine allows the editor to run the film at various speeds, backwards and forwards, to stop on any single frame, and to view the film closely through a magnifying device.

Muddy scene a scene which is inadequately or badly lighted.

Multiple exposure (double exposure) two or more exposures made on the same series of frames.

Multiple images special effects method which produces any number of images of the same shot or subject in a frame, or a variety of separate images in the same frame and shot.

Mushroom floods floodlights used in series for general illumination.

Music editor (also **music cutter**) assigned as technical aid and assistant to the composer.

Mute negative negative of sound film not including the sound track.

Mute print positive print of sound motion picture not including the sound track.

Narrative editing see **Continuity editing.**

Negative cost the total expense of making a film.

Negative cutter a specialist at the photographic laboratory, responsible for matching the original negative, frame by frame, with the final work print created by the film editor, to create the master film.

Negative cutting the editorial work done at the photographic laboratory to match the original negative with the final work print.

Neorealism (Italian: *réalismo*) post-World War II movement in Italian cinema, lasting into the 1950s; characterized by a direct and simple style of filmmaking, and use of natural settings and unprofessional actors.

New Wave (French: *nouvelle vague*) a contemporary movement in French filmmaking, based upon the concept of the director as *auteur*; developed by critics writing for *Cahiers du Cinéma*, some of whom have since proved theory in practice, directing distinguished films.

Newsreels filmed shorts of recent news events widely shown in theaters prior to the development of television and TV news programs; significant in the development of the documentary film.

Nonsynchronous sound (distinguished from **synchronous sound** in which a sound effect is precisely matched to the visual image apparently producing the sound) the use of the sound without the visual image, the sound substituting for and implying the visual image; also applied to unrealistic sound in which the sound does not derive directly from the visual image but comments on it, as, for example, a scene showing the stockmarket with stockbrokers shouting, but the sound is of barking dogs and roaring beasts.

Objective camera by careful application of various techniques, the director seeks to divert audience attention away from any sense of filmmaking and to present the subject in a seemingly objective manner, as if the camera were merely recording events.

Obscured frame a shot in which an image or object in foreground blocks a large part of the frame.

Off-camera (also **off-frame, of,** and **off-screen, os**) any action or dialogue or sound taking place out of view in a particular shot, scene, or sequence.

On-camera (also **on-screen**) action, dialogue, or sound happening in frame, directly experienced by the spectator in a particular shot, scene, or sequence.

On the nose any aspect of a film, visual, auditory, or narrative, presented in an explicit and conventional fashion; perjoratively, a cinematic cliché.

Optical cues conventional visual devices (dissolves, montage sequences, pages of a calendar, etc.) used to indicate passage of time or change of time and space.

Optical effects any effects carried out or created in the optical department of a film-processing laboratory; in addition to a variety of laboratory effects, many effects usually created by camera or editing can be created in the laboratory by complex processes.

Optical printer a device which makes it possible for images from one film to be photographed on another film.

Optical sound track sound track made photographically during actual filming.

Optical zoom a simulated **zoom shot** created in the laboratory.

Out of sync when lip movements and other sound-producing actions on film do not synchronize with sounds on the track.

Out-take any take that is not used in the completed film.

Overlap   in sound or dialogue; a sound or words from one shot or scene intruding upon another, either carried over from a previous scene or anticipating the next.

Overlap shots   a series of shots of the same action from different angles with the effect of extending the time and distance covered by the action.

Overlap sound cut   the overlapping of sound accompanying one scene or shot with the visual transition from that scene or shot to the next.

Overlay   one sound track superimposed on another in dubbing.

Overshooting   the practice by most film directors of shooting and printing far more film of a given scene than can be used in the finished film, for the purpose of allowing maximum flexibility and creativity during editing; an average feature film, 8,100 feet, is reduced by editing from 200,000 feet of printed takes.

Over-shoulder shot   shot, sharing the viewpoint of a character, but including a portion of the character's back and shoulders in the foreground.

Package   subject of film to be made, together with basic staff, cast, and crew available and interested to work on it; and frequently including a draft of the screenplay, along with a breakdown.

Paint in   to add objects, by various means, to a photographed scene as a special effect.

Pan (also **panoramic shot**)   to rotate the camera head on its pivot or axis in a horizontal plane in order either to keep a moving subject in view or to move across a stationary scene. See also **Swish-pan.**

Pan down/pan up (British)   to move the camera in a vertical plane, down or up, towards the subject. See also **Tilt shot.**

Parallel editing (also **parallel action**)   an editing technique of presenting separately shot sequences of action happening in different locations as related to each other by shifting the audience viewpoint back and forth between the separate sequences. See also **Cross-cut.**

Peep show (also **kinetoscope**)   one of the earliest forms of motion picture involving the use of a vertically moving, sprocketed film strip, seen by a single viewer through a slit or eyehole.

Photography to playback   reversal of usual process of dubbing; here actors are filmed moving and acting to a sound track; sometimes used for musical production numbers, songs, etc.

Photofloods   small, bright lights used for general illumination.

Photoplay   in early days (1914), a euphemism for movies, result of a contest for an appropriate term; a film version of a stage play, with minimal adaptation for cinema.

Pickups   shots filmed after the completion of the regular shooting schedule and during the editing phase of production; refers to minor material, not involving extensive reshooting, but merely shots needed for transitions, continuity.

Pistol grip   grip handle at the base of a camera allowing the operator to shoot without use of a tripod.

Playback   use of a recorded sound track during shooting or in looping in order to synchronize action, sound, lip movements, and dialogue.

Point of view (POV)   an aspect of **subjective camera**; calls for the camera to simulate, by position, angle, and distance, the view of a subject in the scene of action taking place in that scene; unlike the over-shoulder shot, a point of view shot does not usually include the observing subject or subjects in its frame.

Polecats   single ceiling-to-floor poles used as mounts for light fixtures.

Position   camera position is defined as static (fixed) or moving.

Premix   preliminary stage of mixing sound tracks in which several tracks are blended together to reduce the number of tracks to be used for the final mix.

Prescoring   any music **scored** before production of a film.

Print   a positive copy of negative film; a **take** indicated to be sent to the laboratory for processing and reproduction.

Process shot (also **back projection, rear projection**)   a scene shot against the background of a moving picture, which is projected through a transparent screen behind the actions being filmed; thus the process shot joins together the two separate units of film in one unit; a conventional example is the shot of two actors in an automobile with a shot of moving traffic projected behind them for verisimilitude.

Producer   financier, and responsible overall for the making of a film, from idea through theatrical release, domestic and foreign.

Production designer   an art director with exceptional responsibility and control, including costumes, props, makeup, decorations, and style, as well as sets.

Production manager   see **Unit production manager.**

Production still   any still photograph taken of any aspect of a film in production.

Prop   any object seen or used on any set except painted scenery and costumes.

Prop box   wheeled, portable, piano-size boxes containing all materials necessary for props and their maintenance; also applied to any portable vehicle, including moving van, used by the prop man.

Prop man (also **property master**)   responsible for all objects used in the action of a film, excluding scenery and costumes.

Property   the story of subject matter of a film to be produced; or a finished film.

Post-synchronize (British; **looping** [U.S.])   recording dialogue with projected film.

Publicity still   any still photograph taken before, during, or after the shooting of a film for the purposes of publicity and advertising, including display photographs often used at the entrance of theaters.

Pull back (PB)   a camera direction indicating that the camera moves, or seems to move, back away from the subject.

Put in   (a special effect)   to create an effect by augmenting or increasing something actually photographed; for example, flames of a fire may be *put in* a scene.

Quartz light (also **halogen**)   specially designed incandescent light capable of extremely high intensity and heat; thus a powerful source of illumination.

Quick cutting   editing of film in short shots for an effect of rapidity.

Raw stock   film that has not yet been used, exposed, or processed.

Reaction shot   a shot featuring the response or reaction of one or more characters to an action already seen or about to be seen.

Reduction (opposite of enlargement and **blowup**)   process by which a film made in one width is produced in a smaller width; for example, 35 MM is *reduced* to 16 MM or 8 MM prints.

Reel   a strip of film on a spool; standard reel is 2,000 feet for American 35 MM projectors.

Reflector light   a light with a built-in reflector; may be either a spotlight for concentrated light beam or floodlight with evenly diffused illumination.

Reflectors   reflecting boards used to control, boost, and direct sunlight or lighting.

Relational editing   editing of separate shots to link them together associatively and intellectually.

Release print   a film for general theatrical showing.

Release script (British)   script version of the finished film. See also **Combined continuity.**

Remake   another filmed version of a previously produced property.

Rembrandt lighting   dramatic and shadowed lighting; term is attributed to Cecil B. De Mille upon receipt of a telegram complaining that sender "couldn't even see the characters' faces half the time" in a De Mille film. "Tell him it's Rembrandt light," De Mille replied.

Retakes   takes made again of unsatisfactory material already shot and viewed in rough form.

Reverse angle shot   a shot made in opposite direction, that is, *reversed*, from the preceding shot.

Reverse motion   camera photographing with film running backward so that when projected the actions or movements appear in reverse sequence; important for special effects.

Riffle book (also **flip book** and **kineograph**)   an early (1868) patented precursor of the motion picture in which a succession of parts of a movement are depicted on pages of a book so that by swiftly thumbing the pages, the viewer enjoys the illusion of a moving image.

"Roll it" (also **"roll 'em"**)   a director's cue for the start of filming or projection of a film.

Rough cut print a first assembly of the total film in rough form and without music and dubbed sound effects.

Rough in arrangement and blocking of lighting on the set prior to shooting.

Running lines rehearsing dialogue.

Running shot a shot in which the camera moves or seems to move keeping up with a moving actor or object.

Running time the length of time a film will take to be projected at standard projection speed.

Rushes see **Dailies.**

Scenario (also **production script**) see **Script.**

Scene a series of **shots** taken at same setting or location from any number of camera angles and positions.

Scoring call assignment of musicians and conductor for purpose of recording the music track for a film.

Scoring stage special sound stage designed for scoring the music track of a film during projection of the sequences to be scored.

Screening showing a film.

Screenplay preproduction, written version of film including settings, scenes, characters, dialogue, and usually some indicated camera directions.

Scrim framed netting used in order to soften, diffuse, or eliminate light on the set.

Script (**shooting script**) a version of the screenplay as revised and prepared for production.

Script supervisor (also **script clerk**) keeps track of everything happening during shooting, that is, logs the shooting in terms of the shooting script; serves as reminder and prompter; prepares combined continuity when filming and editing are complete.

Second unit a self-contained production unit for the filming of scenes and sequences not requiring the director or principals of the cast.

Seconds assistants to the assistant director.

Sequence a number of scenes linked together by time, location, or narrative structure to form a unit of a motion picture.

Serials brief one- or two-reel films involving the same central characters, and presented on a continuing basis; traditionally each unit ending with an unresolved problem or situation (a cliffhanger) which is resolved at the outset of the next episode.

Series short films involving the same chief characters, and each film a complete episode in itself.

Set any place, exterior or interior, on location or in a studio, designated and prepared for shooting in the production of a film.

Set decorator furnishes and decorates the set.

Set dresser responsible for details of settings and locations during production.

Set painter responsible for painting, maintaining, aging all painted parts of the set, also for eliminating reflections.

Setup relationship between the location of the camera, the area of the set or scene, and the actors; a single camera position.

Set up shot a shot involving little or no camera movement.

Shadowmakers devices in many sizes and shapes used by cameramen to create shadows and to filter light.

Sharpness the extent or relative degree in which details in a shot are presented with photographic clarity and definition; when details are clear and distinct, easily identified and perceived, they are said to be *sharp*.

Shoot to film a shot, scene, sequence, or entire motion picture.

Shoot up/down to shoot from a low angle or a high angle on the subject.

Shooting ratio the ratio of film shot to the final footage of the completed film.

Shooting schedule an advance schedule of work assignments, together with sets, cast, costumes, and equipment required.

Short any standard film of less than 3,000 feet in length.

Shot (1) a single continuous unit of film taken at one set and from one camera setup; (2) a single photograph or frame; (3) a notation of camera angle, distance, movement involved in one setup; (4) a printed **take;** editorially, any consecutive strip of frames; (5) **cut** is sometimes used for any shot or part of a take in editing.

Shotgun microphone a special microphone designed to pick up and isolate particular sounds against a noisy background.

Shoulder brace a strap and brace permitting the camera to rest on the operator's shoulder during shooting.

Skip framing a laboratory simulation of accelerated motion; printing only a portion of the original negative frames gives effect of speeded-up action; opposite of **double framing**, which slows down action.

Slow motion effect of slowing down natural action or rhythms; either by filming actions at faster rate than usual, then projecting at standard rate, or by optical effects in the laboratory.

Sneak preview an unannounced trial showing of a new film before a regular theater audience.

Soft focus effect derived from shooting slightly out of focus.

Sound an integral part of all but silent films consisting of dialogue, music, and sound effects.

Sound boom a boom for placing the recording microphone close to the actors in a scene.

Sound crew all technicians on the set charged with the recording of dialogue and sounds and the dialing out of unwanted noise during shooting; a separate unit from the camera crew, but working in close coordination with them.

Sound effects editor   responsible for overseeing the preparation of separate tracks and for the final dubbing of the sound track.

Sound montage   use of dialogue, music, or sound effects to relate separate settings or sequences.

Special effects   technical tricks in photography or processing designed to create illusions; anything added to the film after shooting, in the laboratory or in editing.

Special effects expert   handles the design, mechanics, and engineering of any required special effects which cannot be created in camera or by laboratory.

Splicing   joining together separate pieces of processed film.

Split focus   maintaining sharp focus on two or more objects at different distances from the camera.

Split screen (also **half-wipe**)   frame in which two or more images are simultaneously seen.

Spotlight   any light which projects an intense and narrow beam.

Stand-in   an extra who takes the place of an actor during times of light arrangement and camera adjustment.

Star   a principal member of the cast with a leading dramatic role in the film; a major box-office attraction, not necessarily an actor or actress.

Static position   a setup in which the camera is in a fixed position and does not move or seem to move; for example, though actors move about within the frame or move out of the frame, the camera does not move with them or follow, but continues throughout the shot to shoot from an established angle, recording the same fixed frame.

Steal a shot   to photograph subjects who are not aware of being filmed.

Step outline (also **synopsis**)   a brief story outline indicating the dramatic structure of a screenplay yet to be written.

Stock shot (**stock footage**)   use of film not specifically photographed for the motion picture being produced.

Stop camera (also **stop photography**)   two separate camera operations film the same shot, the two shots becoming one shot in viewing.

Stop motion   exposure of one frame at a time.

Stop printing   the repetition of a single frame or image, created in laboratory, to **freeze** or stop action.

Story   preproduction, it is the narrative line of the script augmented by the storyboard; in filming and after, the story is the organization of shots and sequences into continuity.

Story analyst   a professional reader, preparing synopses and analyses of published material and recommending likely film properties.

Storyboard (also **continuity sketches**)   a preliminary, cartoon-strip form version, in sketches, prepared from the shooting script, breaking down action into a controlled sequence of possible shots.

Storyboard cards   graphic representation of important scenes, shot by shot, prepared in advance of shooting and including all pertinent information required for shooting.

Straight cut (also **direct cut**)   a cut called for where, by convention, another kind of editorial linking or transition might be expected.

Stretch out   a bus-type limousine for transportation to and from locations.

Structured rhythm (also **structural rhythm**)   generally applied to the overall sense of harmonious order of a film, deriving from the director's artistry and control; in film the elements are multiple, including and combining the basic narrative structure of the story, the patterns and arrangements of sound, music, and dialogue, the composition of light and shadow, the angles and movement of the camera, the editorial devices for separating and joining shots, scenes, and sequences; more specifically, structural rhythm in film refers to the purely visual aspects of the director's art, ranging from the composition of individual frames and shots to the relationships, established by likeness and contrast, of sequences, and their significance within the complete aesthetic experience of the film.

Studio driver   all-purpose professional vehicle driver; also drives cranes, fork-lifts, trucks, tractors.

Studio stock   wardrobe, props, and other materials in possession of a studio.

Stunt   any piece of action requiring the use of a professional stuntman.

Stunt coordinator   experienced stuntman who acts as foreman of any group of stuntmen.

Stunt double   a stuntman who bears a close photographic resemblance to a particular actor.

Stuntman   a professional performer of all potentially dangerous action—leaps, falls, horse falls, fights, fainting—in a film.

Subjective camera (also **subjective shots**)   shots created so that the audience views them as if from the literal or subjective point of view of a character; shots indicative of the filmmaker's feelings and attitudes towards characters, objects, events, when the process of filmmaking has been established, explicitly or implicitly, as part of the cinematic experience.

Subtitles   (1) in silent films, the insertion of printed dialogue, comment, and description into filmed scenes or between scenes on subtitle cards; (2) in foreign language films not dubbed into English, the use of white letters on some dark part of the frame to give a translation of dialogue; (3) any title other than the main title.

Sun gun   small, battery-powered unit used chiefly in documentary filming for night shooting, following a subject from exterior to interior, and as a fill light in sunlight.

Superimposition   two or more shots within the same frame, an effect achieved either by camera or in laboratory; may apply also to sounds on tracks.

Supers direct superimposition of one scene over another, creating rhetorical effect of change which is slower than a cut but more rapid than a dissolve.

Supportive elements the musical score, sound effects, voice-over dialogue, etc., which contribute to the primary elements (visual images and dialogue) of the film.

Survey search for and establishment of the locations for various shots to be used in a film.

Swish-pan (also **whip shot**) a rapid panning movement of the camera from one viewpoint or position of the set to another with the effect of blurring intermediate details in movement.

Sync dialogue track basic sound track, consisting of all dialogue and noises recorded during filming and looping.

Synchronous sound sound timed and simultaneous with visual images.

Tail slate a slate held upside down, clapstick at bottom, used when it is necessary to identify a take at the *end* of shooting.

Take each separate recording made of a shot while filming; a shot may consist of any number of takes; when any take is converted into a positive print from the negative, it becomes a **print;** also, in acting, a strong reaction.

Telephoto lens (also **true telephoto lens**) a lens with an exceptionally long focal length, able to focus on a very narrow angle of a scene.

Tests preliminary examinations, often by shooting film, prior to actual production, designed to check costumes (*wardrobe tests*), makeup, and talent (*screen tests*).

Theme a musical sequence, analogous to *leitmotif,* associated in a film with a character, an action, a place; in film overall, the basic idea or subject of the film.

Thin (1) in sound, a sound too weak or vague for its purpose; (2) in acting, a two-dimensional role; (3) in writing, a part of the narrative which is not strongly created or a character not sufficiently developed.

Tilt shot (**tilt up/tilt down**) shot made by moving camera on its pivot or axis in a vertical plane.

Time lapse regular exposure of single frames at long intervals in order to speed up slow action.

Title any written or printed material used in the context of a film, as distinguished from the **main title** announcing the title of the film itself.

Titler device for holding title cards, camera, and lights in proper relation to each other.

Tracking shots (also **trucking, travelling;** sometimes **dollying**) shots in which a mobile camera, mounted on tracks, a truck or other vehicle, or a dolly, moves with the subject or moves towards or away from the subject of a shot.

Trailer (also **theatrical trailer**) a short sequence of film used to advertise a feature film, and often derived from it, for theatrical showing.

Treatment intermediate stage in development of script, basically narrative in form, between step outline and screenplay.

Trim to cut or shorten in editing.

Trim can (also **out-take**) a film can where marked and numbered frames, cut out of a sequence in editing, are kept.

Trims and outs all frames of unused film left over at any stage of editing; these are stored in studio vaults for any possible future use.

Tripod adjustable stand on which the camera may be mounted during shooting.

Trucking shot loosely, any moving shot with camera on mobile mounting; strictly, a moving shot with camera mounted on a truck or van.

Two-shot shot of two characters, the camera usually as close as possible while keeping both in the shot.

Typage acting use of stock photographs from a film library of faces which, when cut into a dramatic sequence, seem to be reacting to the filmed situation and events.

Undershooting filming sequences with too little footage to permit adequate editorial coverage.

Unit production manager executive officer for the producer; from beginning is charged with execution of all the producer's plans, with budgeting, personnel, scheduling, picking locations, serving as manager and foreman for all crews and departments.

Ultra-slow motion photography at a rate of 100 or more frames per second.

Unit still photographer member of production staff responsible for taking all action, production, publicity, and art still photographs.

Utility man lowest ranking titled member of a production crew; charged with running errands and general janitorial duties on the set.

Viewer a small hand-held lens device with frame lines precisely fitting the subject to be shot, permitting the director and the cameraman to examine possible shots without having to move the camera; the camera operator also has a similar instrument attached to his camera.

Voice over (VO) dialogue, comment, or narration coming from off-screen.

Wardrobe department charged with all aspects of costumes and clothing.

Whip shot (also **zip pan**) see **Swish pan.**

White out (opposite: **white in**) opposite of a **fade out** or **in**; image becomes gradually lighter until screen goes white.

White telephone film a type of film popular in the thirties, characterized by great luxury, opulent settings; often a musical film.

Wide angle lens a lens of shorter focal length than is standard; creates an exaggerated perspective, increasing the apparent distance between the foreground and background of a shot.

Wigwag an automatic red warning light which flashes outside the door of studio sound stages whenever sound is being recorded on the set.

Wild lines dialogue not recorded on camera.

Wild sound (also **wild track**) any sound not recorded to synchronize precisely with the picture taken; may be recorded during shooting or separately.

Wild wall a removable wall on a set.

Wipe a link between two shots, both sharing the screen briefly before the second image replaces the first; there are a wide variety of possible wipes in terms of direction; a *half-wipe* is a split-screen effect; a *soft wipe* has a slightly blurred edge between the two cuts.

Work print (also **copy print, cutting copy**) any initial version of the uncompleted film used for editing, dubbing, preliminary screenings.

Wrangler a handler for horses used in a film.

Zoom (**shot**) a shot made by using a lens of varying focal lengths, permitting the change from wide angle to long lens or vice versa during an uninterrupted shot; camera can *zoom in* or *zoom out;* not as dimensional as an equivalent dolly shot with fixed lens but moving camera; *zoom in* effect can be simulated in laboratory with **optical zoom** in which an area of a frame can be progressively enlarged.

Zoom freeze a zoom shot ending with a **freeze,** or apparent still photograph.

BIBLIOGRAPHY

Reference Works

Aaronson, Charles S. (ed.). *International Motion Picture Almanac* (annual). New York: Quigley, 1970.

Amberg, George (ed.). *The New York Times Film Reviews 1913–1970: A One Volume Selection.* New York: N.Y. Times, 1971.

Arneel, Gene (ed.). *The Film Daily Yearbook of Motion Pictures* (annual). New York: Film Daily, 1970.

Barnet, Sylvan, with Morton Berman and William Burto. *A Dictionary of Literary, Dramatic and Cinematic Terms.* Boston: Little, Brown, 1971.

Courtney, Winifred F. (ed.). *The Reader's Adviser: A Layman's Guide.* Vol. II. New York: Bowker, 1969.

Cowie, Peter (ed.). *International Film Guide* (annual). New York: Barnes, 1969.

Current Film Periodicals in English. New York: Adam Reilly, 1970. Lists more than 100 magazines and newspapers devoted to all aspects of film, with subscription information, description of contents, and information for writers.

Dimmitt, Richard B. *An Actor Guide to the Talkies.* Metuchen, N.J.: Scarecrow, 1967. 2 vols. Vol. 1 lists 8,000 films between 1949 and 1964 in alphabetical order. Typical entry gives title, date, and names of characters together with name of actor playing each. Vol. 2 is an alphabetical index of actors with a reference to each film in Vol. 1 in which the actor has played.

————. *A Title Guide to the Talkies.* Metuchen, N.J.: Scarecrow, 1965. 2 vols. Lists 16,000 feature films from 1927 to 1963 in alphabetical order. Typical entry gives date, company, director, and source.

Fordin, Hugh (ed.). *1970 Yearbook of Motion Pictures and Television.* New York: Arno, 1970.

Gottesman, Ronald and Harry M. Geduld. *Guidebook to Film: An Eleven-in-One Reference.* New York: Holt, Rinehart & Winston, 1972.

Greenfilder, Linda B. (ed.). *The American Film Institute's Guide to College Film Courses* (annual). Chicago: American Library Assoc., 1971.

Halliwell, Leslie. *The Filmgoer's Companion: Third Edition, Again Revised and Enlarged.* New York: Hill and Wang, 1970. A useful compendium of information listed alphabetically. Includes entries on actors, directors, individual films, etc., as well as larger topics and specialized movie terminology. Inevitably, each user will find omissions, but a very thorough listing of titles, credits, dates, awards, with helpful bibliography.

Jordan, Thurston C., Jr. *Glossary of Motion Picture Terminology.* Menlo Park, Calif.: Pacific Coast, 1968.

Kirkton, Carole M. (ed.). *Teacher Training Films: A Guide.* Urbana, Ill.: National Council of Teachers of English, 1971.

Levitan, Eli L. *An Alphabetical Guide to Motion Picture, Television, and Videotape Production.* New York: McGraw-Hill, 1970.

Limbacher, James. *Four Aspects of Film.* New York: Brussell, 1969.

McCarty, Clifford. *Published Screenplays: A Checklist.* Kent, Ohio: Kent State University, 1971.

Maynard, Richard. *The Celluloid Curriculum: An Educator's Guide to Movies in the Classroom.* New York: Hayden, 1971.

Michael, Paul (ed.). *The American Movies Reference Book: The Sound Era.* Englewood Cliffs: Prentice-Hall, 1969. Excellent illustrations. Non-technical, but a very thorough listing of titles, credits, dates, awards, with helpful bibliography.

Munden, Kenneth W. (ed.). *The American Film Institute Catalog of Motion Pictures in the United States: Feature Films 1921–1930* (2 vols.). New York: Bowker, 1971.

Neverman, John (ed.). *International Directory of Back Issue Vendors: Periodicals, Newspapers and Documents.* New York: Special Libraries Association, 1968.

The New York Times Film Reviews, 1913–1968. 6 vols. New York: The New York Times, 1970.

Sarris, Andrew. *The American Cinema: Directors and Directions, 1929– .* New York: Dutton, 1968. An entry for each director treated. Includes a list of his films with dates and brief (one to four pages) critical comment.

Schewer, Steven. *Movies On T.V., 1969–1970.* New York: Bantam, 1969.

Spottiswoode, Raymond (ed.). *The Focal Encyclopedia of Film and Television Techniques.* New York: Hastings House, 1969. Well illustrated with charts and drawings. Thorough and extremely useful.

Steele, Robert. *Cataloguing and Classification of Cinema Literature.* Metuchen, N.J.: Scarecrow, 1967.

Thompson, Howard (ed.). *The New York Times Guide To Movies On T.V.* Chicago: Quadrangle, 1970.

Wagner, Robert, and David Parker. *A Filmography of Films About Movies and Movie Making.* Rochester: Eastman Kodak, 1970.

Weber, Olga S. *Audiovisual Market Place* (annual). New York: Bowker, 1970.

The Yearbook of Motion Pictures. New York: *The Film Daily,* 1918–1957. A key source of statistics, survey articles, lists of films (with credits), awards, distributors, etc.

Zwerdling, Shirley (ed.). *Film & TV Festival Directory.* New York: Backstage, 1970.

Film Art, History

Alloway, Lawrence. *Violent America: The Movies 1946–1964.* New York: Museum of Modern Art, 1971.

Alpert, Hollis. *The Barrymores.* New York: Dial, 1964.

Altshuler, Thelma C. *Responses to Drama: An Introduction to Plays and Movies.* Boston: Houghton Mifflin, 1967.

Amelio, Robert, with Anita Owen and Susan Schaefer. *Willowbrook Cinema Study Project.* Dayton: Pflaum, 1970.

Anderson, Joseph L., and Donald Richie. *Japanese Film: Art and Industry.* New York: Grove, 1960.

Anobile, Richard (ed.). *Why A Duck?: The Marx Brothers' Greatest Scenes in Words and Pictures.* New York: Graphic Arts, 1971.

Armes, Roy. *The Cinema of Alain Resnais.* New York: Barnes, 1968.

————. *French Film.* New York: Dutton, 1970.

————. *Screen Series: French Cinema.* New York, Barnes, 1970.

Arnheim, Rudolf. *Film as Art.* Berkeley: University of California, 1957.

————. *Visual Thinking.* Berkeley: University of California, 1969.

Astor, Mary. *A Life on Film.* New York: Delacorte, 1971.

Bainbridge, John. *Garbo.* New York: Doubleday, 1955.

Balazs, Béla. *Theory of the Film.* New York: Roy, 1953.

Balcon, Michael. *Twenty Years of British Films, 1925–1945.* Falcon, 1947.

Ball, Robert Hamilton. *Shakespeare on Silent Film.* New York: Theatre Arts, 1968.

Balshoffer, Fred J., and Arthur C. Miller. *One Reel a Week*. Berkeley: University of California, 1968.

Barbour, Alan G., with Alvin H. Marrill and James Robert Parish. *Karloff*. Kew Gardens, N.Y.: Cinefax, 1969.

————. *Days of Thrills and Adventures: An affectionate pictorial history of the movie serial*. New York: Collier, 1971.

Bardeche, Maurice, and Robert Brasillach. *History of Motion Pictures*. New York: Norton, 1938.

Barker, Felix. *The Olivers*. London: Hamish Hamilton, 1953.

Barnouw, Erik, and S. Krishnaswamy. *Indian Film*. New York: Columbia University, 1963.

Barr, Charles. *Laurel and Hardy*. Berkeley: University of California, 1968.

Barry, Iris. *D. W. Griffith: American Film Master*. New York: Museum of Modern Art, 1965.

————. *Let's Go to the Movies*. London: Payson & Clarke, 1926.

Battcock, Gregory. *The New American Cinema*. New York: Dutton, 1967.

Baxter, John. *Hollywood in the Thirties: A Complete Critical Survey of Hollywood Films from 1930–1940*. Paperback Library, 1970.

————. *Science Fiction in the Cinema*. New York: Barnes, 1970.

————. *Science Fiction in the Cinema: A Complete Critical Review of SF Films from A TRIP TO THE MOON (1902) to 2001: A SPACE ODYSSEY*. New York: Paperback Library, 1970.

————. *The Gangster Film*. New York: Barnes, 1969; London: Zwemmer, 1971.

Bazin, André (tr. by Hugh Gray). *What is Cinema?* Berkeley: University of California, 1967.

Behimer, Rudy, with Terry-Thomas and Cliff McCarty. *The Films of Errol Flynn*. New York: Citadel, 1969.

Bellone, Julius (ed.). *Renaissance of the Film*. New York: Macmillan, 1970.

Bennett, Joan, and Lois Kibbee. *The Bennett Playbill*. New York: Holt, Rinehart and Winston, 1970.

Benoit-Lévy, Jean. *The Art of the Motion Picture*. New York: Coward-McCann, 1946.

Biberman, Herbert. *Salt of the Earth: The Story of a Film*. Boston: Beacon, 1965.

Blesh, Rudi. *Keaton*. New York: Macmillan, 1966.

Bluestone, George. *Novels into Film*. Berkeley: University of California, 1966.

Blum, Daniel, and John Kobal. *A New Pictorial History of the Talkies*. New York: Grosset & Dunlap, 1970.

Bobker, Lee. *Elements of Film*. New York: Harcourt, Brace & World, 1969.

Bogdanovich, Peter. *The Cinema of Alfred Hitchcock*. New York: Museum of Modern Art, 1963.

―――. *The Cinema of Howard Hawks.* New York: Museum of Modern Art, 1962.

―――. *The Cinema of Orson Welles.* New York: Museum of Modern Art, 1961.

―――. *John Ford.* Berkeley: University of California, 1970.

Bowser, Eileen. *Film Notes.* New York: Museum of Modern Art, 1969.

Brodsky, Jack, and Nathan Weiss. *The Cleopatra Papers: A Private Correspondence.* New York: Simon and Schuster, 1963.

Brown, Frederick. *An Impersonation of Angels: A Biography of Jean Cocteau.* New York: Viking, 1968.

Brownlow, Kevin. *How It Happened Here.* New York: Doubleday, 1968.

―――. *The Parade's Gone By.* New York: Alfred Knopf, 1968.

Bucher, Felix. *Germany.* London: Zwemmer, 1971.

Budgen, Suzanne. *Fellini.* London: British Film Institute, 1966.

Butler, Ivan. *Religion in the Cinema.* New York: Barnes, 1969.

―――. *"To Encourage the Art of the Film": The Story of the British Film Institute.* London: Robert Hale, 1971.

―――. *Cinema of Roman Polanski.* New York: Barnes, 1970.

―――. *The Horror Film.* New York: Barnes, 1967.

Calder-Marshall, Arthur. *The Innocent Eye: The Life of Robert J. Flaherty.* New York: Harcourt, Brace & World, 1963.

Callenbach, Ernest. *Our Modern Art: The Movies.* Chicago: Center for the Study of Liberal Education for Adults, 1955.

Cameron, Ian (ed.). *The Films of Jean-Luc Goddard.* New York: Praeger, 1970.

―――. *The Films of Robert Bresson.* New York: Praeger, 1970.

―――. *Second Wave.* New York: Praeger, 1970.

―――, and Elizabeth Cameron. *Dames.* New York: Praeger, 1969.

―――, and Robin Wood. *Antonioni.* New York: Praeger, 1969.

Capra, Frank. *The Name Above the Title.* New York: Macmillan, 1971.

Carey, Gary. *Lost Films.* New York: Museum of Modern Art, 1970.

―――. *Cukor & Co.: The Films of George Cukor and His Collaborators.* New York: Museum of Modern Art, 1971.

Carmen, Ira H. *Movies, Censorship, and the Law.* Ann Arbor: University of Michigan, 1966.

Carr, Larry. *Four Fabulous Faces.* New York: Arlington House, 1971.

Carrick, Edward. *Art and Design in the British Film.* London: Dennis Dobson, 1948.

Casty, Alan Howard. *The Dramatic Art of Film.* New York: Harper & Row, 1970.

―――. *The Films of Robert Rossen.* New York: Museum of Modern Art, 1969.

Cavell, Stanley. *The World Viewer: Reflections on the Ontology of Film.* New York: Viking, 1971.

Ceram, C. W. *Archaeology of the Cinema.* New York: Harcourt, Brace & World, 1965.

Chaplin, Charles. *My Autobiography.* New York: Simon and Schuster, 1966.

Chaplin, Charles, Jr., with N. and M. Rau. *My Father, Charlie Chaplin.* New York: Random House, 1960.

Christian, Linda. *Linda: My Own Story.* New York: Crown, 1962.

Clair, René. *Reflections on the Cinema.* London: Kimber, 1953.

Clarens, Carlos. *Horror Movies.* Berkeley: University of California, 1968.

————. *An Illustrated History of the Horror Film.* New York: Putnam, 1967.

Cocteau, Jean. *Cocteau on the Film.* New York: Roy, 1954.

————. *On the Film.* Chester Springs, Pa.: Dufour, 1954.

Contemporary Polish Cinematography. Warsaw: Polonia, 1962.

Conway, Michael, and Mark Ricci. *The Films of Marilyn Monroe.* New York: Citadel, 1964.

————, Dion McGregor, and Mark Ricci. *The Films of Greta Garbo.* Introduced by Parker Tyler. New York: Citadel, 1963.

————, and Mark Ricci. *The Films of Jean Harlow.* New York: Citadel, 1965.

Cooke, Alistair. *Douglas Fairbanks, the Making of a Screen Character.* New York: Museum of Modern Art, 1940.

————. *Garbo and the Night Watchmen.* London: Cape, 1937.

Cooper, John C., and Carl Skrade (eds.). *Celluloid and Symbols.* Philadelphia: Fortress, 1970.

Coorey, Philip. *The Lonely Artist: A Critical Introduction to the Films of Lester James Peries.* Ceylon: Lake House, 1971.

Coplans, John (with essays by Calvin Tompkins and Jonas Mekas). *Andy Warhol.* New York: Grove, 1970.

Cotes, Peter, and Thelma Niklaus. *The Little Fellow: The Life and Works of Charlie Chaplin.* New York: Citadel, 1965.

Cowie, Peter. *The Cinema of Orson Welles.* New York: Barnes, 1965.

————. *International Film Guide, 1964.* New York: Barnes, 1965.

————. *International Film Guide, 1965.* New York: Barnes, 1966.

———— (ed.). *Concise History of The Cinema* (2 vols.). London: Zwemmer, 1971.

————. *Sweden 1.* London: Tantivy, 1971.

————. *Sweden 2.* London: Tantivy, 1971.

————. *Screen Series: Sweden.* New York: Barnes, 1970.

————. *Seventy Years of Cinema.* New York: Barnes, 1969.

————. *Three Monographs: Antonioni, Bergman, Resnais.* New York: Barnes, 1963.

Crone, Ranier. *Andy Warhol*. New York: Praeger, 1970.

Crowther, Bosley. *The Lion's Share*. New York: Dutton, 1957.

———. *Movies and Censorship*. New York: Public Affairs Committee, 1962.

Culkin, Jon. *Julius Caesar: As a Play and As a Film*. New York: Scholastic Books, 1963.

Curtis, David. *Experimental Cinema*. New York: Universe, 1971.

Curtiss, Thomas Quinn. *Von Stroheim*. New York: Farrar, Straus & Giroux, 1971.

Davies, Hunter. *The Beatles: The Authorized Biography*. New York: McGraw-Hill, 1968.

Davy, Charles (ed.). *Footnotes to the Film*. Oxford, 1937.

De Bartolo, Dick (illus. by Jack Davis). *The Return Of A Mad Look At Old Movies*. New York: New American Library, 1970.

De Mille, Cecil B. (ed. by Donald Harper). *Autobiography*. Englewood Cliffs, N.J.: Prentice-Hall, 1959.

de Mille, William C. *Hollywood Saga*. New York: Dutton, 1939.

Deming, Barbara. *Running Away From Myself: A Dream Portrait of America Drawn from the Films of the Forties*. New York: Grossman, 1969.

Deschner, Donald. *The Films of Spencer Tracy*. New York: Citadel, 1969, 1972.

Deren, Maya. *An Anagram of Ideas on Art, Form, and Film*. Yonkers, N.Y.: Alicat Book Shop, 1946.

Dickens, Homer. *The Films of Gary Cooper*. New York: Citadel, 1970.

———. *The Films of Marlene Dietrich*. New York: Citadel, 1969.

———. *The Films of Katharine Hepburn*. New York: Citadel, 1971.

Dickinson, Thorold, and Catherine De la Roche. *Soviet Cinema*. London: Falcon, 1948.

Dimmitt, Richard B. *Actor's Guide to the Talkies*. 2 vols. Metuchen, N.J.: Scarecrow, 1967.

———. *Title Guide to the Talkies*. 2 vols. Metuchen, N.J.: Scarecrow, 1965.

Dolan, Robert Emmet. *Music in the Modern Media*. New York: G. Schirmer, 1967.

Donner, Jorn. *The Personal Vision of Ingmar Bergman*. Bloomington: Indiana University, 1964.

Douglass, Drake. *Horror*. New York: Collier Books, 1969.

Dunne, John Gregory. *The Studio: A Cinéma Vérité Study of Hollywood at Work*. New York: Farrar, Straus & Giroux, 1968.

Durgnat, Raymond. *The Crazy Mirror: Hollywood Comedy and the American Image*. New York: Horizon, 1969.

———. *A Mirror For England: British Movies From Austerity To Affluence*. London: Faber & Faber, 1971.

————. *Eros in the Cinema.* New York: Fernhill, 1966.

————. *Films and Feelings.* Cambridge, Mass.: M.I.T., 1967.

————. *Luis Buñuel.* Berkeley: University of California, 1970.

————. *Nouvelle Vague: The First Decade.* Loughton (Essex), Eng.: Motion Publications, 1966.

————, and John Kobal. *Greta Garbo.* New York: Dutton Pictureback, 1965.

Eisenstein, Sergei M. *Film Form.* New York: Harcourt, Brace, 1949. Paperback by Meridian, New York, 1957.

————. *The Film Sense.* New York: Harcourt, Brace, 1942. Paperback by Meridian, New York, 1957.

———— (ed. by Jay Leyda). *Film Essays and a Lecture.* New York: Praeger, 1970.

Eisner, Lotte H. (tr. by Roger Greaves). *The Haunted Screen: Expressionism in the German Cinema and the Influence of Max Reinhart.* Berkeley: University of California, 1969.

Elton, Arthur, and Peter Bunson. *The Film Industry in Six European Countries.* Paris: UNESCO, 1950.

Enser, G. S. *Filmed Books and Plays, 1928–1967.* New York: British Book Centre, 1969.

Essoe, Gabe. *The Films of Clark Gable.* New York: Citadel, 1969.

————. *Tarzan of the Movies: A Pictorial History of More Than Fifty Years of Edgar Rice Burroughs' Legendary Hero.* New York: Citadel, 1968.

An Evaluative Guide to Films on Jobs, Training and the Ghetto. New York: American Foundations on Automation and Employment, 1970.

Everson, William K. *The American Movie.* New York: Atheneum, 1963.

————. *The Bad Guys: A Pictorial History of the Movie Villain.* New York: Citadel, 1964.

————. *The Films of Laurel and Hardy.* New York: Citadel, 1969.

————. *A Pictorial History of the Western Film.* New York: Citadel, 1969.

————. *The Art of W. C. Fields.* New York: Merrill, 1967.

Eyles, Allen. *The Marx Brothers: Their World of Comedy.* New York: Barnes, 1966.

————. *The Western: An Illustrated Guide.* New York: Barnes, 1963.

Farber, Manny. *Manny Farber's America.* New York: Chelsea House, 1965.

Fast, Julius. *The Beatles: The Real Story.* New York: Putnam, 1968.

Feldman, Joseph, and Harry Feldman. *Dynamics of the Film.* New York: Hermitage, 1952.

Fenin, George N., and William K. Everson. *The Western.* New York: Orion, 1962.

Fensch, Thomas. *Films on the Campus.* New York: Barnes, 1970.

Feyen, Sharon. *Screen Experience: An Approach to Film.* Dayton: Pflaum, 1970.

Field, R. D. *The Art of Walt Disney.* New York: Macmillan, 1942.

Films 1968: A Comprehensive Review of the Year. New York: Catholic Office for Motion Pictures, 1968.

Film Teaching. London: British Film Institute, 1964.

Finkler, Joel. *Stroheim*. Berkeley: University of California, 1970.

Fischer, Edward. *The Screen Arts*. New York: Sheed and Ward, 1960.

Five Catalogues of the Public Auction of the Countless Treasures Acquired From Metro-Goldwyn-Mayer. 5 vols. Los Angeles: David Weisz, 1970.

Flaherty, Frances H. *The Odyssey of a Filmmaker: Robert Flaherty's Story*. Urbana: University of Illinois, 1960.

Ford, Charles. *Histoire du Western*. Paris: Pierre Horay, 1964.

Franklin, Joe. *Classics of the Silent Screen: A Pictorial Treasury*. New York: Bramhall House, 1959.

Fredrik, Nathalie. *Hollywood and the Academy Awards*. Beverly Hills, Calif.: Hollywood Awards Pub., 1971.

Fulton, A. R. *Motion Pictures: The Development of an Art Form From Silent Films to the Age of Television*. Norman: University of Oklahoma, 1960.

Geduld, Harry M. (ed.). *Focus on D. W. Griffith*. Englewood Cliffs, N.J.: Prentice-Hall, 1971.

————, and Ronald Gottesman (eds.), *Sergei Eisenstein and Upton Sinclair: The Making and Unmaking of Que Viva Mexico*. London: Thames and Hudson, 1971.

Gessner, Robert. *The Moving Image: A Guide to Cinematic Literacy*. New York: Dutton, 1970.

Getlein, Frank, and Harold C. Gardiner, S.J. *Movies, Morals, and Art*. New York: Sheed and Ward, 1961.

Giannetti, Louis D. *Understanding Movies*. Englewood Cliffs, N.J.: Prentice-Hall, 1972.

Gibson, Arthur. *The Silence of God: Creative Response to the Films of Ingmar Bergman*. New York: Harper & Row, 1969.

Gidal, Peter. *Andy Warhol: Films and Paintings*. New York: Dutton, 1971.

Gifford, Denis. *British Cinema—An Illustrated Guide*. New York: Barnes, 1968.

————. *Science Fiction Film*. New York: Dutton, 1971.

Gilson, Rene. *Jean Cocteau*. New York: Crown, 1969.

Gish, Lillian (with Ann Pinchot). *The Movies, Mr. Griffith and Me*. Englewood Cliffs: Prentice-Hall, 1969.

Glucksmann, André. *Violence on the Screen*. London: British Film Institute, 1970.

Goodman, Ezra. *The Fifty Year Decline and Fall of Hollywood*. New York: Simon and Schuster, 1961.

————. *Bogey: The Good-Bad Guy*. New York: Lyle Stuart, 1965.

Gottesman, Ronald (ed.). *Focus on Citizen Kane*. Englewood Cliffs, N.J.: Prentice-Hall, 1971.

Gow, Gordon. *Suspense in the Cinema*. New York: Barnes, 1968.

————. *Hollywood In The Fifties.* London: Zwemmer, 1971.

Graham, Peter. *A Dictionary of the Cinema.* New York: Barnes, 1964.

————. *New Wave: Critical Landmark.* New York: Doubleday, 1968.

Graham, Sheilah. *Confessions of a Hollywood Columnist.* New York: Morrow, 1969.

————. *The Garden of Allah.* New York: Crown, 1970.

Green, Abel, and Joe Laurie, Jr. *Show Biz.* New York: Holt, 1951.

Grierson, John. *Grierson on Documentary.* Berkeley: University of California, 1970.

Griffith, Mrs. D. W. *When the Movies Were Young.* New York: Dutton, 1925.

Griffith, Richard. *The Cinema of Gene Kelly.* New York: Museum of Modern Art, 1962.

————. *Fred Zinneman.* New York: Museum of Modern Art, 1958.

————. *Marlene Dietrich: Image and Legend.* New York: Museum of Modern Art, 1959.

————. *The Movie Stars.* New York: Doubleday, 1970.

————. *Samuel Goldwyn: The Producer and His Films.* New York: Museum of Modern Art, 1956.

————. *The World of Robert Flaherty.* London: Gollancz, 1953.

————, and Arthur Mayer. *The Movies.* New York: Simon and Schuster, 1957.

————, and Paul Rotha. *The Film Till Now.* New York: Funk and Wagnalls, 1949.

Guarner, Jose Luis. *Rossellini.* New York: Praeger, 1970.

Guback, Thomas H. *The International Film Industry: Western Europe and America Since 1945.* Bloomington: Indiana University, 1970.

Guild, Lee. *Zanuck: Hollywood's Last Tycoon.* Los Angeles: Holloway, 1970.

Guiles, Fred Lawrence. *Norma Jean: The Life of Marilyn Monroe.* New York: McGraw-Hill, 1969.

Halas, John, and Roger Manvell. *Design in Motion.* New York: Hastings House, 1962.

Hall, Stuart, and Paddy Whannel. *The Popular Arts.* New York: Pantheon, 1965.

Hampton, Benjamin B. *A History of the Movies.* New York: Covici, Friede, 1931.

Handel, Leo A. *Hollywood Looks at Its Audience: A Report of Film Audience Research.* Urbana: University of Illinois, 1950.

Harding, James. *Sacha Guitry: The Last Boulevardier.* New York: Scribner, 1968.

Hardy, Forsyth. *Scandinavian Film.* London: Falcon, 1952.

Hardy, Phil. *Samuel Fuller.* New York: Praeger, 1970.

Henderson, Robert M. *D. W. Griffith: The Years at Biograph.* New York: Farrar, Straus & Giroux, 1970.

Hendricks, Gordon. *The Edison Motion Picture Myth.* Berkeley: University of California, 1970.

Henri, Jim. *The World's Most Sensual Films.* Chicago: Merit Books, 1965.

Heyer, Robert, and Anthony Meyer. *Discovery in Film.* Paramus, N.J.: Paulist, 1969.

Hibbin, Nina. *Screen Series: Eastern Europe.* New York: Barnes, 1970.

————. *Eastern Europe.* London: Tantivy, 1970.

Higham, Charles. *Hollywood in the Forties.* New York: Barnes, 1968.

————, and Joel Greenberg. *Hollywood In The Forties: A Complete Critical Survey of Hollywood Films 1940–1950.* New York: Paperback Library, 1970.

Hill, Norman (ed.). *The Lonely Beauties.* New York: Popular Library, 1971.

Hodgkinson, Anthony W. *Screen Education.* New York: UNESCO, 1963.

Hofmann, Charles. *Sounds for Silents.* New York: D. B. S. Publications, 1970.

Houston, Penelope. *The Contemporary Cinema.* Baltimore: Penguin, 1963.

Huaco, George. *The Sociology of Film Art.* New York: Basic Books, 1965.

Huettig, Mae D. *Economic Control of the Motion Picture Industry.* Philadelphia: University of Pennsylvania, 1944.

Huff, Theodore. *Charlie Chaplin.* New York: Schuman, 1951.

Hughes, Robert (ed.). *Film Book 1.* New York: Grove, 1959.

———— (ed.). *Film: Book II—Films of Peace and War.* New York: Grove, 1962.

Hull, David Stewart. *Films in the Third Reich.* Berkeley: University of California, 1969.

Hunnings, Neville. *Film Censors and the Law.* New York: Hillary, 1967.

Huss, Roy, and Norman Silverstein. *The Film Experience: Elements of Motion Picture Art.* New York: Harper & Row, 1968.

———— (eds.). *Focus On "Blow Up."* Englewood Cliffs, N.J.: Prentice-Hall, 1972.

Isaksson, Folke, and Leif Furhammar. *Politics and Film.* London: November Books, 1970.

Ivens, Joris. *The Camera and I.* New York: International Publishers, 1969.

Jacobs, Lewis. *The Rise of the American Film.* New York: Teachers College, Columbia University, 1967.

———— (ed.). *The Emergence of Film Art.* New York: Hopkinson and Blake, 1969.

————. *Introduction to the Art of the Movies.* New York: Noonday, 1960.

———— (ed.). *The Movies As Medium.* New York: Farrar, Straus & Giroux, 1970.

Jarratt, Vernon. *The Italian Cinema.* New York: Macmillan, 1951.

Jarvie, I. C. *Movies and Society.* New York: Basic Books, 1970.

Jensen, Paul. *The Cinema of Fritz Lang.* New York: Barnes, 1969.

————, and Arthur Lennig. *Karloff and Lugosi: Titans of Terror.* New York: Atheneum, 1971.

Jobes, Gertrude. *Motion Picture Empire.* Hamden, Conn.: Archon, 1966.

Jones, Ken D., with Arthur F. McClure and Alfred E. Twomey. *The Films of James Stewart.* New York: Barnes, 1970.

Kahn, Gordon. *Hollywood on Trial.* New York: Boni and Gaer, 1948.

Kanin, Garson. *Tracy and Hepburn: An Intimate Memoir.* New York: Viking, 1972.

Kirschner, Allen, and Linda Kirschner. *Film: Readings in the Mass Media.* New York: Odyssey, 1971.

Kitses, Jim. *Horizons West: Anthony Mann, Budd Boetticher, Sam Peckinpah: Studies of Authorship Within the Western.* Bloomington: Indiana University, 1970.

Knef, Hildegard (tr. David Cameron Palastanga). *The Gift Horse.* New York: McGraw-Hill, 1971.

Knight, Arthur. *The Liveliest Art: A Panoramic History of the Movies.* New York: Macmillan, 1957.

Kobal, John. *Gotta Sing Gotta Dance: A Pictorial History of Film Musicals.* New York: Hamlyn, 1971.

————. *Marlene Dietrich.* New York: Dutton, 1968.

Kracauer, Siegfried. *From Caligari to Hitler.* New York: Noonday, 1959.

————. *Theory of Film.* New York: Oxford University, 1960. Paperback by Galaxy, New York, 1965.

Kuhns, William. *Themes: Short Films for Discussion.* Dayton: Pflaum, 1970.

————, and Thomas F. Giardino. *Behind the Camera.* Dayton: Pflaum, 1970.

————, and Robert Stanley. *Teaching Program: Exploring the Film.* Dayton: Pflaum, 1970.

————, and Robert Stanley. *Exploring the Film.* Dayton: Pflaum, 1970.

Kyrou, Ado (tr. by Adrienne Foulke). *Luis Buñuel.* New York: Simon and Schuster, 1963.

Lahue, Kalton C. *Collecting Classic Films.* New York: Amphoto, 1970.

————. *Continued Next Week.* Norman: University of Oklahoma, 1964.

————. *A World of Laughter: The Motion Picture Comedy Short, 1910–1930.* Norman: University of Oklahoma, 1966.

————. *Ladies In Distress.* New York: Barnes, 1971.

Larsen, Otto N. *Violence and the Mass Media.* New York: Harper & Row, 1970.

Latham, Aaron. *Crazy Sundays: F. Scott Fitzgerald in Hollywood.* New York: Viking, 1970.

Lauritzen, Einar. *Swedish Films.* New York: Museum of Modern Art, 1962.

LaValley, Albert J. (ed.). *Focus on Hitchcock.* Englewood Cliffs, N.J.: Prentice-Hall, 1971.

Lawson, John Howard. *Film: The Creative Process.* New York: Hill and Wang, 1964.

————. *Film in the Battle of Ideas.* New York: Mainstream, 1953.

Leahy, James. *The Cinema of Joseph Losey.* New York: Barnes, 1967.

Lebel, J. P. (tr. by P. D. Stovin). *Buster Keaton.* New York: Barnes, 1967.

Lee, Raymond. *Fit for the Chase: Cars and the Movies.* New York: Barnes, 1969.

————. *The Films of Mary Pickford.* New York: Barnes, 1970.

————, and Gabe Essoe. *De Mille: The Man and His Pictures.* New York: Barnes, 1970.

————, and B. C. Van Hecke. *Gangsters and Hoodlums.* New York: Barnes, 1970.

————, and Manuel Weltman. *Pearl White: The Peerless, Fearless Girl.* New York: Barnes, 1970.

Leprohon, Pierre. *Michelangelo Antonioni.* New York: Simon and Schuster, 1963.

Levin, Martin (ed.). *Hollywood and the Great Fan Magazines.* New York: Arbor House, 1970.

Leyda, Jay. *Kino: A History of the Russian and Soviet Film.* New York: Hillary and House, 1960.

Limbacher, James I. *Using Films: A Handbook for the Program Planner.* New York: Educational Film, 1967.

Linden, George. *Reflections on the Screen.* Belmont, Calif.: Wadsworth, 1970.

Lindgren, Ernest. *The Art of the Film.* New York: Macmillan, 1948. 3rd ed. 1968.

————. *The Cinema.* New York: Macmillan, 1960.

————. *Picture History of the Cinema.* Chester Springs, Pa.: Dufour, n.d.

Lindsay, Vachel. *The Art of the Moving Picture.* Introduction by Stanley Kauffmann. New York: Liveright, 1970.

Low, Rachel. *The History of the British Film (1896–1906, 1906–14, 1914–18).* London: Allen & Unwin, 1948–50.

————. *The History of the British Film: 1918–1929.* London: Allen & Unwin, 1971.

Lynch, William F., S.J. *The Image Industries.* New York: Sheed and Ward, 1959.

MacCann, Richard Dyer. *Film and Society.* New York: Scribner's, 1964.

————. *Hollywood in Transition.* Boston: Houghton Mifflin, 1962.

———— (ed.). *Film: A Montage of Theories.* New York: Dutton, 1966.

MacLaine, Shirley. *Don't Fall Off the Mountain.* New York: Norton, 1970.

Madsen, Axel. *Billy Wilder.* Bloomington: Indiana University, 1969.

Malerba, Luigi, and Carmine Sinscalco (eds.). *Fifty Years of Italian Cinema.* Rome: Carlo Besteti, 1954.

Maltin, Leonard. Movie Comedy Teams. New York: New American Library, 1970.

————. *TV Movies.* New York: New American Library, 1969.

Manoogian, Haig P. *The Film-Maker's Art.* New York: Basic Books, 1966.

Manfull, Helen (ed.). *Additional Dialogue: Letters of Dalton Trumbo, 1942–1962.* New York: M. Evans, 1970.

Manvell, Roger. *The Film and the Public.* Baltimore: Penguin, 1955.

———. *Films.* Harmondsworth (Middlesex), Eng.: Penguin, 1950.

———. *The Living Screen.* London: Harrap, 1936.

———. *New Cinema in Europe.* New York: Dutton, 1965.

———. *New Cinema in the USA: The Feature Film Since 1946.* New York: Dutton Picturebacks, 1968.

———. *Shakespeare and the Film.* London: Dent, 1971.

———, and Heinrich Fraenkel. *The German Cinema.* London: Dent, 1971.

———, and John Huntley. *Technique of Film Music.* New York: Hastings House, 1957.

———. *What Is a Film?* London: Macdonald, 1965.

——— (ed.). *Experiment in the Film.* London: Grey Wall, 1949.

Mast, Gerald. *A Short History of the Movies.* New York: Pegasus, 1971.

Matthews, J. H. *Surrealism and Film.* Ann Arbor, Mich.: University of Mich., 1971.

Mayer, Arthur. *Merely Colossal: The Story of the Movies From the Long Chase to the Chaise Lounge.*

Mayer, Jacob P. *Sociology of Film: Studies and Documents.* London: Faber and Faber, 1946.

Mayersberg, Paul. *Hollywood the Haunted House.* New York: Stein and Day, 1968.

McBride, Joseph (ed.). *Persistence of Vision.* Madison: Wisconsin Film Society, 1968.

McCaffrey, Donald W. (ed.). *Focus On Chaplin.* Englewood Cliffs, N.J.: Prentice-Hall, 1972.

———. *Four Great Comedians: Chaplin, Lloyd, Keaton and Langdon.* New York: Barnes, 1968.

McCrindle, Joseph F. (ed.). *Behind the Scenes: Theater and Film Interviews from "The Transatlantic Review."* New York: Holt, Rinehart and Winston, 1971.

McDonald, Gerald, with Michael Conway and Mark Ricci (eds.). *The Films of Charlie Chaplin.* New York: Crown, 1965.

McGuire, Jerimiah. *Cinema and Value Philosophy.* New York: Philosophical Library, 1968.

McKowen, Clark, and William Sparke. *It's Only a Movie.* Englewood Cliffs, N.J.: Prentice-Hall, 1971.

McVay, J. Douglas. *The Musical Film.* New York: Barnes, 1968.

Michael, Paul. *The Academy Awards: A Pictorial History.* New York: Bonanza Books, 1964.

———. *The American Movies Reference Book: The Sound Era.* New York: Prentice-Hall, 1969.

———. *Humphrey Bogart: The Man and His Films.* Indianapolis: Bobbs-Merrill, 1965.

Milne, Tom (ed.). *Losey On Losey*. New York: Doubleday, 1968.

————. *The Cinema of Carl Dreyer*. New York: Barnes, 1970; London: Zwemmer, 1971.

Minus, Johnny, and William Storm Hale. *The Movie Industry Book: How Others Made and Lost Money in the Movie Industry*. Hollywood: Seven Arts, 1970.

Montagu, Ivor. *Film World: A Guide to Cinema*. Baltimore: Penguin, 1965.

————. *With Eisenstein in Hollywood*. New York: International Publishers, 1969.

Morella, Joe, and Edward Epstein. *Judy*. Introduction by Judith Crist. New York: Citadel, 1969.

————, Joe and Edward Z. Epstein. *Lana: The Public and Private Lives of Miss Turner*. New York: Citadel, 1971.

————, Joe and Edward Z. Epstein. *Rebels: The Rebel Hero in Films*. New York: Citadel, 1971.

Morin, Edgar (tr. by Richard Howard). *The Stars*. New York: Grove, 1960.

Moussinac, Leon (tr. by D. Sandy Petrey). *Sergei Eisenstein*. New York: Crown, 1970.

Munsterberg, Hugo. *The Photoplay, a Psychological Study*. New York: Appleton, 1916.

Murphy, George (with Victor Lasky). *Say . . . Didn't You Used to Be George Murphy?* New York: Bartholomew House, 1970.

Murray, Ken. *Golden Days at San Simeon*. New York: Doubleday, 1971.

Museum of Modern Art Film Library. *Film Notes, Part I, The Silent Film*. New York: Museum of Modern Art, 1949.

Mussman, Toby (ed.). *Jean-Luc Goddard*. New York: Dutton, 1968.

Neergaard, Ebbe. *Carl Dreyer: A Film Director's Work*. London: British Film Institute, 1950.

Negri, Pola. *Memoirs Of A Star*. New York: Doubleday, 1970.

Nemcek, Paul. *The Films Of Nancy Carrol*. New York: Lyle Stuart, 1970.

Nemeskurty, Istvan. *Word and Image*. Budapest: Corvina, 1969.

Nicoll, Allardyce. *Film and Theatre*. New York: Crowell, 1936.

Nilsen, Vladimir. *Cinema as Graphic Art*. New York: Hill and Wang, 1959.

Nitsch, Hermann. *Orgies Mysteries Theatre*. Darmstadt: Marz Verlag, 1969.

Niven, David. *The Moon's a Balloon*. New York: Putnam, 1972.

Nizhny, Vladimir. *Lessons With Eisenstein*. New York: Hill and Wang, 1963.

Nowell-Smith, Geoffrey. *Luchino Visconti*. New York: Doubleday, 1968.

Null, Gary. *Black Hollywood: The Negro in Motion Pictures*. New York: Citadel, 1971.

O'Dell, Paul. *Griffith And The Rise of Hollywood*. London: Zwemmer, 1971.

O'Leary, Liam. *The Silent Cinema*. New York: Dutton, 1965.

Osborne, Robert. *Academy Awards*. New York: Schwords, 1969.

Parish, James Robert. *The Fox Girls: starring 15 beautiful vixens and one adorable cub.* New York: Arlington House, 1971.

Pate, Michael. *The Film Actor.* New York: Barnes, 1970.

Payne, Robert. *The Great God Pan.* New York: Hermitage House, 1952.

Pechter, William S. *Twenty-four Times a Second.* New York: Harper & Row, 1970, 1971.

Pensel, Hans. *Seastrom and Stiller in Hollywood.* New York: Vantage, 1970.

Peters, J. M. L. *Teaching About the Film.* New York: UNESCO, 1961.

Perry, George. *The Films of Alfred Hitchcock.* New York: Dutton Picturebacks, 1965.

Playboy's Sex In Cinema 1970. Chicago: MHM Publishing, 1971.

Powdermaker, Hortense. *Hollywood, the Dream Factory.* Boston: Little, Brown, 1950.

Pratley, Gerald. *The Cinema of Otto Preminger.* London: Zwemmer, 1971.

————. *The Cinema of John Frankenheimer.* New York: Barnes, 1970.

Quigley, Martin, Jr. *Magic Shadows: The Story of the Origin of Motion Pictures.* Washington, D.C.: Georgetown University, 1948.

————, and Richard Gertner. Films in America. New York: Golden Press, 1970.

Quirk, Lawrence J. *The Films of Fredric March.* New York: Citadel, 1971.

————. *The Films of Ingrid Bergman.* New York: Citadel, 1971.

————. *The Films of Joan Crawford.* New York: Citadel, 1969.

————. *The Films of Paul Newman.* New York: Citadel, 1971.

Ramsaye, Terry. *A Million and One Nights.* New York: Simon and Schuster, 1926.

Randall, Richard S. *Censorship of the Movies.* Madison: University of Wisconsin, 1968.

Ray, Man. *Self Portrait.* London: Andre Deutsch, 1963.

Reed, Rex. *Conversations in the Raw: Dialogues, Monologues, and Selected Short Subjects.* New York: World, 1970.

————. *Do You Sleep in the Nude?* New York: New American Library, 1969.

Renan, Sheldon. *An Introduction to the American Underground Film.* New York: Dutton, 1967.

Rhode, Eric. *Tower of Babel: Speculations on the Cinema.* New York: Chilton, 1967.

Ricci, Mark, and Steve Zmvewshy. *The Films of John Wayne.* New York: Citadel, 1970.

Richardson, Robert. *Literature and Film.* Bloomington: Indiana University, 1969.

Richie, Donald. *The Films of Akira Kurosawa.* Berkeley: University of California, 1970.

————. *Illustrated History of Japanese Movies.* Rutland, Vt.: Japan Pub. Trading Co., 1965.

————. *Japanese Movies.* Rutland, Vt.: Japan Pub. Trading Co., 1961.

————. *George Stevens: An American Romantic*. New York: Museum of Modern Art, 1970.

Ringgold, Gene (with DeWitt Bodeen). *The Films of Cecil B. De Mille*. New York: Citadel, 1969.

Rissover, Fredric. *Mass Media and The Popular Arts*. New York: McGraw-Hill, 1971.

Robinson, David. *Buster Keaton*. Bloomington: Indiana University, 1969.

————. *The Great Funnies*. New York: Dutton, 1968.

————. *Hollywood in the Twenties*. New York: Barnes, 1968.

————. *Hollywood in the Twenties: A Complete Critical Survey of Hollywood Films from 1920–1930*. New York: Paperback Library, 1970.

Robinson, W. R. (ed.). *Man and the Movies*. Baltimore: Penguin, 1969.

Rondi, Gian L. *Italian Cinema Today*. New York: Hill and Wang, 1965.

Rosenberg, Bernard, and Harry Silverstein. *The Real Tinsel*. New York: Macmillan, 1970.

Rosenthal, Alan. *The New Documentary in Action: A Casebook in Filmmaking*. Berkeley: University of California, 1971.

Ross, Lillian. *Picture*. New York: Rinehart, 1952.

————, and Helen Ross. *The Player: A Profile of an Art*. New York: Simon and Schuster, 1962.

Ross, T. J. (ed.). *Film and the Liberal Arts*. New York: Holt, Rinehart and Winston, 1970.

Rotha, Paul. *Rotha on the Film*. New York: Oxford University, 1958.

Roud, Richard. *Godard*. New York: Doubleday, 1968.

————. *Jean-Marie Straub*. London: Secker & Warburg, 1971.

Ruesch, Jurgen, and Weldon Kees. *Nonverbal Communication: Notes on the Visual Perception of Human Relations*. Berkeley: University of California, 1969.

Sadoul, Georges. *French Film*. Falcon, 1953.

Salachas, Gilbert. *Federico Fellini*. New York: Crown, 1969.

Samuels, Charles (ed.). *A Casebook on Film*. New York: Van Nostrand, 1970.

Sanders, George. *Memoirs of a Professional Cad*. New York: Putnam, 1960.

Sarris, Andrew. *The American Cinema: Directors and Directions*. New York: Dutton, 1968.

————. *Interviews With Film Directors*. New York: Avon, 1967.

———— (ed.). *The Film*. Indianapolis: Bobbs-Merrill, 1968.

————. *The Films of Joseph von Sternberg*. New York: Museum of Modern Art, 1968.

Savary, Louis M., and J. Paul Carrico. *Contemporary Film & The New Generation*. New York: Association Press, 1971.

Schary, Dore. *Case History of a Movie*. New York: Random House, 1950.

Scheuer, Stephen H. (ed.). *Movies on T.V.* 4th ed. New York: Bantam, 1968.

Schickel, Richard. *The Disney Version: The Life, Times, Art and Commerce of Walt Disney*. New York: Simon and Schuster, 1968.

————. *Movies: The History of an Art and an Institution*. New York: Basic Books, 1964.

Schmidt, Georg, with Werner Schmalenbach and Peter Bachlin. *The Film: Its Economic, Social and Artistic Problems*. London: Falcon, 1948.

Schramm, Wilbur, with Philip H. Coombs, Friedrich Kahnert, and Jack Lyle. *The New Media: Memo to Educational Planners*. Paris: UNESCO, 1967.

Schrelvogel, Paul. *Films in Depth* (separate booklets for study, including the following titles: *An Occurrence at Owl Creek Bridge, No Reason to Stay, Overture—Overture/Nyitany, The Language of Faces, Orange and Blue, Toys, Timepiece, Night and Fog, Sunday Lark. Flavio, The Little Island, A Stain on His Conscience*). Dayton: Pflaum, 1970.

Schumach, Murray. *The Face on the Cutting Room Floor*. New York: Morrow, 1964.

Screen Greats: Hollywood Nostalgia. New York: Barven, 1971.

Seldes, Gilbert. *The Public Arts*. New York: Simon and Schuster, 1956.

Sennett, Mack. *King of Comedy*. New York: Doubleday, 1954.

Sennett, Ted. *Warner Brothers Presents: The Most Exciting Years—from The Jazz Singer to White Heat*. New York: Arlington House, 1971.

Seton, Marie. *Sergei M. Eisenstein*. New York: A. A. Wyn, 1952.

Sharp, Dennis. *The Picture Palace and Other Buildings for the Movies*. New York: Praeger, 1969.

Shelby, H. C. *Stag Movie Review*. Canoga Park, Calif.: Viceroy, 1970.

Sherman, Eric, and Martin Rubin. *The Director's Event: Interviews with Five American Film-Makers*. New York: Atheneum, 1970.

Shipman, David. *The Great Movie Stars: The Golden Years*. New York: Crown, 1970.

Shulman, Irving. *Valentino*. New York: Trident, 1967.

Silva, Fred (ed.). *Focus on "Birth of a Nation."* Englewood Cliffs, N.J.: Prentice-Hall, 1971.

Sitney, P. Adams (ed.). *Film Culture Reader*. New York: Praeger, 1970.

Slide, Anthony. *Early American Cinema*. London: Zwemmer, 1971.

Snider, Robert L. *Pare Lorentz and the Documentary Film*. Norman: University of Oklahoma, 1968.

Sohn, David A. *Film: The Creative Eye*. Dayton: Pflaum, 1970.

Solmi, Angelo (tr. Elizabeth Greenwood). *Fellini*. New York: Humanities, 1968.

Spottiswoode, Raymond. *A Grammar of the Film: An Analysis of Film Technique*. Berkeley: University of California, 1950.

Spraos, John. *The Decline of the Cinema: An Economist's Report*. London: Allen and Unwin, 1962.

Springer, John. *The Fondas*. New York: Citadel, 1970, 1971.

Stack, Oswald. *Pasolini on Pasolini: Interviews with Oswald Stack*. Bloomington: Indiana University, 1969.

Stedman, Raymond Williams. *The Serials: Suspense and Drama by Installment.* Norman: University of Oklahoma, 1970.

Steene, Birgitta. *Ingmar Bergman.* New York: Twayne, 1968.

Steen, Mike. *A Look at Tennessee Williams.* New York: Hawthorn, 1969.

Steiger, Brad. *Monsters, Maidens, and Mayhem: A Pictorial History of Hollywood Film Monsters.* Chicago: Camerarts, 1965.

Stephenson, Ralph, and Jean R. Debrix. *The Cinema as Art.* Baltimore: Penguin, 1965.

Stewart, David C. *Film Study in Higher Education.* Washington, D.C.: American Council on Education, 1966.

Strick, Philip. *Antonioni.* Loughton (Essex), Eng.: Motion Publications, 1965.

Sussex, Elizabeth. *Lindsay Anderson.* New York: Praeger, 1970.

Svensson, Arne. *Japan.* London: Zwemmer, 1971.

Swindell, Larry, *Spencer Tracy.* New York: World, 1969.

Tabori, Paul. *Alexander Korda.* London: Oldbourne, 1959.

Talbot, Daniel (ed.). *Film: An Anthology.* Berkeley: University of California, 1966.

Taylor, Deems. *Walt Disney's Fantasia.* New York: Simon and Schuster, 1940.

Taylor, Elizabeth. *Elizabeth Taylor: An Informal Memoir.* New York: Harper & Row, 1965.

Taylor, John Russell, *Cinema Eye, Cinema Ear: Some Key Film-makers of the Sixties.* New York: Hill and Wang, 1964.

——, and Arthur Jackson. *The Hollywood Musical.* London: Secker & Warburg, 1971.

Thomas, Bob. *Selznick.* New York: Doubleday, 1970.

——. *Selznick & Thalberg.* London: W. H. Allen, 1971.

——. *Thalberg: Life and Legend.* New York: Doubleday, 1969.

Thomas, Tony. *Ustinov in Focus.* London. Zwemmer, 1971.

Thompson, David. *Movie Man.* New York: Stein and Day, 1967.

Thorp, Margaret. *America at the Movies.* New Haven: Yale University, 1937.

Torme, Mel. *The Other Side Of the Rainbow: With Judy Garland on "The Dawn Patrol."* New York: Bantam, 1971.

Truffaut, François. *Hitchcock.* New York: Simon and Schuster, 1967.

Tyler, Parker. *Classics of the Foreign Film: A Pictorial History.* New York: Citadel, 1962.

——. *Magic and Myth of the Movies.* Introduction by Richard Schickel. New York: Simon and Schuster, 1970.

——. *The Hollywood Hallucination.* Introduction by Richard Schickel. New York: Simon and Schuster, 1970.

——. *The Three Faces of the Film.* New York: Yoseloff, 1960.

——. *Underground Film: A Critical History.* New York: Grove, 1970.

Tynan, Kenneth. *Alec Guinness*. New York: Macmillan, 1964.

————. *Tynan Right and Left: Plays, Films, People, Places and Events*. New York: Atheneum, 1968.

Vallance, Tom. *The American Musical*. London: Zwemmer, 1971.

Vardac, A. Nicholas. *Stage to Screen*. Cambridge: Harvard University, 1949.

Verdone, Mario. *Roberto Rossellini*. Paris: Editions Seghers, 1963.

Vidor, King. *A Tree Is a Tree*. New York: Harcourt, Brace, 1953.

Von Sternberg, Joseph. *Fun in a Chinese Laundry*. New York: Macmillan, 1965.

Wagenknecht, Edward. *Movies in the Age of Innocence*. Norman: University of Oklahoma, 1962.

Walker, Alexander. *The Celluloid Sacrifice: Aspects of Sex in the Movies*. New York: Hawthorn, 1967.

————. *Sex in the Movies*. Baltimore: Penguin, 1966.

————. *Stardom*. New York: Stein and Day, 1970.

Ward, John. *Alain Resnais, or the Theme of Time*. New York: Doubleday, 1968.

Warshow, Robert. *The Immediate Experience*. New York: Doubleday, 1962.

Weaver, John T. *Forty Years Of Screen Credits*. Metuchen, N.J.: Scarecrow, 1970.

Weinberg, Herman G. *Joseph von Sternberg*. New York: Dutton, 1967.

————. *The Lubitsch Touch: A Critical Study of the Great Film Director*. New York: Dutton, 1969.

————, with preface by Fritz Lang. *Saint Cinema: Selected Writings 1929–1970*. New York: Drama Book Specialists, 1970.

Weise, E. (ed. and tr.). *Enter: The Comics—Rodolphe Topffer's Essay on Physiognomy and the True Story of Monsieur Crepin*. Lincoln: University of Nebraska, 1965.

Wenner, Jann. *Lennon Remembers: The Rolling Stone Interviews*. San Francisco: Straight Arrow, 1971.

Whitaker, Rod. *The Language of Film*. Englewood Cliffs, N.J.: Prentice-Hall, 1970.

White, David Manning, and Richard Averson (eds.). *Sight, Sound, and Society—Motion Pictures and Television in America*. Boston: Beacon, 1968.

Whyte, Alistair. *New Cinema in Eastern Europe*. New York: Dutton, 1971.

Wilde, Larry. *Great Comedians Talk About Comedy*. New York: Citadel, 1969.

Wilk, Max (ed.). *The Wit and Wisdom of Hollywood: From the Squaw Man to the Hatchett Man*. New York: Atheneum, 1971.

Williams, Clarence, and John Debes (eds.). *Visual Literacy*. London: Pitman, 1970.

Willis, John. *Screen World 1949– *. Annual, 21 vols. New York: Crown, 1970.

Wolfenstein, Martha. *Movies*. New York: Macmillan, 1950.

————, and Nathan Leites. *Movies: A Psychological Study*. New York: Atheneum, 1970.

Wollen, Peter. *Signs and Meaning in the Cinema*. Bloomington: Indiana University, 1969.

Woolenberg, H. H. *Anatomy of the Film*. London: Marsland, 1947.

————. *The Miracle of the Movies*. London: Burke, 1947.

Wood, Robin. *Arthur Penn*. New York: Praeger, 1970.

————. *Hitchcock's Films*. New York: Barnes, 1965.

————. *Hitchcock's Films: A Complete Critical Guide to the Films of Alfred Hitchcock*. New York: Paperback Library, 1970.

————. *Howard Hawks*. New York: Doubleday, 1968.

————, and Michael Walker. *Claude Chabrol*. New York: Praeger, 1970.

Wood, Tom. *The Bright Side of Billy Wilder, Primarily*. New York: Doubleday, 1970.

Youngblood, Gene. *Expanded Cinema*. New York: Dutton, 1970.

————. (Introduction by Buckminster Fuller). *Expanded Cinema*. New York: Dutton, 1971.

Zalman, Jan. *Films and Film-Makers in Czechoslovakia*. Prague: Orbis-Prague, 1968.

Zierold, Norman. *The Moguls*. New York: Coward-McCann, 1969.

Zimmerman, Paul D., and Burt Goldblatt. *The Marx Brothers at the Movies*. New York: Putnam, 1968.

Zinman, David. *Fifty Classic Motion Pictures: The Stuff That Dreams Are Made Of*. New York: Crown, 1970.

Screenplays and the Process of Filmmaking

Agee, James. *Agee on Film*. Boston: Beacon, 1964.

————. *Agee on Film: Five Film Scripts*. Boston: Beacon, 1958.

Agel, Jerome (ed.). *The Making of Kubrick's 2001*. New York: New American Library, 1970.

Alton, John. *Painting with Light*. New York: Macmillan, 1949.

Anderson, Lindsay (ed.). *Making a Film: The Story of "Secret People."* London: Allen and Unwin, 1952.

Aitken, Gillon, and Ronald Harwood. *The Making of One Day in the Life of Ivan Denisovich*. New York: Ballantine, 1971.

Anderson, Robert. *I Never Sang For My Father*. New York: New American Library, 1971.

Antonioni, Michelangelo. *Screenplays of Michelangelo Antonioni*. New York: Orion, 1963.

————. *Blow-Up: a Film by Michelangelo Antonioni*. London: Lorrimer, 1971.

Baddeley, W. Hugh. *The Technique of Documentary Film Production.* New York: Hastings House, 1963.

Baker, Fred. *Events: The Complete Scenario of the Film.* New York: Grove, 1971.

Bare, Richard L. ("Foreword" by Robert Wise) *The Film Director: A Practical Guide To Motion Picture and Television Techniques.* New York: Macmillan, 1971.

Beckett, Samuel, and Alan Schneider. *Film By Samuel Beckett.* New York: Grove, 1969.

Bellocchio, Marco. *China Is Near.* New York: Orion, 1969.

―――. *Viridiana, The Exterminating Angel, Simon of the Desert.* New York: Orion, 1969.

Bergman, Ingmar. *Four Screenplays of Ingmar Bergman.* New York: Simon and Schuster, 1960.

――― (tr. by Paul Britten Austin). *A Film Trilogy: "The Silence," "Through a Glass Darkly," "A Winter Light."* New York: Grossman, 1968.

Bobker, Lee. *Elements of Film.* New York: Harcourt, Brace & World, 1969.

Boyer, Deena (tr. by Charles Lam Markmann). *The Two Hundred Days of 8½.* Afterword by Dwight Macdonald. New York: Macmillan, 1964.

Buñuel, Luis. *Belle de Jour: A Film by Luis Buñuel.* London: Lorrimer, 1971.

―――. *L'Age d'Or and Un Chien Andalou.* New York: Simon and Schuster, 1968.

―――. *Buñuel's Screenplays.* New York: Orion, 1969.

―――. *Tristana: A Film by Luis Buñuel.* London: Lorrimer, 1971.

Burder, John. *The Technique of Editing 16MM Films.* New York: Hastings House, 1968.

Butler, Ivan. *The Making of Feature Films: A Guide.* Baltimore: Penguin, 1971.

Campbell, R. (ed.). *Photographic Theory For The Motion Picture Cameraman.* London: Zwemmer's, 1971.

――― (ed.). *Practical Motion Picture Photography.* London: Zwemmer, 1971.

Capote, Truman, with Eleanor and Frank Perry. *Trilogy.* New York: Macmillan, 1969.

Carlson, Verne, and Sylvia Carlson. *Professional 16/35 mm Cameraman's Handbook.* New York: Hastings House, 1970.

Carne, Marcel. *Children of Paradise.* New York: Simon and Schuster, 1968.

Carrick, Edward. *Designing for Moving Pictures.* New York: Studio, 1947.

Carson, L. M. Kit. *David Holzman's Diary: A Screenplay.* New York: Noonday, 1970.

Cassavetes, John, and Al Ruban. *Faces.* New York: New American Library, 1970.

Caunter, Julien. *How To Make Movie Magic in Amateur Films*. New York: Amphoto, 1971.

The Citizen Kane Book: Raising Kane by Pauline Kael and The Shooting Script by Herman J. Mankiewicz and Orson Welles. Boston: Little, Brown, 1971.

Clair, René (tr. by Piergiuseppe Bozzetti). *Four Screenplays: Le silence est d'or, La beauté du diable, Les belles-de-nuit, Les grandes manoeuvres*. New York: Orion, 1970.

Cocteau, Jean (ed. by Robert Morris Hammond). *Beauty and the Beast*. New York: N.Y.U., 1970.

———. (tr. by Lily Pons). *The Blood of a Poet*. New York: Bodley Head, 1947.

———. (tr. by Carol Martin-Sperry). *Two Screenplays: The Blood of a Poet, The Testament of Orpheus*. New York: Orion, 1968.

——— (tr. by Ronald Duncan). *Diary of a Film*. New York: Roy, 1950.

——— (tr. by Carol Martin-Sperry). *Screenplays and Other Writings on the Cinema*. New York: Grossman, 1968.

Coleman, H. La. *Making Movies—Student Films to Features*. New York: World, 1969.

Corry, Will, and Rudolph Wurlitzer. *Two-Lane Blacktop*. New York: Award Books, 1971.

Cross, Brenda (ed.). *The Film Hamlet: A Record of its Production*. London: Saturn, 1948.

Curry, George. *Copperfield '70: The Story of the Making of the Omnibus-20th-Century-Fox Film*. New York: Ballantine, 1970.

Cushman, George. *Movie Making in 18 Lessons*. New York: Amphoto, 1971.

De Sica, Vittorio. *Miricale in Milan*. New York: Orion, 1968.

Dreyer, Carl (tr. by Oliver Stallybrass). *Four Screenplays*. London: Thames and Hudson, 1970.

Dukore, Bernard F. (ed.). *Saint Joan: A Screenplay by Bernard Shaw*. Seattle: University of Washington, 1970.

Duras, Marguerite (tr. by Richard Seaver). *Hiroshima Mon Amour*. Picture editor Robert Hughes. New York: Grove, 1961.

Eastman, Charles. *Little Fauss and Big Halsy*. New York: Pocket Books, 1970.

Eisenstein, Sergei M. *Ivan the Terrible*. New York: Simon and Schuster, 1962.

——— (tr. by Gillon Aitken). *Potemkin*. New York: Simon and Schuster, 1968.

Eisler, Hans. *Composing for the Films*. New York: Oxford University, 1947.

Eliot, T. S., and George Hoellering. *The Film of Murder in the Cathedral*. New York: Harcourt, Brace, 1952.

Fellini, Federico (tr. by Howard Greenfield; ed. by Tullio Kezich). *Federico Fellini's Juliet of the Spirits*. New York: Ballantine, 1965.

————. *La Dolce Vita.* New York: Ballantine, 1961.

———— (tr. by Judith Green). *Three Screenplays: I Vitelloni, Il Bidone, The Temptations of Doctor Antonio.* New York: Orion, 1970.

———— (tr. by Judith Green). *Fellini's Early Screenplays.* New York: Orion, 1970.

————. *Fellini's Satyricon.* New York: Ballantine, 1970.

———— (ed. by Robert Steele). *Eight and a Half.* New York: Ballantine, 1970.

———— (ed. by Robert Steele). *La Strada.* New York: Ballantine, 1970.

———— (tr. by Eugene Walter and John Matthews; ed. by Dario Zanelli). *Satyricon.* New York: Ballantine, 1970.

Ferguson, Robert. *How to Make Movies: A Practical Guide to Group Film-Making.* New York: Viking, 1969.

Fielding, Raymond. *The Technique of Special Effects Cinematography.* New York: Hastings House, 1965.

Fonda, Peter, with Dennis Hopper and Terry Southern. *Easy Rider.* New York: New American Library, 1969.

Foote, Horton. *The Screenplay of To Kill a Mockingbird.* New York: Harcourt, Brace & World, 1964.

Ford, John, and Dudley Nichols. *Stagecoach.* London: Lorrimer, 1971.

Forman, Milos. *Taking Off.* New York: New American Library, 1971.

Fry, Christopher. *The Bible.* New York: Pocket Books, 1966.

Gardner, Herb. *Who is Harry Kellerman and why is he saying those terrible things about me?: a screenplay.* New York: New American Library, 1971.

Gassner, John (ed.). *Best Film Plays of 1943/44.* New York: Crown, 1945.

————. *Great Film Plays.* New York: Crown, 1959.

———— (ed. with Dudley Nichols). *Best Film Plays of 1939/40.* New York: Crown, 1941.

Geduld, Harry M. (ed.). *Film Makers on Film Making: Statements on their Art by Thirty Directors.* Bloomington: Indiana University, 1967.

Gelmis, Joseph. *The Film Director as Superstar.* New York: Doubleday, 1970.

Gilliatt, Penelope. *Sunday Bloody Sunday.* New York: Bantam, 1971.

Godard, Jean-Luc. *The Married Woman.* New York: Berkeley, 1965.

Goldman, William. *Butch Cassidy and The Sundance Kid.* New York: Bantam, 1969.

Goode, James. *The Story of The Misfits.* Indianapolis: Bobbs-Merrill, 1963.

Gordon, George N., and Irving A. Falk. *Your Career In Film Making.* New York: Julian Messner, 1969.

Griffith, Richard. *The Anatomy of a Motion Picture.* New York: St. Martin's, 1959.

Hamill, Pete. *Doc.* New York: Paperback Library, 1971.

Herman, Lewis. *A Practical Manual of Screen Playwriting: For Theater and Television Films*. New York: World, 1966.

Higham, Charles. *Hollywood Cameramen: Sources of Light*. London: Thames and Hudson, 1970.

————, and Joel Greenberg. *The Celluloid Muse: Hollywood Directors Speak*. New York: New American Library, 1970.

Hopper, Dennis. *The Last Movie*. New York: New American Library, 1970.

Isaksson, Ulla. *The Virgin Spring*. New York: Ballantine, 1960.

Kantor, Bernard R., with Irwin A. Blacker and Anne Kramer (eds.). *Directors at Work*. New York: Funk and Wagnalls, 1970.

Kurosawa, Akira. *Seven Samurai*. London: Lorrimer, 1971.

Larson, Rodger, Jr. *A Guide for Film Teachers to Filmmaking by Teenagers*. New York: Cultural Affairs Foundation, 1968.

———— and Ellen Meade. *Young Filmmakers*. New York: Avon, 1971.

Lawson, John Howard. *Theory and Technique of Playwriting and Screenwriting*. New York: Putnam, 1949.

Lewis, Colby. *The TV Director-Interpreter*. New York: Funk and Wagnalls, 1968.

Lewis, Herman. *A Practical Manual of Screen Playwriting*. New York: World, 1966.

Lewis, Jerry. *The Total Film-Maker*. New York: Random House, 1971.

Leyda, Jay. *Films Beget Films*. New York: Hill and Wang, 1964.

Lidstone, John, and Don McIntosh. *Children As Film Makers*. New York: Van Nostrand, 1970.

Livingston, Don. *Film and the Director*. New York: Macmillan, 1953.

London, Kurt. *Film Music*. London: Faber and Faber, 1936.

Lowndes, Douglas. *Film Making In Schools*. New York: Watson-Guptill, 1968.

Maddux, Rachel, with Stirling Silliphant and Neil D. Issacs. *Fiction Into Film: A Walk in the Spring Rain*. Knoxville: University of Tennessee, 1970.

Madsen, Roy. *Animated Film*. New York: Interland, 1969.

Mailer, Norman. *Maidstone: A Mystery*. New York: New American Library, 1971.

Mankiewicz, Joseph L. *All About Eve: A Screenplay*. New York: Random House, 1951.

Manoogian, Haig P. *The Film-Maker's Art*. New York: Basic Books, 1966.

Manvell, Roger. *Three British Screenplays: Brief Encounter, Odd Man Out, and Scott of the Antarctic*. London: Methuen, 1950.

Mascelli, Joseph V. *The Five C's of Cinematography: Motion Picture Filming Techniques Simplified*. Los Angeles: Cine/Grafic Publications, 1965.

———— (ed.). *American Cinematographer Manual*. Hollywood: American Society of Cinematographers, 1966.

Maugham, Somerset, with R. C. Sheriff and Loel Langley. *Encore*. New York: Doubleday, 1952.

————. *Trio*. New York: Delta, 1950.

Maysles, Albert, and David Maysles. *Salesman*. New York: New American Library, 1969.

McGowan, Kenneth. *Behind the Screen: The History and Techniques of the Motion Picture*. New York: Delacorte, 1965.

Menzel, Jiri, and Bohumil Hrabal (tr. Josef Holzbecher). *Closely Watched Trains*. New York: Simon and Schuster, 1971.

Mercer, John. *An Introduction to Cinematography*. Champaign, Ill.: Stipes, 1970.

Meyer, Nicholas. *The Love Story*. New York: Avon, 1971.

Miller, Arthur. *The Misfits*. New York: Viking, 1961.

Miller, Merle, and Evan Rhodes. *Only You, Dick Darling, or How to Write One Television Script and Make $50,000,000*. New York: Bantam Books, 1964.

Montagu, Ivor. *With Eisenstein in Hollywood*. New York: International Publishers, 1969.

Mosley, Raymond. *Battle of Britain: The Making of a Film*. New York: Ballantine, 1969.

Naumburg, Nancy (ed.). *We Make the Movies*. New York: Norton, 1937.

Nilsen, Vladimir. *The Cinema as a Graphic Art*. New York: Hill and Wang, 1959.

Nurnberg, Walter. *Lighting for Photography*. New York: Hastings House, 1956.

Oringel, Robert S. *Audio Control Handbook*. New York: Hastings House, 1956.

Osborne, John. *Tom Jones*. London: Faber, 1964.

———— (ed. Robert Hughes). *Tom Jones: A Film Script*. New York: Grove, 1964.

Pabst, G. W. *Pandora's Box Lulu: A Film By G. W. Pabst*.

Parker, Norton S. *Audiovisual Script Writing*. New Brunswick: Rutgers University, 1968.

Pasolini, Pier Paolo. *Oedipus Rex: A Film By Pier Paolo Pasolini*. London: Lorrimer, 1971.

Peebles, Melvin Van. *Sweet Sweetback's Baadasssss Song*. New York: Lancer, 1971.

Pennebaker, D. A. *Bob Dylan—Don't Look Back*. New York: Ballantine, 1968.

Petrow, Mischa. *Efficient Film-Making Practices: Rules, Forms & Guides*. New York: Drama Book Specialists, 1970.

Petzold, Paul. *All-In-One Movie Book*. New York: Hastings House, 1969.

Pincus, Edward, and Jairus Lincoln. *Guide to Filmmaking*. New York: New American Library, 1969.

Pinter, Harold. *Five Screenplays*. London: Methuen, 1971.

Provisor, Henry. *8MM/16MM Movie-Making*. New York: Chilton, 1970.

Pudovkin, V. I. *Film Technique and Film Acting*. New York: Grove, 1960.

Quigley, Martin, Jr. (ed.). *New Screen Techniques*. Quigley, 1953.

Rattigan, Terence. *The Prince and the Showgirl*. New York: New American Library, 1957.

Reisz, Karel. *The Technique of Film Editing*. New York: Hastings House, 1968.

Renoir, Jean. *The Rules of the Game*. London: Lorrimer, 1970.

Reynertson, A. J. *The Work of the Film Director*. New York: Hastings House, 1971.

Rilla, Wolf. *A–Z of Movie Making*. London: Studio Vista, 1970.

Robbe-Grillet, Alain. *Last Year at Marienbad*. New York: Grove, 1962.

———. *L'Immortelle*. Paris: Editions de Minuit, 1963.

Roberts, Kenneth H., and Win Sharples, Jr. *A Primer for Film Making*. New York: Bobbs-Merrill, 1972.

Serling, Rod. *Patterns*. New York: Simon and Schuster, 1957.

Shavelson, Melville. *How to Make A Jewish Movie*. Englewood Cliffs, N.J.: Prentice-Hall, 1971.

Sherwood, Robert E. *The Best Moving Pictures of 1922–1923*. New York: Small, Maynard, 1923.

Shoman, Vilgot (tr. by Martin Minow and Jenny Bohman). *I Am Curious (Blue)*. New York: Grove, 1970.

———. *I Am Curious (Yellow)*. New York: Grove, 1968.

———. *I Was Curious—Diary of the Making of a Film*. New York: Grove, 1968.

Skillbeck, Oswald. *ABC of Film and TV Working Terms*. New York: Focal, 1960.

Smallman, Kirk. *Creative Film-Making*. New York: Macmillan, 1969.

Sontag, Susan. *Duet for Cannibals: A Screenplay*. New York: Farrar, Straus & Giroux, 1970.

Southern, Terry. *The Journal of The Loved One: The Production Log of a Motion Picture*. With photography by William Claxton. New York: Random House, 1965.

Souto, H. Mario Raimondo (ed. by Raymond Spottiswoode). *The Technique of the Motion Picture Camera*. New York: Communications Arts Books, 1967.

Spottiswoode, Raymond. *Film and Its Techniques*. Berkeley: University of California, 1951.

Stroheim, Erich von. *Greed: A Film By Erich von Stroheim*. London: Lorrimer, 1971.

Taylor, Theodore. *People Who Make Movies*. New York: Doubleday, 1967.

Teshigahara, Hiroshi. *Woman in the Dunes*. New York: Phaedra, 1971.

Thomas, Dylan. *The Doctor and The Devils And Other Scripts*. New York: New Directions, 1966.

Thompson, Robert E. *They Shoot Horses, Don't They?* New York: Avon, 1969.

Trapnell, Coles. *Teleplay*. San Francisco: Chandler, 1966.

Truffaut, François, with Helen G. Scott. *Hitchcock*. New York: Simon and Schuster, 1966.

Vadim, Roger. *Les Liaisons Dangereuses*. New York: Ballantine, 1962.

Vardac, A. Nicholas. *Stage to Screen: Theatrical Method from Garrick to Griffith*. New York: Blom, 1949.

Visconti, Luchino (tr. by Judith Green). *Three Screenplays: White Nights, Rocco and His Brothers, The Job*. New York: Orion, 1970.

————. *Two Screenplays: La Terra Trema, Senso*. New York: Orion, 1970.

Walter, Ernest. *The Technique of the Film Cutting Room*. New York: Hastings House, 1960.

Wanger, Walter, and Joe Hyams. *My Life With Cleopatra*. New York: Bantam, 1963.

Warhol, Andy. *Blue Movie*. New York: Grove, 1970.

Welles, Orson. *The Trial*. London: Lorrimer, 1971.

West, Jessamyn. *To See the Dream*. New York: Harcourt, Brace, 1957.

Wexler, Norman. *Joe*. Introduction by Judith Crist. New York: Avon, 1970.

Wilder, Billy and I. A. L. Diamond. *Irma La Douce*. New York: Midwood-Tower, 1963.

Wilk, Max. *The Beatles in the Yellow Submarine*. New York: New American Library, 1968.

Wilson, Michael. *Salt of the Earth*. Hollywood: Hollywood Quarterly, 1953.

Wolfe, Maynard Frank. *The Making of "The Adventurers."* New York: Paperback Library, 1970.

Published screenplays are now becoming available, in various forms, for study and appreciation.

(a.) Under the general editorship of Robert Hughes, a highly regarded film editor, Grove Press has released a series of scenarios, "reconstructed from the finished film," and offering many illustrations from the film. A section of "Interviews and Criticism" in each volume is a useful gathering of material. Among the screenplays so far published in this series are *The 400 Blows* by François Truffaut, *Masculine Feminine* by Jean-Luc Goddard, *L'Aventura* by Michelangelo Antonioni, and *Rashomon* by Akira Kurosawa.

Simon and Schuster has two separate series of screenplays. These series are presented under two general titles—"Modern Film Scripts" and "Classic Film Scripts." The Modern Film Scripts series includes such works as Truffaut's *Jules and Jim*, Godard's *Alphaville*, De Sica's *The Bicycle Thief*, Bergman's *The Seventh Seal*, Kurosawa's *Ikiru*, and *The Third Man*, written by Graham Greene and directed by Carol Reed. The Classic Film Series makes available such films as *Grand Illusion, Potemkin, L'Age d'or, Un chien andalou, The Blue Angel, Les enfants du Paradis,* and *M.*

Some Criticism

Adler, Renata. *A Year In The Dark.* New York: Berkeley, 1970.

Agee, James. *Agee on Film: Reviews and Comments.* Boston: Beacon, 1964.

Alpert, Hollis. *The Dreams and the Dreamers.* New York: Macmillan, 1962.

————, and Andrews Sarris. *Film 68–69: An Anthology by the National Society of Film Critics.* New York: Simon and Schuster, 1969.

Boyum, Jay Gould, and Adrienne Scott. *Film as Film: Critical Responses to Film Art.* Boston: Allyn and Bacon, 1970.

Crist, Judith. *The Private Eye, the Cowboy, and the Very Naked Girl.* New York: Holt, Rinehart and Winston, 1968.

Crowther, Bosley. *Great Films: Fifty Golden Years of Motion Pictures.* New York: Putnam, 1967.

Ephron, Nora. *Wallflower At The Orgy.* New York: Viking, 1970.

Farber, Manny. *Negative Space: Manny Farber on the Movies.* New York: Praeger, 1971.

Huss, Roy (ed.). *Focus on Blow Up.* Englewood Cliffs, N.J.: Prentice-Hall, 1971.

Kael, Pauline. *Going Steady.* Boston: Atlantic-Little, Brown, 1970.

————. *I Lost It at the Movies.* Boston: Little, Brown, 1965.

————. *Kiss Kiss Bang Bang.* New York: Bantam, 1969.

Kauffmann, Stanley. *World on Film.* New York: Harper & Row, 1967.

————. *Figures of Light: film criticism and comment.* New York: Harper & Row, 1971.

Lejeune, C. A. *Chestnuts in Her Lap,* 1936–1946. London: Phoenix, 1947.

Lewis, Leon, with William David Sherman. *Lanscape of Contemporary Cinema.* Buffalo: Buffalo Spectrum, 1967.

Macdonald, Dwight. *Dwight Macdonald on Movies.* Englewood Cliffs: Prentice-Hall, 1969.

Manvell, Roger, and others (eds.). *Shots in the Dark.* New York: British Book Centre, 1952.

Reed, Rex. *Big Screen, Little Screen.* New York: Macmillan, 1971.

Sarris, Andrew. *Confessions of a Cultist.* New York: Simon and Schuster, 1970.

Schickel, Richard. *Movies.* New York: Basic Books, 1964.

———— (ed. with John Simon). *Film 67/68: An Anthology by the National Society of Film Critics.* New York: Simon and Schuster, 1968.

Simon, John. *Acid Test.* New York: Stein and Day, 1963.

————. *Private Screenings: Views of the Cinema of the Sixties.* New York: Macmillan, 1967.

————. *Movies into Film: Film Criticism 1967–1970.* New York: Dial, 1971.

Sontag, Susan. *Against Interpretation.* New York: Farrar, Straus & Giroux, 1966.

Tyler, Parker. *Magic and Myth in the Movies.* New York: Holt, Rinehart and Winston, 1947.

Zinsser, William K. *Seen Any Good Movies Lately?* Introduction by Elia Kazan. New York: Doubleday, 1958.

Notes and Suggestions for Further Research

One of the basic problems facing the student, who is not a specialist in films and has no plans for being a professional, is where to begin. Above and beyond the many books, some of them with fine bibliographies and references, the student must seek out certain useful reference books and periodicals.

To search out articles and reviews of pictures, the student is directed to *The Reader's Guide to Periodicals* in the library, where this material is to be found under the heading of "Moving Pictures."

In addition to the "key" reviews of films by the small number of establishment reviewers centered in and around New York—reviews in the New York *Times, The New Yorker, New Republic, Commonweal, Life, Time, Newsweek,* the New York *Post, Cue, The Village Voice, New York Magazine, The New Leader,* the New York *Daily News,* etc.—there are regular reviews in many if not most of the big national "slick" magazines as well. Among those regularly offering film reviews are *Vogue, Cosmopolitan, Cavalier, Playboy, Redbook, Good Housekeeping, Psychology Today, Ladies Home Journal,* and *Esquire.* Similarly, on an irregular basis, there are articles about films, actors, and directors, etc., in most of these magazines.

Some of the chief quarterlies now offer some film criticism and review on a fairly regular schedule. Among these are *Contempora, The Hudson Review, Partisan Review, Georgia Review, Trace,* and *The Yale Review.* More infrequently film criticism is found in other quarterlies such as *The Virginia Quarterly Review* and *The Kenyon Review.*

Among the many serious publications devoted exclusively to the study of films and readily accessible in this country are *Cahiers du Cinéma, Cinema, Continental Film Review* (London), *Film Comment, Film Culture, Film News, Film Quarterly, International Film Art News,* and *Sight and Sound* (London). (See "Selective List of U.S. Film Magazines" below.)

For films produced and released over the past ten years, *Film Facts* offers a basic listing of cast and credits, together with a summary of the chief reviews. In the annual index there is a listing of all awards and prizes garnered by these films.

For more professional reaction to films within the film industry, see such trade publications as: *Daily Cinema* (London), *Daily Variety, Film Daily, Hollywood Reporter,* and *Motion Picture Daily.*

A great deal of film criticism, together with articles, interviews, and general information, is to be found in local newspapers throughout the country.

There are certain very useful reference books available for the interested student. Among these are *Foremost Films of 19* , *A Yearbook of the American Screen 1939–* , edited by Frank Vreeland (Chicago: Pitman).

The most ambitious and extensive encyclopedia of film, in six volumes up to 1967, unfortunately for most students still untranslated from the Italian, is *Film-lexicon Degli Autori e Delle Opere* (Rome: Edizioni di Bianco e Nero).

There is, as yet, a shortage of reference books, encyclopedias, and dictionaries of film in English. Among those, in various languages, commonly used by students of film are:

Bessy, Maurice, and Jean-Louis Chardans. *Dictionnaire du Cinéma et de la télévision.* Paris: J.-J. Pauvert, 1965. Illustrated.

Boussinot, Roger (ed.). *L'encyclopédie du cinéma.* Paris: Bordas, 1967. Illustrated.

Cameron, James Ross, and Joseph S. Cifre. *Cameron's Encyclopedia: Sound Motion Pictures.* Coral Gables, Fla.: Cameron, 1959.

Enciclopedìa dello Spettàcolo. 9 vols. Rome: Maschere, 1954–62.

Enciclopedìa dello Spettàcolo, 1955–1965. Rome: Unione editorale, 1966. Illustrated.

Enciclopedìa dello Spettàcolo, 1963– 6 vols. Venice: Istituto per la collaborazióne culturale, 1963– . Illustrated.

Guide to Government-Loan Film. Alexandria, Va.: Serina, 1969. Contains more than 900 synopses of films from 53 federal agencies, plus 2,000 titles and sources.

Guide to Military-Loan Film. Alexandria, Va.: Serina, 1969. Contains synopses of 1,430 16MM service films.

The International Film and Television Council Directory of Organizations and their National Branches. London: International Film and Television Council (Rome), 1963. Published in French and English in parallel columns on opposite pages.

Motion Pictures from the Library of Congress Paper Print Collection, 1894–1912. Berkeley: University of California, 1969.

Multi-Media Instructional Materials Catalog. New York: Universal Education and Visual Arts, 1970.

Saldoul, Georges. *Dictionnaire des films.* Paris: Editions du Seuil, 1965.

Standards for Cataloguing, Coding and Scheduling Educational Media. Washington, D.C.: N.E.A. Publication, 1970.

Theatrical Variety Guide. Los Angeles: Theatrical Variety Publications, 1966. "The dictionary of the entertainment industry issued on behalf of American Guild of Variety Artists."

An extremely valuable guide for schools, film groups, and students is James L. Limbacher's *Feature Films on 16: A Directory of 16 MM Sound Films Available for Rental from Major Distributors in the United States* (New York: Continental 16, 1966).

Also useful is *The Filmviewer's Handbook* by Emile G. McAnany, S.J., and Robert Williams, S.J. (Glen Rock, N.J.: Paulist Press, 1965).

Specifically related to the interests of the general and appreciative audience to whom this textbook is addressed are *The Motion Picture and the Teaching of English* by Marion C. Sheridan, with Harold H. Owen, Jr., Ken Macrorie, and Fred Marcus (New York: Appleton-Century-Crofts, 1965); and *Film Study in Higher Education,* edited by David C. Stewart (Washington, D.C.: American Council on Education, 1966). Both of these books contain a great deal of information useful to the student of film, including addresses and locations of archives and libraries.

Selective List of U.S. Film Magazines

(Prepared by Thomas Atkins, Professor of Drama at Hollins College, and Editor of *Cinema Critic*.)

Cinéaste 27 West 11th Street, New York, N.Y. 10011. Editor: Gary Crowdus. Illustrated quarterly. $.60 per issue; $2.00 four issues.

Offbeat magazine focusing chiefly on *cinéma engagé*—films which protest or explore social problems, new trends in ideological and political use of film. Articles, interviews with "radical filmmakers," book reviews, abstracts of U.S. and foreign film magazines not readily available at newsstands, news of festivals and film events, unclassifieds carrying information wanted, film magazines and equipment for sale, rent, trade.

Cinema 9661 Wilshire Boulevard, Beverly Hills, Calif. 90212. Editor: Paul Schrader. Illustrated triyearly. $1.25 per issue; $5.00 four issues.

In the past **Cinema** has been stronger on visuals than on text, with covers featuring sexy starlets and pictorial tributes inside to big Hollywood or foreign screen personalities; recent issues indicate an upgrading of the contents to appeal to academia. Interviews, articles, current film reviews. New feature: "Lost Films."

Film Comment   100 Walnut Place, Brookline, Mass. 02146. Editor: Richard Corliss. Illustrated quarterly. $1.50 per issue; $6.00 four issues.

Under its founder and former editor, Gordon Hitchens, ***Film Comment*** was noted for elucidating social causes related to cinema: censorship, blacklisting, propaganda and documentary film, civil liberties in mass media, etc. The first issue edited by its new head, Richard Corliss, suggests that in the future the magazine may become less socially engaged, more concerned with film criticism and aesthetics—that is, more like other film magazines. Articles, interviews with directors, current film reviews, book reviews, and news of film schools and festivals. New feature under Corliss: "Film Favorites," in which critics analyze their favorite American films.

Film Culture   G.P.O. Box 1499, New York, N.Y. 10001. Editor: Jonas Mekas. Illustrated quarterly. $1.00 per issue; $4.00 four issues.

Published since 1955, ***Film Culture*** has become the official journal of the New American Cinema—*avant garde*, experimental filmmakers (Kenneth Anger, Stan Brakhage, Bruce Conner, Ed Emshwiller, Ron Rice, Jack Smith, Andy Warhol, *et al.*) whose works are distributed by such organizations as Film-Makers' Cooperative in New York and Canyon Cinema in San Francisco. Articles by and about experimental filmmakers, historical articles and documents, Herman G. Weinberg's column "Coffee, Brandy and Cigars," occasional book reviews. Special issues devoted to single topics: D. W. Griffith, Erich von Stroheim, Andrew Sarris on American directors, with chronology, 1915–1962, etc. Annual Independent Film Award made to outstanding creative filmmaker.

Filmfacts   P.O. Box 213, Village Station, N.Y. 10014. (Now a publication of The American Film Institute, 1815 H Street, N.W., Washington, D.C. 20006.) Editor: Ernest Parmentier. Illustrated fortnightly. $25.00 annual subscription.

Now in its tenth year, publishes information on every motion picture (domestic and foreign) released in the U.S. Story synopsis, reviews from major critics, complete cast and production credits. Annual film awards supplement.

Film Heritage   University of Dayton, Dayton, Ohio 45409. Editor: F. Anthony Macklin. Illustrated quarterly. $.60 per issue; $2.00 four issues. Small academic journal, with conservative reputation, publishing critical reviews of current films and revaluations of older films, occasional interviews with directors, bibliographies, and book reviews.

Film Library Quarterly   Film Library Information Council, 101 Putnam Avenue, Greenwich, Conn. 06830. Editor: William Sloan. Illustrated quarterly. Subscription included with membership in FLIC: individual voting membership $10.00, individual nonvoting $8.00, student $5.00. Informative journal publishing articles and reviews on "aspects of library film and media services, the documentary, avant-garde, and short film." News of film schools, conferences, and information about film distributors.

Filmmakers Newsletter   80 Wooster Street, New York, N.Y. 10012. Editor: Suni Mallow. Illustrated monthly. $.75 per issue; $4.00 eleven issues.

Aims to provide independent and student filmmakers with hard-core information about filmmaking techniques and equipment, distributors, festivals, conferences, film schools. Articles by and about independent filmmakers. Lists equipment for sale, rent, trade; jobs wanted or positions open for filmmakers; plus calendar of independent film events.

Film News   250 West 57th Street, New York, N.Y. 10019. Editor-publisher: Rohama Lee. Illustrated bimonthly. $6.00 six issues.

Recently celebrated its thirtieth anniversary of providing information about new audiovisual materials and equipment. Addressed primarily to educators using film in schools and libraries, each issue features articles about conferences, festivals, technical innovations, and educational experiments; plus 20 to 50 short reviews of films and filmstrips, brief comments on film and TV books, abstracts of film and TV periodicals, and a calendar of educational film events. Special feature: descriptive listings of films according to topics—Black-themed films, films about the American Indian, etc.

Film Quarterly   University of California Press, Berkeley, Calif. 94720. Editor: Ernest Callenbach. Illustrated quarterly. $1.25 per issue; $5.00 four issues.

Addressed chiefly to the film scholar and student, this magazine emphasizes film history/aesthetics and has a somewhat highbrow and stuffy reputation. Critical and historical articles, interviews with directors, reviews of current features and short films, and book reviews; occasionally runs two differing opinions of same film. In recent ad for overseas readers, ***Film Quarterly*** described itself as a publication of "intricate analysis, rigorous argument, lengthy articles and reviews"; it uses a difficult vocabulary and makes "no attempt to be popular."

Film Society Review   American Federation of Film Societies, 144 Bleecker Street, New York, N.Y. 10012. Editor: William A. Starr. Illustrated monthly. $.50 per issue: $5.00 twelve issues (included in membership dues: $10.00 or $25.00 annually).

Official magazine of the American Federation of Film Societies, prints reviews of current films, excerpts from major critics, abstracts of U.S. and foreign film magazines, book reviews, news of film festivals, Supplement to **FSR**, ***Film Society Bulletin***, carries AFFS news and listings of latest film offerings from distributors' catalogues. Primary audience: campus and community film societies, libraries, museums.

New Cinema Review   80 Wooster Place, New York, N.Y. 10012. Editor-publisher: Suni Mallow. Illustrated monthly. $.75 per issue; $4.00 eleven issues.

Motto: "We review only special films"—independent/*avant garde*/ experimental films made outside of Hollywood and the major studios. Interviews with experimental filmmakers, articles on the state of the *avant garde* here and abroad, rental information about films reviewed, and listings of independent film screenings around the country.

Selected Film Distributors

Many of these companies have branch offices around the country; only the main office is listed. Most send free catalogues on request.

Brandon Films & Audio Film Center (recently merged under Crowell-Collier and Macmillan) 34 MacQuesten Parkway South, Mount Vernon, N.Y. 10550.

Canyon Cinema Cooperative Room 220, Industrial Center Building, Sausalito, Calif. 94965.

Columbia Cinematheque 741 Fifth Avenue, New York, N.Y. 10022.

Contemporary Films/McGraw-Hill Princeton Road, Hightstown, N.J. 08520.

Film-makers' Cooperative 745 Lexington Avenue, New York, N.Y. 10016.

Films Incorporated 35-01 Queens Boulevard, Long Island City, N.Y. 11101.

Grove Press Film Library 214 Mercer Street, New York, N.Y. 10012.

Institutional Cinema Service 915 Broadway, New York, N.Y. 10010.

Janus Films 745 Fifth Avenue, New York, N.Y. 10022.

Museum of Modern Art Film Library 11 West 53rd Street, New York, N.Y. 10019.

Pyramid Films Box 1048, Santa Monica, Calif. 90406.

Radim Films 17 West 60th Street, New York, N.Y. 10023.

Roa's Films 1696 N. Astor Street, Milwaukee, Wis. 53202.

Twyman Films 329 Salem Avenue, Dayton, Ohio 45401.

United Artists 729 Seventh Avenue, New York, N.Y. 10019.

United Films Inc. 1122 So. Cheyenne, Tulsa, Okla. 74119.

United World Films 221 Park Avenue, New York, N.Y. 10003.

Walter Reade 16 241 East 34th Street, New York, N.Y. 10016.

Warner Bros., Inc. Nontheatrical Division, 666 Fifth Avenue, New York, N.Y. 10019.

Willoughby-Peerless Film Library 115 West 31st Street, New York, N.Y. 10001.

Reference Source

Feature Films on 8mm and 16mm: Directory of Feature Films Available for Rental, Sale and Lease in the United States, compiled and edited by James L. Limbacher. Continental 16, 241 East 34th Street, New York, N.Y. 10016. 2nd ed., $7.50.

Film Scripts Series

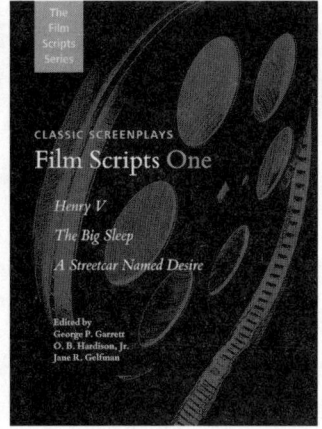

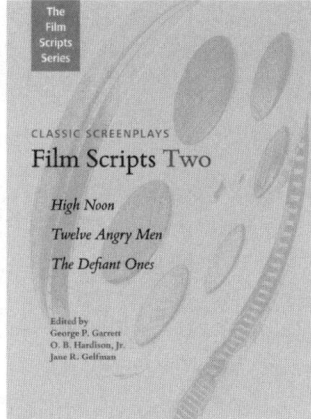

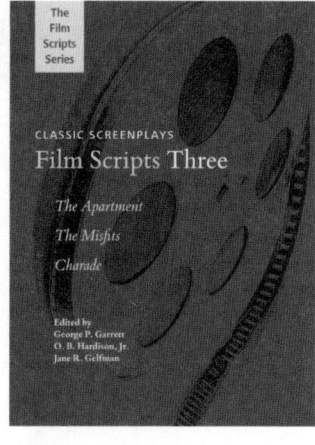

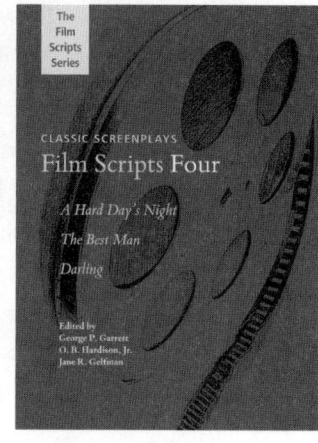

FILM SCRIPTS ONE
Henry V, The Big Sleep, A Streetcar Named Desire
edited by George P. Garrett,
O.B. Hardison, Jr.,
Jane R. Gelfman
9781480342033.........$27.99

FILM SCRIPTS TWO
High Noon, Twelve Angry Men, The Defiant Ones
edited by George P. Garrett,
O.B. Hardison, Jr.,
Jane R. Gelfman
9781480342040.........$27.99

FILM SCRIPTS THREE
The Apartment, The Misfits, Charade
edited by George P. Garrett,
O.B. Hardison, Jr.,
Jane R. Gelfman
9781480342057.........$27.99

FILM SCRIPTS FOUR
A Hard Day's Night, The Best Man, Darling
edited by George P. Garrett,
O.B. Hardison, Jr.,
Jane R. Gelfman
9781480342064.........$27.99

APPLAUSE
THEATRE & CINEMA BOOKS

AN IMPRINT OF

HAL•LEONARD®

www.applausebooks.com

Prices, contents, and availability subject to change without notice.